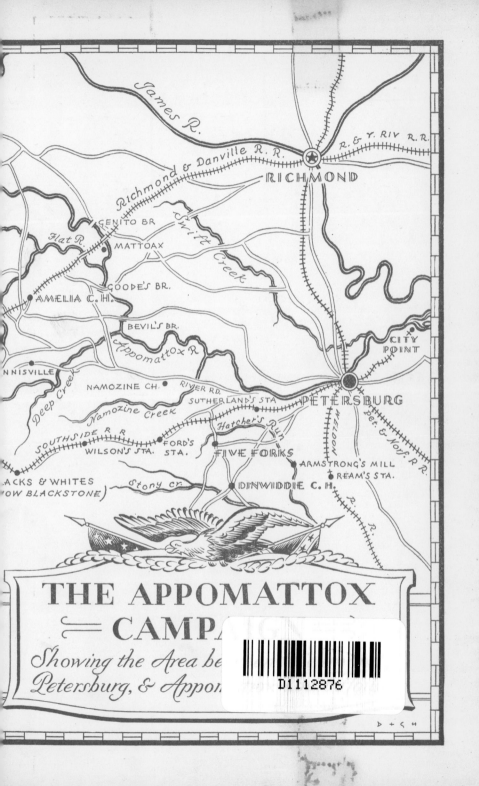

AN END TO VALOR

The Last Days of the Civil War

OTHER CIVIL WAR BOOKS
BY PHILIP VAN DOREN STERN

The Man Who Killed Lincoln

The Life and Writings of Abraham Lincoln

The Drums of Morning

*The Assassination of President Lincoln
and the Trial of the Conspirators
(the original Pitman report)*

PHILIP VAN DOREN STERN

AN END TO VALOR

The Last Days of the Civil War

Illustrated with maps,
photographs, and drawings

1 9 *5 8*

HOUGHTON MIFFLIN COMPANY BOSTON

𝕿𝖍𝖊 𝕽𝖎𝖛𝖊𝖗𝖘𝖎𝖉𝖊 𝕻𝖗𝖊𝖘𝖘 𝕮𝖆𝖒𝖇𝖗𝖎𝖉𝖌𝖊

First Printing

Copyright © 1958
by Philip Van Doren Stern
All rights reserved including the right to
reproduce this book or parts thereof in any form
Library of Congress Catalog Card Number: 58-7783

Part of Chapter 1 (Lincoln's second inauguration) has appeared in
American Heritage. *Copyright © 1958 by American Heritage Pub-*
lishing Company. Some of Chapter 13 (Lincoln's visit to Richmond)
was first published, in somewhat different form, in Collier's. *Copy-*
right © 1956 by Crowell-Collier Publishing Company.

𝕿𝖍𝖊 𝕽𝖎𝖛𝖊𝖗𝖘𝖎𝖉𝖊 𝕻𝖗𝖊𝖘𝖘
Cambridge · Massachusetts
Printed in the U.S.A.

*This book is dedicated
to those devoted public servants,
the librarians and archivists
who keep, preserve, and make available
the manuscripts and printed material
which are the living record
of our past*

Contents

Illustrations

following page 242

Lincoln's Second Inauguration, March 4, 1865

Mr. and Mrs. Lincoln

> Mrs. Lincoln wearing one of the elaborate costumes for which she ran up enormous debts without her husband's knowledge.
> One of the last four photographs made of the living Lincoln. Taken in Washington by Alexander Gardner on April 10, 1865.

Two of the Easy-Money Boys

> Orville Hickman Browning and James Washington Singleton

The *River Queen*

The *Malvern*

Winslow Homer's Sketch of Lincoln, Tad, and Grant

City Point and the *Monohansett,* which took Mrs. Lincoln to Washington

The Peacemakers

> G. P. A. Healy's painting of the conference in the cabin of the *River Queen,* portraying Sherman, Grant, Lincoln, and Admiral Porter.

The Two Great Adversaries

> Ulysses S. Grant, U.S.A., and Robert E. Lee, C.S.A.

An End to Valor

> Union weapons neatly stacked on the streets of Petersburg, April 2, 1865. Confederate weapons—not so neatly arranged—in a trench outside the town.

The War as Seen by an Artist. Two pencil sketches made by
A. R. Waud, one of the roving illustrators for *Harper's
Weekly*.

The burned-out ruins of the Turnbull house, Lee's headquarters west
of Petersburg.
Custer receiving the flag of truce on the field at Appomattox Court
House, April 9, 1865.

Richmond

The burning of Richmond and the flight across Mayo's Bridge.
The former tobacco warehouse that became Libby Prison.

The Country Village That History Made Immortal

Wilmer McLean's private residence at Appomattox Court House.
The court house surrounded by Union troops and townspeople.

No More Parades

The Lincoln funeral procession on Pennsylvania Avenue, Washington.
The decorated stand in front of the White House for the grand review.

Maps

Spring: 1865

As the earth, forever spinning on its axis, moves
in its stately orbit around the sun, it leaves the
sign of the Fishes and enters the sign of the
Ram. For one brief moment, at the vernal
equinox, the axis of the earth is perpendicular
to a line drawn from it to the sun, and all over
the world day and night are of equal length. In
the northern hemisphere, spring — the season of
rebirth and resurrection — begins at this moment. This is the time when all creatures want
most to be alive. But men have always believed
that the gift of life has to be paid for dearly.
From earliest pagan ceremonies to modern
commemorations of the return of the season of
growth, the crossing of the vernal equinox has
been celebrated universally by sacred rites of
welcome. And these rites have often called
for a sacrifice — sometimes for the
sacrifice of human life.

AN END TO VALOR

The Last Days of the Civil War

1

Lincoln's Second Inauguration

Friday, March 3, to Monday, March 6

THE WINTER of 1864–1865 had been unusually cold, with ice on the Potomac so thick that it could support crowds of skaters who were in a gay mood despite the war. But in Petersburg and Richmond, where the war was very real, the remnants of Lee's Army of Northern Virginia clung grimly to the elaborate network of fortifications and trenches that guarded the two cities. Only a few hundred yards away, their Union counterparts opposed the Confederate lines. The two armies had been locked together since the previous summer, when Grant had begun his siege. Fighting had never stopped, but action had slowed down considerably while the soldiers huddled in their dugouts for warmth. Farther south, Sherman's victorious army had swept through Georgia and South Carolina and was moving into North Carolina with Goldsboro as its immediate goal.

On March 4 it had been raining for two days all through the East. It was a good time to stay indoors, because the roads were almost impassable. Sherman took refuge from the weather at Cheraw, in northern South Carolina, where luncheon was served for him in the dining room of a private home. Eight wagonloads of confiscated Confederate wine, which had been sent inland for safety's sake by wealthy Charleston families, were distributed to the army, and the fine old vintages were heartily enjoyed by their captors.

The rain poured down on the men in the field and in the trenches. Land warfare came temporarily to a stop, but maritime operations went on as usual. Grant had his headquarters at City Point, less than twenty miles southeast of Richmond and ten miles northeast of Petersburg, at the confluence of the Appomattox and the James. Here supplies were being unloaded from merchant ships and transports for the great spring offensive.

In Washington, the rain had come down in torrents at daybreak and then had let up so that by half-past ten the enormous crowds, which had flocked to the city to see the second inauguration of their wartime President, ventured hopefully into the streets. People kept looking anxiously at the sky, for rain at noon would mean that the President would have to take his oath of office inside the Capitol, where only the favored few who held tickets could witness the ceremony. Ten minutes later it began to rain again. Hardy blue-coated veterans, who were used to being soaked to the skin for days, watched scornfully while civilians and their women fled to shelter. But the crowds were so dense that it took time to clear the streets, and many got drenched in the sudden downpour.

Even worse than the rain, though, was the mud. The New York *Herald*'s correspondent said of it: "There is mud in Pennsylvania Avenue and all the other avenues. There is also mud in the streets that cross Pennsylvania Avenue and all the other avenues. . . . The streets are flooded and afloat with a vile yellow fluid, not thick enough to walk on nor thin enough to swim in. This yellow material added to the holiday appearance of the people, marking them with gay and festive spots from head to heel. All the backs were yellow with it, and all the horses, and all the little boys — all the world floundered about in it, and swore at it, and laughed at it. In Pennsylvania Avenue it was not so deep as in many other places, for as that street is paved, it was possible to touch bottom there. It was blacker there, however . . . and when it spattered on people it did not look so much like golden spangles."

The President was already at the Capitol, signing last-minute bills before the Thirty-eighth Congress adjourned at noon. In Lafayette Square and in the grounds around the White House there was a great deal of stirring about as soldiers, marshals, volunteer firemen, and civilians got ready to take their places in the grand procession up Pennsylvania Avenue to the Capitol. About eleven o'clock the procession began to form. Mrs. Lincoln got into a closed carriage; after a long delay she began to worry about being late and ordered the coachman to go ahead and drive quickly. As her carriage hurried to the Capitol everyone took it for granted that the President was inside, and the crowd cheered him *in absentia* all along the way.

Mrs. Lincoln's haste upset the carefully planned arrangements for the procession, but at last it began to move. The bells of the city rang out, military bands played lustily, and on one of the floats, a miniature replica of the *Monitor,* sailors fired blank charges from the cannon in the turret. Another float, which advertised the Washington *Daily Chronicle,* had a printing press in full operation, with handbills being tossed to the crowd as fast as they were printed. The uncertain weather had spoiled the effect which a float carrying a Temple of Liberty was expected to achieve. The pretty girls in white dresses who were supposed to grace the temple refused to risk their costumes on such an undependable day, and their places were taken by badly behaved small boys who made a lark out of what was intended as a dignified display. But the visiting firemen from Philadelphia and their Washington hosts put on an impressive show as their beautifully decorated and shined-up engines moved along the muddy street. And, for the first time in the history of Washington, two companies of Negro troops and a lodge of Negro Odd Fellows in full regalia took part in an inauguration parade.

The Thirty-eighth Congress had worked all night to finish the final business of the session, while the President and his Cabinet had stayed at the Capitol on the evening of March 3 until after midnight. During the time he was there, a telegram from Grant arrived. It indicated that the end of the war was very near. General E. O. C. Ord, Commander of the Army of the James, when in conference on prisoners of war with General James Longstreet, the head of Lee's First Army Corps, had persuaded Longstreet to try to get Lee to sound out Grant about possible peace terms. As a result, Lee had written a letter to Grant on March 2, in which he broached "the possibility of arriving at a satisfactory adjustment of the present unhappy difficulties by means of a military convention."

Lincoln was with his Secretary of War, Edwin M. Stanton, when Lee's letter and Grant's covering message arrived at the Capitol. The President's first reaction was to encourage a negotiated peace, but his trigger-tempered Secretary of War was furious. He reminded Lincoln that he was about to be inaugurated for the second time and said: "Your work is already achieved — all but reconstruction. If any other authority than your own . . . be recognized; or if terms of peace be agreed upon that do not emanate from yourself, and do not imply that you are the supreme head of the nation — you are not needed. You should not consent to act in the humiliating capacity of a mere figure-head. . . ."

Lincoln was convinced by Stanton's argument. He wrote out the body of the following dispatch, which he then asked the Secretary of War to date and sign:

March 3, 1865

Lieutenant General Grant
The President directs me to say to you that he wishes you to have no conference with General Lee unless it be for the capitulation of Gen. Lee's army, or on some minor, and purely military matter. He instructs me to say that you are

not to decide, discuss, or confer upon any political question. Such questions the President holds in his own hands; and will submit them to no military conferences or conventions. Meantime you are to press to the utmost, your military advantages.

EDWIN M STANTON
Secretary of War

By some mischance no copy of this important policy-making document was sent to Sherman — an oversight which was to cause much trouble in the difficult days after Appomattox.

The military situation was shaping up rapidly in the field where everything was going in favor of the Union cause. General Philip H. Sheridan had completed his devastation of the Confederacy's main source of food supplies, the fertile Shenandoah Valley, and had beaten Early's army at Waynesboro, thus eliminating all organized Confederate resistance in the Valley. A body of rain-soaked, mud-covered Union cavalrymen clattered across the mountains to Charlottesville, where their advance guard, under the command of General George Armstrong Custer, was met outside the town on March 3 by the mayor, "who surrendered the town with medieval ceremony, formally handing over the keys of the public buildings and of the University of Virginia." On March 9, Sheridan's whole Army of the Shenandoah (about 10,000 mounted men) left the Valley and, acting under orders, followed the course of the James River to join Grant at City Point in order to be in at the kill.

When members left the House and Senate Chambers early in the morning of March 4, they found that people who had not been able to get accommodations in the overcrowded city were sleeping in the Capitol. It was raining so hard that no one had the heart to turn them out, although the building soon had to be cleared for the ceremonies of the day.

The President had returned to the Capitol and was in the ornately decorated room set aside for him in the Senate wing, so busy reading bills that he had not had time to remove his tall hat. He sat there all morning with it on, reading the bills and affixing the signature "A. Lincoln" to those he wanted to approve. (One of the bills he signed in the closing days of the Thirty-eighth Congress was for extra pensions for the last five survivors of the American Revolution.) Senators Foster and Henricks were with the President, while pages kept running in and out of the room. They heard the inaugural procession reach the Capitol; then they heard the footsteps and subdued murmurs of many people crowding through the halls.

The President was due to appear in the Senate Chamber at noon, but when noon came the Senate was not yet ready for him. One of the pages told the men in the little room that Vice-President-elect Andrew Johnson was speaking longer than had been expected. The people around the President grew more and more impatient. They sent a marshal to make sure that Chief Justice Chase was on hand; then they escorted the President down the hall to the Senate Chamber. The spectators they encountered on the way for once were polite; instead of pushing and shoving forward as they usually did when they saw a celebrity, they were quiet, and some of the men even took off their hats.

Johnson was still speaking when the Presidential party entered the Senate Chamber. His face was red and his voice boomed above all the rustle and bustle of the densely crowded room. When Lincoln unobtrusively took his seat at the end of the Clerk's desk, there was audible whispering from the ladies in the galleries, and there was much craning of necks while comment buzzed everywhere. Johnson spoke even more loudly in order to be heard, and then, as the noise died away, his voice was left stranded on a peak of sound.

The two men who were about to be sworn in as the highest

officials of the land had several things in common. Lincoln had been born in a border state, Kentucky; Johnson, although born in North Carolina, had spent most of his life in a border state, Tennessee. Both were strongly pro-Union; both were moderates on the slavery issue; both were shrewd professional politicians who knew how to get out the vote. And they were both of humble origin, self-educated and self-made — typical products of the westward-moving American frontier.

But here the resemblance ended. Lincoln was a master of words, by far the most eloquent of all our Presidents. Johnson was a stump speaker who could rouse a backwoods audience. He had been the war governor of Tennessee and had had much more experience in Washington in both the House and the Senate than Lincoln. But he had few friends in the Capitol; his uncertain political position as a lifelong Democrat who had consented to run for office with a Republican President on the Union ticket had made him distrusted and unpopular.

Lincoln had outgrown his log-cabin background, but Johnson was still suffering from a poor-boy complex. He liked to boast of his lowly origin, of being a tailor by trade, a man of the people, but when he spoke, he used long words of Latin or Greek derivation to show how learned he had become. He enjoyed calling himself a plebian. The word had caught his fancy; it was the kind of word that conjured up images of immense crowds in the Roman forum, where a white-robed speaker swayed the multitudes and through them ruled an empire. He had seized upon this word and had made it his own. But the magic word was to betray him on this, the most important day of his life.

He had been seriously ill in Nashville for many weeks with a fever that was probably malarial, and he had not felt well enough to travel to Washington for the inauguration. He had even written to the Chief Clerk of the Secretary of the Senate to find out whether it was absolutely necessary for him to be present that day and was told that six previous Vice Presidents

had been sworn in months after Inauguration Day. But Lincoln
had urged him to come to Washington, saying that he and
several members of his Cabinet had unanimously concluded
"that it is unsafe for you not to be here on the fourth of March.
Be sure to reach here by that time."

Once the dutiful Johnson had decided to go to Washington,
neither illness nor the very real possibility of assassination
could stop him. His friends warned him that guerrillas might
attack the railroad, but he had always been disdainful of
threats of physical violence. He arrived safely in Washington
on March 1 and immediately secluded himself in a hotel,
ignoring Brady's plea to make a photographic portrait and
declining all other invitations while he nursed his illness. On
the morning of Inauguration Day, Senator J. R. Doolittle of
Wisconsin called for him at his hotel and escorted him to the
Vice President's room in the Capitol, where he met his predecessor, Hannibal Hamlin. What happened that morning is
explained in a newspaper clipping from the Boston *Commonwealth* which was sent to Johnson by one of his admirers and
which he carefully preserved for the rest of his life: "There was
nothing unusual in his [Johnson's] appearance, except that he
did not seem in robust health. . . . Conversation proceeded on
ordinary topics for a few minutes, when Mr. Johnson asked Mr.
Hamlin if he had any liquor in the room, stating that he was
sick and nervous. . . . Brandy being indicated, a bottle was
brought by one of the pages. It was opened, a tumbler provided, and Mr. Johnson poured it about two-thirds full. . . .
when near 12 . . . Mr. Hamlin rose, moved to the door near
which the Sergeant-at-Arms stood, and suggested to Mr. Johnson to come also. The latter got up and . . . said, 'Excuse me a
moment,' and walked hastily back to where the bottle was
deposited. Mr. Hamlin saw him . . . pour as large a quantity as
before into the glass and drink it down like water. They then
went into the Senate chamber."

An American Presidential inauguration is an elaborate public ceremony. Every moment of the day is carefully planned, and events have to run on an exact schedule. The rain had made everything uncertain, for it was still an open question whether the Presidential part of the great spectacle could be staged outdoors. The Vice President customarily took his oath of office in the Senate Chamber, and just seven minutes had been allowed for his speech.

The big room was filling up rapidly when the Vice-President-elect came in, leaning rather heavily on Hamlin's arm. The galleries were already well filled, and the ladies' section was even noisier than usual, for the stylishly dressed women seated there had no intention of allowing anyone to hush them up. Several Senators had made requests for silence, but the privileged ladies who held official tickets of admission were so engrossed in their own conversation that they did not even hear what was being said on the floor.

In order to accommodate the visitors, extra chairs, sofas, and settees had been brought in. A New York *Herald* correspondent described the scene: "In the seats at the rear of the Senators' desks were gathered officers of the Army and Navy. . . . Farragut, with his usual modesty, quietly remained almost hidden in one of the large Senatorial seats. . . . A noise was heard in the diplomatic gallery. All eyes were turned in that direction. The noise that attracted attention arose from one of the representatives of a South American government getting his feet entangled with a mass of crinoline, losing his balance, and rolling down the aisle in the gallery."

Hamlin took the chair and began his farewell message to the Senate. While he was speaking, members of the Cabinet and seven of the ten Justices of the Supreme Court entered the room. Chief Justice Salmon P. Chase was carrying a copy of the Constitution and also a Bible so he could administer the oath of office to the President. Heads were turned toward the diplo-

matic gallery when Mrs. Lincoln appeared there. Reporters
noted dutifully that she was wearing "a black velvet dress
trimmed with ermine." Then representatives of various foreign
governments, resplendent with medals and insignia of rank,
were seated behind the Justices of the Supreme Court.

While Hamlin spoke, many of his listeners must have recalled with amusement the unconscious slip he had made at a
previous joint session of Congress on February 8, when 212
electoral votes were cast for Lincoln, while only 21 were tallied
for his opponent on the Democratic ticket, General George B.
McClellan. Hamlin had then said: "I therefore declare
Abraham Lincoln elected President of the United States for
four years from the fourth day of March, 1835." The members
of the House and Senate had laughed good-naturedly at the
wrong date, but Hamlin was unaware of his error until Schuyler
Colfax, the Speaker of the House, whispered to him. He smiled
and made a correction.

Hamlin's farewell address was a short and gracious speech in
which he simply thanked the Senators for their kindness to him.
At its conclusion he turned to Johnson and asked him if he was
ready to take the oath of office as Vice President. Johnson stood
up and said that he was, but instead of waiting for Hamlin to
administer the oath, he plunged abruptly into what was
apparently intended to be his speech of acceptance. Only the
newspaper accounts of the day give a truthful approximation
of what he actually said.*

The New York *World,* an opposition paper which was to
plague Johnson with his own words for weeks afterward, reported the speech as follows: "By choice of the people, he said,

---

* On March 9, Johnson wrote to Richard Sutton, Chief Reporter of the
Senate, saying: "I see from the *Congressional Globe* that the proceedings of
Saturday, the 4 inst. have not as yet been published, and as I understand there
has been some criticism ... will you ... preserve the original notes ... and bring
me an accurate copy of your report of what I said on that occasion." The
speech, as published in the *Globe* on March 17, is obviously rewritten.

he had been made presiding officer of this body, and, in presenting himself here in obedience to the behests of the Constitution of the United States, it would, perhaps, not be out of
place to remark just here what a striking thing the Constitution
was. It was the Constitution of the people of the country, and
under it, here today, before the American Senate, he felt that
he was a man and an American citizen. He had a proud
illustration of the fact that, under the Constitution, a man
could rise from the ranks to occupy the second place in the
gift of the American people and of the American government.
Those of us who have labored our whole lives for the establishment of a free government knew how to cherish its great bless-
ings. He would say to Senators and to others before him – to
the Supreme Court, which sat before him, that they all got
their power from the people of this country. Turning toward
Mr. Chase, Mr. Johnson said: 'And your exaltation and position
depend upon the people.' Then turning toward the Cabinet,
he said: 'And I will say to you, Mr. Secretary Seward, and to
you, Mr. Secretary Stanton, and to you, Mr. Secretary – ' (To
a gentleman nearby, *sotto voce,* 'Who is Secretary of the Navy?'
The person addressed replied in a whisper, 'Mr. Welles') – 'and
to you, Mr. Secretary Welles, I would say, you derive your
power from the people.' Mr. Johnson then remarked that the
great element of vitality in this government was its nearness and
proximity to the people. He wanted to say to all who heard
him in the face of the American people, that all power was
derived from the people. He would say in the hearing of the
foreign ministers, for he was going to tell the truth here today,
that he was a plebian – he thanked God for it."

By this time, despite the chattering of the women in the
gallery, Johnson's audience, which was expecting the brief,
formal speech that was customary for the occasion, had caught
on to the fact that something was wrong. The speaker's florid
face and peculiar manner of speaking caused the unruly crowd

to fall silent. The silence emphasized the lack of meaning in what was being said. The loud, pompous voice went on to boast several times more about its plebian origin; then it drifted off to Tennessee, where God was again thanked that it was still a state in the Union although "there had been an interregnum, a hiatus." It was obvious to everyone now that the Vice-President-elect was trying to show off his political vocabulary but could not put the high-sounding words together to make sense.

Johnson's speech had originally been scheduled to end before members of the diplomatic corps entered the Senate Chamber. But the timing had gone wrong, and the Vice-President-elect rambled on while the august gentlemen from abroad listened with impassive faces. The members of the House were crowding in before anyone could stop the hapless speaker. The Democrats were secretly delighted at what was happening, but the Republicans took it badly. Senator Zachariah Chandler of Michigan wrote later to his wife: "I was never so mortified in my life. Had I been able to find a small hole, I should have dropped through it out of sight."

Amid audible remarks of "What a shame!" and "Tell him to stop," Johnson was temporarily silenced. Hamlin then tried to administer the oath of office quickly. But Johnson was in no condition to be hurried. Hamlin had to read the oath by single sentences and sometimes prompt the befuddled man. According to the *World,* Johnson "stumbled, stammered, repeated portions of it several times over. The moment that he concluded this task, Mr. Johnson turned to the audience and commenced another speech, giving to those assembled his ideas of the oath which he had just taken. He had uttered but two or three sentences when some of the officials standing near him had the good sense to stop him."

Hamlin then adjourned the old Senate, and the new Vice President called the new Senate to order. J. W. Forney, the

Clerk of the Senate, read a proclamation convening an extraordinary session which was needed to confirm various military and governmental appointments. But Johnson's ordeal was not yet over. Eight newly elected Senators were called upon to take their oath of office. Johnson held out a Bible to them, so they could touch it and bow their heads. Then he dismissed them without formally giving them the oath. Some of the bewildered Senators began leaving the stand. Forney had to take over and recall them so he could administer the official oath of office. Since the weather was rapidly improving, he then announced that the procession to the east front of the building should be formed.

The great occasion had begun badly, and there was much shaking of heads when the people who had been in the Senate Chamber went outside to seek places on the platform. This temporary structure had been built over the grand central staircase between the two statuary groups that symbolize America's beginnings. It was the first inauguration to be held in front of the new iron dome, which had been completed on December 2, 1863, when the head of Thomas Crawford's statue of Freedom was hauled into place.

The New York *Herald*'s correspondent tells how the platform quickly filled up with people: "Ladies, Senators, Negroes, Justices, secretaries, diplomats, and people generally, tumbled upon the platform pell-mell. As the ladies moved on to the north entrance there was a grand national display of ankles. Representative ankles were exhibited by the fair dames and lasses of every state in the Union. The variety of shape and size of hose was perfectly bewildering; but every foot was muddy and every skirt bedraggled. . . . Colored persons innumerable flocked around, though none were admitted to the Capitol. Soldiers off duty were present in large numbers. . . . Men, women, and children soaked about quietly, caught cold, and waited for something to see. . . . The rain had taken all the starch out of them.

"Stanton and Seward retired to the left at some distance from the President and sat down together. They seemed very friendly. Stanton had his arm around Seward's neck and constantly whispered in his ear. Welles sat by himself, and Justice Chase sat erect and dignified, evidently reflecting that he ought to be in Lincoln's place. Senator Sumner stood prominently forward as if to attract attention. . . . The President smiled to himself and seemed greatly to enjoy the sunshine which now streamed upon him. He was dressed in black, with a plain frock coat. In his hand he held a printed copy of his inaugural address. The marshals of the day were grouped around the President, swelling with pride, and often excluding him from sight. The planks of the platform were wet, and the airy position rather chilly. The bands played away most lustily, and their 'Hail to the Chief' could scarcely be stopped.

"From the platform nothing could be seen but a sea of faces below and a sea of mud beyond. . . . In the Capitol all the windows were filled with ladies, and the steps and esplanade at the north wing presented the same dense crowd that the central steps did, while on the unfinished parts of the south wing, on all the scaffolding, hundreds of soldiers had clambered up and decorated all that part with the army blue. . . . As the President came forward there was a cheer but not a great one, and at the same time the sun burst through the clouds, and, though pretty well to the south, lighted up the whole east face very brilliantly. . . . Out by the colossal statue of Washington that faced the president with a monitory finger pointed to Heaven . . . [Greenough's seated, semi-nude marble figure, now in the Smithsonian] the crowd was scattered thinly; but . . . toward the Capitol it grew denser at every step, until it became a packed mass impossible to penetrate. This mass surged in silence below. Above this was the central mass about the President. . . .

"At about one o'clock ... the President rose and stepped forward to the reading desk. He was greeted with very faint applause; indeed there was no enthusiasm throughout the address. It was not strictly an inaugural address, since it was read before Mr. Lincoln took the oath. It was more like a valedictory. The President read in a very loud, clear voice, and hundreds of the audience could hear it.

"During the delivery of the speech Stanton and Seward were remarkably attentive, rising and bending forward to listen. The crowd kept pushing nearer and nearer the platform. Sumner smiled superciliously at the frequent scriptural quotations. Negroes ejaculated 'Bress de Lord' in a low murmur at the end of almost every sentence. Beyond this there was no cheering of any consequence. Even the soldiers did not hurrah much. The statement that 'the progress of our arms ... is, I trust, reasonably satisfactory and encouraging to all' met with no response, although the President paused significantly. The declaration that we accepted the war 'rather than let the nation perish' drew the first cheer. The remark that slavery would cease with the war was applauded. The satirical observation that men ask God's assistance in wringing bread from other men's faces caused a half-laugh. These were the only marks of approbation until the close of the address. After a brief pause the President and Chief Justice rose together and the oath of office was administered. The voice of the Chief Justice was inaudible, but the workings of his countenance could be distinctly seen as he labored to be impressive. Then there was a cheer, and the President came forward and bowed and smiled. During the whole ceremony he looked unusually handsome. When delivering his speech his face glowed with enthusiasm, and he evidently felt every word that he uttered.

"Cries for Andy Johnson next ensued. There was a momentary delay and then the Vice President presented himself and waved both hands. There were calls of 'Speech! Speech!' and some applause when Andy appeared. He rubbed his red face with his hands as if to clear up his ideas, but did not succeed and said nothing. A lane was then opened through the crowd on the platform, and the Presidential party retired into the Capitol amid the thunders of artillery in Capitol Square and the music of the bands."

One incident that went almost unnoticed had to do with the strange actions of a man who had a card of admission to the Capitol which he had probably procured through Senator John T. Hale of New Hampshire, for he was secretly engaged to marry the Senator's daughter. This good-looking young man tried to force his way through the line of police as the President passed. He was forcibly ejected from the Rotunda, but, oddly enough, was not arrested. Weeks later, when the nation-wide man hunt for the President's assassin was under way, a photograph of this man was shown to Benjamin B. French, Commissioner of Public Buildings, who had been present when the intruder behaved so oddly. He identified the picture as a portrait of John Wilkes Booth, the celebrated actor of an even more celebrated theatrical family. And one of Booth's friends testified that the violently pro-Southern actor had said: "What an excellent chance I had to kill the President, if I had wished, on inauguration day!"

Unaware of the presence in the Capitol of the man who was destined to slay him just forty-one days later, Abraham Lincoln, now inaugurated as President of the United States for the second time, was led to his waiting carriage to return to the White House. As the President's carriage was about to leave, his eleven-year-old son, little Tad, scrambled into it. Mrs. Lincoln and their first-born son, Robert Todd Lincoln, who had just been made a captain on Grant's staff, followed in other carriages.

Walt Whitman wrote about Lincoln's return to the White House: "He was in his plain two-horse barouche, and looked very much worn and tired; the lines, indeed, of vast responsibilities, intricate questions, and demands of life and death, cut deeper than ever upon his dark brown face; yet all the goodness, tenderness, sadness, and canny shrewdness [showed] underneath the furrows."

And so ended one of the most memorable inaugurations in American history. The Senators re-entered the Senate Chamber, paying little attention to the President's speech but discussing Johnson's behavior with the petty spite of washerwomen gossiping over a backyard fence. They waited for the new Vice President to appear, so he could officially adjourn the Senate, but he never came and thus brought more malicious comment down upon himself. Finally the Senators departed by ones and twos, and the great halls of the Capitol became silent.

At Lincoln's first inauguration in 1861, which had been held in front of an unfinished Capitol with part of the dome still open to the sky, and with armed guards posted in the windows to protect the first Republican President from possible violence, Lincoln's course of action was still unknown, even to himself. He then faced a divided nation, and nothing he had said on his long journey from Springfield to Washington had given anyone reason to believe that he had the strength or the wisdom to guide the nation through the troubled times that were ahead. But as iron gains strength when beaten upon an anvil, four years of war had made the peace-loving prairie lawyer tougher-minded, more eloquent, and much wiser. And the people of the Northern states, recognizing this, had given his administration a vote of confidence by a return of 55 per cent of the popular vote in the Presidential election of 1864.

The great issue of human slavery which had divided the country for so long was at last nearing a final solution. Two border states, Missouri and Tennessee, had recently voted to abolish slavery of their own accord; this meant that the necessary two-thirds majority of states needed to propose an amendment to the Constitution had been reached. And the Thirteenth Amendment, which would end slavery forever in the United States, had been passed by both the House and the Senate. It had only to be ratified by the legislatures of three-fourths of the states, and seventeen of them had already done so. (The Amendment went into effect on December 18, 1865.) With the end of the war and slavery in sight, the re-elected President could look forward confidently to a second term of office during which he would be busy rebuilding the nation instead of trying to hold it together by force of arms.

As Lincoln stood on the wind-swept platform in front of the Capitol on that changeable March day in 1865, he could look beyond the crowd to see the brick walls and iron-barred windows of the Old Capitol and Carroll Prisons, which were reserved for political offenders, spies, and soldiers charged with serious crimes. He knew, as did everyone in Washington who read a newspaper, that less than twenty-four hours before, a Union soldier found guilty of the attempted rape of a fifteen-year-old girl, had been executed in the prison yard of the Old Capitol by a firing squad of eight men from the Twelfth Volunteer Reserve Corps. The President, whose well-known readiness to pardon was sometimes imposed upon, had made no attempt to save the life of a man who had committed a criminal act under particularly brutal circumstances.

Lincoln is sometimes thought of as having been too lenient and easygoing, but he could be firm when the situation required strength and decisiveness. The next to the last sentence of the address he delivered that day shows how determined he was to finish the stern task to which he was committed. But the harsh attitude of the Old Testament changes quickly in the famous peroration, which is much nearer to the New Testament in thought and words:

Fondly do we hope — fervently do we pray — that this mighty scourge of war may speedily pass away. Yet, if God wills that it continue, until all the wealth piled by the bondsman's two hundred and fifty years of unrequited toil shall be sunk, and until every drop of blood drawn with the lash, shall be paid by another drawn with the sword, as was said three thousand years ago, so still it must be said "the judgments of the Lord are true and righteous altogether."

With malice toward none; with charity for all; with firmness in the right, as God gives us to see the right, let us strive on to finish the work we are in; to bind up the nation's wounds; to care for him who shall have borne the battle, and for his widow, and his orphan — to do all which may achieve and cherish a just, and a lasting peace, among ourselves, and with all nations.

American reaction to the President's Second Inaugural Address followed party lines as usual. The unfriendly New York *World* called it "a prose parody of John Brown's hymn" and said that it substituted piety for much needed ideas of statesmanship. Then it came out with what many people must have been thinking privately: "The pity of it, that the life of this Chief Magistrate should be made precious to us by the thought that he at least excludes from the most august station in the land the person who defiled our chief council chamber . . . with the spewings of a drunken boor." Pro-administration papers were naturally kinder in their comment, but few people seemed to realize that the President had said anything out of the ordinary. Charles Francis Adams spoke well of the speech, and so did Thurlow Weed, who wrote a complimentary letter to the President, but Weed, who was a shrewd politician, may just have been flattering. In England, where more impartiality was to be expected, the powerful London *Times* was mildly favorable, but the *Spectator* said unreservedly that the "short state paper, for political weight, moral dignity, and unaffected solemnity, has had no equal in our time. . . . No statesman ever uttered words stamped at once with a seal of so deep a wisdom and so true a simplicity."

The President's arduous day was not yet over. He had to greet several thousand people at a White House levee that evening. It was still an American tradition that anyone could attend such a public reception who had the patience and the strength to wait for hours to gain admission. It was also a tradition that the President must stand in the receiving line to shake each person's hand and utter a few meaningless words of greeting.

Instead of getting some rest for the occasion, Mr. and Mrs. Lincoln drove out that afternoon in an open barouche. They stopped on the way at Willard's Hotel so Mrs. Lincoln could see one of her friends.

After dinner, Cabinet members and their families began arriving early at the White House in order to have a few moments with the President before the crowd got in. A temporary wooden platform had been erected at one of the East Room windows so the long line of visitors could be channeled past the President across the room and then out through the high window to the side street. At eight o'clock, when the gates were thrown open, some two thousand people tried to storm the main entrance. The doors to the White House were opened for only a few minutes at a time in order to control the rate of entry. Even with this precaution the *Chronicle* reported that "some of the more unfortunate females, who were caught in the surging mass, actually shrieked with pain while several fainted and were carried away."

When the visitors got inside they had to carry their hats and coats, for no provision had been made for checking anything. They were hurried through the halls to the East Room, where the Marine Band was playing and where Government and military dignitaries were clustered in exclusive little groups around the formal reception room. There, according to the

Star, "the President, in a plain black suit with white kid gloves, was in excellent spirits . . . and received all visitors cordially. It is estimated that he shook hands with between five and six thousand persons during the course of the evening. Mrs. Lincoln was also kept fully occupied. . . . She was dressed most charmingly in an elegant white satin dress, the skirt tastefully draped with black lace, a rich black lace shawl . . . a costly pearl necklace, etc. etc."

The carpets were covered to protect them from mud brought in on the visitors' feet, and soldiers and police guided the line of eager people through the hallways. But despite these precautions, the visitors did some damage as they always did when they were permitted to invade the White House. Even the watchful soldiers and Metropolitan Police could not entirely prevent the souvenir hunting and actual vandalism that was characteristic of American sightseers in the mid-nineteenth century. William H. Crook, one of the President's four body-guards, said that "a great piece of red brocade, a yard square almost, was cut from the window-hangings of the East Room, and another piece, not quite so large, from a curtain in the Green Room. Besides this, flowers from the floral design in the lace curtains were cut out, evidently for an ornament for the top of pincushions or something of the sort."

The crush went on all evening. Those who came by carriage had to wait for several hours while the long line of vehicles ahead of them slowly unloaded passengers. At eleven o'clock a large crowd was still trying to gain admission, but the doors were firmly closed on the hour, and the latecomers had to go home without seeing the President. Just before midnight the Marine Band played "Yankee Doodle," and the White House was then cleared of guests so rapidly that the downstairs rooms were dark before the clock struck twelve.

News stories about the inauguration were telegraphed to the

Pacific Coast on the line that had replaced the Pony Express during the first year of the war. It was raining over parts of the long route, and the imperfectly insulated wires were affected by the wet weather, but detailed descriptions of the inaugural ceremonies got through. The news was sent by wire to all the major cities of the Northern States and Canada; communication with the states still under the control of the Confederacy, however, had been cut off for nearly four years. Word had to be dispatched to Europe by ship, for the Atlantic cable, which had been completed in August 1858, had sputtered a few signals and then had slowly faded into inaudibility because its defective insulation could not withstand the corrosive effects of salt water. The cable was not restored to service until July 1866.

The Senate, sitting in extra session on Monday, March 6, was called to order at noon by the new Vice President. As soon as the formalities of the day were over, Henry Wilson of Massachusetts got up to ask for the floor. When Vice President Johnson recognized him and gave him the right to speak, he proposed a resolution that was intended to be a deliberate insult to the Senate's new leader. It directed "the sergeant-at-arms to remove from the Senate side of the Capitol the sale of intoxicating or spirituous liquors." Wilson said that he was willing to let his resolution lie over until the next day, but his colleague from Massachusetts, Charles Sumner, got up to ask very coolly, "Why not act upon it now?" Everyone must have felt very uncomfortable, but no one dared to offer an objection, so the resolution was considered passed. The sergeant-at-arms promptly closed the bar known as "The Hole in the Wall," and the sign over it which read EXCLUSIVELY FOR SENATORS was turned to the wall.

The public reception at the White House on Saturday evening had been a minor affair compared with the great Inauguration Ball that was held in the Patent Office on Monday night. The north wing had just been completed, and the building formed an enormous quadrangle with an open court in the center. Its high-ceilinged second story was designed for displaying the thousands of patent models that had been accumulating ever since the disastrous fire of 1836 destroyed the earlier ones. It was also a national museum, where the original copy of the Declaration of Independence, Franklin's printing press, and various relics of Washington, Lafayette, Jefferson, Jackson, and other historic figures were on public view. Part of the building's spacious halls had served as a military hospital from October 1861 to March 1863.

All four of the enormous second-story rooms, each approximately 270 feet long and 60 feet wide, were used for the ball. The south wing, with its elaborate and colorful English tiled floor, tall pillars, and large glass showcases, was the main entrance. The east wing was used as a promenade leading to the north wing, which was to be the main ballroom. The elaborate supper was served at midnight in the west wing.

The engraved tickets cost ten dollars each; this price entitled a gentleman to bring as many ladies as he wished. The local newspapers had made it clear that — contrary to rumor — Negroes would not be admitted to the ballroom, although many of them were, of course, employed as waiters and servants. Three orchestras were used; the one that provided the dance music was conducted by Professor William Withers, Jr., leader of the orchestra at Ford's Theatre.

The north hall was described by the Washington *Morning Chronicle* as being "magnificently decorated with our glorious national emblem, large banners being festooned from the ceiling to the floor. Between the windows were artistically disposed guidons and corps insignia, bearing the marks of the various army corps, brigades, and regiments of the United States service, while miniature American flags were crossed and placed at intervals on the walls. Over the main entrance approaching from the east, on a balcony, was stationed a fine military band, and midway in the hall, on the southern side, upon another balcony, tastefully decorated, as was the former, with bunting, was placed the orchestra under the care of Mr. Withers. So, between the two bands, the music . . . was kept up continually. On a raised dais immediately opposite the latter balcony, and on the northern side of the hall, were placed handsome sofas of blue and gold adornment . . . as seats of honor for the President and his suite." The New York *World* was unhappy about the dais and its gold chairs, muttering editorially that "it needed but little imagination to transform them into thrones."

The main entrance to the building was brilliantly illuminated by ten powerful calcium lights. Their dazzling hard-shadowed glare gave an illusion of depth to the Doric-columned portico which made the building look like an American version of a Greek temple. The first guests arrived shortly before nine o'clock and were sent down the long dirty halls where puddles of water had been left by hurrying waiters and where department clerks still sat with feet propped up on their desks, puffing vigorously on their cigars while they inspected the pretty girls in their colorful evening dresses. People kept coming until midnight, by which time some four thousand guests had arrived. The party began at ten, when the military band in the north hall played a "National Inauguration March" especially composed for the occasion; after this a grand promenade around the ballroom was staged with much ceremony. Quadrilles, lancers, schottisches, polkas, and waltzes then followed. The New York *World* had a poor opinion of the crowd and the dancing, saying that "the men threw their legs around like the spokes of a wheel; the women hopped, skipped, and jumped about in a manner which would have made a French dancing master commit suicide. They appeared to think that every other dance was a waltz and acted accordingly and exhibited the greatest science when they were kicking up the most dust."

About half-past ten there was a sudden pause; the military band took over and struck up "Hail to the Chief," while a passageway was formed through the crowd for the entrance of the Presidential party. The President came down the aisle with Schuyler Colfax, followed by Mrs. Lincoln, who was escorted by Senator Charles Sumner. The *Chronicle* said that "the procession promenaded the entire length of the hall. . . . Mrs. Lincoln was attired in faultless taste. She wore a white silk skirt, a berthe of point lace and puffs of silk, and a white fan, trimmed with ermine and silvered spangles, white kid gloves and lace handkerchief, and a necklace, bracelet, and earrings of pearls. Her hair was brushed closely back from her forehead, and a head-dress, composed of a wreath of white jessamines and purple violets, with long trailing vines, completed a most *recherché* costume. The President was dressed in a full suit of black, with white kid gloves."

Later in the evening members of the Cabinet and the diplomatic corps made their entry. Vice President Johnson was apparently well enough to attend, and his appearance, after his rebuff in the Senate that day, started tongues wagging. The crowd pressed in close around the central platform to stare at the President and the other celebrities there. Among the notables on the platform was Captain Robert Todd Lincoln in full-dress uniform, paying close attention to the daughter of the Senator from Iowa, Mary Eunice Harlan, whom he was later to marry.

Much of the gossip during the evening centered around the Lincoln family. Little Tad's imperious manner in dealing with the Black Horse Cavalry, which had been detailed to guard the White House, was a favorite topic of discussion. It was said that he issued orders like a major general, would not let his favorite soldiers be sent away from Washington, and forced his father to make speeches to the troops. Worst of all, it was rumored that he commanded the members of the band to play serenades at any hour of the day or night. "Are we to have a Prince Imperial?" the New York *Herald* asked querulously.

Few people had anything against Tad except that they often called him a spoiled brat. His older brother's appointment as a captain on Grant's staff had come in for some criticism, but now that he was at last in the Army, the public had lost much of its hositility toward him. Mrs. Lincoln, however, had many real enemies. Her relatives in the Confederacy, her extravagance in costume, and her expenditures for decorating the White House in war time made her unpopular. The *Herald* went out of its way to report that as she sat on the platform "her face bore an expression which assured all observers that she was the wife of the President." And caustic remarks were being made about what she would do to punish the Congressmen who had defeated the omnibus bill to provide $40,000 for still further refurnishing the White House.

During the evening there was a brief fight in the temporary kitchen set up in the Patent Office for the preparation of the midnight supper. For no ascertainable reason one temperamental cook threw a bowl of chicken salad at another. The police promptly arrested the thrower and took him to court, where he was fined one dollar. Meanwhile, the other cooks worked busily getting the great feast ready. The bill of fare as reported in the *Star* read:

Oyster stews, terrapin do., oysters pickled. Beef — Roast beef, filet de beef, beef a la mode, beef a l'anglais. Veal — Leg of veal, fricandeau, veal malakoff. Poultry — Roast turkey, boned do., Roast chicken, grouse, boned and roast. Game — Pheasant, quail, venison. Patetes — Patetete of duck engelee, patete de fois gras. Smoked — Ham, tongue engelee, Tongue plain. Salades — Chickens, lobster. Ornamental Pyramides — Nougate, orange, caramel with fancy cream candy, cocoanut, macaroon, croquant, chocolate, tree cakes. Cakes and Tarts. Almond sponge, belle alliance, dame blanche, macaroon tart, tart a la Nelson, tarte, a l'Orleans, tarte a la Portugaise, tarte a la Vienne, pound cake, sponge cake, lady cake, fancy small cakes. Jellies and Creams — Calfsfoot and wine jelly, Charlotte a la Russe, do. vanilla, blanc mangue [*sic*], creme Neapolitane, do. a la nelson, de chateaubriand, do. a la Smyrna, do. nesselrode, bombe a la vanilla. Ice Cream — vanilla, lemon, white coffee, chocolate, burnt almonds, maraschino. Fruit ices — Strawberry, orange, lemon. Desert — Grapes, almonds, raisins, &c. Coffee and Chocolate.

The President and his party were shown into the big supper room first and were seated at the head of a 250-foot-long table so they could eat in peace before the crowd was admitted. They thus had a chance to see the display in all its gastronomic glory. The center ornament was a huge model of the Capitol made of pastry covered with white icing. This stood on a large pedestal upon which were other pastry models, including one of Fort Sumter with realistic-looking ironclads around it; a group of Washington and his generals; a symbolic statue of Liberty; as well as such abstract ideas as "The Progress of Civilization" and "The Advance of the Arts and Sciences in America."

There were other edible pieces representing the various military services, the most striking of which was one of Admiral Farragut's flagship, the *Hartford,* with that daring officer tied to the mast. Over the army scenes showing the troops in camp and in battle were three eagles carrying these mottoes: "The Union must and shall be preserved" — Andrew Jackson; "Eternal vigilance is the price of liberty" — Thomas Jefferson; "We shall nobly save or meanly lose the last best hope of the human race." [*sic*] — Abraham Lincoln.

It was fortunate that the Presidential party was permitted to begin eating before the crowd was admitted to the supper room. As soon as the doors were opened there was a general rush (according to the *Star*) : "The onset of the crowd upon the tables was frightful, and nothing but the immense reserves of eatables would have supplied the demand, or rather the waste. Numbers ... with more audacity than good taste, could be seen snatching whole patés, chickens, legs of veal, halves of turkies, ornamental pyramids, &c., from the tables, and bearing them aloft over the heads of the shuddering crowd, (ladies especially, with greasy ruin to their dresses impending. . . .)

"The floor of the supper room was soon sticky, pasty and oily with wasted confections, mashed cakes and debris of fowl and meat. The ... appropriaters of eatables from the tables left their plates upon the floor ... adding to the difficulty of loco-motion; and gentlemen, in conscientiously giving a wide berth to a lady's skirt, not unfrequently steered clear of Scylla only to fall upon a Charybdis of greasy crockery. Finally everybody was satisfied, even those who felt bound to 'eat their ten dollars' worth' ... the ball room again filled up, and the dance ... was resumed."

When the President and his party wanted to leave, they found it impossible to pass through the mob that was still raid-ing the food tables. They had to enter an alcove between display cases and then go upstairs to a balcony from which they could make their way through devious and little-used narrow passages to an obscure side exit. No one paid any attention to them as they went, for the guests were so busy getting food, eating it, or chattering while they waited for someone to bring it that they did not care about anything else.

The grand ball went on until the early morning hours, and the sky was beginning to lighten when the party finally broke up.

2

The Singleton-Browning Trading Scheme

Monday, March 6, to Saturday, March 11

WHEN THE LAST REVELER left the Patent Office that morning and daylight came in through the high windows to reveal the unpleasant mess which was all that remained of the once imposing display set out on the supper tables, President Lincoln's second term had been launched officially and socially.

South of the city, nearly halfway to Richmond, a dark cloud of smoke was hanging over the already war-ravaged town of Fredericksburg. There was a rich smell of nearly $400,000 worth of burning tobacco in the air because Grant had sent an order to Colonel S. H. Roberts, telling him that "a very considerable contraband trade is carried on across the Potomac by what is known as the Northern Neck, and through Fredericksburg into Richmond." Roberts' men had marched into town on Monday night and had burned twenty-eight railroad cars, eighteen of which were loaded with tobacco belonging to the Confederate government. This raid on Fredericksburg was not an isolated instance, nor was it an insignificant one, for in this case its reverberations were to reach the White House.

To understand the complex issues involved, one has to remember that the South was poor in mines and machinery but rich in cotton and tobacco. The Confederate government expected to finance its wartime operations by exporting cotton, so it sent agents to Europe to obtain ships, munitions, and medical goods in exchange for the much needed fiber. To prevent this, Lincoln issued a proclamation blockading Confederate ports a few days after Fort Sumter was surrendered.

A situation was then created by which the rest of the world was soon desperately short of cotton while the warehouses of the Confederacy were bursting with it. In the summer of 1862, cotton was worth only ten cents a pound in the South, yet it cost only four cents a pound to ship it to Boston, where it could be sold for thirty cents. In August 1864 it reached a peak price of $1.90 there.

Such a situation was very tempting to unscrupulous traders everywhere. Attracted by the heady smell of easy money, they came swarming from all the ports of the world. Blockade running was popular during the early years of the war before the Federal blockade became effective. Although this illicit enterprise was fairly dangerous and somewhat of a gamble, it was fabulously profitable. A ship could be purchased and outfitted in Europe, sent at night through the Federal fleet, loaded in a Southern port with cotton, and then if it got through the blockade, its precious cargo could be sold in England or France. Many ships were captured but many more got through, and the business was doubly profitable, for money was made not only by selling the cotton at high prices abroad, but also by bringing in weapons, medical supplies, needles, salt, fabrics, and luxury goods, all of which could be sold advantageously in the South.

A great deal has been written about running the Atlantic blockade, which was a romantic and glamorous business with exciting chases at sea and much derring-do. Less is known about the numerous shipments that went through the Federal lines by land. But one thing is certain: the cotton mills of the North never stopped running during the entire war. Consumption dropped off more and more each year, but even in 1864, 220,000 bales of cotton were brought in. Some of it was shipped by sea from the West Indies or Matamoros, Mexico; most of it came north by wagon and rail.

Cotton and tobacco were the chief commercial assets of the Confederacy. Trading in the North in these materials was not always contraband; much of it was legal under the Captured and Abandoned Property Act of March 3, 1863. As defined by the United States Government, "captured" property meant any goods taken by force of arms which were not of a military nature, such as cotton or tobacco. "Abandoned" property was defined as anything belonging to a person who was absent while "aiding or encouraging the rebellion." The Treasury Department was authorized to handle trading in all seized property, and special Treasury agents were appointed to issue trading permits to individuals or companies. In charge of this large corps of men was Hanson A. Risley, Supervising Special Agent of the Treasury Department, whose rulings soon became law on all such permits, although each one had to be personally approved and signed by the President.

Although trading under Treasury permits was legal there was bitter criticism of it, especially from soldiers and Federal employees in the West, where it first went into operation. However, the attitudes of the President and his Cabinet toward such trading are a matter of record. On September 9, 1864, Gideon Welles, Secretary of the Navy, noted in his diary that the Secretary of the Treasury, W. P. Fessenden, had presented some new trade regulations at the Cabinet meeting that day:

> The regulations of Mr. Fessenden met with little favor.... The President objected ... to that part of the plan which threw upon him the odium, and labor, and responsibility of selecting the agents.... Both he and Mr. Fessenden, however, started with the assumption ... that the cotton within the Rebel lines must be sought for and brought out, — trading on the part of the government with the enemy.

Postmaster General Montgomery Blair was outspokenly opposed to the whole scheme, and so was Welles. Yet on December 12, 1864, Lincoln was still defending his policy. In a letter to Major General Edward R. S. Canby, whose headquarters were in New Orleans, he wrote:

> As to cotton. By the external blockade, the price is made certainly six times as great as it was. And yet the enemy gets through at least one sixth part as much in a given period, say a year, as if there were no blockade, and receives as much for it, as he would for a full crop in time of peace. The effect in substance is, that we give him six ordinary crops, without the trouble of producing any but the first; and at the same time leave his fields and his laborers free to produce provisions. You know how this keeps up his armies at home, and procures supplies from abroad. For other reasons we cannot give up the blockade, and hence it becomes immensely important to us to get the cotton away from him. Better give him guns for it, than let him, as now, get both guns and ammunition for it. But even this only presents part of the public interest to get out cotton. Our finances are greatly involved in the matter. The way cotton goes now carries so much gold out of the country as to leave us paper currency only, and that so far depreciated, as that for every hard dollar's worth of supplies we obtain, we contract to pay two and a half hard dollars hereafter. This is much to be regretted; and ... it demands an earnest effort on the part of all to correct it. And if pecuniary greed can be made to aid us in such effort, let us be thankful that so much good can be got out of pecuniary greed.

Lincoln had for many years been a practicing attorney in Illinois, and his work there had brought him into close contact with other lawyers, with whom he had formed friendships and business alliances. When he came to Washington as President, he appointed his friend and former law partner, Ward Hill Lamon, Marshal of the District of Columbia, and he permitted

Leonard Swett, with whom he had often ridden the Eighth Judicial Circuit, to go to California in 1863 armed with a writ to take over the very profitable New Almaden Quicksilver Mine for an Eastern company which Swett represented as an attorney and in which he owned stock. It is therefore not surprising to find Lamon and Swett also benefiting from the trade in seized Confederate property. The records of the Treasury Department show that Robert Lamon (Ward Hill Lamon's younger brother), was issued a permit to bring 45,000 bales of cotton out of the Southern states, and that Leonard Swett was appointed by the Treasury as its official field agent to go into the South to purchase vast amounts of cotton for the Government on a commission basis.

Still more closely connected with the Lincoln family was the huge speculation undertaken late in 1864 by a group of wealthy investors under the guidance of two other Illinois attorneys who knew the President. The first was "General" James Washington Singleton, who had been born in Virginia in 1811. Singleton read medicine and had even practiced it for a short while. Perhaps he thought it too unprofitable a profession to provide a good living in a pioneer land, for he soon switched to law and emigrated to Illinois. He got his title of "General" in 1846 for his work in the ruthless campaign to drive the Mormons out of Nauvoo, which was then the largest city in the state.

Singleton married one of Mrs. Lincoln's numerous cousins. He became a successful railroad attorney, and in 1854 set up an office in Quincy, where he built a fine home. He was elected to the state legislature on the Democratic ticket and often came in contact with Lincoln in both law and politics. It could hardly be said that they were friends, for the only expression of opinion about Singleton that Lincoln left on record (made verbally to John Hay on May 7, 1861) was that he was "a miracle of meanness." Throughout the war Singleton was associated with the subversive Copperhead organization known as the Sons of Lib-

erty, and in November 1864, he went to Canada to confer with
the Confederate commissioners who had been sent with secret
service funds to make war upon the United States from outside
its borders. Singleton was ostensibly trying to establish himself
as a peacemaker, a seemingly well-intentioned go-between who
had good connections with both Lincoln and Jefferson Davis
and who might therefore help to bring the war to an end.

His real intentions and motives are revealed in a diary kept
by his fellow attorney from Quincy, Orville Hickman Browning. This diary, together with letters and papers of Browning,
Singleton, and certain Treasury Department records show that
Singleton was really involved in a gigantic plot to make millions
from speculation in cotton and tobacco. Although he had ready
access to the White House, Singleton was not close to Lincoln,
but Browning was on fairly intimate terms with the President.

Browning had been born in Harrison, Kentucky, in 1806. He
was well educated and had all the assets of handsome appearance
and cultivated manners that Lincoln lacked. To the end of his
life he played the part of the suave Kentucky gentleman, even
to the point of wearing ruffled shirts after they had gone out of
style. He moved to Quincy, Illinois, in 1831, and took part in
the Black Hawk War the next year, during which he may first
have met Lincoln. Law and politics often brought Lincoln and
Browning together after that, and in 1861, when Stephen A.
Douglas died, Governor Richard Yates appointed Browning to
the United States Senate to complete Douglas' unfinished term.
He flourished in wartime Washington, which was exactly
the sort of place where his peculiar talents could best be put
to use.

He was not re-elected in 1863, but he returned to Washington
to enter the practice of law there with two former Senators who
also had good political connections. (One of them was closely
related to General Sherman.) The firm was especially successful
in obtaining favors from Republican leaders for contractors

seeking Government business. Browning's characteristic day in
Washington began with his making the rounds of the various
departments that might be useful to his clients. He also did a
good business in defending Confederates and people charged
with being disloyal. He had been openly against the administration's efforts to emancipate the slaves, and he differed with
Lincoln on many other political principles, but long acquaintance always enabled him to reach the President.

After Singleton had conferred with Confederate commissioner Beverley Tucker in Canada, he got together with Browning to make some easy money. The names Ward Lamon and
Leonard Swett again appear. In testimony taken on February 2, 1865, before a House Committee, Colonel Lafayette C.
Baker, head of the United States Secret Service, testified that
"in . . . November last . . . I was approached . . . for the purpose
of getting Beverley Tucker from Canada, and pass him through
our lines, ostensibly for the purpose of seeing his family, but
really for the purpose of assisting them in getting cotton out."
Baker said that Lamon and Swett — among others — applied to
the President for a pass for Tucker. The man who was chief of
the United States Secret Service during the Civil War was not
always a reliable witness, but if what he said is true, the President's friends, in their eagerness to make easy money, were
bordering on treason.

Baker's superiors in the War Department told him that they
would not let Tucker go through the lines, and they warned him
not to accept money from any of those involved. Since Singleton was in Montreal later that November and in touch with
Tucker on his "peace" mission, he may have taken up where
Baker left off. This raises the interesting possibility that some
of the large capital required for Singleton's operations may have
been supplied by the Confederates.

On December 24, 1864, Browning went to the President to

ask him to let Singleton go to Richmond. And then, on January 5, 1865, Browning made this entry in his diary:

> The President sent me word last night that he wished to see me this morning I had previously talked with him about permitting Singleton to go South to buy Cotton, tobacco &c a scheme out of which he, Singleton, Judge Hughes of the Court of Claims, Senator Morgan myself and some others, hope to make some money, and do the Country some service. He wished to see me upon this subject now. We talked it all over, and before leaving him he gave me two cards for Singleton . . . to pass our lines with ordinary baggage, and go South. . . .
>
> He gave me a history of two of the half sisters of Mrs. Lincoln who are rebels. Mrs Helm and Mrs. White* and wished some of us to see Mrs. Helm, and make some arrangement with her about 600 bales of cotton she claims to have somewhere in the South.

Lincoln's mentioning Mrs. Helm's 600 bales of cotton to Singleton was a stroke of luck for that shrewd speculator. He now had one of the Lincoln family involved in his spiderlike plot, and he meant to use the connection for all it was worth. The deals Singleton made during the two weeks he was in Richmond had the appearance of great success; on his return he told Browning that he had "brought back contracts for seven million dollars worth of Cotton, Tobacco, Rosin and Turpentine, which will make us rich if we can only get it out."

On February 7, Singleton went to New York for ten days to make the necessary arrangements to raise the money to pay for all the produce he had contracted to buy. On the day he left, Browning saw the President, who gave him this letter which Singleton was to deliver to Grant in person:

* The full names of the people involved are: Edwin D. Morgan, Republican Senator from New York; Judge James Hughes, who had resigned from the United States Court of Claims in December 1864, and who later (1866) became cotton agent for the Treasury Department; Mrs. Emilie Todd Helm, widow of General Ben Hardin Helm of the Confederate Army, who had been killed in battle in 1863; and Mrs. Martha Todd White of Selma, Alabama.

Gen. Singleton, who bears you this claims that, he already
has arrangements made if you consent* to bring a large amount
of Southern produce through your lines. For its bearing on our
finances I would be glad for this to be done if it can be
without injuriously disturbing your military operations, or
supplying the enemy. I wish you to be judge and master on
these points. Please see and hear him fully, and decide whether
anything, and if anything, what can be done in the premises.

On the same day Grant telegraphed to General H. W. Halleck
in Washington to notify him that he would be in that city later
in the week. He asked Halleck to inform the Committee on the
Conduct of the War and Congressman Elihu B. Washburne
about his intended visit. Washburne, who was a fellow townsman of Grant's and acted as his unofficial sponsor in Congress,
had evidently communicated to Grant the testimony he had
heard during the previous week about the possible connection
between Beverley Tucker and the men who were speculating in
cotton. Washburne, known as "the watchdog of the Treasury,"
and Grant, who had had his fill of speculators in the West, were
both opposed to the whole business of trading in contraband
goods under Treasury permits. And the fact that such trading
had been made legal only increased their opposition. Grant
arrived in Washington on February 10 and doubtless was told
a great deal about cotton trading during his brief stay in the
city.

Singleton returned from New York on February 17, completely unaware of the trouble that was brewing. On February 22 he and Judge Hughes left for City Point, happily carrying
their letter from the President to Grant. They were probably
too sure of themselves to notice that Lincoln, the careful former
attorney, had inserted the words "if you consent" into the body

---

* Only the three important words "if you consent" and the signature are in
Lincoln's handwriting. The body of the letter was probably written by one of
the President's secretaries.

of the letter. Those three short words gave the President an excuse to bow out and gave Grant full authority to rule on the mission.

Apparently no word of Singleton's difficulties got back to Browning, who was waiting in Washington for a fortune to fall into his lap. Action which he could not know about was going on behind the scenes. On March 8, Grant telegraphed to Stanton, urging that "orders be sent to the Army and Navy everywhere, to stop supplies going to the interior and annulling all permits for such trade heretofore given." Then, in another telegram, he said: "I believe Gen'l. Singleton should be ordered to return from Richmond and all permits he may have should be revoked. Our ... [spies] in Richmond ... send word that Tobacco is being exchanged on the Potomac for Bacon, and they believe Singleton to be at the bottom of it.

"I am also of the opinion that all permits issued to Judge Hughes should be cancelled. I think the same of all other permits heretofore granted, but in the case of Singleton and Judge Hughes, I believe there is a deep laid plan for making millions and they will sacrifice every interest of the country to succeed. I do not know Hughes personally never having seen him but once, but the conviction here expressed is forced upon me."

Lincoln replied to Grant the same day, pointing out that Singleton and Hughes could be in Richmond only by Grant's authority, and he then reminded the general of his letter of February 7, quoting all of it, including its three key words "if you consent." He then went on to say: "However this may be I now authorize you to get Singleton and Hughes away from Richmond, if you choose, and can. I also authorize you, by an order, or in what form you choose, to suspend all operations on the Treasury-trade-permits, in all places South Eastward of the Alleghenies."

On March 10, when Washburne went to City Point to present a medal to Grant, Browning could not have suspected the hidden purpose of his visit. Many years later Ward Lamon revealed the real motive. According to Lamon, when Washburne heard that Lincoln had given Singleton a pass and Treasury trading permits, he "called immediately on Mr. Lincoln, and after remonstrating with him on the impropriety of such a démarche, threatened to have General Grant countermand the permits if they were not revoked. Naturally, both became excited. Lincoln declared that he did not believe General Grant would take upon himself the responsibility of such an act. 'I will show you, sir, I will show you whether Grant will do it or not,' responded Mr. Washburne as he abruptly withdrew."

Grant not only countermanded Singleton's trading permits, but that same day issued his Special Order Number 48, which canceled all trading permits in all Southern states except those under Sherman's control. Once Grant took this stand, Lincoln did not attempt to overrule him. But he did say: "I wonder when General Grant changed his mind on this subject. He was the first man, after the commencement of the war, to grant a permit for the passage of cotton through the lines, and that to his own father."

Not until March 11, when the morning's papers announced the capture and burning of the tobacco trains at Fredericksburg, did Browning learn what was happening to his great venture.

3

More Plots and Counterplots

Tuesday, March 14, to Tuesday, March 21

DESPITE THE FACT that Lincoln had thousands of enemies, many of whom had threatened his life, anyone who wanted to see him — and who had enough patience to wait — could come to the White House and reach him without a letter of introduction. Lincoln felt that this easy availability kept him in touch with the public. But in those days before Civil Service there were many jobs to be filled by appointments, and the constant pressure of avid office seekers was an intolerable nuisance. The President became ill on March 14 and had to stay in bed for a day or two. No visitors except members of his family or of his Cabinet were allowed to see him. Nevertheless, the halls of the White House were as thronged as ever by office seekers who hoped by some miracle to reach the President and press their claims.

One of Lincoln's bodyguards, William H. Crook, describes the room where the sick man lay: "It was handsomely furnished; the bedstead, bureau, and wash-stand were of heavy mahogany, the bureau and washstand with marble tops; the chairs were of rosewood. Like all the other chambers, it was covered with a carpet. . . .

"All night I walked up and down the long corridor which . . . divided the second story of the White House in half. Usu-

ally the household, with the exception of Mr. Lincoln, was
asleep when I began my watch. . . . When in my patrol I came
near to the door of the President's room I could hear his deep
breathing. Sometimes, after a day of unusual anxiety, I have
heard him moan in his sleep. It gave me a curious sensation.
While the expression of Mr. Lincoln's face was always sad when
he was quiet, it gave one the assurance of calm. He never
seemed to doubt the wisdom of an action when he had once
decided on it. And so when he was in a way defenceless in his
sleep it made me feel the pity that would have been almost an
impertinence when he was awake. I would stand there and
listen until a sort of panic stole over me. If he felt the weight
of things so heavily, how much worse the situation of the country must be than any of us realized! At last I would walk softly
away, feeling as if I had been listening at a keyhole."

By the evening of March 15, the President was well enough
to go to Grover's Theatre with Mrs. Lincoln and her young
friend, Miss Clara Harris, to attend a performance of Mozart's
opera *The Magic Flute.* Two days later he had recovered sufficiently to drive out with Tad and also to visit the National
Hotel on Pennsylvania Avenue at Sixth Street to speak at a
ceremony at which a captured Confederate flag was presented
to Governor Oliver P. Morton of Indiana. The President, the
Governor, and some officers of the 19th Regiment of Indiana
Volunteers — who had been captured at Gettysburg and held in
Confederate prisons ever since — stood on the balcony while the
Marine Band played patriotic airs. Lincoln then addressed a
mixed audience of civilians and soldiers of the regiment. He
began his speech to a crowd composed largely of Indiana people
by reminding them that he "was born in Kentucky, raised in
Indiana, and lived in Illinois." Then he went on to discuss the
Confederates' recent efforts to pass a law which would enable
them to use Negroes in their armies. "They have drawn upon

their last branch of resources," he concluded. "And we can now see the bottom. I am glad to see the end so near at hand."

After the presentation of the flag, the President, Governor Morton, and other civil dignitaries and military officers went into the hotel lobby to meet some friends. The President was still looking so unwell that one of the newspapers commented on his poor appearance.

John Wilkes Booth usually stayed at the National Hotel, and the register shows that he had a room there from March 1 to March 21. He was almost surely in the city on the day Lincoln visited the hotel, for he was scheduled to give a performance as Pescara in Richard Taylor Shiel's *The Apostate* at Ford's Theatre the next evening. And it was at this time that his plot to kidnap Lincoln and take him as a prize of war to Richmond was coming to a head. He had been planning such a move for many months and had made several abortive attempts to put his scheme into action. At some time during the next few days he made his final effort to capture the President alive.

Booth spent a great deal of time at an unpretentious boardinghouse located at 541 (now 604) H Street, N.W. This establishment, a three-story-and-attic brick building, was kept by Mrs. Mary E. Surratt, a widow who had gone into business there during the autumn of 1864. She wanted to take only boarders who were known or recommended to her, but on several occasions she had advertised in the Washington *Star* "for two or four gentlemen." Her son, John Harrison Surratt, was a Confederate spy who ran messages between Richmond and Montreal. Booth, evidently thinking that young Surratt might be useful in his plot, cultivated his acquaintance and got himself introduced into the household. Mrs. Surratt owned a tavern in Maryland about ten miles south of Washington, which Booth was planning to use as a stopping place on his escape route.

The handsome twenty-six-year-old actor quickly won the

hearts of Mrs. Surratt, her young daughter Anna, and all the women staying in the pro-Southern boardinghouse. Here he came to consult with John Surratt when the Confederate courier was in town; here too he gave orders to the wretched creatures involved in the kidnaping plot. The only one of these who proved to have enough strength or courage to be useful was a twenty-year-old Confederate veteran named Lewis Paine. He was a ruthless giant who had fought with Mosby and Harry Gilmor in guerrilla operations after having been wounded at Gettysburg. The others were a German carriage painter named George Atzerodt; David Herold, a former Washington druggist's clerk who knew the Maryland countryside, and two companions of Booth's boyhood days in Maryland, Michael O'Laughlin and Samuel A. Arnold, both of whom had been in the Confederate Army.

One evening, probably just before his appearance at Ford's in *The Apostate,* Booth gave a dinner for his followers in a private room at Gautier's Restaurant on Pennsylvania Avenue. At this time his idea was to capture the President while he was driving in the suburbs, or, better still, because it appealed to Booth's exaggerated sense of the dramatic, to seize him in a theater. One of his men was to turn out the gas lights so he could lower Lincoln's trussed-up body to the stage in the darkness and spirit him out the back door.

Tom Taylor, who was the author of the popular comedy *Our American Cousin,* had written another successful play, entitled *Still Waters Run Deep.* This had been playing for more than a month in Washington and was to be given for a charity performance at the Soldiers' Home on the northern edge of the city. Lincoln was supposed to attend this private showing. The conspirators heard of this and rode out, armed, booted, and spurred to capture the fifty-six-year-old President. When they saw that he was not in the carriage, the whole abduction plot collapsed. Surratt went on to Richmond, while Arnold and

O'Laughlin returned to Baltimore. After that the Confederacy began to fall apart so rapidly that Booth would have had trouble taking his prisoner to Richmond even if he had captured him and got him out of Washington.

There is good reason to believe that others besides Booth and his known followers were involved in the plot to kidnap or assassinate the President. After being captured, Paine told one of his interrogators: "You have not got the one half of them." And Herold, in his confession, said that thirty-five or forty others in Washington were connected with the plot.

One ironic note remains: during the very time John Wilkes Booth was planning harm to the President of the United States, his loyal brother Edwin was reaching the climax of his successful acting career by completing an unprecedented run of one hundred performances of *Hamlet* in New York City on March 22.

While Booth was plotting against the President, the sordid Singleton-Browning scheme to profit by trading with the enemy was running into complications. Browning went to see Lincoln as soon as he learned that Federal troops had burned the tobacco at Fredericksburg. The President seemed sympathetic, but Browning felt that he was afraid of his irascible Secretary of War. When Browning volunteered to visit Stanton, Lincoln urged him to do so, saying that he thought Judge Hughes should go to City Point to see Grant. He even promised to issue a pass for Hughes.

On Sunday night, March 12, Browning had a long talk with the Secretary of War. To his consternation he found that Stanton was violently opposed to the whole idea of trading in contraband goods. He wrote in his diary later that night that Stanton "said every man who went thro the lines to buy cotton ought to be shot — that it was trading in the blood of our soldiers, and sacrificing the interests of the Country to enable mercenary scoundrels to amass large fortunes &c, and that he had rather everý pound of tobacco, and every pound of cotton in Richmond should be burnt, than that we should buy it, and pay for it in Green backs.... I showed him the paper Grant had given to Singleton. He expressed his surprise at it — said with great emphasis that if he had given such a guaranty he would never have destroyed the produce afterwards — that the letter needed explanation, and asked me if I had any objection to giving him a copy of it.... Although he occasionally became very much excited on the subject he was perfectly kind and courteous to me."

Lincoln was evidently becoming wary of Browning and Singleton, but he still had a good opinion of Judge Hughes; on March 13 he wrote to Grant suggesting that he see Hughes again. He added that he knew the Judge well and could not believe that "he would knowingly betray any interest of the country and attempt to deceive you...."

Browning spent some time with Lincoln on Thursday, March 16. During the interview the President told him that Stanton had gone to City Point to discuss the whole trading permit problem with Grant. When the troubled attorney said that it would be an outrage for Stanton to ruin Singleton, Lincoln replied "O, no, he [Stanton] has always ... been as much in favor of the trade as I am." He then endorsed a permit for one of Browning's Southern clients, Robert E. Coxe, and issued a pass for him.

Stanton returned from City Point on March 20 and was called upon by Browning the next morning. As they walked from the War Department to the White House, where a Cabinet meeting was about to be held, the usually gruff Secretary of War seemed to be in a jovial mood. He took Browning's arm and said with a hearty laugh, "That was not Singleton's tobacco that was seized at Fredericksburg after all. Strange what stories get in circulation!"

Browning tried to explain how legitimate and aboveboard

Singleton's enterprise was and said that he would hate to see him ruined. "We'll not ruin him bad," Stanton commented grimly.

At the front portico of the White House Browning said he was sorry he had not consulted Stanton about the matter from the beginning. To this the ordinarily arrogant Secretary of War replied with amazing humility, "I am as liable to be mistaken as anybody else. I may be wrong."

The Confederates were in a desperate state and they were resorting to desperate measures. On November 25, 1864, they had made an attempt to set fire to a number of hotels and public buildings in New York City. They had also invaded the Northern states from Canada, seized passenger ships on the Great Lakes, and blown up trains, military depots, and ships by using concealed explosive devices. Confederate agents in Canada and Europe were purchasing commerce-raiding ships, blockade runners, weapons, ammunition, and supplies. The United States Government knew what was going on outside its own borders and had established a network of counterintelligence agents at various places throughout the world. From the American consulate in London a mysterious message to Secretary Seward was sent on March 17. It said that the consulate's secret agent in Paris had uncovered a plot to assassinate Seward and Sherman. Two men were allegedly being sent to the United States who were each to be paid $5000 if they successfully eliminated their appointed victims. The Paris agent claimed to know the man who was to kill Sherman well enough to name and describe him. He said that the hired assassin was a Texan named Clark, who was "five feet nine, rather slender, thin in flesh, high cheekbones, a long forehead, eyes dark and sunken, very quiet, seldom if ever speaking in company unless spoken to. Has large dark brown mustache and large long goatee. Hair much darker than his whiskers. Complexion rather sallow. He wore grey clothes and a wide-awake slouch hat."

This man was supposed to join Sherman's army, and then, in the heat of battle, shoot him down. The Paris agent went on to say that the Confederates wanted to eliminate Sherman because they believed that he was "the only real general the Yankees had" and that there was no one to take his place.

The agent had practically no information about the other man except that his name was Johnston and that he had come to Paris from Canada via Liverpool. He was to go to Washington and assassinate Seward at the earliest opportunity.

Whether there was anything to this secret agent's story or not, the Government took it very seriously. When the message arrived at the State Department several weeks later, the War Department informed Sherman of the plot to kill him. He evidently believed the story and put himself on guard.

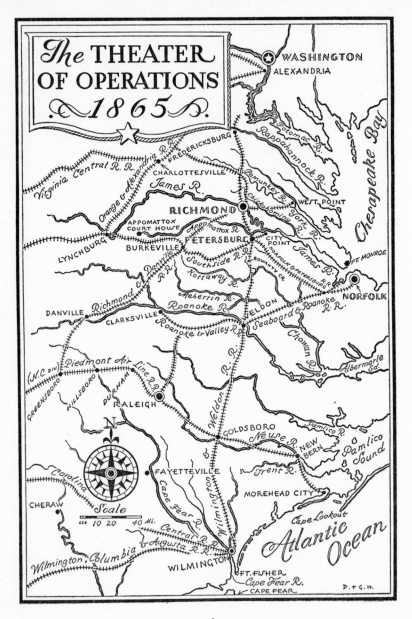

The THEATER OF OPERATIONS 1865

WASHINGTON
ALEXANDRIA

Chesapeake Bay

Potomac R.

Rappahannock R.

Virginia Central R. R.

FREDERICKSBURG

CHARLOTTESVILLE

Orange & Alexandria R.R.

James R.

Pamunkey R.

Chickahominy R.

WEST POINT

York R.

RICHMOND

APPOMATTOX COURT HOUSE

Appomattox R.

PETERSBURG

CITY POINT

NORFOLK & PETERSBURG R.R.

James R.

FT. MONROE

LYNCHBURG

BURKEVILLE

Southside R.R.

Nottaway R.

Richmond & Danville R.R.

NORFOLK

ROWANTY CR.

Meherrin R.

Roanoke R.

WELDON

Seaboard & Roanoke R.R.

DANVILLE

CLARKSVILLE

Roanoke & Valley R.R.

Chowan R.

Albermarle Sd.

(N.C. DIV.)

Piedmont Air Line R.R.

GREENSBORO

HILLSBORO

DURHAM

RALEIGH

Weldon R.R.

GOLDSBORO

Neuse R.

NEW BERN

Pamlico R.

Pamlico Sound

N

Carolina

FAYETTEVILLE

Trent R.

MOREHEAD CITY

CHERAW

Scale
0 10 20 40 Mi.

Cape Fear R.

Wilmington

Central R.R.

Cape Lookout

Atlantic Ocean

Wilmington, Columbia & Augusta R.R.

WILMINGTON

FT. FISHER
Cape Fear R.
CAPE FEAR

D. + G. H.

4

The Lincolns Go to City Point

Monday, March 20, to Friday, March 24

THERE HAD BEEN a white frost on the ground in Washington on Sunday morning, but on Monday, March 20, spring began officially at 8:58 A.M., when the earth passed the vernal equinox. The Washington weather, as if taking its cue from the cosmic circumstance, immediately began to improve. The overcast sky cleared; the sun came out in all its springtime splendor, and the temperature rose to 69 degrees in the shade by midafternoon.

Grant's huge army was almost ready to move; only a few days of fair weather were needed to dry out the roads and fields. Thousands of horses had been brought to City Point, where the blacksmiths' forges burned late into the night, while the steady ringing of hammers pounding horseshoes on scores of anvils resounded throughout the camp. Most important of all, Sheridan with his thousands of cavalrymen had arrived the day before at White House, Virginia, only twenty-five miles northeast of City Point. Sheridan and his men had circled north of Richmond, continuing their policy of burning and destroying everything in sight. The damage they did to railroads and to the James River Canal made it almost impossible to bring enough supplies into Richmond to feed its citizens and the soldiers defending the city.

The sun beamed warmly on the Eastern states. It was a day
for beginnings, for movement, for the rush and stir of active life.
On that day Major General Edward R. S. Canby began his final
assault against Mobile; George Stoneman rode out of Knoxville
with 5000 cavalrymen to drive through eastern Tennessee
toward Lynchburg, Virginia; and at City Point, with Sheridan
close by, Grant could start breaking down his over-all campaign
plans into specific orders to be sent to his various commanders.
And that morning at ten o'clock, perhaps because he had heard
that Lincoln had been ill, Grant sent a wire to Washington
inviting the President to visit City Point for a day or two.
Grant added that he thought the rest would do him good.

The telegram reached the White House at 3:20 P.M., after
which time there must have been a hurried conference with
Mrs. Lincoln, for at six o'clock the President sent a wire to
Grant saying:

> Your kind invitation received. Had already thought of going
> immediately after the next rain. Will go sooner if any reason
> for it. Mrs. L. and a few others will probably accompany me.
> Will notify you of exact time, once it shall be fixed upon.

Mrs. Lincoln probably decided to accompany her husband
in order to see their son Robert, who was with Grant at City
Point. The next day Lincoln telegraphed to Robert that they
expected to start on Thursday, March 23. Evidently they intended to stay for only a short time, for Mrs. Lincoln wrote to
Senator Charles Sumner on the morning of their departure:
"On our return, about Wednesday [March 29], we trust you
will be inclined to accompany us to the Italian opera. *Ernani*
is set aside for that evening." The opera was scheduled to be
performed at Ford's Theatre, where Mrs. Lincoln had ordered
a private box, but the President's appointment there with destiny had already been assigned to a later evening in the eternal
book of dates.

Mrs. Lincoln's decision to go with the President to City Point immediately caused complications. He was supposed to travel on the *Bat,* a captured blockade runner described by her commander as a steel-hulled steamer with four powerful engines that drove two side paddle wheels fast enough to reach a speed of eighteen knots.

G. V. Fox, Assistant Secretary of the Navy, who was returning to Washington on the *Bat,* telegraphed to Lincoln from Norfolk that the ship was the fastest vessel on the river and was well armed. He added significantly: "I think it would be best for you to use her."

Lieutenant Commander John S. Barnes, the naval officer in command of the *Bat,* was ordered to report to the White House, where the President, who seemed tired, worried, and rather embarrassed about the whole matter, informed him that Mrs. Lincoln and her maid were going to be with him. The President wanted to know whether the *Bat* could offer them suitable accommodations. Barnes recorded his predicament: "The *Bat* was in no respect adapted to the private life of womankind, nor could she be made so. I ventured to state some of the difficulties — as delicately as I could. 'Well,' said the President, 'I understand, but you will have to see mother'; — and I was soon ushered into the presence of Mrs. Lincoln. She received me very graciously, standing with arms folded, and at once opened the conversation by saying that she had learned from one of her friends, Miss Clara Harris, daughter of Senator Ira Harris, of New York, that I was an old acquaintance and relative. I expressed my great satisfaction at the recognition and remarked that Miss Harris was one of my best friends also.

"Mrs. Lincoln then said, 'I am going with the President to City Point, and I want you to arrange your ship to take me, my maid and my officer, as well as the President....' In great consternation I went to Mr. Fox at the Navy Department and explained to him the situation; how utterly impossible it was to make the *Bat* at all suitable for the reasonable requirements of the wife of the President. He recognized the impossibility, and we went again to the White House, where we were again received by Mr. Lincoln, when in very funny terms the President translated our difficulties, and Fox promised another and better craft for his use.... The steamer *River Queen* was chartered for the Presidential party; a river passenger side-wheeler, with the ordinary civilian officers and crew, and no armament....

"I was directed to accompany her ... and was placed under the immediate direction of the President, and charged with his safe conduct to City Point and return."

The *River Queen** had been used by the President before; in fact the fruitless peace conference of February 3, 1865, with the three Confederate commissioners, Alexander H. Stephens, R. M. T. Hunter, and John A. Campbell, had been held on board her while she lay anchored in Hampton Roads.

An attempt was made to keep the President's plans secret, but information about the movements of troops and important persons could seldom be withheld from the public during the Civil War. Word of the President's departure appeared in Northern newspapers, which were regularly quoted a day later by Richmond editors.

While the *River Queen* was being made ready, one of the Baltimore *American*'s writers visited the White House on March 21 to gather material for an account of what the President did on an average day. He must have heard about the intended voyage to City Point, but his paper, the only one in pro-Confederate Baltimore that was loyal to the administration, did not reveal Lincoln's plans to go to the front. The story appeared on March 23 under the title:

---

* This historic old steamer was kept in active service as an excursion boat to carry sightseers from Washington to Mount Vernon until 1911, when she was destroyed by fire.

A DAY AT THE WHITE HOUSE

"The President commenced to receive visitors at ten o'clock, but at half-past eleven o'clock the Cabinet session commenced, and continued until nearly two o'clock. So soon as the Cabinet members had withdrawn, the reception of visitors was resumed, those having members of Congress with them taking precedence. At two o'clock, however, the doors were thrown open and all that remained in the anteroom were invited to enter and take seats. The President then commenced to dispose of them in his frank, cordial, and candid manner, the presence of 'a cloud of witnesses' enabling him to get through with them much more rapidly than if each had been granted a private interview.

"The first case was that of an old gentleman whose sons had been killed in battle, and who had come to Washington in hope of being able to obtain some kind of employment. The President replied that Washington was the worst place in the country for anyone to seek to go to better their condition, and advised him to go home again by the first train. He wished some species of saffron tea could be administered to produce an eruption of those already in Washington and make this migration fever strike out instead of striking in. The supplicant replied that he had not the means to go, and hoped that the President would give him a note to one of the quartermasters, who might probably give him some form of employment. After thinking a minute, he wrote something on a piece of paper and gave it to him, when the old man's countenance brightened, and with profuse thanks he retired.

"A gentleman largely engaged in bringing out cotton, etc. from the rebel states, inquired of the President whether it was his intention to sustain the recent order issued by General Grant putting a stop to the whole business. The President replied that in no case would he interfere with the wishes of General Grant. He held him responsible for inflicting the hardest blows possible on the enemy, and as desirable as it was to possess the cotton, if he thought that bacon was of more importance to the enemy at this moment than cotton to us, why we must do without the cotton. General Grant was no lawyer, and consequently he used no unnecessary words to amplify his order; but the President understood him to mean that this trade was giving aid and comfort to the enemy, and consequently it must stop. 'Under no circumstances,' concluded the President, 'will I interfere with the orders of General Grant.'

"The next was an applicant for a small country post office, accompanied by a Democratic member of Congress. On reading his application, he responded at once, 'You shall have it,' and endorsed his approval on the back. The member remarked, 'I presume, Mr. President, that is because I trouble you so little that you promptly grant my request.' The President responded, 'That reminds me of my own experience as an old Whig member of Congress. I was always in the opposition, and I had no troubles of this kind at all. It was the easiest thing imaginable to be an opposition member — no running to the departments and the White House.'

"Next came an old gentleman who wished to get a man pardoned from the penitentiary, convicted of stealing two pairs of pantaloons and a box of shoes belonging to the government from a box he was hauling on his dray. A statement of the case from the State's attorney was presented, which admitted that one witness had testified that he had sold him a pair of shoes. 'Yes,' said the President, 'so much for the shoes but nothing about the pantaloons. The jury had the whole facts before them, and convicted the man, and I am bound to regard him as guilty. I am sorry for his wife and children, sir, but the man must be punished.'

"Next was the case of a youth who had been arrested as a deserter in Baltimore. . . . He was on his way to his home to see a sick sister, who had subsequently died; had no intention of deserting, but merely intended to overstay his time on his pass and return to camp. He was now at the Dry Tortugas under a three-year sentence, with a ball and chain on his leg. The President, in view of his recent proclamation to deserters who had been arrested, promptly pardoned him.

"A young widow, the mother of three children, whose husband had been killed in a battle, presented an application for the appointment of postmistress of a small town in Orange County, New York. The President received her very kindly — told her to leave all her papers with him, and that he would examine the matter thoroughly, and would do the best he could for her case. She was advised to return home and trust her case in his hands, as he would attend to it as well in her absence as if she were present. He 'could not act on it at once; for, although he was President, she must remember that he was but one horse in the team, and that if the others pulled in a different direction it would be a hard matter for him to outpull them.' The lady left much pleased with her interview.

"A wounded officer was an applicant for an office, and presented a memorial signed by a large number of citizens of his district. The President replied that he was disposed to favor the application, but that he must wait to hear from the member of Congress from that district. He would be forever in hot water if he did not pay some deference to the wishes of members on these appointments.

"An applicant for the discharge of a minor from service, assured him that an officer, whom he named, had said that the case was one deserving of executive interference. The President immediately remarked, 'Bring me his opinion to that effect in writing, and I will promptly discharge him. His word will be sufficient for me; I will require no argument on the subject.'

"A man who wished to escape from the draft on the plea of being in the employ of the government and of being physically disabled, was told that the President could not take exception against the army surgeons, and he doubted that there were not a dozen gentlemen in the room who would not gladly relieve him of his government employment. 'I don't know why it is that I am troubled with these cases,' said the President; 'but if I were, by interfering, to make a hole through which a kitten might pass, it would soon be large enough for the old cat to get through, also.'

"Several other applicants for executive interference in small matters were kindly received and their cases promptly disposed of, all retiring apparently well pleased with their reception and in most cases gratified with the decision of the President.

"A singular case occurred at an early hour in the morning, of a young woman who presented herself to the usher with three children, one almost an infant. She demanded to see the President, and on being told that the Cabinet was in session and that she could not see him, she set the children on the floor in the East Room, declaring that her husband had been killed in battle, she had brought her children to the President and intended to leave them with him. She was ascertained to be a poor deranged creature, whose afflictions had overbalanced her mind, and by directions of Mrs. Lincoln was properly cared for.

"We would also add as a matter of special interest that the President looked extremely well, seemed in excellent spirits, and bore none of those evidences of debility or failing health ... is lithe and elastic, his features firm and expressive of energy and vigorous thought, and his manner of receiving his visitors was indicative of all that kindness of heart for which he is so distinguished. Indeed there is good reason to hope that he will not only live many years to witness the future of his restored country, but should the people so decide, retain the physical and mental ability to administer executive functions even beyond his present term of office."

Despite heavy rain on Tuesday evening, Mr. and Mrs. Lincoln went to Grover's Theatre to see Boieldieu's then popular opera, *La Dame Blanche*. Its preposterous plot, put together by Eugène Scribe from two of Walter Scott's books, would be laughed at today, but the audience applauded it enthusiastically. The Lincolns went to the theater again the next night when Gounod's *Mireille* was performed for the first time in America.

Then on Thursday, March 23, the day scheduled for their departure, Mr. and Mrs. Lincoln, with little Tad, Mrs. Lincoln's maid, the President's bodyguard, Crook, and Captain Charles B. Penrose (whom Mrs. Lincoln called "her officer") drove to the Sixth Street wharf on the Potomac River.

The wind kept rising as they approached the river, and at one o'clock, when the *River Queen* left the wharf, the surface of the water was broken by ugly-looking whitecaps. The *Bat*, which had been lying at anchor farther downstream, joined them fifteen minutes later in the midst of a howling windstorm.

Stanton and his wife arrived at the dock just too late to see the Presidential party off. The wind tore at his long beard and dashed spray wildly in his face. He disgustedly told his carriage driver to go to the Navy Yard, perhaps with some idea of intercepting the *River Queen* in a fast tugboat. By the time he got to the Navy Yard the ship was out of sight.

By two o'clock the wind had reached gale force. It tore the roof off a foundry in Washington, killed a man and his horses, and sank a schooner lying alongside the wharf. Then it slowly began to die down, but the afternoon was cold and unpleasant, and occasional gusts of wind made the *River Queen*'s deck uncomfortable. Crook reported that the President stayed outside until the ship passed Alexandria and then took refuge in the cabin. He was entertained during the evening by Captain Bradford, the steamer's master, who knew the Maryland and Virginia shores well and could tell tale after tale about the Confederate spies and blockade runners who regularly crossed the Potomac under cover of darkness.

At half-past eight the escorting vessel *Bat* turned into St. Mary's River near the mouth of the Potomac to anchor for the night. The *River Queen* dropped anchor nearby with much rattling of chain and calling of voices from vessel to vessel. Armed lookouts were posted on the deck of the *Bat*. The passengers retired early, for the ship was due to sail before sunrise.

At 5:15 A.M., on March 24, the *Bat* hauled up her anchor and started toward the open waters of Chesapeake Bay, followed by the *River Queen*. It was half an hour before sunrise, and the water kept getting rougher and rougher.

Crook, who was sharing a stateroom with Tad, was awakened just before dawn by someone entering the cabin. It was Mrs. Lincoln, who said reassuringly: "It is I, Crook. It is growing colder, and I came in to see if my little boy has covers enough on him."

As they steamed out of the Potomac and down the wide bay, the west wind piled the water into high waves, causing the *River Queen* to roll heavily. Crook, who was not used to traveling on ships, became seasick. But the President seemed well and ate fish for breakfast. Perhaps it was the fish that upset his stomach, for just before noon, when they came to anchor near Fortress Monroe, a boat was sent ashore to obtain fresh drinking water for the President, who by this time was not feeling well. There was some delay about getting the water, which caused Major William I. James, the acting quartermaster, to write a letter of apology to the President. Gracious as always under such circumstances, Lincoln wrote a few words on the back of the letter and returned it to its sender. The words were: "I am not at all impatient, and hope Major James will not reproach himself or deal harshly with the officer having the matter in charge. Doubtless he, too, has met some difficulty."

At two o'clock they got under way again and turned west at Newport News to enter the historic James River. They passed the three lightships marking the channel and steamed along the shores of the peninsula where Cornwallis had surrendered to Washington in 1781. Across these same redoubts and trenches McClellan's men had fought the Confederates in the ill-fated Peninsular Campaign of 1862 to take Richmond. They sailed on up the wide river, the broad waterway that had opened up the Tidewater country of Virginia when the North American continent was first being settled by white men. They steamed past the 200-foot-long red brick mansion, Carter's Grove, standing high above the shore, and they came in sight of Jamestown Island, where the ruins of the ancient church tower marked the site of the first permanent British colony in America. It was here that the seeds of slavery had been sown in the summer of 1619, when the captain of a Dutch man-of-war sold twenty Negroes to the Jamestown colonists. From that small beginning had come millions of bondsmen and endless strife, and now the great fratricidal war was taking its toll of hundreds of thousands of young men's lives in expiation for the centuries-old crime. As they sailed past the island only a few miserable huts were to be seen; beyond them two or three gaunt chimneys of burned-out houses rose starkly above the trees.

Farther up the river they passed the elaborate mansions of the wealthy planters — Claremont Manor, the two Brandons, Westover, and Berkeley. From the deck of the *River Queen* these magnificent houses of men who had backed the Confederacy may have seemed as impressive as ever, but closer inspection would have shown that they had been seriously damaged during the war. Westover's east wing was in ruins, and the main house bore the scars of battle. Many fine houses had been burned to the ground; the once rich Tidewater plantations had been devastated by marching armies and had been blasted by shells fired from passing Federal ships by crews who wanted to "get even with the Rebels."

The two Treasury agents most concerned with the issuing of cotton and tobacco trading permits, Hanson A. Risley and William P. Mellen, had intended to accompany the Lincolns on the *River Queen,* but at the last moment they sent the President a note saying that the Treasury Department was providing them with a revenue cutter and that they would meet him at City Point. Something was evidently going on behind the scenes that made these two agents want to reach Grant first. Whatever they hoped to accomplish — or cover up — was past doing, for nothing would now move Grant's determination to stamp out trading with the Confederates. The Northern newspapers for March 29 mention the Treasury agents' return to Washington but say nothing about the purpose of their mission.

On March 24, the day the Lincolns were due to arrive at City Point, a flag-of-truce boat came down the river from Richmond carrying exchanged prisoners of war and "General" James W. Singleton, who was accompanied by two ladies, one of whom was related to Singleton, while the other was Mrs. Lincoln's half sister, Mrs. Helm. The conniving "General," still eager to make use of Mrs. Helm's 600 bales of cotton, had urged her to leave Richmond with him, saying that the city was about to fall into Federal hands. Robert Lincoln met his aunt accidentally when the little steamer docked at City Point. They greeted each other affectionately, and the young captain obtained permission to accompany the boat to its next stop. He told his aunt that he felt his mother had never completely recovered from a fall she had had in a carriage accident two years before. Then there was some talk about their widely scattered relatives, after which Robert bade his aunt farewell and returned to City Point to await the arrival of his parents.

Near Berkeley, the *Bat,* which had fallen farther and farther behind because of engine trouble, had to cease acting as an escort. She came to anchor off Harrison's Landing at 8:25 P.M., while the *River Queen* sailed on through the darkness to reach City Point shortly before nine o'clock on March 24.

More than a hundred Union vessels of all kinds were anchored there. Since the idea of a blackout was then almost unknown, lights burned brightly on the ships and on the shore, where a huge tangle of wharves, warehouses, and railroads lay just below the bluff on which Grant's headquarters were located.

It had been a busy day for Grant, for he had had to send numerous written orders to his commanders to start their armies in motion on March 29, the date he had set for the beginning of his spring campaign. He was gambling on the weather, hoping that the rainy season was past and that the wet ground would be dry by then. And he was afraid that Lee might suddenly pull his troops out of the fortifications around Petersburg and Richmond and try to join General Joseph E. Johnston to continue the fighting in territory farther south. Grant was on edge because he knew the war was rapidly coming to a grand climax. It was a time when one had to be exactly right, make all the correct decisions, think clearly, act quickly, and outguess Lee, the wily gray fox who had held off all his pursuers since June 1862, when he had been given command of the Army of Northern Virginia.

When word of the *River Queen*'s arrival reached Grant, he left the log cabin that served as his headquarters and went down the steep wooden stairs leading to the wharves below. He boarded the steamer to welcome the Lincolns and tell the President how matters stood in the field.

5

The Confederates Try
to Break the Union Lines
Saturday, March 25

THE IMPASSE at Petersburg had been a long time in the
making. More than a year before, on March 12, 1864, when
Grant was formally placed in command of all the Union armies,
he had decided to take active charge of the campaign in Virginia and leave the West and the deep South to Sherman and
McPherson.* The stalemate at Richmond needed the man
who had taken Vicksburg and had fought with grim determination in the West. The campaign in the Virginia area had
broken a long succession of Northern generals, and the cry
"On to Richmond," which had been so popular earlier in the
war, had become an ironic joke. Grant at once made preparations for a tremendous drive on the Confederate capital, which
began on May 3, 1864, when Ben Butler started an expedition
up the Peninsula to draw attention away from the main assault.
The next day, Grant's armies started south and were held off
with enormous losses in the bloody fighting which began in the
Wilderness on May 5 and ended at Cold Harbor on June 3
with a loss of 55,000 men. Unable to break through Lee's
rapidly moved defenses, Grant changed his strategy and swung
east and south to lay siege to Petersburg, an important railroad center twenty-three miles below Richmond.

---

* Brigadier General James B. McPherson was killed by skirmishers four months
later.

The Confederates were well aware of Petersburg's strategic importance and after fending off McClellan's Peninsula Campaign in 1862, had started to fortify the city at that time by constructing an elaborate ten-mile-long series of earthworks and trenches. When Grant turned toward Petersburg, this strongly built line was so lightly manned that the 10,000 men led by General William F. ("Baldy") Smith could have walked through it when they arrived on June 15. But, by a series of the kind of errors in command that had plagued the Army of the Potomac since the beginning of the war, they did not even try. By morning, Confederate reserves had been rushed into position, and what had been an opportunity to take the city without much of a fight became a battle that dragged on fruitlessly for days until Grant decided to dig in and begin a formal siege. Both armies then went to work to construct what eventually became the largest battlefield anywhere in the Western world. It covered 170 square miles, and its interconnected forts and batteries ran for nearly 50 miles.

When it became evident that such massive works could not be taken by direct assault, long tunnels were dug and mines were laid under the opposing fortifications. On July 30 Union miners ignited four tons of gunpowder which they had placed under one of the main Confederate works in the center of the line. The explosion tore a hole 170 feet long and 30 feet deep in the earth, and through this gigantic crater Federal troops were supposed to rush and overwhelm the paralyzed Confederates. It was a brilliant idea, and it should have worked, but again by the error and stupidity — and in this case, criminal cowardice and drunkenness — of some of those in command, the assault was late in getting under way. By the time Union troops reached the hole in the lines, the Confederates had recovered from their surprise, hurried replacements into the breech, and were waiting there, fighting mad. The crater became a blood bath in which the Union Army lost nearly 4000 men.

A few days later the Confederates exploded a much smaller mine, which had little effect. Both sides then settled down to more digging. The Federals kept reaching toward the west, and in February 1865 there was active fighting around Dinwiddie Court House and Dabney's Mill — places which had to be fought over again when the Appomattox Campaign began.

By the spring of 1865 the defenses around Richmond and Petersburg had become fine examples of the art of field fortification as it was known to the military engineers of the day. Earthworks, strengthened and shored up by timbers, had been found to be far more effective in stopping explosive shells than stone walls. Besides, they were quicker, easier, and cheaper to construct. Strung out in front of the forts and batteries were advanced picket posts, which were either rifle pits or one-man dugouts. These could be reached by long trenches or covered ways so the pickets could reach their positions without being seen.

Since the nearly horizontal trajectory of cannon or rifles rendered them almost useless in this kind of stalemate, mortars were brought up. These very short, stubby, heavy iron or bronze cannon could lob an explosive shell high into the air and drop it with reasonable accuracy into a fort or trench. In order to protect the troops during heavy firing, bombproof shelters were dug deep into the ground and covered with timbers, sheet iron, and earth. These underground refuges became more and more elaborate as the siege dragged on. Sleeping quarters warmed by fireplaces were built for comfort, and men lived like moles beneath the surface of the earth.

Along the tops of the earthworks and rifle pits heavy timbers or iron rails were placed to stop bullets. Small spaces were left between these so that sharpshooters, equipped with especially accurate rifles (which sometimes had telescopic sights), could be stationed at the openings to pick off anyone unwary enough to raise his head above the opposite parapet.

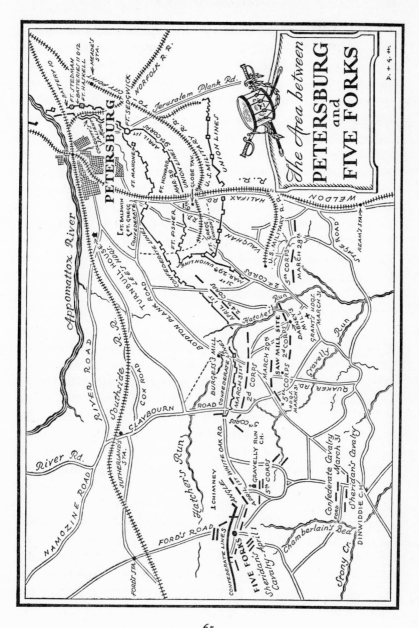

The Area between PETERSBURG and FIVE FORKS

To ward off a surprise mass attack — particularly at night — the ground in front of the picket lines was protected by thousands of closely placed, long, sharp-pointed saplings with their butts buried in the ground so their points faced the enemy. This bristling defense was called an abatis, or fraise. More portable were the chevaux-de-frise, which consisted of long timbers with holes bored in them so sharp-pointed stakes, set close, could be driven through. A continuous line of chevaux-de-frise could be chained or tied together with telegraph wire to make an unbroken barricade of forbidding spikes, the sharpened points of which were breast-high.

Union and Confederate fortifications faced each other for miles, so close together in some places that the opposing pickets could call out a message across the intervening ground. In several low-lying areas, streams had been diverted and dammed to form ponds which served to protect the lines.

The more important forts were solidly constructed, with four high earthen walls surrounded by water-filled moats. But many of the smaller forts and gun or mortar batteries were left open in the rear. Since the Confederates had less manpower than the Union forces, their earthworks tended to be less substantially built. They often used slave labor to do the digging, and when the work had to be done under fire, the slaves were understandably reluctant to risk their lives for a cause that was against their own interest.

The men who faced each other in these fortified lines were well-trained troops sharpened to a razor's edge by long and bitter experience. The bungled slaughter of raw recruits at First Manassas and Shiloh was far behind. Those who had survived had learned how to keep alive in that hardest of all schools — the battleground, where a single mistake can send a man to a hospital or a grave. And these veterans had taught the newcomers to their ranks all they knew so that they too could stay alive and help in the fighting that was still to come.

This elaborately fortified front had been relatively quiet for a long time, with only occasional firing between the picket lines. Lee had not made an offensive attack since Spotsylvania, nearly a year before, and Grant had been busy building up supplies and reinforcements for a final crushing blow. But Lee was now ready to make a surprise attack, preparations for which had been going on for weeks.

This assault had been under consideration since the night of March 3, when Lee had summoned thirty-three-year-old General John B. Gordon, commander of the Second Corps, to his headquarters in the Turnbull house at Edge Hill on the western outskirts of Petersburg. Gordon had risen rapidly as one of the bright young combat officers needed to replace the older Confederate leaders who had been eliminated by four years of war.

It was about 3 A.M. in bitterly cold weather when the young general entered the Turnbull house. Gordon left a record of the meeting: "As I entered, General Lee, who was entirely alone, was standing at the fireplace, his arm on the mantel and his head resting on his arm as he gazed into the coal fire burning in the grate. He had evidently been up all . . . night. For the first time . . . I saw a look of painful depression on his face. Of course he had experienced many hours of depression, but he had concealed from those around him all evidence of discouragement. He had carried the burden in his own soul — wrapping his doubts and apprehensions in an exterior of cheerfulness and apparent confidence. The hour had come, however, when he could no longer carry alone the burden, or entirely conceal his forebodings of impending disaster. . . . To me he had the appearance of one suffering from physical illness. In answer to my inquiry as to his health, he stated that he was well enough bodily. . . . In his room was a long table covered with recent reports from every portion of his army. . . . He motioned me to a chair on one side of the table, and seated

himself opposite me. I had known before I came that our army
was in desperate straits; but when I entered that room I realized
at once, from the gravity of the commander's bearing, that I
was to learn of a situation worse than I had anticipated. The
interview was a long one, intensely absorbing, and in many
respects harrowing. . . .

"Each report was bad enough, and all the distressing facts
combined were sufficient, it seemed to me, to destroy all co-
hesive power and lead to the inevitable disintegration of any
other army that was ever marshalled. Of the great disparity
of number between the two hostile forces I was already apprised.
I had also learned much of the general suffering among the
troops; but the condition of my own command . . . was not a
fair measure of the suffering in the army. I was not prepared
for the picture presented by these reports of extreme destitu-
tion — of the lack of shoes, of hats, of overcoats, and of blankets,
as well as of food. Some of the officers had gone outside the
formal official statement as to numbers of the sick, to tell in
plain, terse, and forceful words of depleted strength, emaciation,
and decreased power of endurance among those who appeared
on the rolls as fit for duty. Cases were given, and not a few,
where good men, faithful, tried, and devoted, gave evidence of
temporary insanity and indifference to orders or to the consequences of disobedience — the natural and inevitable effect
of their mental and bodily sufferings. My recollection is that
General Lee stated that, since the reports from A. P. Hill's
corps had been sent in, he had learned that those men had
just been rationed on one sixth of a pound of beef, whereas
the army ration was a pound of beef per man per day, with
the addition of other supplies. . . .

"When I had finished . . . General Lee began his own analysis
of the situation. He first considered the relative strength of his
army and that of General Grant. The exact number of his
own men was given in the reports before him — about 50,000,

or 35,000 fit for duty. Against them he estimated that General Grant had in front of Richmond and Petersburg, or within his reach, about 150,000. Coming up from Knoxville was Thomas with an estimated force of 30,000 superb troops. . . .

" 'From the Valley,' he said, 'General Grant can and will bring upon us nearly 20,000.' . . . This made an army of 200,000 well-fed, well-equipped men which General Grant could soon concentrate upon our force of 50,000, whose efficiency was greatly impaired by suffering. Sherman was approaching from North Carolina, and his force, when united with Schofield's, would reach 80,000. What force had we to confront that army? General Beauregard had telegraphed a few days before that, with the aid of Governor Vance's Home Guards, he could muster probably 20,000 to 25,000. But General Joseph E. Johnston had just sent a despatch saying in substance that General Beauregard had over-estimated his strength, and that it would be nearer the truth to place the available Confederate force at from 13,000 to 15,000. So that the final summing up gave Grant the available crushing power of 280,000 men, while to resist this overwhelming force Lee had in round numbers only 65,000."*

Lee then asked Gordon what he thought should be done under the circumstances. Somewhat awed by their difference in rank, the junior officer hesitated and then said: "General, it seems to me there are but three courses: First, make terms with the enemy, the best we can get. Second, if that is not practicable, the best thing to do is to retreat — abandon Richmond and Petersburg, unite by rapid marches with General Johnston in North Carolina, and strike Sherman before Grant can join him; or lastly, we must fight, and without delay."

In the conversation that followed, Lee indicated that as a soldier he did not think he had the right to advise the Con-

* See the Appendix for a discussion of Civil War battle statistics.

federate civil authorities except on matters having to do with
the conduct of the war. He went on to explain the difficulties
of uniting his forces with Johnston's in North Carolina because
his men and horses were in such poor condition. He smiled
then and said that he had received a verbal message from
General Grant that morning when a Federal officer came
through the lines under a flag of truce to ask for a cease-fire
so the dead lying between the lines could be buried. This
officer told Lee that Grant had sent him his compliments and
then instructed him to say "that I keep in such close touch
with him that I know what he eats for breakfast every
morning."

Lee smiled grimly and said: "Tell General Grant that there
must be some mistake, for unless he has fallen from grace since
I last saw him, he would not permit me to eat such breakfasts
as mine without dividing his with me." Then he added:
"Present my compliments to General Grant, and say to him
that perhaps I know as much about his dinners as he knows
about my breakfasts."

The day after this session with Gordon, Lee went to Richmond to consult with Jefferson Davis. He found the Confederate president unalterably opposed to any means of
ending the war that did not guarantee independence for the
South. When Lee returned to Petersburg, he quietly told
Gordon that nothing could be done at Richmond and said
that the only thing left to do was fight. He asked the young
officer to work out the tactical details of a major assault on
the Union lines.

He did not have to tell Gordon how important it was that
the attack succeed. Both men knew that the life of the Confederacy would be at stake when the thinning gray army went
out to fling itself on the well-fed, well-armed, blue-clad troops
that so vastly outnumbered them. Gordon has stated just what
they hoped to accomplish by such an attack:

"The purpose of the movement was not simply the capture of Fort Stedman. . . . The tremendous possibility was the disintegration of the whole left wing of the Federal army, or at least the dealing of such a staggering blow upon it as would disable it temporarily, enabling us to withdraw from Petersburg in safety and join Johnston in North Carolina. The capture of the fort was only the breasting of the first wave in the ocean of difficulties to be encountered. It was simply the opening of a road through the wilderness of hostile works nearest to us in order that my corps and the additional forces to be sent me could pass toward the rear of Grant's lines and then turn upon his flanks."

But at least one Confederate authority, Brigadier General John G. Walker, who took part in the fighting that day, said the attack had an even more important objective. According to him, a way was to be opened for a cavalry force to dash through the Union lines, press on to City Point, seize Grant at his headquarters, and bring him back as a prize of war. And Confederate secret agents may have known that the *River Queen*, with the President of the United States on board, would be at City Point when their cavalry was supposed to arrive.

In preparation for the attack, Gordon moved his troops into the Confederate earthworks as quietly as possible. Then he and his staff began to study every inch of the terrain along the opposing front. The sector in which the Confederates became especially interested was a rather small square earthwork named Fort Stedman, which was armed with four twelve-pound guns. It was located in a pleasant grove of trees, some of which had been allowed to stand inside the fort to provide shade. The winter rains had weakened the walls, and the fort was so near the Confederate lines that practically no repair work could be done. To its right, and so close as to be almost a part of it, was Battery Ten, which had been left open at the rear. This battery had two three-inch rifles, three small Coehorn mortars, and four eight-inch mortars. Three-eighths of a mile to the south was Fort Haskell, a much larger and better built work with six guns and a battery of mortars.

The opposing fortified positions were only 613 feet apart where Colquitt's Salient faced Fort Stedman, and there the pickets were so close together that they could talk to each other. This section of the lines was only about half a mile north of the huge crater left by the explosion of the ill-fated mine which the Federals had dug under the Confederate earthworks in July 1864.

Before presenting his battle plan to Lee, Gordon and his staff worked out all the tactical details of timing, movement, supply, and reinforcement. The plan seemed almost foolproof when Gordon explained it, but there were two serious errors which no one foresaw. Gordon was new to the area; he had come to Petersburg from the Shenandoah Valley only a few months before and was unfamiliar with the much fought-over ground that lay before him. He saw what he thought were three Union forts above and behind Fort Stedman; he expected to storm them from the rear and then turn their captured guns against Stedman. But these were ghost forts, the remains of works that had been constructed during the campaign of the previous summer and had been abandoned. The useless effort to take them was going to use up men and time, neither of which could be spared in so crucial a battle.

The attack was set for four o'clock in the morning of March 25. There was no moon, so the troops would have more than an hour of darkness to make their assault before the sky first began to lighten. Actual sunrise was due at four minutes before six.

During the day Gordon sent his pregnant young wife to the drygoods stores in Petersburg to buy yards of cheap white cloth. She then worked late into the night, tearing this cloth into strips so 300 picked men could tie them over their right

shoulders and under their left arms in order to tell friend from
foe in the dark.

Lee had telegraphed orders for Pickett's Division to be sent
down by train to serve as reinforcements, but he warned
Gordon that he did not think the troops could arrive until late
in the day — too late to be of much use. Long before the time
set for the attack, the gray-haired general who was playing his
last trump card rode out of Petersburg on his famous horse
Traveller to wait in the dark cold hours before the dawn on a
slope above Colquitt's Salient. Better than anyone else, Lee
knew that if the attack failed, the Union Army was almost
certain to stage a counterattack that would still further reduce
the already depleted Confederate forces.

Lee was familiar with all the details of Gordon's plan of
battle. He knew that the bristling chevaux-de-frise protecting
his own front were fastened together with iron chains and
telegraph wires which would have to be removed stealthily
while nearby Federal pickets were listening for suspicious
sounds. And he knew that fifty sturdy axmen wearing the
identifying white cloth strips were waiting to rush forward
the moment they heard the go-ahead signal. They were to
reach the elaborate network of sharpened rails that guarded the
ground in front of Fort Stedman and start slashing out passage-
ways for the troops. Then the 300 shock troops with bayoneted
muskets, who also wore identifying strips of white cloth, were
to capture or kill the Union pickets and clear a way for three
columns of men who were to concentrate on the nonexistent
garrisons of the ghost forts. In order to make sure that these
assaulting parties did not get lost, Lee had combed his army
for three local men who said they knew the ground. One of
these guides was to accompany each column while the three
officers in charge were to assume the names of three Union
officers stationed in or near Fort Stedman. Once they got
through, they were to pretend to be leading Federal troops

that had been driven back from the front and were to attempt
to throw their adversaries into a panic by crying: "The Rebels
have carried Fort Stedman and our front lines!" as they hurried
to the Union rear. The cavalry force was waiting in readiness;
some of its men were carrying the tools needed to cut telegraph
wires and pull up railroad tracks. Their immediate objective
was to sever Grant's communications between City Point and
his far-flung lines beyond Petersburg. Waiting to follow these
advance troops were about half of all the men Lee had in his
forces south of the James River.

The Federals had been offering rewards to deserters who
brought in their weapons when they surrendered. Business
had been good as the Confederacy's chance of winning the war
became more remote each day, but in the early morning of
March 25, the trade in surrendered arms began to soar. Starting about 3 A.M., so many Confederate deserters crawled into
the Union picket trenches near Fort Stedman that the officer
of the guard there could not send them in as prisoners and had
to order them detained in the line. At Battery Eleven, Major
Charles T. Richardson of the 29th Massachusetts Volunteers
became suspicious and sent word to Fort Stedman about the
sudden influx of deserters. But no one in the fort even suspected that an assault was to be made on that negligently held,
highly vulnerable position. In fact, at that very moment an
all-night poker game was going on in the quarters of a staff
officer of the fort, and the leaders who should have been on
the alert had their senses dulled by too much whisky and too
little sleep. Major Richardson's warning was ignored.

Gordon told how the attack began: "All things ready, at
4 A.M. I stood on the top of the breastworks, with no one at my
side except a single private soldier . . . who was to fire the signal
shot. . . . There still remained near my works some of the
debris of our obstructions . . . which I feared might retard
the rapid exit of my men; and I ordered it cleared away. The

noise made by this removal, though slight, attracted the attention of a Union picket who stood on guard only a few rods from me, and he called out: 'What are you doing over there, Johnny? What is that noise? Answer quick or I'll shoot.'

"The pickets of the two armies were so close together at this point that there was an understanding between them, either expressed or implied, that they would not shoot each other down except when necessary. . . . The quick mother-wit of the private soldier at my side came to my relief. In an instant he replied: 'Never mind, Yank. Lie down and go to sleep. We are just gathering a little corn. You know rations are mighty short over here.'

"There was a narrow strip of corn which the bullets had not shot away still standing between the lines. The Union picket promptly answered: 'All right, Johnny; go ahead and get your corn. I'll not shoot at you while you are drawing your rations. . . .'

"The last of the obstructions . . . were removed, and I ordered the private to fire the signal for the assault. He pointed his rifle upward, with his finger on the trigger, but hesitated. . . . He evidently felt that it was hardly fair to take advantage of the generosity and soldierly sympathy of his foe who had so magnanimously assured him that he would not be shot while drawing his rations from the little field of corn. His hesitation surprised me, and I again ordered: 'fire your gun, sir.' He at once called to his kindhearted foe and said: 'Hello, Yank! Wake up; we are going to shell the woods. Look out; we are coming.' And with this effort to satisfy his conscience and even up accounts with the Yankee picket, he fired the shot and rushed forward in the darkness."

When that single rifle shot broke the silence, the dark ground in front of Fort Stedman began to boil with action. The Confederate "deserters" who were already in the Union picket trenches suddenly turned on their captors and disarmed or killed them. The fifty axmen leaped forward and began to demolish the obstructions blocking their way. Close behind them came the three columns of men wearing white strips of cloth. They jumped down into the Union trenches and helped the pretended deserters overwhelm their guards. Following them swarmed more than 10,000 of Lee's veteran fighters arrayed in three attacking columns; one went to the left of Battery Ten, one between Fort Stedman and Battery Eleven, while the third concentrated on the fort.

The men at Battery Ten were taken by surprise. They were able to fire their two three-inch rifles only once, and the flash of the guns showed the attackers where the emplacements were located. They made a sudden rush, seized the cannoneers and threw them over the ditch, wounded one of their officers, and killed two others. In a short time they had possession of the battery. Since Battery Ten was so near to Stedman as to be practically a part of it, it was now impossible to defend the main fort for long. But the cannoneers manning Stedman's four guns fired a dozen rounds of canister into the faces of the invaders and were desperately trying to hold off a hundred Confederate sharpshooters armed with fine British Whitworth rifles.

Captain Joseph P. Carson, who was in command of the sharpshooters, told about his experiences in front of Fort Stedman that night: "At the flash of their guns, darkness disappeared, and at intervals, as the guns were discharged, it was light as day. . . . We struck the middle line of brush, climbing, falling, and rolling over into the open ground beyond. Then the wind from the cannon and flying balls was so strong that we could not keep our hats on, while the frightful roar of the guns drowned every other sound. We went the balance of the way with hats and guns in hand till we reached the last line of obstructions. . . . In a few minutes we were in the moat. We had struck the fort about the middle. The infantry in the fort was . . . firing straight down upon us. Lieutenant Gay of the Fourth Georgia Company fell at this time, mortally wounded, and would have drowned had we not carried him out of the water and placed him on the bank, where he died. We were in the dark, while the enemy above us were faintly outlined against the sky. I shouted to the men to shoot every man who showed himself. They began firing at once, and in a few moments the works were cleared. It was but thirteen feet up, and my men were sharpshooters. . . . Word was quietly passed from the right of our line that a low place had been found. . . . We filed along until the place was reached and scrambled into the fort. Forming my line, we struck the enemy at right angles, and they in a few minutes surrendered."

With Battery Ten and Fort Stedman in their possession, the Confederates turned the captured guns around to sweep the Federal lines north and south. They then made a determined effort to take Fort Haskell, and laid down a heavy barrage to drive out the Union soldiers who had taken refuge there. The invaders quickly captured Battery Eleven and kept pushing on. A large mass of Confederate infantry was working its way north up the Union line, and the three columns that were supposed to occupy the ghost forts above Stedman groped ahead in the darkness. One by one, their guides got lost or separated from the troops. Word of the fact that these three columns were going astray reached Gordon, who sent the bad news back to Lee. This was the first intimation he had of disaster, for from his position on the slope, the rapid firing and the soaring mortar shells over Fort Haskell must have led him to believe that the attack was going to be successful.

Two factors were now holding up the Confederate advance. The half-starved men, finding plenty of food in the forts and dugouts they had captured, were stopping to eat and load up with provisions. While they were losing time, the covering darkness was fading away, for the earth, revolving like the hands of a celestial clock, was bringing the morning sun nearer and nearer to the eastern horizon. The gray light of dawn hung over the battlefield, and things that had been hidden by the night were coming into view.

Brigadier General McLaughlen, of the 57th Massachusetts Infantry, had been awakened by the first sound of firing. He hurried from his headquarters to Fort Haskell, which he found strongly garrisoned with men ready to stand off an attack, so he went up the line to Battery Twelve, where everything also seemed all right. He then proceeded toward mortar Battery Eleven, but before he got there he met the Major Richardson who had earlier been suspicious of so many Confederates coming into the Union lines as deserters. When Richardson told McLaughlen that mortar Battery Eleven was already in enemy hands, both men hurried back to Battery Twelve. There McLaughlen ordered the guns turned on Battery Eleven, and three shots were fired. He also ordered the 59th Massachusetts Veteran Volunteers to try to recapture Battery Eleven. When they had regained this key position, McLaughlen, thinking that he had mended the only break in the line and knowing nothing of what had happened farther north, walked into Fort Stedman while it was still dark. He gave orders to the dim figures he saw standing there, and his orders were promptly obeyed. A little while later, when the sky was beginning to brighten he saw someone walk across the parapet. By then there was enough light for him to see that the man was wearing a Confederate uniform. He questioned him sharply and asked him his regiment. The troops around him who had been so obedient suddenly became aware of the fact that they had a Union general in their midst. They promptly seized McLaughlen and sent him to General Gordon, to whom he surrendered. He must have been embarrassed when Gordon asked him who he was, for his given name was Napoleon Bonaparte.

From the slope where Lee sat watching the tide of battle slowly turn against him, it was impossible to get more than a general idea of what was happening where the fighting was at its thickest. Nor did the coming of daylight make the scene much clearer. The dispatches brought in from the front gave the Confederate commander a better understanding of what was going on than anything he could see.

Confederate artillerymen manning the guns in Fort Stedman and along the ridge behind the Confederate front kept pounding away at Fort Haskell. One of the Union soldiers in the fort described the heavy firing:

"The air was full of shells, and on glancing up one saw, as it were, a flock of blackbirds with blazing tails beating about in a gale. At first the shells did not explode. Their fuses were too long, so they fell intact, and the fires went out. Sometimes they rolled about like foot-balls, or bounded along the parapet and landed in the watery ditch. But when at last the Confederate gunners got the range, their shots became murderous. We held the battalion flag in the center of the right parapet, and a shell aimed there exploded on the mark. A sergeant of the color company was hoisted bodily into the air by the concussion. Strange to say, he was unharmed, but two of his fellow-soldiers ... were killed, and the commandant, Houghton, who stood near the flag, was prostrated with a shattered thigh. This was all the work of one shell. Before our commander could be removed, a second shell wounded him in the head and in the hand. . . .

"Lieutenant Julius G. Tuerk, of Woerner's Battery, had an arm torn off by a shell while he was sighting the angle gun. Captain Woerner relieved him, and mounted the gun-carriage, glass in hand, to fix a more destructive range. He then left the piece with a corporal, the highest subordinate fit for duty, with instruction to continue working it on the elevation just set, while he himself went to prepare another gun for closer quarters. The corporal leaped upon the gun-stagings and was brained by a bullet before he could fire a shot. The Confederate column was preceded, as usual, by sharpshooters, and these, using the block-houses of the cantonments along the trenches for shelter, succeeded in getting their bullets into the fort, and also gaining command of our rear sally port. All of our outside supports had been driven off, and we were virtually surrounded. The flag-pole had been shot away, and the post colors were down. To make matters still worse, one of our own batteries, a long range siege-work away back on the bluff near the railroad, began to toss shell into the fort. We were isolated, as all could see; our flag was from time to time depressed below the ramparts, or if floating was enveloped in smoke; we were reserving our little stock of ammunition for the last emergency, the hand-to-hand struggle that seemed inevitable. The rear batteries interpreted the situation with us as a sign that Haskell had yielded, or was about to yield. . . .

"Captain Woerner . . . held his fire, having three pieces on the north front loaded with grape. Suddenly a great number of little parties or squads, of three to six men each, rose with a yell from their hidings down along those connecting parapets, and dashed toward us. The parapets joined on to the fort, and upon these the Confederates leaped, intending thus to scale our walls. But Woerner had anticipated this; the rear angle embrasure had been contrived for the emergency, and he let go his grape. Some of the squads were cut down, others ran off to cover, and not a few passed on beyond our right wall to the rear of the work and out of reach of the guns."

It was now after seven o'clock, and the attack had passed its peak. Federal artillerymen had moved their guns in closer and were firing at the Confederates in Fort Stedman and the area around it. Farther up the long slope to the east, Major General John F. Hartranft was massing Union forces for a major assault.

The 200th Pennsylvania went in first; it was not strong enough to force the Confederates back, but it stopped them at great cost to itself. Then at half-past seven, the 211th Pennsylvania came over the top of the hill and swept down the long slope in one of the spectacular closed-rank charges that were still the pride of military men. Other Union troops joined them in the action, and in a matter of minutes the Confederates' hold on Fort Stedman was broken. Prisoners were taken by the hundreds, whole stands of battle flags were captured, and the routed remnants of Gordon's troops found themselves trapped, for there was no way to get back to their own lines except by crossing open ground swept by Union crossfire. At eight o'clock, Lee, who was watching the action from his position above Colquitt's Salient, ordered his troops to fall back, and the quick urgent notes of the bugler's recall with its long final summoning signal sounded across the field where men were still dying and more were yet to die.

A Union observer who watched the trapped Confederates trying to get back said: "My mind sickens at the memory of it — a real tragedy in war — for the victims had ceased fighting, and were now struggling between imprisonment and death or home."

From two until four o'clock that afternoon there was a truce for removing the dead and wounded from the area between the lines. Burial squads were sent out from both sides, and stretcher-bearers carried badly wounded men to ambulances. The tent hospitals behind the lines were crowded, and the ghastly business of performing emergency operations in the field went on all night.

6

Mr. and Mrs. Lincoln Visit the Front

Saturday, March 25, to Monday, March 27

GORDON'S RAIDERS succeeded in cutting the telegraph
line to City Point. As a result, Grant's headquarters there received only fragmentary information about the magnitude of
the attack on Fort Stedman. General George Gordon Meade,
head of the Army of the Potomac, and General O. C. Ord, head
of the Army of the James, were both at City Point for an all-
night conference, so command devolved upon General John
Parke, of the Ninth Corps of the Army of the Potomac, but he
was unwilling to take the responsibility for ordering an immediate counterattack upon the weakened Confederate lines,
although such a move was clearly called for. It was not until
later in the morning, when couriers brought word to City Point
of what had happened at the front, that a counterattack was
made. More Confederates were killed, wounded, or captured
then, bringing their gross losses for the day to nearly 5000,
while the Union casualties were about 2000.

The signs and portents were beginning. Fishermen, hauling
their nets in one of the little creeks running into the Potomac
near Washington, came up with a strange catch. The fish,
which ran from seven to ten inches in length, were reddish
gold in color. No one had ever seen such creatures in that area

before. There was much comment about them, and the local newspapers sent reporters to the markets to examine the remarkable catch and write stories about the golden fish.

At City Point, on the morning after their arrival, the Lincolns had breakfast on the *River Queen*. Robert Lincoln came on board to tell his father that a promised midday review of the troops would have to be postponed because of the firing at the front. He also said that the reports which had been received at headquarters were meager but it was known that the assault had been repelled. The President then wrote out a telegram to be sent to Stanton. He was to regret the last sentence of it before the day was over, for it read: "Robert just now tells me there was a little rumpus up the line this morning, ending about where it began."

Accompanied by a group of officers who had come to pay their respects, Lincoln went ashore to visit General Grant at his headquarters. He had been at City Point briefly in June of the previous year, but the supply depot had been expanded enormously since then. Its strategic importance was due to its location, for this important base was at the confluence of the James and the Appomattox Rivers and was ideal for launching an attack on Petersburg. The beautiful old Eppes mansion stood (and still stands) on a bluff with a splendid view of both rivers. On its grounds Grant and his officers had built their headquarters camp of log cabins and tents. For half a mile behind this stretched barracks, camps, hospitals, stables, and the other buildings needed to operate a major base of supply and operation. Down below, and for an equal distance south along the James, were the warehouses, wharves, and railroad yards for storing and transporting arms and ammunition. From this point army engineers had built a hastily constructed military railroad that ran westward behind the Union lines for nearly fifteen miles.

Although Lincoln had great admiration for Grant, he did not know him well. Both men were probably a little in awe of each other and were therefore rather reserved when they were together. Grant was more complex than is generally believed. The stories of his taciturnity, his unrelenting belligerence as a commander, and his cigar smoking and drinking habits are well known, but there is more to him than that. Grant, who had been called a butcher after the dreadful slaughter in the campaign from Wilderness to Cold Harbor, disliked firearms, could not bear the thought of killing an animal, or tolerate meat unless it was so well cooked that no trace of blood remained.

He was superbly good in handling horses, but he was incredibly naïve in his dealings with men, as a story he told about his boyhood shows: "There was a Mr. Ralston living within a few miles of the village, who owned a colt which I very much wanted. My father had offered twenty dollars for it, but Ralston wanted twenty-five. I was so anxious to have the colt, that after the owner left, I begged to be allowed to take him at the price demanded. My father yielded, but said twenty dollars was all the horse was worth, and told me to offer that price; if it was not accepted I was to offer twenty-two and a half, and if that would not get him, to give the twenty-five. I at once mounted a horse and went for the colt. When I got to Mr. Ralston's house I said to him: 'Papa says I may offer you twenty dollars for the colt, but if you won't take that, I am to offer twenty-two and a half, and if you won't take that, to give you twenty-five.' It would not take a Connecticut man to guess the price finally agreed upon. . . . I could not have been over eight years old at the time. This transaction caused me great heartburning. The story got out among the boys of the village, and it was a long time before I heard the last of it."

Because of early incidents like this and because he had failed at everything he had tried to do in the world of business, Grant had come to have a very low opinion of himself. Even the great success he had made in his military career did not entirely dispel this deeply rooted feeling of inadequacy. Assistant Secretary of War Charles A. Dana said of him: "Of all men he is the slowest to anger. He has been heard to say that even under the severest insult he never became indignant till a week after the offense has been given, and then only at himself for not having sooner discovered that he had been insulted or misused. This arises rather from an unconscious self-abnegation than from any incapacity for choler."

Adam Badeau, who was Grant's aide-de-camp and military secretary, said: "I found him a man like other men, with feelings as profound as those of the most passionate, but with a power of concealing them almost without example. His reserve, however, was natural in part, as well as in part the result of intention. At times there was a positive inability to reveal emotion, a sort of inarticulate undemonstrativeness as far as possible from stolidity. He had few affections, but these were intense; he did not hate many, but he could be implacable. He was not what is usually called ambitious, but after he had been long in power he was not insensible to the sweets of possession, and was decidedly averse to relinquishing what he had enjoyed. He was not vain, but he knew his own qualities, and, though he had the faculty of receiving adulation with a greater appearance of equanimity than any other human being I have known, he was not indifferent to the recognition of the world or the praises of his friends. He who never betrayed on that imperturbable countenance that he relished the plaudits of the multitude has told me often with delicious frankness afterward of the compliments he had received; he who seemed so careless of censure or criticism — after some little attempt at a speech of four or five lines, has looked around shyly as he sat down, and whispered: 'Was that all right?' "

Grant's reticence was perhaps due to his unwillingness to commit himself to words before he had a chance to be certain that what he was about to say expressed exactly what he meant. He was much surer of himself when he could put his ideas down on paper, and his reports and his *Memoirs* show that he could express himself clearly in writing.

He was devoted to his wife. She was apparently the only woman he ever loved, and it was when he was separated from her that he took to drink to escape from the dreadful loneliness which terrified him. Many of the accounts of his intemperance were exaggerated, but he was the sensitive, self-searching, unsure type of man who needed an occasional flight into temporary forgetfulness in order to keep firm control of himself the rest of the time.

The morning of March 25 was cool. Mist shrouded the river at City Point in the early hours but traffic on that busy waterway never ceased; there was a constant going up and coming down of many Federal vessels, all on wartime missions. And from the encampment came the sounds of drums and bugles, of men marching in drill formation, and of the endless ringing of hammers on anvils as the war horses were being shod.

When the President arrived at Grant's headquarters, the general told him about the battle that was going on at Fort Stedman and said that the outcome would surely be favorable to the Union and that Lee's sudden attack probably presaged an early withdrawal of the Army of Northern Virginia from Petersburg and Richmond. Lincoln wanted to go to the front to see the fighting but Grant was reluctant to expose the President of the United States to unnecessary danger. Later in the morning, however, when the telegraph line had been repaired and reports from the front seemed better, Grant had a special train made up that was ready to leave at noon with Mr. and Mrs. Lincoln, Mrs. Grant, Barnes, the commander of the *Bat,* and Adam Badeau.

The train carried the Presidential party over the uneven

roadbed of the Military Railroad, which General Horace Porter said was like "a corrugated washboard." As they approached the area behind Fort Stedman, where the Confederate advance had swept over the railroad tracks, the ground was still covered with the dead and those who were so seriously wounded that they could not be moved. Men in blue uniforms and gray lay closely huddled together, and around them red blood was darkening in the sun.

Horses were provided for the men at Meade's Station, while Mrs. Lincoln and Mrs. Grant rode in an army ambulance in company with Adam Badeau, who occupied a seat facing the two ladies.

Stories of Mrs. Lincoln's eccentric behavior were common in Washington. There is no doubt that the unhappy woman was well on the way to the actual insanity which caused her son Robert to commit her to an institution for a nine-month stay in 1875. What happened on this day and the next is an indication of how far her mental deterioration had already gone. Badeau reported the journey some twenty years later:

"I chanced to mention that all the wives of officers at the army front had been ordered to the rear — a sure sign that active operations were in contemplation. I said not a lady had been allowed to remain, except Mrs. Griffin, the wife of General Charles Griffin, who had obtained a special permit from the President. At this Mrs. Lincoln was up in arms, 'What do you mean by that, sir?' she exclaimed. 'Do you mean to say that she saw the President alone? Do you know that I never allow the President to see any woman alone?' She was absolutely jealous of poor, ugly Abraham Lincoln.

"I tried to pacify her and to palliate my remark, but she was fairly boiling over with rage. 'That's a very equivocal smile, sir,' she exclaimed: 'Let me out of this carriage at once. I will ask the President if he saw that woman alone.' Mrs. Griffin, afterward the Countess Esterhazy, was one of the best known and most elegant women in Washington, a Carroll, and a personal acquaintance of Mrs. Grant, who strove to mollify the excited spouse, but all in vain. Mrs. Lincoln again bade me stop the driver, and when I hesitated to obey, she thrust her arms past me to the front of the carriage and held the driver fast. But Mrs. Grant finally prevailed upon her to wait till the whole party alighted, and then General Meade came up to pay his respects to the wife of the President. I had intended to offer Mrs. Lincoln my arm, and endeavor to prevent a scene, but Meade, of course, as my superior, had the right to escort her, and I had no chance to warn him. I saw them go off together, and remained in fear . . . for what might occur. . . . But General Meade was very adroit, and when they returned Mrs. Lincoln looked at me significantly and said: 'General Meade is a gentleman, sir. He says it was not the President who gave Mrs. Griffin the permit, but the Secretary of War.' Meade was the son of a diplomatist, and had evidently inherited some of his father's skill.

"At night, when we were back in camp, Mrs. Grant talked over the matter with me, and said the whole affair was so distressing and mortifying that neither of us must ever mention it; at least, I was to be absolutely silent, and she would disclose it only to the General."

While this unhappy scene was going on, President Lincoln was riding over that part of the battlefield where the fighting had been at its thickest earlier in the day. Farther down the line shells were bursting in the air, and small arms as well as cannon were being fired. The Presidential party saw burial squads at work, and watched surgeons attending to the wounded. Hundreds of Confederate prisoners, dirty, emaciated, and sometimes wearing homemade bandages which they had used to bind up their wounds, were being rounded up for removal to the bull pen at City Point. Barnes, who had been exploring the battlefield on his own, told Lincoln about a Confederate drummer boy he had seen die from a mortal head wound. The President, already moved by the dreadful scenes around him, was visibly touched by Barnes's description of the child's death. Lincoln had been under fire at Fort Stevens on July 11, 1864, but he had never seen the naked face of war all bloodied and terrible like this. Yet he had to do his duty as Commander in Chief of the United States Army, so he followed the course of the battle by referring to a map on which he had marked troop positions.

At three o'clock, the military review which had been postponed from noon was held in a quiet sector well away from the front. Drums beat as the colors dipped, and the men of the Fifth Corps of the Army of the Potomac passed in formal parade before their Commander in Chief, who sat astride one of Grant's horses while he watched the troops march by.

While his men were preparing to cross the James, Sheridan came up the river by boat at Grant's request and arrived at City Point very early the next morning (March 26). Of all the commanders in the Union Army, Major General Philip Henry Sheridan was probably the most popular with his own men and with the public. He had fought in the West with Grant and Sherman, but it was his campaign in the Shenandoah Valley that made him famous. He was one of the few men in the Union Army who really enjoyed fighting. He made it his policy to be in the thick of the battle with his men, and his many narrow escapes from death were fabulous. This hard-riding, wiry little Irishman was America's last great cavalry leader to have the opportunity of maneuvering large masses of men and horses in a major encounter.

When he arrived at City Point, Sheridan was greeted with enthusiasm by Grant's friend and chief of staff, Major General

John A. Rawlins. While leading him to headquarters, Rawlins told Sheridan that Grant intended to send him and his men south to join Sherman. Their combined forces were then to overwhelm Johnston and march north to help Grant conquer Lee. Rawlins was opposed to the idea and candidly said so. He escorted Sheridan to Grant's quarters but did not enter.

Grant greeted his top cavalry commander with his customary quietly spoken "How are you?" and waited for him to begin the conversation. Sheridan went into some detail about his long march from Winchester, slanting his words so as to lead up to his objections about being sent to join Sherman. Grant ignored the implications of what he was saying and told him that he "was to cut loose from the Army of the Potomac by passing . . . to the southward . . . and, after crossing the Roanoke River, join General Sherman." He then handed Sheridan a copy of his order of March 24. It contained the sentence "General Sheridan will . . . move independently under other instructions which will be given him." Sheridan naturally assumed that what Grant had just said about joining Sherman had to do with the "other instructions." He began to argue, saying that his cavalry belonged to the Army of the Potomac, which he felt should be allowed to destroy Lee's army without help from any other force.

In his *Memoirs* Grant told what happened: "I saw that after Sheridan had read his instructions he seemed somewhat disappointed at the idea, possibly, of having to cut loose again from the Army of the Potomac, and place himself between the two main armies of the enemy. I said to him: 'General, this portion of your instructions I have put in merely as a blind;' and gave him the reason for doing so. . . . I told him that . . . I intended to close the war right here, with this movement, and that he should go no farther. His face at once brightened up, and slapping his hand on his leg he said: 'I am glad to hear it, and we can do it.' "

The telegraph tent at City Point, where Captain Samuel H. Beckwith, Grant's cipher operator was in charge, was the listening post to which news from the various fronts was immediately flashed. Lincoln spent a good deal of time there, keeping himself informed of what was going on. On the morning of Sheridan's arrival he visited Beckwith, who gave him a dispatch from Stanton filed the night before in reply to one the President had sent about his inspecting the battlefield. Stanton said: "The rebel rooster now looks a little the worse as he could not hold the fence. . . . I hope you will remember Gen. Harrison's advice to his men at Tippecanoe, that they 'can see as well a little further off.' "

The President then began an exchange of telegrams with Stanton about setting a date for the celebration of the fourth anniversary of the fall of Fort Sumter (which he consistently misspelled Sumpter). It was finally decided that April 14 was the most satisfactory day for the ceremony that was to be held in the recaptured fort, since it was on April 14, 1861, that the Federal garrison had abandoned this key to Charleston Harbor.

At eleven o'clock, the President, General and Mrs. Grant, General Sheridan, General Horace Porter, Lieutenant Commander Barnes, and Adam Badeau left to go up the James by steamer to watch Sheridan's men cross the river and also to review General Ord's troops. On their way they passed Malvern Hill, where Major General John Bankhead Magruder had launched a savage attack on McClellan's army as it withdrew from its attempt to take Richmond in 1862. Both Sheridan and Porter noted that Lincoln was depressed during the short run up the river, but he was more cheerful later when they arrived at the place where Sheridan's cavalrymen, nearly 10,000 strong, were crossing the James. Barnes describes the lively scene: "A pontoon bridge had been thrown across the river, and Sheridan's men were passing over it in a stream, while the bank was lined with others, some bathing and watering their horses, laughing and shouting to each other and having a fine time. They soon found out that the President was watching them, and cheered vociferously. . . . Then the *River Queen* turned and passed through the naval flotilla, ranged in double line, dressed with flags, the crews cheering as we passed. Porter had sent his orders ahead before starting, and the ships made a brave show. The President was apparently delighted, and the Admiral naturally very proud of his command. Mr. Lincoln, as he passed each vessel waved his high hat, as if saluting old friends in his native town, and seemed as happy as a school boy.

"On reaching the *Malvern*, [Admiral] Porter's flagship, the *Queen* went alongside, and we found there a grand lunch spread out in her cabin. How Porter could have got it up on so short notice was a source of wonder to Mr. Lincoln, as to everyone else. It was the cause of funny comments and remarks by the President, contrasting army and navy life, as was witnessed by the laughter among the group immediately about him, of which he was the moving spirit. Luncheon over, we all returned to the *Queen* and to Aiken's Landing, where the horses and ambulances were put ashore. Many officers of Ord's division were waiting to accompany and escort the President to the field review, which was to be reached over a rough corduroy road leading to the pontoon bridge close by.

"The arrangements were that Mr. Lincoln should go on horseback, accompanied by Grant and Ord, with their respective staffs, then Mrs. Lincoln and Mrs. Grant were to be conducted to the ground in an ambulance, under the special escort of General Horace Porter and Colonel Badeau. The distance to Ord's camp was three or four miles. The President wore a long-tailed black frock coat, not buttoned, black vest, low cut, with . . . a rather rumpled shirt-front, a black, carelessly tied necktie, black trousers without straps, which as he rode, gradually worked up and displayed some inches of white socks. He wore a high silk hat, rather out of fashion, and innocent of a brush. He rode with some ease, however, with very long stirrup leathers, lengthened to their extreme, to suit his extraordinarily long legs. His horse was gentle, with an easy pacing, or single-foot gait, and progress was rapid; but owing to the luncheon and delay in starting, we reached the parade-ground at a late hour.

"The division was drawn up in a wide field, at 'parade rest' and had been so for several hours. After hurried conferences with the commanding officer General Ord reported to General Grant, who referred to the President with the statement that the soldiers' dinner time was long past, and asked whether the review should await the coming of Mrs. Lincoln and Mrs. Grant. ... Mr. Lincoln exclaimed against any postponement, and in a few moments the review began; the President, with Grant and Ord leading, proceeded to the right of the line and passed in front, the bands playing, colors dipping, and the soldiers at 'present arms.' Mrs. Ord asked me whether it was proper for her to accompany the cavalcade, now very numerous. I replied that I was ignorant of army usages and ceremonies, but a staff officer, to whom I referred the question, said, 'Of course! Come along!' and gladly enough we ... followed the reviewing column. Half way down the line the missing ambulance with the ladies drove in upon the line. Seeing it Mrs. Ord exclaimed 'There come Mrs. Lincoln and Mrs. Grant — I think I had better join them.' Reining out of the crowd we galloped across the field and drew up beside the ambulance. Our reception was not cordial; it was evident that some unpleasantness had occurred. Porter and Badeau looked unhappy, and Mrs. Grant was silent and embarrassed. It was a painful situation, from which the only escape was to retire."

Adam Badeau told what had happened during his second ride with Mrs. Lincoln: "I was detailed as before to act as escort, but I asked for a companion in the duty; for after my experience, I did not wish to be the only officer in the party.

Mrs. Ord accompanied her husband; as she was the wife of the commander of an army she was not subject to the order for return; though before that day was over she wished herself in Washington or anywhere else away from the army, I am sure. She was mounted, and as the ambulance was full, she remained on her horse and rode for a while by the side of the President. . . .

"As soon as Mrs. Lincoln discovered this her rage was beyond all bounds. 'What does the woman mean,' she exclaimed, 'by riding by the side of the President? and ahead of me? Does she suppose that *he* wants *her* by the side of *him?*' She was in a frenzy of excitement, and language and action both became more extravagant every moment. Mrs. Grant again endeavored to pacify her, but then Mrs. Lincoln got angry with Mrs. Grant; and all that Porter and I could do was to see that nothing worse than words occurred. We feared she might jump out of the vehicle and shout to the cavalcade. Once she said to Mrs. Grant in her transports: 'I suppose you think you'll get to the White House yourself, don't you?' Mrs. Grant was very calm and dignified, and merely replied that she was quite satisfied with her present position; it was far greater than she had ever expected to attain. But Mrs. Lincoln exclaimed: 'Oh! you had better take it if you can get it. 'Tis very nice.' Then she reverted to Mrs. Ord, while Mrs. Grant defended her friend at the risk of arousing greater vehemence.

"When there was a halt Major Seward, a nephew of the Secretary of State, and an officer of General Ord's staff, rode up, and tried to say something jocular. 'The President's horse is very gallant, Mrs. Lincoln,' he remarked; 'he insists on riding by the side of Mrs. Ord.' This of course added fuel to the flame. 'What do you mean by that, sir?' she cried. Seward discovered that he had made a huge mistake, and his horse at once developed a peculiarity that compelled him to ride behind, to get out of the way of the storm.

"Finally the party arrived at its destination and Mrs. Ord came up to the ambulance. Then Mrs. Lincoln positively insulted her, called her vile names in the presence of a crowd of officers, and asked what she meant by following up the President. The poor woman burst into tears and inquired what she had done, but Mrs. Lincoln refused to be appeased, and stormed till she was tired. Mrs. Grant still tried to stand by her friend, and everybody was shocked and horrified. But all things come to an end, and after a while we returned to City Point.

"That night the President and Mrs. Lincoln entertained General and Mrs. Grant and the General's staff at dinner on the steamer, and before us all Mrs. Lincoln berated General Ord to the President, and urged that he should be removed. He was unfit for his place, she said, to say nothing of his wife. General Grant sat next and defended his officer bravely. Of course General Ord was not removed.

"During all this visit similar scenes were occurring. Mrs. Lincoln repeatedly attacked her husband in the presence of officers because of Mrs. Griffin and Mrs. Ord, and I never suffered greater humiliation and pain on account of one not a near personal friend than when I saw the Head of the State, the man who carried all the cares of the nation at such a crisis — subjected to this inexpressible public mortification. He bore it as Christ might have done; with an expression of pain and sadness that cut one to the heart, but with supreme calmness and dignity. He called her 'mother,' with his old-time plainness; he pleaded with eyes and tones, and endeavored to explain or palliate the offenses of others, till she turned on him like a tigress; and then he walked away, hiding that noble, ugly face that we might not catch the full expression of its misery."

Barnes's ordeal was not yet over. He went to bed early but was summoned to the *River Queen* at eleven o'clock that night. He reported that he found "Mr. and Mrs. Lincoln awaiting me in the upper saloon. He seemed weary and greatly distressed.

... He took little part in the conversation ... which evidently
followed some previous discussion with Mrs. Lincoln, who had
objected very strenuously to the presence of other ladies at the
review; and had thought that Mrs. Ord had been too prominent
in it; that the troops were led to think she was the wife of the
President, who had distinguished her with too much attention.
Mr. Lincoln very gently suggested that he had hardly remarked
her presence; but Mrs. Lincoln was not to be pacified, and
appealed to me to support her views. Of course I could not
umpire such a question, and could only state why Mrs. Ord and
myself found ourselves in the reviewing column, and how immediately we withdrew from it upon the appearance of the
ambulance with Mrs. Lincoln and Mrs. Grant.

"I extricated myself as well as I could ... and asked permission to retire, the President bidding me goodnight sadly and
gently.

"The next morning I reported as usual to the President, who
received me with marked kindness. I inquired for Mrs.
Lincoln, hoping she had recovered from the fatigue of the
previous day. Mr. Lincoln said she was not at all well, and
expressed the fear that the excitement of the surroundings was
too great for her, or for any woman."

In the morning the President told Barnes that he was going to
Grant's headquarters and asked him to accompany him. They
went on foot through the busy landing area, where trains and
boats were being loaded and unloaded. As they looked down
from the bluff at the wharves below, Barnes was reminded of
the very feminine controversy that was going on between Mrs.
Lincoln and Mrs. Grant. He said that for "convenience in
landing and returning the *River Queen* had been placed alongside the dock and a gang plank connected her with the wharf.
The [*Mary*] *Martin,* a boat similar to the *Queen* was also tied
up to the dock. She was General Grant's headquarters boat,

and on her Mrs. Grant and family were living. It was sometimes a question of precedence as to which boat should lie next
the dock — a question not raised by Mr. Lincoln. But Mrs.
Lincoln thought that the President's boat should have place,
and declined to go ashore if she had to do so over the *Martin:*
so several times the latter was pushed out and the *Queen* in,
requiring some work and creating confusion, despite Mr.
Lincoln's expostulations. The two craft came to be called 'Mrs.
Lincoln's boat' and 'Mrs. Grant's boat,' and the open discussions between their respective skippers were sometimes warm.
Of course neither Mr. Lincoln nor General Grant took any
notice of such trivialities."

Barnes returned to the *Bat* for lunch. Shortly afterward
Robert Lincoln came on board to extend an invitation from
the President to go on an excursion to Point of Rocks. A young
Navy officer cannot very well turn down a personal invitation
from the President of the United States, although Barnes said,
"I was doubtful about the expediency of my going, but Captain
Lincoln said his father expressly desired it; so I went aboard
the *Queen* which at once pushed out from the wharf and started
up the river. I found Mr. Lincoln in his office, where he made
me sit down and we talked for awhile — mainly, I could see,
to put me at my ease. 'Tad' was with him as usual hanging or
half sitting on his father's knees. The only other persons
aboard were Mrs. Grant, Mrs. Lincoln, and Captain Lincoln
and I think Captain Penrose.

"Leaving Mr. Lincoln I joined Mrs. Grant who was alone in
the forward cabin, and inquired for Mrs. Lincoln. She pointed
her out standing on the uncovered deck, near the pilot house.
. . . She was alone, and at Mrs. Grant's suggestion I pushed out
of the door a large upholstered arm chair, bade Mrs. Lincoln
good morning . . . and suggested that she should occupy the
chair; which she declined. Finding my presence unwelcome, I
returned to Mrs. Grant, who had witnessed my failure. Very

soon Mrs. Lincoln beckoned to her, she joined her and an animated conversation ensued between them; Mrs. Grant returned to the cabin and told me Mrs. Lincoln objected to my presence aboard the *Queen* and requested her to so inform me. This made things rather uncomfortable for a pleasure party, so on our arrival at Point of Rocks, Mrs. Grant and I stayed behind while the Lincoln party rambled in the woods. Before their return, upon consultation with Mrs. Grant, I had the captain put me ashore on the other side of the Appomattox, where I got a horse from the quartermaster, with an orderly to show me the way and bring back the horse. Thus I rode, discomfitted, back to City Point. I had gone upon the trip with some misgivings. I am sure the President's invitation was in desire to bring about more pleasant relations between Mrs. Lincoln and myself. It is only proper to add that, in these perhaps unnecessary allusions to Mrs. Lincoln there can be found the cause of the sadness and melancholy which were at times so apparent in Mr. Lincoln's expression. She was at no time well; the mental strain upon her was great, betrayed by extreme nervousness approaching hysteria, causing misapprehensions, extreme sensitiveness as to slights or want of politeness or consideration. I had the greatest sympathy for her, and for Mr. Lincoln, who I am sure felt deep anxiety for her. His manner towards her was always that of the most affectionate solicitude, so marked, so gentle and unaffected that no one could see them together without being impressed by it."

7

Lincoln Sets the Surrender Terms

Monday, March 27, and Tuesday, March 28

SHERIDAN HAD ARRIVED on March 26, fresh from his conquest of the Valley; now, on March 27, Sherman arrived from North Carolina, fresh from his victorious march that had cut the Confederacy in two. The *Malvern* had been summoned by telegraph to come down the river to City Point so Admiral Porter could represent the Navy at the forthcoming meeting of the high command. The flagship dropped anchor near the wharves at 6:15 P.M. in time to greet Sherman's arrival with a salute of fifteen guns.

Grant, Horace Porter, and other officers from headquarters hurried down the wooden stairs to the wharf, where Sherman had already landed. Porter describes their greeting as they shook hands: "Their encounter was more like that of two schoolboys coming together after a vacation than the meeting of the chief actors in a great war tragedy. Sherman ... walked up to headquarters, where Mrs. Grant extended to the illustrious visitor a cordial greeting. Sherman then seated himself with the others by the camp-fire, and gave a most graphic description of the stirring events of his march through Georgia. The story was the more charming from the fact that it was related without the manifestation of the slightest egotism. His field of operations had covered more than half of the entire theater of war; his orders always spoke with the true bluntness of the soldier; he had fought from valley depths to mountain heights, and marched from inland rivers to the sea. Never were listeners more enthusiastic; never was a speaker more eloquent. The story, told as he alone could tell it, was a grand epic related with Homeric power. At times he became humorous, and in a nervous, offhand, rattling manner recounted a number of amusing incidents of the famous march. . . .

"Sherman . . . went on to talk about his famous 'bummers,' saying: 'They are not stragglers or mere self-constituted foragers, as many have been led to suppose, but they are organized for a very useful purpose from the adventurous spirits who are always found in the ranks. They serve as 'feelers' who keep in advance and on the flanks of the main columns, spy out the land, and discover where the best supplies are to be found. They are indispensable in feeding troops when compelled, like my army, to live off the country, and in destroying the enemy's communications.'"

Grant then reminded Sherman that President Lincoln was at City Point and suggested that they pay him a brief visit before dinner. In 1872, Sherman wrote about this meeting with the President, whom he had not seen since the beginning of the war, when he had formed a very poor opinion of Lincoln.

"We had met in the early part of the war, and he recognized me and received me with a warmth of manner and expression that was most grateful. . . . Mr. Lincoln made many inquiries about . . . the march from Savannah to Goldsboro. . . . When in lively conversation his face brightened wonderfully, but if the conversation flagged his face assumed a sad and sorrowful expression. General Grant and I explained to him that my next move . . . would bring my army, increased to 80,000 men by Schofield's and Terry's reinforcements, in close communication with General Grant's army . . . and that unless Lee could effect his escape . . . he would soon be shut up in Richmond . . . and

would have to surrender. Mr. Lincoln was extremely interested
in this view of the case, and when we explained that Lee's only
chance was to escape, join Johnston, and being then between
me in North Carolina, and Grant in Virginia he . . . could
choose which to fight. Mr. Lincoln seemed unusually impressed
with this, but General Grant explained that at the very
moment of our conversation Gen. Sheridan was passing his
cavalry across the James River . . . that he would . . . reach the
South Shore Road [Southside Railroad] and that if Lee should
'let go' his fortified lines, he [Grant] would follow him so close
that he could not . . . fall on me alone. . . . I . . . expressed the
fullest confidence that my army in North Carolina was willing
to cope with Lee & Johnston combined till Grant could come
up. But we both agreed that one more bloody battle was likely
to occur before the close [of] the war.

"Mr. Lincoln . . . more than once exclaimed, 'Must more
blood be shed! Can not this last bloody battle be avoided!' We
explained that we had to presume that General Lee was a real
General, that he must see that Johnston alone was no barrier
to my progress, and that if my army of 80,000 veterans should
reach Burkeville, he in Richmond was lost, and that we were
forced to believe he would not await that inevitable conclusion,
but make one more desperate effort."

When Grant and Sherman returned to headquarters, Mrs.
Grant asked them if they had paid their respects to Mrs. Lincoln. Grant said no, and Sherman explained that he had not
even known she was on the ship. The two top generals of the
Union Army then dutifully promised to make amends by asking solicitously for Mrs. Lincoln the next time they went
aboard the *River Queen*.

Various officers called during the evening to consult with
Sherman, but Sheridan did not arrive until midnight. The
fiery-tempered cavalry commander, who ordinarily traveled on

horseback, unfortunately had come to City Point by train. He came in cursing and fuming at all railroads and particularly at the miserably built Military Railroad, which ran back of the lines, for his train had gone off the tracks and had delayed him for hours. His bad mood was made even worse when the subject he hoped was closed for good was reopened — that of his joining Sherman instead of attacking Lee. Grant came to his rescue, and Sheridan left, hoping that the vexatious question was settled for ever. But the tenacity for which Sherman was noted would not allow him to let matters rest. He came to Sheridan's quarters in the morning while the cavalry leader was still in bed and again tried to persuade him to join him in North Carolina. Fortunately, both men had a good sense of humor, so the situation ended amicably, with Sheridan remaining with Grant to fight with him in the campaign that was to end at Appomattox.

Later that morning Sherman and Admiral Porter spent some time with Grant; then all three went aboard the *River Queen* for the last high-level policy meeting of the war.* Before beginning the business of the day, Grant was careful to inquire about Mrs. Lincoln. The President went to her cabin and returned to say that she was not feeling well and would be unable to appear.

Grant left no known record of the celebrated conference which then took place, but Adam Badeau, who was very close to him, wrote what he knew about Grant's behavior at the meeting: "There was nothing like a council of war, for Grant never held one in his life. He listened always with proper deference to the views of those of his subordinates who were entitled to offer them, and was never unwilling to receive ideas or information from any source; but his plans were his own,

---

* G. P. A. Healy painted his well-known picture, "The Peacemakers," which portrays the four men in the after-cabin of the *River Queen*, from data supplied to him by Sherman, Porter, and Grant. The original hangs in the White House.

and were invariably announced in the shape of orders. Even when he seemed to adopt the views that were presented to him, those who offered them never knew it at the time, nor did they ever know whether he had conceived them in advance. He never claimed to have originated them, nor did he ever acknowledge an indebtedness. All was left in that obscurity which enveloped so much of his intellectual individuality, and he never allowed any one, friend or follower, no matter how intimate, to know his intentions or convictions before they were fully formed. In this crisis, he asked no advice on military matters from the President, who offered none; and he listened to Sherman's eager and restless eloquence, suggestive and advisory, yet deferential and subordinate, but said nothing in return more definite than he had already written. If there was a man living whose advice in such matters he would have sought, that man was certainly Sherman; and, as he had written and said, if Sherman had been his superior Grant would have obeyed absolutely, but it was never his nature to seek advice; he sought only information, and without vanity or self-assertion, he came to his own conclusions. He did this always. He did so now."

Sherman wrote only a brief account of the conference for his *Memoirs,* because he knew that Porter had made notes of the meeting shortly after it was held. He therefore used Porter's version, written in 1866, in his book. It is the only detailed account made by any of the four men who were present. The part which deals with the President's ideas of the peace terms is particularly important, especially when viewed in light of what happened after Lincoln's death, when Sherman followed what he believed were his dead Commander in Chief's wishes in arranging the surrender terms with Johnston. Porter wrote:

"My opinion is, that Mr. Lincoln came down to City Point with the most liberal views toward the rebels. He felt confident that we would be successful, and was willing that the enemy should capitulate on the most favorable terms. . . . He wanted peace on almost any terms, and there is no knowing what proposals he might have been willing to listen to. His heart was tenderness throughout, and, as long as the rebels laid down their arms, he did not care how it was done. I do not know how far he was influenced by General Grant, but I presume, from their long conferences, that they must have understood each other perfectly, and that the terms given to Lee after his surrender were authorized by Mr. Lincoln. I know that the latter was delighted when he heard that they had been given, and exclaimed, a dozen times, 'Good!' 'All right!' 'Exactly the thing!' and other similar expressions. Indeed, the President more than once told me what he supposed the terms would be: if Lee and Johnston surrendered, he considered the war ended, and that all the other rebel forces would lay down their arms at once.

"In this he proved to be right. Grant and Sherman were both of the same opinion, and so was every one else who knew any thing about the matter.

"What signified *the terms* to them, so long as we obtained the actual surrender of people who only wanted a good opportunity to give up gracefully? The rebels had fought 'to the last ditch,' and all that they had left them was the hope of being handed down in history as having received honorable terms.

"After hearing General Sherman's account of his own position, and that of Johnston, at that time, the President expressed fears that the rebel general would escape south again by the railroads, and that General Sherman would have to chase him anew, over the same ground; but the general pronounced this to be impracticable. He remarked: 'I have him where he cannot move without breaking up his army, which, once disbanded, can never again be got together; and I have destroyed the Southern railroads, so that they cannot be used again for a long time.' General Grant remarked, 'What is to prevent their laying the rails again?' 'Why,' said General Sherman, 'my bummers don't do things by halves. Every rail, after having been placed over a hot fire, has been twisted as crooked as a ram's-horn, and they never can be used again.'

"This was the only remark made by General Grant during the interview, as he sat smoking a short distance from the President, intent, no doubt, on his own plans, which were being brought to a successful termination.

"The conversation between the President and General Sherman about the terms of surrender to be allowed Jos. Johnston, continued. Sherman energetically insisted that he could command his own terms, and that Johnston would have to yield to his demands; but the President was very decided about the matter, and insisted that the surrender of Johnston's army must be obtained on any terms.

"General Grant was evidently of the same way of thinking, for, although he did not join in the conversation to any extent, yet he made no objections, and I presume had made up his mind to allow the best terms himself.

"He was also anxious that Johnston should not be driven into Richmond, to reenforce the rebels there, who, from behind their intrenchments, would have given us incalculable trouble.

"Sherman, as a subordinate officer, yielded his views to those of the President, and the terms of capitulation between himself and Johnston were exactly in accordance with Mr. Lincoln's wishes. He could not have done any thing which would have pleased the President better.

"Mr. Lincoln did, in fact, arrange the (so considered) liberal terms offered General Jos. Johnston, and, whatever may have been General Sherman's private views, I feel sure that he yielded to the wishes of the President in every respect. It was Mr. Lincoln's policy that was carried out, and, had he lived long enough, he would have been but too glad to have acknowledged it."

A newspaper correspondent who saw the men in command of the Union war efforts as they walked along the shore on the second day of the conference described how they looked: "Lincoln, tall, round-shouldered, loose-jointed, large-featured, deep-eyed, with a smile upon his face, is dressed in black, and wears a fashionable silk hat. Grant is at Lincoln's right, shorter, stouter, more compact; wears a military hat with a stiff, broad brim, has his hands in his pantaloons' pockets, and is puffing away at a cigar while listening to Sherman. Sherman, tall, with high, commanding forehead, is almost as loosely built as Lincoln; has sandy whiskers, closely cropped, and sharp, twinkling eyes, long arms and legs, shabby coat, slouched hat, his pantaloons tucked into his boots. He is talking hurriedly, gesticulating now to Lincoln, now to Grant, his eyes wandering everywhere. Meade, also tall, with thin, sharp features, a gray beard, and spectacles, is a little stooping in his gait. Sheridan, the shortest of all, quick and energetic in all his movements, with a face bronzed by sun and wind, is courteous, affable, and a thorough soldier."

These were the men who were to shape America's destiny during the next few days. The two conferences on the *River Queen* were intended to set the terms for surrender and guide the nation through the difficult years of reconstruction that were ahead.

8

Soldiers in the Rain

Wednesday, March 29, and Thursday, March 30

LINCOLN HAD several times expressed his uneasiness about Sherman's being separated from his army at so crucial a moment. Therefore as soon as the conference on the *River Queen* was over, Sherman boarded the *Bat* with several of his fellow officers and his brother, Senator John Sherman, to go back to New Bern. The *Bat* left City Point at 3:15 P.M., March 28, on what turned out to be a tedious voyage: again the former blockade runner had trouble with her engines. Seven miles short of his destination the impatient Sherman hurried off in the ship's gig, leaving the *Bat* to make her way up the Neuse River under sail.

During the voyage, Barnes told Sherman about Mrs. Lincoln's strange behavior. Sherman was so impressed by what he heard that he printed Barnes's version of Mrs. Ord's unhappy encounter with Mrs. Lincoln in his *Memoirs,* which were published in 1875 — the year in which the President's unfortunate widow was declared insane.

When Sherman left City Point, it was agreed that his army was to start on April 10 from Goldsboro, North Carolina, to Raleigh, and then drive on toward the railroad junction at Burkeville, Virginia, to intercept Lee's army there if it abandoned Richmond and Petersburg. The only two Confederate

escape routes still open (the Southside and the Richmond
Danville Railroads) led to Lynchburg and Danville. Since the
two lines crossed at Burkeville, anyone commanding that strategic junction could prevent Lee from moving troops or
supplies by train. The military situation was still rather fluid,
for much depended upon what Lee would do next, and Johnston's army in the Carolinas, even though it had dwindled to
hardly more than 14,000 men, was still a factor.

Nothing had changed Grant's determination to begin his
campaign on March 29. The weather had been generally clear
for some time, and the roads seemed to be dry enough to support wagons and cannon. The long siege was ending, and as
darkness came on that night, closing in over the vast tangle of
trenches, earthworks, and forts, the men in the units that were
to march the next morning knew they were about to see action.
Joshua L. Chamberlain, the Maine general who was to play
an important part in the Appomattox Campaign, recorded his
impressions of that last night before Petersburg: "The solemn
notes of the last tattoo rang 'Lights out!' through the deepening
shades, echoed from point to point of wooded hill and earth-
piled parapet, floating away northward ... toward the homes
our hearts reached after, the lingering echoes sweeping the
heartstrings as they died away."

Grant's strategy in opening his spring campaign was simple.
He would move troops westward to try to cut the Southside
Railroad, thus forcing Lee to strip his thinly held fortifications
in order to defend his army against this new threat. The same
troops would also attempt to turn Lee's westernmost lines and
force them back. If and when it was thought that the Confederate fortifications around Petersburg were so lightly
manned that a direct assault could be made on them without
disastrous losses, such an attack would be made. The long
stalemate was ending. Grant, with his vast superiority in men

and matériel, could now afford to force Lee's hand. The earthworks around Petersburg and Richmond had already become obsolete.

On the night of March 27, 17,000 men from Ord's Army of the James were moved south and then west around the Army of the Potomac to relieve Humphreys' Second Corps. Beginning at three o'clock in the morning of March 29, still more thousands of troops started to leave their long held, strongly fortified positions below Petersburg to head west into the open country beyond the farthest Union and Confederate earthworks. Obscure country roads now began to take on military and historic significance. The Boydton Plank Road was the chief one; it roughly paralleled the Southside Railroad and the Appomattox River. South of it was the Vaughan Road, which joined the Boydton Plank Road at Dinwiddie Court House.

This section had been fought over early in February when two infantry corps and Major General David Gregg's cavalry had been sent out to damage the Southside Railroad. There had been some sharp skirmishes, in which one of the Confederacy's best generals, John Pegram, was killed. Gregg's men got as far as Dinwiddie Court House, but nothing much came of the expedition except that it gave Union commanders a chance to examine the terrain. They were unanimous in agreeing that the back-country Virginia roads were "the worst possible."

Grant and his staff were waiting in camp for their train to be loaded with their horses and gear. Headquarters were being shifted to the field that morning, and City Point would soon become only a prison stockade, an army hospital, and a base of supplies for the westward marching armies.

At 8:30 Lincoln arrived at the cabin on the bluff to bid farewell to the headquarters staff. While they waited for the train to be made ready, Grant told the President some of the many crackpot schemes that had been proposed for conquering the Confederacy. One was to build a high wall around Richmond and then pump in enough water from the James River to drown all the citizens and soldiers. Another was to supply Union soldiers with bayonets a foot longer than those of their opponents, who would then — in theory — be unable to reach them.

Grant said good-by to his wife; then everybody walked down the steep wooden stairs to the railroad tracks. Lincoln wished his son luck and formally shook hands with each officer in turn; the train whistle blew, and, as the engine pulled away, Grant's staff saluted the President by raising their hats. He returned the salute; then the train slowly moved off toward the end of the Petersburg lines and the contested country beyond.

When the last station on the Military Railroad was reached, the horses were unloaded, and Grant and his officers rode to a cornfield south of the Vaughan Road near Gravelly Run. Here the headquarters tents were pitched, and the previously deserted field became the temporary center of Union operations.

All day long Union troops moved out of the area south of Petersburg in the elaborate series of withdrawals and replacements that were needed to keep the fortified lines defended yet release men for the major thrust to the west. And as they went, wary and watchful Confederate troops moved parallel to them — or, in some cases anticipated them, for Lee's intelligence service had kept him well informed of Grant's plans.

As Union cavalry and infantry poured out in an onrushing flood, there were constant clashes with the Confederates. Sporadic musket fire could be heard again and again in the woods where the trees were just beginning to bear the tender leaves of spring. The country into which the Union Army was advancing was gently rolling with several streams cutting through sand and clay. It was a poor section, thinly settled, and much of it had never been worth clearing, so only a few open fields alternated with long stretches of scrawny woods.

The day was cloudy, with a constant threat of rain hanging heavily in the air, which depressed the spirits of the men and made their commanders worry about getting wagons and cannon through. Since all the bridges had been destroyed, the troops often had to wait until temporary structures could be put across the fast-running streams. The Confederates had tried to block the narrow wood roads by cutting down trees. Foot soldiers and mounted men could go around the fallen trunks, but these barricades had to be dragged out of the way to let wheeled vehicles and cannon pass.

During the day, while Union troops spread out over new terrain, the Confederates did their best to delay the inexorable advance of the blue-clad soldiers who would soon vastly outnumber them in the field. The infantrymen in the Second and the Fifth Corps were meeting with resistance all the way.

The Confederates had a small fort on the far side of Hatcher's Run. When they saw Union battle lines forming on the other side of the little creek they hastily abandoned the fort. Only a single sergeant "gathered up a pile of rifles that his comrades had thrown away, and took his stand at an angle of the fort, behind a tree. The stream was deep, and [the] only means of crossing was on the trunk of a fallen tree. A Union soldier sprang upon the log. There was a flash of a rifle in the fort, and the soldier fell.... Another followed, and fell in like manner. Another and yet another, another, and yet another, went down before the unerring aim until seven ... men were dead.... The advance of the whole line was checked, and no one volunteered to step forth to certain death. But in this moment of uncertainty, a sharpshooter from a tree top some little distance in the rear saw the rebel sergeant. He took careful aim; a bullet went singing through the air, and he was dead." The Union soldiers admired the grim courage of the slain man so much that they gathered up his personal effects to send them to his family. Then they buried him in the fort he had defended so bravely and put a pine slab bearing his name, regiment, and an account of his deed at the head of the lonely grave.

Unnamed back roads running through the forest suddenly became important and were fought for so marching armies and the ever-advancing guns could move over them. Men died as the greening branches of spring were torn by shot and shell; and the walking wounded went back through the woods to seek medical attention, while those who had been badly hit lay where they had fallen, hoping someone would come to find them. These were only skirmishes, some of the many minor encounters that were to take place along the roads leading to Appomattox, but men died in them or were hurt.

An infantry action typical of many which were fought that day along the widely extended front was one in which General Joshua L. Chamberlain took part. He was in command of the first of the three brigades making up Griffin's 1st Division, which was one of the three divisions belonging to Warren's Fifth Corps. Chamberlain, probably because of his previous vocation, was more articulate than most military men, so he left a graphic account of what he saw during the Appomattox Campaign. He had been Professor of Modern Languages at Bowdoin College until July 1862, when he was given a two-year leave of absence to study in Europe. Instead, be became Lieutenant Colonel of the 20th Regiment of Maine Volunteers and rose rapidly in the Union Army, for he was not only a gifted teacher but a born soldier. He was awarded the Congressional Medal of Honor for gallantry of action at Gettysburg, and the next year, while leading a charge against the fortified lines around Petersburg, was badly wounded by a rifle shot that went through both hips, maiming him for life. Grant was so impressed by this volunteer soldier that he made him a brigadier general while he lay wounded on the field.

About noon on this gray and dismal March 29, Griffin ordered Chamberlain to push up the Quaker Road to attack the Confederates who were known to be waiting along the north side of Gravelly Run, where they had destroyed the bridge. There was only one way to cross the stream and that was to wade. Chamberlain's troops plunged into the cold water, holding their arms and ammunition high over their heads to keep them dry. The Confederates poured a devastating fire into the temporarily helpless men, cutting many of them down. The wounded had no chance and were quickly drowned, but the survivors emerged on the other bank, fighting mad, and drove the Confederates back for about a mile to some breastworks made of earth topped by heavy logs. It was almost impossible to capture such a strongly held position. Chamberlain's men hesitated and then began to fall back. The Confederates, seeing them waver, poured out of their fortifications to attack them in the open. A hand-to-hand struggle took place which was brought to an abrupt end by the arrival of Union reinforcements. The Confederates were driven back into their earthworks, and the ever-changing pattern of warfare shifted again.

Near a portable sawmill deep in the woods was a huge pile of sawdust, which Lee's battle-wise veterans knew would stop a bullet or shell more certainly than any harder material. They made this the center of their line, and posted sharpshooters in the trees behind it to pick off individuals in the attacking Union forces. A direct charge had to be made upon the men protected by the sawdust, so Chamberlain urged his horse forward in advance of his troops. The horse, excited by the crashing sounds of battle and the wildly yelling men, began to run too fast. Chamberlain brought the animal up so sharply that it reared up on its hind legs, and just at that split second, a bullet from one of the sharpshooters' rifles, aimed directly at the general's heart, came zinging through the woods.

The heavy bullet went through the strong muscle of the horse's neck. This did not deflect the piece of lead from its destined course but did slow it down. It struck Chamberlain right over the heart, went through a leather case containing a sheaf of orders, smashed a brass-backed pocket mirror, and then ricocheted so violently that it hit a revolver carried in the belt of the general's aide and knocked the astonished lieutenant out of his saddle.

Chamberlain fell to the ground unconscious but not seriously injured. His superior officer, General Charles Griffin, came by to pick him up and to say to his aides that he was afraid the wound was mortal. The invincible down-Easter regained consciousness just in time to hear his commander's words and a rebel yell as part of his line was broken by the fiercely fighting Confederates. He staggered to his feet, found that the bullet had ripped open his sleeve and rendered his left arm temporarily useless. Streaming with blood and swaying unsteadily, he insisted on remounting his wounded horse to rally his men who were beginning to retreat from the break in the line. When Chamberlain had straightened things out there, he rode his faltering horse back to his former command post and on the way was cheered not only by Union troops but by the Confederates as well.

His badly wounded horse collapsed under him, so Chamberlain drew his sword with his good right hand and went ahead on foot. In the action that followed, he became separated from his men and found himself surrounded by a band of Confederates who seemed uncertain as to whether this blood-covered, bare-headed, dingy-coated officer was a Yankee or not. He pretended to be a Confederate commander and succeeded in urging the men forward so rapidly that they were taken prisoner.

At this point a major from the 20th Maine Regiment offered the wounded general a drink from his pocket flask. The alcohol so confused the already dazed man that he did not know how he found himself suddenly mounted on a strange white horse spattered with mud. But dazed or not, the stalwart Maine soldier knew what to do — hold the field until artillery arrived. Ten minutes of desperate hand-to-hand fighting followed, and Chamberlain recorded that never-to-be-forgotten moment when the guns appeared: "Now they come . . . with headlong speed, horses smoking, battery thundering with jolt and rattle, wheeling into action . . . while the earth flew beneath the wheels — magnificent, the shining, terrible Napoleons." The guns were quickly unlimbered, brought into position, loaded, aimed, and fired. "It was splendid and terrible: the swift-served, bellowing, leaping big guns; the thrashing of the solid shot into the woods; the flying splinters and branches and treetops coming down upon the astonished heads; shouts changing into shrieks at the savage work of these unaccustomed missiles; then answering back the burst of fire oblique upon the battery, where there was a desperate attempt to carry it by flank attack; [which was] repulsed . . . thus leaving clear range for closer cutting projectiles, when now case shot and shell, now a blast of canister, poured into the swarming, swirling foe."

Finally the day's cruel work was over, the Confederates were driven north, and Chamberlain, sore and aching from the bullet that had pounded his chest and arm, after seeing to it that his wounded horse was taken care of and given shelter in a farmshed, rode through the rain to look thoughtfully at the dead that lay tumbled in grotesque attitudes around the captured breastworks. The former teacher of languages (who had also been an instructor in Natural and Revealed Religion) tortured himself with the problem that has always plagued those who fight and kill and then wonder about what they have done. In those rain-swept, darkening woods, where the guns were at last still, he asked the eternally unanswerable question: "Was it God's command we heard, or His forgiveness we must forever implore?"

Then he went to a candle-lit house filled with the wounded, to write a letter to a friend in Philadelphia whose son, entrusted to his command, had been killed that afternoon.

One soldier, at least, was enjoying the day's action and was eagerly looking forward to the decisive battles to come. This was Sheridan, who early in the morning of March 29 had led 9000* mounted men south to Ream's Station on the defunct Petersburg and Weldon Railroad, where the torn-up tracks had been twisted by fire and left in a tangled jumble of rusted iron. The Second Corps had done some serious fighting there in August 1864. The deserted trenches, reinforced by railroad ties, still remained as reminders of the fruitless and forgotten battle that had been fought along the abandoned railroad line.

The head of the mounted column crossed the railroad bed and turned west toward Dinwiddie Court House, following an almost unopposed line of march that ran south of the area where the infantry was engaged with the Confederates. The country through which they were passing was wet and swampy, and the roads, which had been miserable to start with, were quickly cut up by the hoofs of thousands of horses and the wheels of countless supply wagons and artillery. When rain began falling during the late afternoon, the wagons sometimes got stuck so badly that they had to be unloaded and lifted by sheer manpower to more solid ground.

General George Armstrong Custer, who was to meet his destiny at Little Big Horn eleven years later, and who was known more for his fighting prowess and daring conduct in battle than for digging out wagons, had been given the job of

* See the Appendix

getting the supply train through. He rode up and down the long line of wagons, cursing and cajoling the drivers to keep them at their work. Custer was a very young man who wore his yellow hair in long locks and favored a crimson scarf, which he habitually tossed back over one shoulder, but despite his tendency to be a show-off, he worked hard to keep things moving.

Just before the advance guard of Sheridan's cavalry reached Dinwiddie Court House, they encountered a party of North Carolinians outside the village. Seeing that they were outnumbered, the Confederates quickly withdrew, and the tiny hamlet was Sheridan's for the taking. As a town it did not amount to much, but its location, commanding several important roads, was of great strategic value. Sheridan felt that Lee had made a serious error in giving it up without a fight.

There were only about a dozen buildings clustered around the crossroads. The red brick court house was in fair condition except for its roof, which was propped up on the outside by heavy timbers. Near it was a dingy-looking jail, a post office, a small church, a few weather-beaten houses, and, most important of all, a tavern with a long portico facing the road. Sheridan established his headquarters in this building, which was so badly kept that his tired officers refused to sleep in the filthy beds. But there was a piano, and staying temporarily in the hotel were some "lovely ladies," the feminine backwash of the war who had gone from Charleston to Petersburg and from Petersburg to this lonely crossroads where their friends in the Confederate Army had left them to shift for themselves. The girls cheerfully made coffee for the Union officers (there was no food because the supply wagons were mired somewhere on the road), and then everyone gathered around the piano to sing choruses and forget the black night outside.

After dark the rain began to fall again, first in big drops and then in solid sheets. It drummed down on the tavern's roof, ran down the sides, and started to invade the building with cold, probing, wet tentacles. Sheridan's troops sought refuge under anything that would serve as shelter, even making use of the long, low, wagon sheds which were rich with the aroma of many years' accumulation of manure. Their horses stood outside in the rain with their heads held low and their hides glistening in the lantern light as water ran down their sides and trickled down their legs. Everything was wet, everyone was miserable, and from privates to staff officers, every man in the Army was wondering why this day of all days had been chosen to launch a major campaign.

The rain poured down during the night and kept falling all the next day. The morning was foggy, and drops of water hung on the branches of the trees and along the eaves of the houses. There was no sleeping for the men in the invading army. Sheridan was up early, bristling with impatience. Dispatches began arriving from Grant, suggesting that some of the cavalry horses should be returned to Humphreys' Station on the Military Railroad, where there was adequate forage for them. But this meant turning back, and Sheridan wanted to go forward. He ordered his commanders to send out scouting parties northward over the water-soaked roads and fields and then had his big gray pacer, Breckinridge, saddled. He chose this horse because its long legs would carry him through the mud. Strangers who had never seen Sheridan ride always wondered how the diminutive general could mount a large horse, and there was a legend in the Army that he did it by climbing up his sword. Actually he was one of the world's finest horsemen; he literally vaulted into the saddle, and then, in absolute command of the huge animal, rode like a centaur.

With his adjutant general, Colonel Frederick C. Newhall, and a dozen troopers, he galloped up the Boydton Road, heedless of the fog and the rain. His men could see from the furious way he rode that he was annoyed; he was even more annoyed when some Union pickets fired at his little party. They got through this outpost, went along the Vaughan Road, and finally arrived at the rain-sodden cornfield where Grant had his headquarters. Sheridan's long-legged pacer had to wade through the soft earth there, pulling up each hoof with effort and then sinking far down at each new step. A campfire was burning near Grant's tent, and around it, standing uncomfortably on planks to keep them from being swallowed up in the all-enveloping mud, were the officers of the headquarters staff.

Sheridan, with "water dripping from every angle of his face and clothes," approached the disconsolate little group who had been debating the advisability of waiting for drier weather, and greeted them with amazing cheerfulness. When they asked his opinion of the situation, he scoffed at any thought of delay and said: "I can drive in the whole cavalry force of the enemy with ease, and if an infantry force is added to my command, I can strike out for Lee's right, and either crush it or force him to so weaken his intrenched lines that our troops in front of them can break through and march into Petersburg."

And when asked about forage for his horses he said forthrightly: "I'll get up all the forage I want. I'll haul it out, if I have to set every man in the command to corduroying roads, and corduroy every mile of them from the railroad to Dinwiddie. I tell you, I'm ready to strike out tomorrow and go to smashing things."

The officers standing in the rain were so impressed by Sheridan's confidence and optimistic energy that they wanted him to talk to Grant. One of them went into Grant's tent and got permission to bring Sheridan in, but when the belligerent cavalry commander arrived there he saw that an argument was going on between Grant and Rawlins, so he quickly made an excuse to go outside to warm himself at the fire. Grant soon followed him out. They borrowed General Rufus Ingalls' tent, where they could talk in private for a fateful twenty minutes, during which the indomitable Sheridan put the case for pressing on to battle so well that he convinced Grant not to delay the campaign.

Sheridan pointed out that cavalry could move in any kind of weather, but he asked to be reinforced by Horatio Wright's Sixth Corps of infantry which had fought with him in the Shenandoah Valley. Grant told him that Wright's distant position in the line in front of Petersburg made this impossible and that he would have to take the country between Dinwiddie Court House and the Southside Railroad with his own cavalry.

Sheridan went off to rejoin his troops, but on the way he stopped at the headquarters of the commander of the Fifth Corps, Major General Gouverneur Kemble Warren, probably because he knew that the Fifth Corps was the nearest infantry at hand. And here begins one of the most controversial, cruelest, and saddest incidents of the high command during the entire war.

Warren at this time was thirty-five years old; he had been graduated from West Point with high honors and then had done valuable work in the West with the Topographical Engineers. In 1859 he had been asked to return to West Point to teach mathematics. Under ordinary circumstances Warren might have remained at the Academy for the rest of his life, leading a useful but uneventful life. Like his contemporaries he had been caught up in the war and became a combat officer, serving with distinction during the campaigns in Virginia since early in 1861. Warren had gained a national reputation at Gettysburg during the second day's battle, when he saw that the strategic hill, Little Round Top, at the southern end of the Union lines, was practically undefended. Acting quickly and pressing into service any troops he could get, he garrisoned the rocky hilltop and saved it from falling into the Confederates' hands. From this commanding position, a few well-placed guns could have swept the Union lines from one end to the other.

Warren was promoted rapidly after that. But by 1865, the overworked general had been wounded several times and was exhausted from the previous day's fighting in the rainy woods. When Sheridan arrived at Warren's tent, the commander of the Fifth Corps was asleep. Sheridan did not ask that the sleeping man be awakened; instead he spent some time talking to one of Warren's staff officers, a colonel he had known in Oregon. Warren woke up, and then, according to Sheridan, they "had a short conversation, he [Warren] speaking rather despondently of the outlook, being no doubt influenced by the depressing weather."

Sheridan returned to Dinwiddie, ordering Newhall to ride north and instruct Major General Wesley Merritt to send a brigade across the rain-swept fields to see what they could find. This brigade (Gibbs's) easily pushed back a few widely scattered Confederates to the place where the White Oak Road met other country roads to form a complicated intersection known locally as Five Forks. There were no houses at this uninhabited crossroads — only a few open fields surrounded by pine woods. The almost worthless land could have been bought for a few cents an acre, but every foot of it was about to be paid for in blood.

The energetic Custer was making superhuman efforts to get the guns and the wagons through, but many of the discouraged teamsters had given up and were sitting under their wagons for shelter, leisurely smoking their pipes. Horses and mules had been unhitched and were standing around sniffing hungrily at their empty feed boxes. There was only one way to make the long-stalled line move again and that was to provide a firm enough footing to support the heavily loaded wheels. Instruc-

tions were given to corduroy the roads, and the sound of axes
was soon heard in the forests. Trees began to fall, were skillfully trimmed of their branches, and were then dragged into
position to be placed one alongside the other like so many
pencils pushed together on a desk to form a flat surface. It was
hard, backbreaking work for troopers, teamsters, cooks, horses,
and mules, but it had to be done. Meanwhile the rain never
stopped falling, and there was mud all over everything as men
and animals slipped and floundered to bring the heavy logs to
the bottomless roads. One joke became so popular that it
spread quickly through the Army. Question: "If anybody ever
asks you if you have been through Virginia, what will you say?"
Answer: "I sure have — in a number of places."

   While Custer and everyone who could be spared were busy
bringing up the wagon trains, Merritt reached the White Oak
Road but was pushed back. Late in the day more Confederate
cavalry and a large division of infantry led by General George
E. Pickett took over the strategically important White Oak
Road. Like Warren, Pickett was best known for what he had
done — or, in this case, for what he had not done — at Gettysburg. His name will be forever associated with the last desperate charge which ended that celebrated battle when his
division tried to break through the strongly held Union lines
on Cemetery Ridge and was hurled back in a repulse that
marked the beginning of the end for the Confederacy. Pickett
now commanded a miscellaneous group of reserves — the only
troops available, in the area — and so was put in charge of the
entire operation west of the Petersburg lines.
   Because of the continuing rains there was relatively little
action in front of Dinwiddie Court House on March 30. Sheridan learned that the Confederates were entrenching along the
White Oak Road near Five Forks, and early that evening he
notified Grant that Pickett's infantry and more cavalry had

arrived on the scene. The situation was becoming dangerous, so he again asked for the Sixth Corps to be sent to his support and again was told it was too far away to make this possible.

It was obvious that whoever held the White Oak Road would be in a strong position, for it was practically the only solid ground in swampy, wooded, very rough country through which it was almost impossible to move except on this road. But the Confederates, who were fully aware of the vital road's military importance, had long ago fortified it strongly at Burgess's Mill, just south of the stream called Hatcher's Run. Pickett was therefore able to march his men easily to Five Forks. But Grant and Meade also saw the need for gaining control of the now essential road, and orders were sent to Warren to extend his lines to the west and north in an effort to seize the road.

The rain never stopped falling; it came down on Union and Confederate troops alike as they stood without shelter in the dark, rain-soaked woods, occasionally taking a pot shot at each other. Sometimes fieldpieces roared out, but it was tricky work trying to charge the wide barrel of a muzzle-loader with powder in wet weather.

It was a disappointing day for both Sheridan and Warren, for neither of them was able to carry out any decisive action. The Confederates did somewhat better: Pickett's infantry, aided by cavalry under the command of Fitzhugh Lee, W. H. F. Lee, with six fieldpieces in charge of young Colonel William Johnson Pegram, got through to Five Forks and were able to dig themselves in along the White Oak Road at that crucial point.

9

Dinwiddie Court House

Friday, March 31

ABOUT TEN O'CLOCK in the morning, Confederate cavalry appeared on the western side of a swampy creek locally called Chamberlain's Bed. So few people lived in this neighborhood that the stream flowing through the swamp was not thought worth bridging; it was customarily crossed by two fords, now deeper than usual because of the spring rains. Several Union cavalry brigades were guarding these fords and the higher ground east of them. They held their positions until midafternoon, when Pickett's infantrymen came to the support of the Confederate cavalry, waded across the creek, and steadily pressed back the Union horsemen until they were in sight of Dinwiddie Court House. Sheridan was in a desperate spot; he hastily sent dispatch riders to Custer to leave the wagon trains and bring up two brigades. When Custer's hard-worked cavalrymen came dashing up, most of them were ordered to dismount* so they could fight on foot. Horse artillery rushed

---

* Since horse cavalry is now extinct in the United States Army, few people know how it operated in a Civil War battle. During the early part of the war it was used mostly for guarding wagon trains and establishing communications. Then, under such brilliant improvisers as J. E. B. Stuart and Sheridan, it began to act as an independent unit that could move rapidly and strike swiftly. But it was also found that cavalry was almost useless in heavily wooded or swampy country, and that it was not at its best when employed against well-trained and determined infantrymen like those in Lee's army. Under such conditions cavalrymen rode to the battle area and then fought on foot. But this is not as simple

in field guns, and a strong line of breastworks made of hastily dug earth topped by fence rails was established on the ridge in front of Dinwiddie. After days of rain and heavily covered skies, the sun had at last come out, and this final scene was played against a romantic-looking sky with the reddish rays of the setting sun breaking through dark, menacing clouds that were being rolled away by the west wind.

Sheridan believed in inspiring his men with martial music. His military bands were mounted on picked gray horses, and the musicians were instructed to play loudly without stopping. The bands, posted at several places along the line, all began to play at once. The notes of "Hail, Columbia," "Lanigan's Ball," "Johnny Fill Up the Bowl," "Yankee Doodle," and "Hail to the Chief" drifted across the open field, punctuated by the sounds of faraway Confederate muskets, quick reports from Custer's Spencer carbines, and the deep, low booming of the Union artillery stationed on the ridge. Confederate cavalry made an attempt to charge the Union lines, but a heavy burst of fire quickly discouraged them. Then the celebrated foot soldiers of the Army of Northern Virginia appeared; they came on, according to a Union observer, with "an air of

---

as it sounds, for the horses had to be taken care of. One of Sheridan's officers describes what this involved: "When a command is obliged to dismount . . . every fourth man remains mounted to care for four horses. . . . The horses are then located in an open field, if possible, sheltered from the fire and observation of the enemy, and where the animals will be liable to no sudden panic. Of course with any considerable change in the relative positions of the troops these horses must be moved to correspond, an operation often extremely hazardous. . . . To maneuver these masses of led horses for miles across a thickly wooded country without any defined roads was no inconsiderable task. Did you ever ride one horse and at the same time lead two or perhaps three others? Try it in a grove of young trees; imagine an enemy in close pursuit, when, consequently, you are rather hurried, you may feel well assured that if two of the animals go with you to the left of a tree, the other two will inevitably choose the opposite side. Under these circumstances is it not quite likely that you would feel some solicitude and perhaps yield to profanity? On this day horses and trees were seriously intermingled. Moreover, the saddles were filled with blankets, overcoats, rations, sabers, forage, 'nicknacks,' and all the paraphernalia appertaining to a campaigner."

abandon, a sort of devil-may-care swing in their long stride."

Sheridan, mounted on his black charger Rienzi, which had
carried him to fame at Winchester, handed his field glass to
a staff officer. Then, according to Sheridan's own account:
"Accompanied by Generals Merritt and Custer and my staff, I
now rode along the barricades to encourage the men. Our
enthusiastic reception showed that they were determined to
stay. The cavalcade drew the enemy's fire, which emptied
several of the saddles — among others Mr. Theodore Wilson,
correspondent of the New York *Herald,* being wounded. In
reply our horse-artillery opened on the advancing Confederates,
but the men behind the barricades lay still till Pickett's troops
were within short range. Then they opened, Custer's repeating
rifles pouring out such a shower of lead that nothing could
stand up against it. The repulse was very quick, and as the
gray lines retired to the woods from which but a few minutes
before they had so confidently advanced, all danger of their
taking Dinwiddie or marching to the left and rear of our
infantry line was over."

At that moment and with that repulse, the once great Army
of Northern Virginia had lost its final chance. Now, although
most Southerners were not yet aware of their government's
plight, the heart of the Confederacy was thrown into the
dreadful irregular flutter that marks the terminal phase which
leads inevitably to death.

Warren's Fifth Corps was still in the dark, wet woods west
of the Petersburg lines. On the morning of March 31, his
three division commanders were told "that there would be no
troop movements that day, because of the almost impassable
conditions of the roads and country." But no one had counted
on what the ever resourceful Lee might do. In a blinding
downpour he rode out to the western end of his lines to order
four of his brigades to leave their fortifications near Burgess's

Mill and attack the Fifth Corps. This surprise assault in the rain hit the Union lines hard. The men in Ayres's division,* who held an advance position, broke and rushed back, paying no attention to their general's frantic commands to stop; their panic infected Crawford's division, which also broke and retreated to a place in the woods where Griffin and Chamberlain were standing together. Chamberlain got permission to use artillery to stem the tide; while he was busy ordering the guns to be brought in, Warren and Griffin came riding up.

"General Chamberlain," Griffin said bitterly, "the Fifth Corps is eternally damned!"

Then Warren turned to the Maine professor to ask: "General Chamberlain, will you save the honor of the Fifth Corps? I'll have a bridge ready here in less than an hour. You can't get men through this swamp in any kind of order."

Chamberlain said impatiently, "A bridge may do to come back on; but we can't stop for it now. My men will go straight through."

He gave the necessary orders to his troops, whom he described as "wet and worn and famished." They put their cartridge boxes up high on their bayonet sockets and waded through the swirling waters of the creek. Once they got across, the Confederates withdrew. But there was no stopping the men of the Fifth Corps now. Just as they had been driven back before, they plunged forward to push the Confederates across the White Oak Road in such a dashing and determined charge that Brigadier General Eppa Hunton, who commanded one of Lee's four brigades, later said admiringly: "I thought it was one of the most gallant things I had ever seen."

The Confederates had failed to break Sheridan's lines in front of Dinwiddie Court House, but his cavalry was still in

---

* The division commanders for Warren's Fifth Corps were: 1st Division, Brigadier General Charles Griffin; 2nd Division, Brigadier General Romeyn B. Ayres; 3rd Division, Brigadier General Samuel W. Crawford.

a precarious position there. Warren heard the sound of firing
coming from the west and sent General William F. Bartlett's
brigade to help. Then darkness closed in, and a terrible night
for Warren began. His superiors, Meade and Grant, could not
know how matters stood in the black, wet, battle-littered woods
several miles from their headquarters. And because of the
dampness, the hurriedly strung temporary telegraph line kept
going out of commission during the night and had to be repaired again and again. A series of orders was sent to Warren
to make sure he would go to Sheridan's support at the earliest
possible moment.

Grant informed Sheridan that he could expect Warren's
infantry to reach him by midnight — which was obviously
impossible, for thousands of foot soldiers could not be pulled
out of the lines and moved through rough, wooded country in
so little time — especially at night. Nor did Grant or Meade
know that the Confederates had destroyed the Boydton Road
Bridge over Gravelly Run. Warren, who was closer to the
scene of action, sent an engineer with a crew to the place where
the bridge was out, and they worked furiously by lantern light
to build a forty-foot wooden structure strong enough to support
the marching ranks of infantrymen. By two o'clock in the
morning they had their new crossing ready, and Ayres's men
were passing over it on their way to the Dinwiddie area.

No one in the Fifth Corps had a chance to sleep that night.
At Warren's headquarters south of Mrs. Butler's house, telegraph messages and dispatches brought in by mounted riders
kept arriving to add confusion and contradiction to an already
difficult situation. Nevertheless, troops got under way and
were marched westward to support Sheridan.

10

The Battle of Five Forks

Saturday, April 1

THE NEXT MORNING Sheridan and his staff left the Dinwiddie tavern before daybreak. The fog was so thick that even when daylight came it was difficult to see more than a few yards ahead. Sheridan rode out to the line where Custer's pickets had been waiting all night in the rain. Several fieldpieces had been brought up there and loaded with rifled shells.

When the fog began to lift, Sheridan, Custer, Merritt, and their respective staffs rode ahead to find out what the mist-covered fields might hide. There was much discussion as to whether or not the Confederates had withdrawn during the night, and everyone knew, of course, that Warren's eagerly awaited infantry might be marching toward them.

Out of the fog, the distant shapes of dismounted men and officers on horses began to emerge. The generals halted and used their field glasses to try to determine whether the moving figures wore blue or gray uniforms. In order to settle the question quickly, one of Custer's officers rode forward to investigate. The generals and their staffs sat on their horses, intent upon the little scene that was being enacted against the backdrop of white mist. One of Sheridan's staff officers recorded the incident: "We heard a 'Halt!' a question, and an answer . . . then the sharp report of a pistol, and Custer's officer came galloping back through the muddy field, and was able to report positively that the line was gray — a very gray gentleman having shot at him and called him some highly improper names."

Sheridan barked sudden commands. An officer bent low over his horse to dash to Dinwiddie and bring up the main body of cavalry. While the Confederates began to disappear into the misty woods, the gun crews sent several rifled shells howling after them. These shots were also intended to notify Warren — if he was near enough to hear them — that the cavalry was starting into action. Meanwhile Sheridan had one of his bands play "John Brown's Body" so Warren's men could identify the troops on the ridge as friends.

Bugles began sounding, and masses of Sheridan's cavalrymen were seen coming on from Dinwiddie. The relatively small body of Confederates left to guard the approaches to Five Forks knew they were heavily outnumbered, so they fell back — but not without fighting all the way, even stopping at two places to build temporary breastworks. The Confederate withdrawal had started early; everything on wheels had been hauled back to the White Oak Road before midnight, and the infantry and then part of the cavalry had followed at 2 A.M.

Some of the Union cavalrymen went by horse up the road leading to Five Forks, while others, dismounted because of the dense thickets and swampy ground, advanced on foot. When the mounted troops came to a lane leading in from the Boydton Plank Road they caught sight of blue-coated infantrymen from Ayres's division. These were the first tangible evidence that Warren's infantry support was on its way.

The Confederates also saw the Union infantrymen; they promptly turned west to cross Chamberlain's Bed and made their way back to the White Oak Road, keeping the stream between themselves and their attackers. Rifles and carbines cracked angrily in the pine woods and swamps, but the Confederates' single-shot muzzle-loaders were no match for the seven-shot Spencer repeating carbines carried by Sheridan's men. By midday the Confederates had retired behind the rough breastworks made of earth, pine logs, and fence rails which extended for nearly two miles along the White Oak Road. Young Colonel William Johnson Pegram had three guns in position at the western end of the line and three others at Five Forks, near the center. McGregor's six guns were at the eastern end, where the sharp terminal angle turned northward for about a hundred yards.

So far matters had been relatively quiet; now there was a lull in the firing, which had been going on since daybreak. The dismounted Union cavalrymen were busy bringing up more ammunition, while the Confederates waited behind their protecting earthworks.

The countryside had been stirring with life as spring came on. Frogs were peeping in the swamps, and shadfish had come up the larger streams from the depths of the ocean, driven, like salmon, by some instinctive urge to spawn in the fresh water in which they had been born. Two days before, when General Thomas L. Rosser's Confederate cavalrymen had crossed the upper reaches of the Nottaway River, one of his men had seen the large dark shapes of the migrating fish moving upstream. The half-starved officers had excitedly borrowed a seine and had caught a fine haul of fish. They had eaten all they could and then had loaded the rest into several ambulances and hurried on to keep their rendezvous at Five Forks.

Since Rosser had been wounded and was in poor physical condition, he was sent north of Hatcher's Run to an open field nearly two miles from the White Oak Road to guard the Confederate wagon trains. On the fateful morning of April 1, he invited his fellow generals, Fitzhugh Lee and George E. Pickett, to a shadbake. No one in that pathetically hungry army could turn down such a tempting invitation. The successful action of the previous day had made them overconfident, and they did not know how near thousands of Warren's infantrymen were. The two generals rode gaily off to their promised luncheon, leaving General Thomas T. Munford in command of the highly vulnerable angle at the eastern end of the line. Perhaps they felt a bit guilty about what they were doing, for they did not tell Munford where they were going or why they were leaving the front at such a time.

Warren arrived with Crawford's big infantry division and met Sheridan about 11 A.M. The two leading generals greeted each other cordially, but Sheridan was impatient to get the fighting started, while Warren, as always, was methodical and precise, wanting to make sure that everything was in order before the attack began. In the past, they had had very little contact with each other, although both had been in the campaign from Wilderness to Cold Harbor. It was at this time that Warren's troubles with Meade and Grant had begun.

Warren was an able soldier and a brave commander who had proved his personal courage in battle after battle. He was the very opposite of the headlong, devil-may-care Sheridan. Sheridan was outgoing; when he was angry or excited he cursed and swore and thus worked off his violent emotions. Warren was reserved and quiet; his facial expression seldom showed what he was feeling.

But Grant had placed Sheridan in complete command of the combined operation, and had therefore made him the final judge of a man so unlike himself that Sheridan could not understand him.

Sheridan rode off to keep an eye on his cavalrymen while Warren went toward Gravelly Run Church. The road was cluttered with supply wagons and horses left behind by dismounted cavalrymen. Troops were arriving everywhere. Ma-

jor General Ranald Mackenzie had come up before dawn with
more than a thousand mounted men from the Army of the
James, and Warren's three infantry divisions under command
of Ayres, Griffin, and Crawford, tired out from long marches
and several days of hard fighting, were trying to get some rest
while they waited in a large field south of the church. Some
of them were washing and drying their clothes, for the sun was
shining brightly. At one o'clock Warren received an order to
bring up his infantry; he sent out the necessary commands, and
then remained near the church with his staff.

Sheridan rode up to the little church, bursting with energy
as usual. He knew exactly what he wanted to do; his plan of
battle was complete. Warren and his generals listened to his
crisp, brusque words, and watched, fascinated, while the always
positive cavalry commander drew a sketch of the Confederate
line in the sand with the point of his saber. The first step in
his plan of attack was for Custer's troops to make a mounted
charge at the extreme western end of the line in order to draw
attention there. Then Warren's three infantry divisions (about
12,000 men) were to assault the other end. Ayres's 2nd Division was to march northwest and head for the angle, while
Griffin's 1st Division and Crawford's 3rd Division were to swing
around in a wheeling maneuver so they could fall upon the
Confederates from the rear. As soon as the infantry began
firing, Sheridan's dismounted cavalrymen were to make a
frontal assault on the nearly two-mile-long Confederate front.
Meanwhile Mackenzie's troopers were to ride around the infantry to guard the White Oak Road from any possible attack
from the Confederates stationed in the western end of the
fortified lines around Petersburg.

It was a good plan, beautifully conceived, and skillfully
coordinated. But no one had taken the trouble to find out
just where the angled end of the Confederate line really was.
It was believed to be near the point where the Gravelly Run

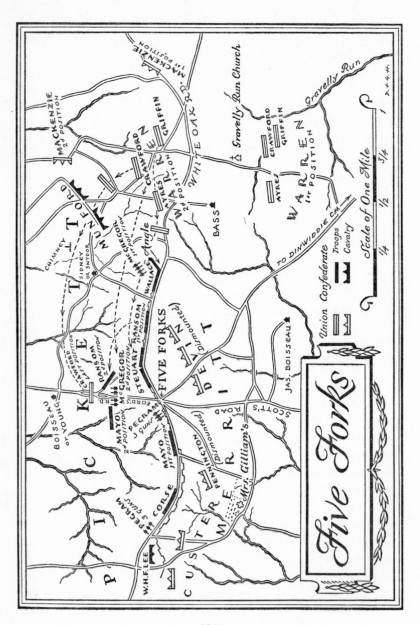

MACKENZIE
1st POSITION

MACKENZIE
2d POSITION

Gravelly Run Church

Gravelly Run

CRAWFORD
GRIFFIN

CRAWFORD
GRIFFIN

WARREN
1st POSITION

AYRES
GRIFFIN

WARREN
2d POSITION

AYRES
2d POSITION

WHITE OAK R.D.

T. L. FORD

MUNFO

CHIMNEY HILL

SIDNEY
OR SNYDOR

McGREGOR
WALLACE'S Angle

WALLACE

BASS

TO DINWIDDIE C.H.

CRAWFORD
LAST POSITION

RANSOM
2d POSITION

McGREGOR
2d POSITION

STUART RANSOM
1st POSITION

FORD'S

FIVE FORKS

DEVIN
(Dismounted)

BOISSEAU
OR YOUNG'S

PICKETT

MAYO
2d POSITION

McGREGOR

PEGRAM

MAYO
1st POSITION

FORD'S ROAD

PENNINGTON
(Dismounted)

SCOTT'S ROAD

JAS. BOISSEAU

BOISSEAU

Mrs. Gilliam's

CORSE

PEGRAM's GUNS

W.H.F. LEE

CUSTER

Union
Confederate
Troops
Cavalry

Scale of One Mile

¼   ½   ¾   1

Five Forks

Church Road made a T with the White Oak Road, but actually it was seven or eight hundred yards west of that point. Warren made copies of a map based on the faulty intelligence he had received and distributed them to his division commanders. Sheridan's scouts were considered to be the best in the Army; ordinarily, he got more accurate military intelli-

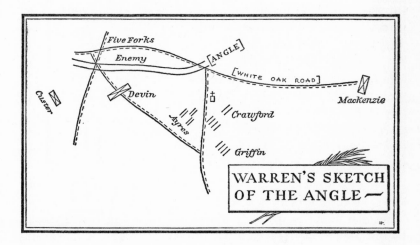

WARREN'S SKETCH OF THE ANGLE

gence than any other general. But this time the information was wrong, and Warren made the mistake of accepting it without sending out his own scouts to check.

Sheridan, who was usually lighthearted and good-natured, was undoubtedly in a bad mood on this day. He was smarting because the Confederates had driven his men back to Dinwiddie during the previous afternoon; he was doubtless irritated by adverse comments on this from headquarters; he hadn't wanted Warren's Fifth Corps to begin with; and he had probably heard army gossip that Warren was in disfavor with Grant because the commanding general thought he had been slow in moving up his troops at Spotsylvania the year before.

Chamberlain said significantly that "a voice of doom was in the air" that day. Actually, Warren's position was worse than anyone suspected. Earlier in the morning Rawlins had sent an artillery officer to Warren's former headquarters. There he discovered the Fifth Corps' adjutant general trying to get some much needed sleep. The suddenly awakened man stammered out something about not having heard from his corps commander since the night before, when Warren had gone off to order the bridge built over Gravelly Run. This news, of course, was nearly half a day old at a time when events were moving with extraordinary swiftness. The artillery officer carried the outdated news back to Rawlins, Rawlins passed it on to Grant, and then, in the hearing of his staff, Grant instructed Colonel Orville E. Babcock to go to Sheridan and tell him that if he thought one of the Fifth Corps' division commanders could do better than Warren, he was authorized to relieve him from command and order him to report to headquarters.

Babcock rode to a field below Five Forks and a little before noon met Sheridan and delivered Grant's verbal message. Sheridan now began to watch Warren suspiciously. He waited — but not patiently — for the already doomed infantry commander to get his men into position.

Time passed. The led cavalry horses and supply wagons had to be removed from the road. The ground was still soft and muddy, and the infantrymen were physically tired and weary of fighting. Some of them were complaining that they had been marched to the field "the long way around," while Sheridan's mounted troopers had been allowed to go the short way. And there was the ever present resentment of the infantryman, who has to go on foot, against the man who rides to the battle area.

By this time Warren may have sensed that a cloud was hanging over him. Some word of Grant's instructions to Sheridan may have leaked out, especially since Grant had spoken the fatal words in the presence of his staff. Sheridan and some of his officers later said that Warren "seemed gloomy and despondent" that afternoon. Sheridan had several conversations with him. He said that during one of them, Warren, instead of being inspired by his own enthusiasm, had muttered something about " 'Bobby' Lee getting people into difficulties." Sheridan then decided to accompany the Fifth Corps instead of staying with his own beloved cavalry.

Sensing Sheridan's dissatisfaction, Warren told him that his men could not be ready before four o'clock, but that he was perfectly willing to begin the attack immediately with whatever troops he had on hand and let the others follow when they arrived. But Sheridan held to his original plan. By four o'clock Warren had his three divisions, made up of three brigades each, arrayed along a marching line 3000 feet wide. There was no artillery; it had been left behind to guard the woods where the previous fighting had been done.

While the infantry was being massed, Griffin confided to Chamberlain that Grant had been hard on Sheridan for his failure to hold the line in front of Dinwiddie Court House the day before. Then he went on to say that he had heard that Grant had given Sheridan authority to remove Warren from command.

It was under this ominous cloud of suspicion and doubt that the Fifth Corps started forward just before four o'clock. The sun, which was already low in the early spring sky, was due to set at 6:21.

Crawford's big division was the first to cross the White Oak Road. Griffin's division followed it closely. Scattered through the pine woods beyond the road were Munford's dismounted Confederate cavalrymen who started a harassing fire but could not hope to stop the huge body of troops that kept steadily advancing. The men in these two divisions had been instructed to keep the sun over their left shoulders, so they would eventually come in behind the Confederate line.

Sheridan stayed with Ayres's division, which was the smallest of the three. Ayres was an old professional soldier who could be depended upon to make a highly competent assault, but Sheridan wanted to be on hand when the infantry attacked. The Confederates' angle was in the woods, so it was impossible for Ayres's men to see the low breastworks as they marched across a large open field. Sheridan, accompanied by his staff and with his headquarters flag flying, rode ahead of the massed infantry. Battle-trained Rienzi "plunged and curveted, whisking his broad tail, champing his bit, and tossing impatient flicks of foam in the air as if ... eager for the fray."

A body of Union cavalry clattered up the White Oak Road at top speed. At their head was Mackenzie, who hurried over to report to Sheridan that he had driven what Confederate cavalry he had found into their fortifications protecting Petersburg. Sheridan told him to go around the advancing infantry and come down Ford's Road to strike at Five Forks from the north.

As Sheridan and Ayres crossed the White Oak Road, not only Munford's men but Confederate infantry pickets concealed in the woods in front of the angle began firing. Since the Union troops were farther east than they were supposed to be, they had to correct their position quickly. Then, when they got close to the dark woods where an armed Confederate might be lurking behind every tree, some of the skirmishers dropped to the ground for the natural protection a foot soldier is trained to seek. But Sheridan, who made an even better target on his tall charger, lost his temper. He rode in among them, alternately cursing at them for cowardice and urging them to get up and keep going. The troops, inspired by his example and perhaps encouraged by the crackling sound of carbines which they heard coming from the left where the dismounted

Union cavalrymen were making their promised frontal attack on the Confederates' earthworks, again surged forward.

Ayres's men plunged into the woods and soon came in sight of the hastily constructed angle where anything that came to hand had been thrown together to protect the troops at the eastern end of the Confederate line. Beyond this short run of earthworks was an open field where the bright sunlight made the dense pine woods around the angle seem even gloomier. Here the Confederates had brought up McGregor's four field-pieces, which were loaded with deadly canister that could literally tear a hole through a line of men. Young William Johnson Pegram, the ranking Confederate artillerist on the field, was riding from the other end of the line to take personal charge of the defense here. The fieldpieces were fired into the mass of advancing infantrymen, blasting dreadful gaps in their ranks. Then the guns were quickly and expertly reloaded.

These guns had to be captured, and to take them by a frontal assault was the most terrifying job Civil War fighting men had to do. Chamberlain, who knew from actual experience just what this involved, describes such an action: "Plowed through by booming shot; torn by ragged bursts of shell; riddled by blasts of whirling canister; straight ahead to the guns hidden in their own smoke; straight on to the red scorching flame of the muzzles, the giant grains of cannon-powder beating, burning, sizzling into the cheek; then in upon them! — pistol to rifle-shot, saber to bayonet, musket-butt to hand-spike and rammer. . . ."

Sheridan was now at his fighting best as a combat general whose conduct was to inspire similar commanders for generations to come. He seized his colors in his own hand, and urging his big black charger forward, went dashing toward the earthworks, which were blazing fire from hundreds of muskets and the four Confederate fieldpieces. His quartermaster was hit, several of his staff officers' horses went down, and farther to

the left, handsome young General Winthrop was killed while
leading his brigade to action. General Horace Porter, who had
been sent to the field as an observer by Grant, said that "Sheridan spurred Rienzi up to the angle, and with a bound the
animal carried his rider over the earthworks." He landed
amidst a lot of frightened Confederates who were trying to
take shelter from the heavy Union fire. They asked Sheridan
what he wanted them to do. His fighting fury quickly calmed
down, and he said good-naturedly, pointing to the Union rear,
"Go right over there. Drop your guns; you won't need them
any more."

Union troops were swarming over the breastworks. They
crowded around the captured cannon, sniffing at the sharp,
acrid odor of burned powder that still lingered around the
blackened muzzles. The gun barrels were still so hot that they
could not be touched with a bare hand. Some of the men had
at least a rudimentary knowledge of handling artillery. They
swung the guns around enthusiastically and pointed them at
the retreating Confederates, but they soon proved to be such
a menace to their own rapidly moving troops that their well-
intentioned but too amateurish firing had to be stopped.

Meanwhile, infantry and cavalry, working together, rolled
back the Confederate line upon itself until the repulse became
a rout. The battle-weary gray-clad troops kept forming small
islands of resistance, but they had little chance against the
victory-hungry Union Army, which outnumbered the broken
ranks of its opponents more than two to one. Sheridan was all
over the field; his cleft red-and-white cavalry guidon with its
two stars clearly showed his presence at the various scenes of
action, but he was never even touched by the bullets that were
cutting down hundreds of others.

The victorious Union troops swept on to the crossroads at
Five Forks, where Pegram had placed three of his guns, but the
young artillerist had already gone down, mortally wounded

like his brother, General John Pegram, hardly two months before.

The sun sank lower in the western sky, but the three Confederate generals who were happily feasting on baked shad in the wagon park north of Hatcher's Run hardly noticed that it was later than they thought. Rumors persisted for years that they had been drinking heavily, but they were not obviously drunk. They had simply not heard the firing, because the dense pine woods masked the sound of battle, which was nearly two miles away. Sometime after four o'clock they sent two mounted couriers southward to make sure everything was all right. The couriers, one riding well in advance of the other, according to custom, quickly crossed an open field between the feasting place and Hatcher's Run. A heavy mist hung over the creek, but the three generals were able to watch their couriers get across the stream safely. Then they were horrified to see a large number of blue-clad infantrymen emerge from the woods to seize the first courier.

Pickett, who was in command of all the Confederate troops in the area, jumped into the saddle and tried to reach Five Forks. On the way he met some of Munford's cavalrymen, who were being pressed back by the inexorable Union advance. One of their young commanders lost his life while trying to hold off the Union infantrymen long enough for the general to get through.

Pickett arrived at Five Forks too late to be of any use. The combined Union infantry and cavalry attack was already close to that vital point. Pickett dismounted and took up a position near the three fieldpieces. A moment later a Yankee cavalryman, perched precariously on a mule, jumped over the breastworks to call out to him to "surrender and be damned!" But before the bold rider could bring his balky mule under control, he was followed by a wave of Union troops that swept over the earthworks. Pickett barely had time to gallop away to join his fleeing army.

After the capture of Five Forks the dismounted Union cavalrymen were ordered to go back and find their horses so they could pursue the fleeing Confederates. All the roads were blocked by strong Union forces, and the Confederates' only chance of escape was to go through fields and woods. Pursuit of the shattered remnants of what had been an important part of Lee's army went on until after dark. It was hard work, for the men who had not already surrendered were determined to get away; they stood together and put up stout resistance every time an organized body of them could be assembled.

The misinformation Warren was given about the location of the angle had made it necessary for Ayres to wheel abruptly to the left, thus breaking contact with Griffin and Crawford, who kept marching blindly away from the scene of action. Warren saw what was wrong and sent orders to both commanders to turn left. Since he felt that the situation would soon be corrected he did not leave his place in the field where he had told his staff officers they could reach him.

But he could hear the firing at the angle grow hotter, and his two errant divisions were still nowhere in sight. Finally, in desperation, he left an officer to stand by to receive information at the designated place; then he galloped along the eastern edge of an open field toward the ruins of a house where only the bare chimneys remained. The sight of a top Union general riding almost alone in such an exposed area caused the Confederates on the other side of the field to shoot at him in the hope of bringing him down. This sudden burst of fire threw some of Ayres's attacking force into temporary disorder and caused Crawford's men to shift even farther away to seek the protection of a tree-covered ridge.

Warren reached Griffin and told him to swing south. Chamberlain's brigade, which belonged to this division, had already gone to Ayres's assistance and was in at the fighting at the angle. Here Sheridan met the former Maine Professor of Languages and said to him: "By God, that's what I want to see — general officers at the front. Where are your [other] general officers?" Chamberlain said that he had seen Warren's flag in the open field to the north and then hurried forward to urge on his men.

Warren caught up with Crawford only after that commander's troops had crossed Ford's Road. Since this led directly south to Five Forks, Warren sent him marching down it. Warren hurried down this road ahead of the troops, found Five Forks already taken and Pegram's three guns captured, so he turned west along the White Oak Road, where he heard the sound of fighting.

Somewhere along the way Warren apparently learned that Sheridan had already given verbal orders to Griffin to take over the command of the Fifth Corps. Chamberlain said that when he met Warren on the road, the unfortunate general told him that he was no longer in command. The kindhearted officer from Maine, hoping to cheer up Warren, remarked that after the battle perhaps everything would be straightened out and that they would all get back to where they belonged.

Chamberlain was still with Warren when they came to what was known as the Gilliam field, where disorganized Union cavalry and infantry were firing at but not advancing against the last strong body of Confederate troops holding out near Five Forks. He tells what happened there: "Here Warren took his leave of the corps, himself under a shadow as somber as the scene and with a flash as lurid as the red light of the battle-edge rolling away into the darkness and distance of the deep woods. When our line was checked at this last angle, Griffin had ordered one of Crawford's colonels to advance. The colonel, a brave and well-balanced man, replied that where soldiers as good as Griffin's men had failed, he did not feel warranted in

going in without proper orders. 'Very well I order you in!' says
Griffin, without adding that he did it as a commander of the
corps. The gallant colonel bows — it is Richardson, of the 7th
Wisconsin — grasps his regimental colors in his own hand . . .
and rides forward in advance of his men. What can they do but
follow such example? General Warren, with intensity of feeling
that is now desperation, snatches his corps flag from the hands
of its bearer, and dashes to Richardson's side. And so the two
leaders ride, the corps commander and his last visible colonel —
colors aloft, reckless of the growing distance between them and
their followers, straight for the smoking line, straight for the
flaming edge; not hesitating at the breastworks, over they go:
one with swelling tumult of soul, where the passion of suffering
craves outburst in action; the other with obedience and self-
devotion, love-like, stronger than death. Over the breastworks,
down among the astonished foe, one of whom, instinct over-
mastering admiration, aims at the foremost a deadly blow,
which the noble youth rushes forward to parry, and shielding
with his own the breast of his uncaring commander, falls to
earth, bathing his colors with his blood. . . . [Richardson was
wounded, but Warren's faithful Irish orderly was killed here,
and Warren's horse was shot from under him.] Slowly Warren
returns over the somber field. At its forsaken edge a staff
officer hands him a crude field order. Partly by the lurid
flashes of the last guns, partly by light of the dying day, he
reads: 'Major-General Warren, commanding the Fifth Army
Corps, is relieved from duty and will at once report for orders
to Lieutenant-General Grant,* commanding Armies of the
United States. By command of Major-General Sheridan.' "

* Warren reported to Grant at his headquarters about ten o'clock that night.
According to Warren, Grant "spoke very kindly of my past services and efforts,
but thought I was too self-reliant in executing my duties, and did not strictly
obey orders and cooperate in his general plans closely enough." Grant then put
him in command of the inactive area around City Point and later sent him to
the Mississippi to do engineering work for the Army there.
   Warren's career in the United States Army was his whole professional life.

Chamberlain was keenly aware of the agony through which Warren was going and said later if that luckless general had been killed in the charge on the Gilliam field he would have been remembered as one of the great heroes of the war. He concludes his story of the tragic affair by saying "With almost the agony of death upon his face, Warren approaches Sheridan and asks him if he cannot reconsider the order. 'Reconsider. Hell! I don't reconsider my decisions. Obey the order!'"

George Alfred Townsend, one of the most competent newspaper correspondents of the Civil War, was at Five Forks during the battle. That evening he wrote an account of the day's action: "I came upon Five Forks ... and ... at the foot of some pines, the victor and his assistants were congregated.

He therefore kept insisting that an official court of inquiry be appointed to rule upon his case. It took him fourteen years to get such a court authorized. A board of highly placed Army officers then heard detailed testimony from Union and Confederate officers (including Grant, Sheridan, and Fitzhugh Lee) who had taken part in the actions west of the lines around Petersburg at the beginning of the Appomattox Campaign.

After nearly three years, the court finally made its opinions public on November 21, 1882. Although it said that Warren should have moved two of his divisions earlier on March 31, the court completely exonerated him against Sheridan's imputations that he had been in any way negligent on April 1 — the day of the Battle of Five Forks.

One can understand why the impetuous Sheridan, during the heat of battle, might remove a man who differed so widely from him in temperament, but it was very unlike the ordinarily generous Sheridan to remain so hostile for years afterwards toward a man whose professional career he had ruined. Apparently Warren's real nemesis was Grant. Nicolay and Hay, who knew all the men in the case well, said that Grant was "implacable" toward Warren.

It is always difficult — and sometimes impossible — to determine the true causes of human behavior. A word, a gesture, a seeming resemblance to someone dimly remembered and disliked, a laugh or even a smile wrongly timed, an expression of disagreement when agreement is expected, may cause the unconscious mind to form a judgment which reason is then forever unable to change. Grant said that Warren was too slow in getting his troops into action at Spotsylvania. Perhaps it was that, or perhaps it was something else.... And Warren had also had differences of opinion with Meade, who as commander of the Army of the Potomac was his immediate superior. Also the fact that Warren had been devoted to McClellan did not help him. *(cont'd next page)*

Sheridan sat by some fagots, examining a topographical map. ... He is opposite me now as I pen these paragraphs by the imperfect blaze of his bivouac fire. He is good-humored and talkative, like all men conscious of having achieved a great work, and has been good enough to sketch for me the plan of the day's operations. ... Close by lies Custer, trying to sleep, his long yellow hair covering his face; and General Griffin, now commanding the Fifth Corps, goes here and there issuing orders, while aides and orderlies ride in and out. ... There are dark masses of horses blackened into the gray background, and ambulances are creaking to and fro. I hear the sobs and howls of the weary, and note, afar off, among the pines, moving lights

---

Warren wrote to his wife the day after his removal from command to say: "Ever since General Grant came here, every chance and favor has been given to the Western generals." Many other old-timers in the Eastern theater of war also believed this, but Warren's difficulties had probably begun on May 7 and 8, 1864, when Grant, then new to the Army of the Potomac, was moving his army from the Wilderness to Spotsylvania. Grant, Sheridan, Meade, and Warren had all been involved in the bitter personal quarrels which followed the bungling of certain troop movements there. Warren, as the fourth one down in rank, was made the sacrificial victim nearly a year later.

According to civilian standards, Warren seems to have been dealt with unjustly by Sheridan and Grant. But it is only fair to state the Army's attitude toward the court's decision even though the court was an instrument of the Army. Sheridan disagreed with the court's findings, and General Sherman, who was the top Army commander in 1882, said "that General Sheridan was perfectly justified in his action in this case, and he must be fully and entirely sustained if the United States expects great victories by her armies in the future."

The men who had been in the Fifth Corps, however, did not agree with the attitude of the high command. One of them, writing in 1882, just before the final decision was made public, said: "We can forgive Sheridan for the injustice of an act performed in a moment of excitement, but to persist in it for seventeen long years, preferring to crush a brother officer rather than acknowledge an error ... is not an honorable course for a brave man to pursue. The old Fifth Corps will stand by their commander, and whether he receives tardy justice or not, he has the sympathy and love of the men he once led to battle."

Warren did not hear the court's favorable ruling: he had died three months before it published its decisions. And, characteristically, he had left orders to be buried in civilian clothes without a military ceremony of any kind. (A lifelike bronze statue of him in uniform stands on the rocky summit of Little Round Top, the key position he had saved at Gettysburg.)

of burying parties, which are tumbling the slain into the trenches. A cowed and shivering silence has succeeded in the late burst of drums, trumpets, and cannon; the dead are at rest; the captives are quiet."

About two miles away, the wounded were being brought to Gravelly Run Church, where the Fifth Corps had been drawn up in battle array earlier that afternoon. Townsend visited the little Methodist meetinghouse during the evening and wrote about the suffering he saw there: "A little frame church, planted among the pines, and painted white, with cool, green window-shutters, holds at its foot a gallery for the Negroes, and at the head a varnished pulpit. I found its pews moved to the green plain over the threshold, and on its bare floors the screaming wounded. Blood ran in little rills across the planks, and, human feet treading in them, had made indelible prints in every direction; the pulpit-lamps were doing duty, not to shed holy light upon holy pages, but to show the pale and dusty faces of the beseeching; and as they moved in and out, and groans and curses of the suffering replace ... the peaceful hymns and the deep responses to the preacher's prayers. Federal and Confederate lay together, the bitterness of noon assuaged in the common tribulation of the night, and all the while came in the dripping stretchers, to place in this golgotha new recruits for death and sorrow."

Five Forks was a decisive battle. General Thomas T. Munford, whose men had had to do the first fighting at the eastern end of the Confederate line, called it "the Waterloo of the Confederacy." The action at that lonely crossroads broke Lee's hold on Petersburg and Richmond. His fortified lines were now vulnerable, and he had to try to move his shattered army toward Danville or Lynchburg in an attempt to join Johnston in North Carolina.

Thousands of Confederates who had fought at Five Forks

were taken as prisoners; many others had thrown their arms away and fled, hoping eventually to reach their far-distant homes. So many Confederate muskets were picked up on the battlefield that they were used to corduroy the worst spots in the muddy roads.

Shortly after dark Horace Porter rode back to headquarters to bring the news of victory to Grant. He had to go past supply wagons, ambulances, and men on foot who were still blocking the way. When he arrived at Grant's headquarters near Dabney's Mill he found the general sitting with his staff around a campfire that was burning brightly in the darkness. Porter was bubbling with youthful eagerness to break the glad news. Everyone jumped up to listen to his shouted words, but Grant remained quietly seated. Even when Porter slapped him on the back in his excitement, the self-contained general merely asked how many prisoners had been taken. When he was told that they would number more than five thousand, he seemed pleased. Then he went to his tent to write out by candlelight the dispatches which ordered a general assault to be made all along the lines.

As soon as Grant and his staff had gone off to the front on March 29, Admiral David Dixon Porter very sensibly tried to distract the President's mind. Lincoln, Tad, and Porter got into the admiral's barge, which was made fast to a Navy tug with a long line and were towed up and down the wide river, where the ships, forts, pontoon bridges, signal towers, and army camps made the scene endlessly interesting.

But even this pleasant diversion could not stop Lincoln from haunting the telegraph tent at City Point while the armies drove west. He was under so much tension that he slept badly. It was on one of these restless nights that he had the most clearly prophetic of all his many prophetic dreams. He told it about ten days later to Ward Lamon, who recorded Lincoln's words:

> There seemed to be a deathlike stillness about me. Then I heard subdued sobs, as if a number of people were weeping. I thought I left my bed and wandered downstairs. There the silence was broken by the same pitiful sobbing, but the mourners were invisible. I went from room to room; no living person was in sight, but the same mournful sounds of distress met me as I passed along. It was light in all the rooms; every object was familiar to me; but where were all the people who were grieving as if their hearts would break? . . . I kept on until I arrived at the East Room [of the White House]. . . . Before me was a catafalque, on which rested a corpse wrapped in funeral vestments. Around it were stationed soldiers who were acting as guards; and there was a throng of people, some gazing mournfully upon the corpse, whose face was covered, others weeping pitifully. "Who is dead in the White House?" I demanded of one of the soldiers. "The President," was his answer; "he was killed by an assassin!" Then came a loud burst of grief from the crowd, which awoke me from my dream. . . .

He also dreamt that the White House was on fire, and this was used as an excuse for Mrs. Lincoln, who had not been well since her public outbursts of anger at the Army reviews, to return to Washington. She left City Point on April 1 and arrived at the White House the next day. Oddly enough, she found that Augur's headquarters across the street had been seriously damaged by fire. The news her husband kept sending by telegraph from the front was so encouraging that she decided almost at once to return to City Point and invited a large party of notable guests to accompany her.

When Mrs. Lincoln had left City Point to return to Washington, Lincoln moved to Porter's flagship, the *Malvern*, a captured blockade runner slightly larger than the *Bat*. Mrs.

Porter came aboard to join the admiral, and during the evening
the band of 114th Pennsylvania Volunteer Regiment visited the
ship to play a serenade.

Admiral Porter told an amusing story about the President's
stay on his ship: "I offered the President my bed, but he . . .
elected to sleep in a small state-room . . . six feet long by four
and a half feet wide — a small room for the President of the
United States . . . but Mr. Lincoln was pleased with it. He
told me, at parting, that the few days he had spent on board
the *Malvern* were among the pleasantest in his life.

"When the President retired for his first night on board, he
put his shoes and socks outside the state-room door. I am
sorry to say the President's socks had holes in them; but they
were washed and darned, his boots cleaned, and the whole
placed at his door. When he came to breakfast he remarked:
'A miracle happened to me last night. When I went to bed I
had two large holes in my socks, and this morning there are no
holes in them. That never happened to me before; it must be
a miracle!'

" 'How did you sleep?' I inquired.

" 'I slept well,' he answered, 'but you can't put a long blade
into a short scabbard. I was too long for that berth.'

"Then I remembered he was over six feet four inches, while
the berth was only six feet. That day, while we were out of
the ship, all the carpenters were put to work; the state-room
was taken down and increased in size to eight feet by six and
a half feet. The mattress was widened to suit a berth of four
feet width, and the entire state-room remodeled.

"Nothing was said to the President about the change in his
quarters when he went to bed, but next morning he came out
smiling, and said: 'A greater miracle than ever happened last
night; I shrank six inches in length and about a foot sideways.
I got somebody else's big pillow, and slept in a better bed than
I did on the *River Queen*. . . .' "

The storm that had delayed the armies on March 30 and 31 blew out to sea, where it caused still more damage. News now began to arrive about the dreadful disaster of March 31 when the transport *General Lyon* had caught fire off Cape Hatteras. The ship was carrying about 600 soldiers and male and female refugees from the war. Aid came quickly when the *General Sedgwick* caught sight of the burning vessel as it drifted toward the roaring breakers, but the rescue ship was able to save only about 30 people. All the others were drowned. More than 200 of the soldiers were from the 56th Illinois Regiment. They had just been mustered out and were returning to Lincoln's home town.

Very early on Sunday, April 2, 1865, Sheridan's cavalry and the infantry of the Fifth and Second Corps were engaged in cleanup operations in the area north of Five Forks. Some of Merritt's cavalrymen reached Ford's Station on the Southside Railroad about ten o'clock and found that although the Confederates had dug trenches there they had abandoned them a few hours before. Not a shot was fired as the Union cavalrymen rode up to the little country way station in the bright spring sunshine. They found a locomotive and some freight cars, in which twelve badly wounded Confederates were lying. Then, down from the upper story of the station house came a procession of deserters eager to surrender. Later in the day Chamberlain's brigade followed the route Merritt's men had taken up Ford's Road, and about one o'clock heard the whistle of a locomotive coming from Petersburg. Chamberlain sent Colonel Cunningham of the 32nd Massachusetts ahead and hurried his own troops forward at the double quick. When they came in sight of the abandoned railroad line they found "Cunningham mounted on the engine pulling the whistle-valve wide open to announce the arrival of the last train that tried to run the gauntlet out of Petersburg under a Confederate flag. This train was crowded with quite a mixed company as to color, character, and capacity, but united in the single aim of forming a personally-conducted southern tour. The officers and soldiers we were obliged to regard as prisoners of war: the rest we let go in peace, if they could find it."

Evidently the train had left Petersburg so early that it had got past the place where some of the men in Wright's Sixth Corps tore up the tracks later in the morning.

Farther east, where an attack was made by the Second Corps on the very westernmost end of the Confederates' fortified lines, the action was confused and uncertain, and the lines were not broken until about three o'clock in the afternoon, after hours of indecisive struggle.

All day long on that warm and springlike Sunday, overwhelming Union forces kept driving the Confederates west of Petersburg toward the Appomattox River, which was running high from the recent rains. Victorious, and with the end of the war in sight, the blue-clad troops were in good spirits. Newhall said that when they encamped at the end of the day "some of the wakeful boys, thinking over it all, startled the owls with sudden yells of satisfaction, and kicked the dying embers of their camp-fire into an astonished gasp of flame."

11

The Attack on Petersburg

Sunday, April 2, and Monday, April 3

WHEN GRANT'S orders were issued for a frontal attack to be made before dawn on the Confederate lines defending Petersburg, the troops received their instructions in gloomy silence because the men felt that they were being sent to certain death. They knew that the opposing lines had long been considered impregnable. But at ten o'clock on Saturday night, when news of Sheridan's victory at Five Forks was announced, and the cannon roared out in glad celebration, the men took heart and began to believe that perhaps Lee's seemingly invincible army could at last be beaten.

The attack was scheduled for 4 A.M., but preparations for it were started at midnight when cannon began firing up and down the line, keeping up a frightful din that made sleep impossible. In the Confederate lines only the gun crews were active as they attempted to return the fire. The pickets huddled close to the protecting walls of the trenches, and all those who could crowd into bombproofs did so while the iron rain fell all around. At two o'clock the Union firing slackened off to allow the guns to cool and to give their crews some rest.

Starting at midnight under the protective cover of the bombardment, 14,000 infantrymen, wearing no equipment that might rattle to betray them, moved into the open ground

between the lines. It was marshy there, but the men were told
to lie down in the wet soil and wait for the signal gun at four
o'clock. When some of their own pickets nervously began firing,
the massed troops moving into position had to take the Confederate counterfire without being able to return it.

After the guns had quieted down it was essential for the
huge body of men to maintain absolute silence while they
waited in the darkness. No sound was heard except the soft
murmur of thousands of feet treading cautiously on the marshy
ground as more troops were brought up. The noise was
described by one observer as sounding like the rustling of the
wind through the leaves of trees in a great forest.

The planning of the attack had been very thorough. Axmen
were ready to cut away the obstructions protecting the Confederate lines, and trained artillerymen were to accompany the
infantry so they could man any guns that were seized and turn
them against their former owners. Just before the main action
began, the 1st Division of the Ninth Corps made a feint attack
toward the east to deceive the Confederates as to where the
major assault was to be directed. They captured 200 yards of
trenches before they were driven back by reinforcements rushed
into the breech from other parts of the thinly held Confederate
line.

The main attack was slow in getting under way. Another
heavy bombardment began a few minutes after four, but it was
decided to hold up the infantry advance until daylight so the
men could see where they were going. As soon as the first faint
light of dawn began to show the outlines of trees and earthworks
against the sky (about 4:40), Wright's Sixth Corps started
forward. They were met with artillery and musket fire from
the Confederates, but the once impregnable lines were manned
by too few troops to hold them. Under the intensive Federal
assault the lines weakened and gave way. Blue-clad infantrymen
kept running until they dashed up and over the earthworks.

Once the attackers got inside the lines, the Confederates had to fall back. The guns in the works were then swung around and fired at the retreating Confederates. More and more Union troops kept pouring through the rapidly widening breech to push the firstcomers forward. They went on beyond the newly captured lines for several miles, until some of them reached the Southside Railroad and began pulling up tracks and cutting telegraph wires. Others overtook a Confederate wagon train and set it on fire.

Farther to the east and along the line of the Jerusalem Plank Road, General John Parke's Ninth Corps went through the Confederate fortifications and drove its defenders back to the inner line around the city. The whole area south and west of Petersburg was now the scene of violent action as Union troops forced the outnumbered Confederates from one position to another.

There had been little sleep for anyone that night. General Lee, who had gone to bed in his headquarters at the Turnbull house on Edge Hill, was awake at four o'clock when General A. P. Hill of the Third Corps arrived there. Longstreet, who commanded the First Corps, was already on hand, waiting for his troops to come to Petersburg by train. Soon an officer hurried into the house to tell them that Union troops were advancing rapidly toward the house. Hill, who had only recently returned from sick leave, ran to his horse so he could join his men; Longstreet went off to meet his troops at the railroad station in Petersburg; Lee, as if anticipating death or disaster, dressed himself in one of his best uniforms, buckled on his finest sword, and went out to ride to a slope on the other side of the road where he could get a better view of the battlefield.

Two youngsters — one a corporal — from the 138th Pennsylvania Infantry, who had been among the first to reach the

Southside Railroad, where they tore up two rails, quickly got bored with such work and started back to find their regiment. On the way they saw some Union troops who had stopped to make coffee and eat breakfast, but they kept on going until they entered a grove of trees near a swamp. While they waited there, wondering which way to go, they saw two men who looked like officers riding toward them. Figuring that any kind of officers would mean trouble, the Pennsylvanians tried to hide behind a large tree. Soon they could see that the rapidly approaching horsemen wore gray uniforms. Almost automatically the two Federal rifles went up, one above the other, while their owners stayed behind the shelter of the tree.

The Confederates were startled to see the two Pennsylvanians. The older officer, a general who was used to command, tried to bluff it out. He called upon them to surrender. "I can't see it," said the one with corporal's stripes, firing. The general fell out of his saddle, shot dead. The other rifle barked out almost simultaneously, but its bullet went wild. The Confederate sergeant at whom it was aimed yanked his horse around, crouched down on its neck, and dug the spurs in so hard that the startled animal leaped away as if propelled by springs. The horse with the empty saddle trotted behind.

As soon as the sergeant got a safe distance away he quickly changed horses, for the animal following him was one of the best in the Confederate Army. He rode to the slope near the Turnbull house to find General Lee. The sergeant had no need to say who had been killed, for the general recognized the familiar horse. He told the sergeant to go with Colonel Palmer to break the news as gently as possible to the widow, Mrs. A. P. Hill.

Telegraph operators went with the Union Army to establish temporary stations where a sword or a bayonet thrust into wet soil served as a ground connection. These stations were hooked up to the well-established line running along the Military Rail-road to City Point, an extension from which had been made to Grant's field headquarters. Dispatch-bearers would carry a message directly to its destination or to the nearest telegraph station, where the operator on duty could send it along the line to the officer to whom it was addressed. The wires were kept busy that day. The first message of victory was filed at 5:15 A.M., when headquarters was informed that the works in front of Petersburg had been taken and that many prisoners were being sent in.

At 6:40 A.M. Grant wired to City Point that both Wright and Parke had broken through the enemy's lines and that the battle was raging furiously. At 8:25 he telegraphed again:

> Wright has gone through the enemy's line, and now has a regiment tearing up the track on the South Side road west of Petersburg. Humphreys, with two divisions, is south of Hatcher's Run crossing the Boydton road. Sheridan with his cavalry, the Fifth Corps, and one division of the Second Corps, is moving from the west toward Petersburg. Ord has gone in with Wright. I do not see how the portion of the rebel army south where Wright broke through (Oak Grove) are to escape. Dispatch just received from Ord states that some of his troops have just captured the enemy's works south of Hatcher's Run, north side, and are pushing on. This is bringing our troops rapidly to a focus with a portion of the rebels in the center.

Shortly after this, Grant's headquarters were moved to Bank's house near the Boydton Plank Road northwest of Fort Fisher. This was much closer to the scene of action. While they were on the way to the new location Grant and his staff were under fire. Adam Badeau reports the incident:

"He [Grant] was met by three thousand prisoners ... march-ing to the rear. Next he came upon a division of the triumphant Sixth corps. ... The cheers of the men ... told that they recog-nized who ... had organized their victory. Grant galloped along, staying neither for prisoners nor cheers, receiving dispatches and instructing generals as he rode. The dead and the wounded showed that the works had not been too easily won....

"The general-in-chief rode up on some high ground to watch the movement. The point was about a mile from the interior rebel line, and not three miles from the heart of Petersburg. Here he dismounted and sat on the ground near a farmer's house, and waited for reports. The rebel artillerists soon turned their guns against the group of officers and orderlies, and the place seemed hot for a while, even to men who were used to battle; but just as the cannonading began, several officers arrived, and Grant remained to receive their intelligence, and write his orders in return. He was thus under fire for nearly a quarter of an hour, and his aides-de-camp, remembering the results that hung upon his life, ventured to suggest a change of position; but he sat unmoved, with his back to a tree, until the reports directed to this spot had all arrived. Then quietly, but rather maliciously, he remarked: 'The enemy seems to have the range of this place. Suppose we ride away.' A long breath, and a quick gallop, and the general-in-chief was out of danger."

The Union troops which had been seen advancing toward the Turnbull house at dawn did not continue in that direction until later in the day. Meanwhile, news was brought to Lee from various sectors of the front, and all of it was bad, for his lines were crumbling everywhere. He told Walter Taylor, his adjutant general, to send a telegram to General John C. Breckinridge, Secretary of War of the Confederate States. It was this telegram, which was received in Richmond at 10:40 A.M., that caused the evacuation of that city and sent the Confederate government into its last wild flight to escape from the trap that was closing around it. The message read:

I see no prospect of doing more than holding our position here till night. I am not certain that I can do that. If I can I

shall withdraw to-night north of the Appomattox, and, if possible, it will be better to withdraw the whole line to-night from
James River. The brigades on Hatcher's Run are cut off from
us; enemy have broken through our lines and intercepted
between us and them, and there is no bridge over which they
can cross the Appomattox this side of Goode's or Beaver's,
which are not very far from the Danville railroad. Our only
chance, then, of concentrating our forces, is to do so near
Danville railroad, which I shall endeavor to do at once. I
advise that all preparation be made for leaving Richmond
to-night. I will advise you later, according to circumstances.

Directly in front of the Turnbull house and only about a
mile from it was Fort Gregg, one of the last of the outer Confederate positions to stand firm against the overwhelming Union
tide. Behind it and even closer to Lee's headquarters was Fort
Baldwin (sometimes referred to as Fort or Battery Whitworth).
In the preparation for the assault on these last two key
positions, the Sixth Corps drove to the left of the two forts
and approached the Turnbull house. Lee had ordered six
brass Napoleons to be brought there, where they were unlimbered and made ready for action in the garden around the
house. Lee now took personal charge of them and waited
for the Union troops to approach. One of the Federal officers
said: "As we advanced . . . over rolling and open country our
batteries galloped to the front and opened fire. . . . Soon a rebel
battery opened on our left . . . and several times, as it was forced
to change position by the fire of the First Maine, we noticed
each time a fine-looking old officer on a gray horse, who seemed
to be directing its movements. At length the guns went into
battery again on a hill near a large house, and their audible
presence became more annoying than ever. By common consent
the three brigades attempted to charge the hill, but the canister
fire was so hot, and the division now so small and weary,
[that] the first attack was a failure. While our men were getting

in shape to charge again, I sent Lt. Nicholls with fifty men of
the First Maine off to the left and around the hill with orders
to shoot the battery horses, as we knew . . . they were probably
standing hitched to the caissons and would be a fine mark from
that side. . . . We started again, this time through a swamp
where many sank to the waist, and were shot, with mud and
water splashing in every direction. . . . The wounded as well as
the dead had to stay there for a time. The first five hundred
men across made a run for the battery, and as we went up the
hill amid the roar of guns and the whirr of canister . . . I detected
the crack of Nicholls' rifles and knew the guns could not be
got away. The din was terrible! Brass Napoleons were never
better served, but they were doomed. . . . Riding through the
guns I could not see the road beyond, where the enemy were
retreating, for dust, and most of the battery horses lay in their
tracks.

"I asked a mortally wounded artillery officer, who was propped
up against a limber, what battery it was. . . . 'Poague's North
Carolina,' he said. 'And who was the officer on the gray horse?'
I continued. 'General Robert E. Lee, sir, and he was the last
man to leave these guns.' "

The deserted Turnbull house, which had already been hit
by several shells, was on fire, and smoke and flames were pouring
from it as Lee and his little band rode off to join what was left
of the Confederate Army in Petersburg. A shell burst so near
them that it killed one of the horses. Lee's face stiffened with
anger, when he saw the dying animal. There was nothing he
could do but ride on grimly through the smoke of battle that
was blotting out the sun.

The last stand of the Confederacy at Petersburg was made
about one o'clock that afternoon at Fort Gregg,* where one of

* Confederate Fort Gregg should not be confused with the Union fort of the
same name, which almost directly faced it across the lines.

the most desperate hand-to-hand struggles of the war took place. As soon as the battery at the Turnbull house was put out of commission, attention was turned to Fort Gregg. A Confederate garrison had been placed there with instructions to hold out at all costs in order to gain time for the orderly evacuation of Petersburg during the night. The two guns in the fort had already fallen into Union hands earlier in the day and had then been recaptured. These two rifled cannon were manned by members of the famous Washington Artillery of New Orleans, while the garrison of some 300 infantrymen was composed of troops from Mississippi and North Carolina.

The fort itself was a square earthwork with a ditch filled with rainwater at the foot of its steeply sloped walls. This moat had not been completed all around the fort; toward the rear there was a level section where rifle pits intended to connect Gregg with nearby Fort Baldwin had been planned but had not been dug. The caissons containing extra ammunition for the two guns had to be left outside, where a heavy concentration of Union fire made it impossible for the besieged garrison to reach them. The gunners inside the fort piled their available ammunition on the wooden platforms, where they could get at it quickly and prepared to defend themselves against about 5000 men of Gibbon's Twenty-fourth Corps, whom they could see advancing across the open fields in three large columns.

The progress of blue-clad troops was temporarily diverted by the remains of a pond which the Confederates had made by damming Indian Town Creek. The dam had been broken, and the pond was almost empty, but the bottom was a morass of mud which the invading army had to go around. The attacking force came on slowly but determinedly, and all the firing from the fort's two guns and hundreds of muskets could not stop them. Soon the fort was entirely surrounded, and more Union troops kept coming on.

The men at the head of the columns jumped into the ditch

and waded across it; some of them clambered up on the bent backs of others to reach the top of the parapet. The Confederates fired straight down at them, and the dead and wounded fell into the water. But the powerful blue wave could not be stopped. Six regimental colors were planted on the parapet, where the smoke of heavy firing made it almost impossible for anyone to see what was happening. Wounded men in the fort loaded rifles taken from the dead and the dying and handed them up to those who could still fight. The two guns of the Washington Artillery poured canister into the ranks of the fiercely attacking Union troops, but nothing could halt their inexorable advance. Some of the men found the level ground at the rear and swarmed over it into the fort, where they were met with bayonets and clubbed muskets. On the other walls the third surge of Union troops broke over the top of the parapet, and yelling, screaming men leaped down into the fort. For twenty-five dreadful minutes, this hand-to-hand struggle went on.

It was literally a battle to the death. When a wave of Federal soldiers broke over the parapet they found a Confederate artillerist about to fire one of the two guns. He had his hand on the lanyard; a pull on it would discharge the loaded piece. The attackers leveled their rifles at him and yelled: "Don't fire that gun! Drop the lanyard, or we'll shoot!" He glanced up and yelled back "Shoot and be damned!" Then he yanked the lanyard. The gun went off, sending a charge of double canister into the still-advancing Union ranks. But the artillerist fell dead at the same instant, his body riddled with bullets.

When they ran out of ammunition, the Confederates threw rocks down at their attackers. But stones will not hold back men armed with rifles, and when the defenders tried to use their bayonets they were shot down. At the very end, when Union troops were pouring into the fort without meeting further resistance, the color-bearer of the 33rd North Carolina

Regiment leapt over the parapet with his flag and made a dash across the open ground outside, zigzagging as he went in order to avoid being hit. Union riflemen tried to bring down the running man, who made a good target with his bright colors flying, but he reached the Confederate inner line unscathed. He was cheered by the troops there as he approached, and men climbed up on the parapet to pull him safely inside the fortified works.

Fort Gregg had to be taken, but the cost for its capture was high. According to General John Gibbon, commander of the Twenty-fourth Corps, the attack cost him 122 men killed and 592 wounded, while he found 55 Confederate dead inside the fort and took about 300 prisoners.

An assault was then launched on Fort Baldwin. Sharpshooters armed with Spencer repeating rifles drove the pickets into the fort. A charge was made on the works, which was met only by rifle fire, for the Confederates, realizing that the position could not be held, were hauling the guns away. When wild cheering burst out from Gregg and the firing ceased there, a final charge was made on Baldwin which easily took the fort because the garrison was rapidly abandoning it. Gregg's two guns were turned on the fleeing Confederates, and shot and shell went screaming over the heads of the Union soldiers who were invading Baldwin. As soon as they had the fort in their possession, they went on to take a small redoubt 200 yards beyond it. With its capture, all the outer Confederate fortifications around Petersburg were in Union hands. Cavalry dashed ahead to reach the Appomattox River, leaving a trail of burning buildings behind them. But most of the men, who had been in action for eighteen hours of almost continual fighting, were glad to settle down in the quarters the Confederates had just vacated.

Since he was now sure that Petersburg was his, Grant did not want to waste his men's lives on an assault against the inner lines, for he felt reasonably certain that the Confederates would evacuate the city during the night. At 4:40 P.M., he telegraphed a summary of the day's work to City Point:

> We are now up, and have a continuous line of troops, and in a few hours will be intrenched from the Appomattox, below Petersburg, to the river above.... The whole captures ... will not amount to less than 12,000 men, and probably 50 pieces of artillery.... A portion of General Foster's division, Twenty-fourth Corps, made one of the most gallant charges and captured a very important fort [Gregg] with its ... entire garrison. All seems well with us, and everything quiet just now. I think the President might come out and pay us a visit to-morrow.

At just about the time Grant was sending this telegram announcing a series of triumphs, young Colonel Walter Taylor, Lee's adjutant general, was composing the detailed instructions for the withdrawal of the Confederate Army from Petersburg and Richmond. Since the troops, wagons, and artillery would have to make a night march over the narrow, rutted, muddy roads of the Virginia countryside, a great deal of planning had to go into the routing of each unit. All the streams were running high because of the recent rains, so pontoons had to be taken along in case any of the bridges had been swept away. The various units had to be dispersed until they all came together again at Amelia Court House, the appointed rendezvous nearly forty miles west of Richmond.

At 8 P.M. some 30,000 men began leaving their long held positions in the trenches and fortifications around Petersburg and Richmond. A few militiamen were sent to occupy the earthworks in order to make a show of life in them, but they were not expected even to attempt to hold the lines.

The tragic day that had begun with the death of A. P. Hill and was ending with the evacuation of Petersburg and Richmond was not without its more cheerful side for at least two of the Confederate high command. General John B. Gordon had been notified that his wife had given birth to a fine healthy baby that day, and Lee's twenty-six-year-old adjutant general, Colonel Walter Taylor, after finishing his paper work, went to his commander to make a request which, under the circumstances, only a very young man who was very much in love would have dared to make. He later wrote an account of the romantic incident: "I asked permission of General Lee to ride over to Richmond and rejoin him early the next morning, telling him that my mother and sister were in Richmond and that I would like to say good-bye to them, and that my sweetheart was there, and we had arranged, if practicable, to be married that night. He expressed some surprise at my entertaining such a purpose at that time, but when I explained to him that the home of the bride-elect was in the enemy's lines, that she was alone in Richmond, and employed in one of the departments of the government, and wished to follow the fortunes of the Confederacy, should our lines be established farther south, he promptly gave his assent to my plans. I galloped to the railroad station . . . where I found a locomotive and several cars, constituting the ambulance train designed to carry to Richmond the last of the wounded of our army requiring hospital treatment. I asked the engineer if he had another engine, when pointing to the one rapidly receding in the direction of Richmond, he replied, 'Yonder goes the only locomotive we have besides the one attached to this train.' Turning my horse over to the courier who accompanied me, with directions to join me in Richmond as soon as he could, I mounted the locomotive in waiting, directed the engineer to detach it from the cars and to proceed to overtake the engine ahead of us. . . . We did not overtake the other locomotive until it reached Falling Creek, about three-quarters of the distance, when I transferred to it and sent the other back to Petersburg. I reached Richmond without further incident and soon after midnight I was married. . . ."

While this gallant young swain was keeping his midnight rendezvous, his commander was riding along a dark country road with his troops. Five different routes were required to move some two hundred guns, more than a thousand wagons, and many thousands of horsemen and foot soldiers. The ammunition that could not be taken along was destroyed in the magazines of the abandoned forts. One after another, the deeply buried stores of gunpowder were blown up. Federal artillerymen, surprised by the sudden explosions, began firing their guns all along the front, and it was to this thunderous accompaniment that the Army of Northern Virginia began its last march.

On the night that Petersburg and Richmond were being evacuated, Lincoln and Porter were sitting on the deck of the admiral's flagship, the *Malvern,* watching the distant guns flash against the sky. The President was nervous and impatient. "Can't the Navy do something now to make history?" he asked Porter.

"The Navy is busy keeping four big Confederate ironclads bottled up in the James River," Porter explained.

"But can't we at least make some noise?"

Porter smiled understandingly and sent a message to the Federal vessels lying above Dutch Gap. He told them to fire all their guns at the Confederate river forts and keep firing as rapidly as possible for one hour. The bombardment soon began, with the guns lighting up the northwestern sky.

Suddenly there was a tremendous explosion, followed by three more. Porter's trained ear knew what had happened. The Confederates had blown up their four ironclads in order to prevent them from falling into Union hands. As soon as the obstructions and floating mines could be removed from the channel, the James would be clear all the way to Richmond.

Grant correctly appraised the situation at Petersburg that night, as is made clear in his telegram to Meade at 7:40 P.M.:

> I think there is nothing in Petersburg except the remnant of Gordon's corps, and a few men brought from the north side to-day. I believe it will pay to commence a furious bombardment at 5 A.M. to be followed by an assault at 6, only if there is good reason to believe the enemy is leaving.

He told Meade to have Parke use his siege guns on the railroad bridge during the night in the hope of hitting it by a random shot.

A young lieutenant in the 2nd Rhode Island Infantry, George V. Peck, Jr., who had never been in battle before, describes the next few hours: "At three o'clock ... I awoke with a start, finding it perfectly dark. I lit my candle, and was opening the door when a corporal rapped and asked if I would like to see Petersburg on fire, pointing to a bright light over that city. About four o'clock an explosion occurred, followed by a marked diminution of the crimson cloud. At light we were ordered to pack. ... We took the Halifax Road for Petersburg. Passing at length through lines of abatis and rows of chevaux-de-frise of most perfect workmanship, we crossed on a bridge composed of two logs over a ditch some twenty feet deep and equally wide, scaled a parapet towering nearly the same distance above our heads, crossed a small tract of very rough country intersected with deep ravines, and found ourselves within the suburbs of Petersburg. Here we halted for an hour near a little grocery that appeared to have no proprietor, hence the boys helped themselves to what they desired. ... The tobacco was promptly removed and distributed. Nothing else was found eatable save a cask of prunes, two or three years old, dry and slightly moldy, not very tempting viands, yet most everyone took a handful. Sundry individuals appropriated little glass vases and statues of china as keepsakes. ... Just as we moved on

I saw smoke pouring from one of the windows. Some vagabond had fired the store."

Petersburg was surrendered on Monday, April 3, at 4:28 A.M. The 6th Michigan sharpshooters ran up their flag on the court house, guards were posted in the streets, and the soldiers began to roam through the town. The invaders at last had a chance to see how destructive their firing had been.

At six o'clock, when Grant was informed that Union forces had possession of Petersburg, he instructed Meade to leave only one division to guard the city and to press on with all the others in pursuit of Lee.

At nine o'clock in the morning Grant rode into town, where he used Thomas Wallace's large brick house on Market Street to interview officers, citizens, and prisoners. He also arranged for the President to meet him there.

Lincoln traveled on the Military Railroad and was met by his son Robert, who had several horses for the Presidential party, which consisted of Tad, Admiral Porter, Barnes (who had just returned from taking Sherman back to New Bern), Crook, and a few soldiers. Petersburg was almost deserted as they rode through its wreckage-strewn streets, and they saw no one until they arrived at the Wallace house. There Lincoln found out that he knew its owner, for they had both campaigned as Whigs when they were younger.

Grant was waiting for him on the porch. He reported the details of their meeting in his *Memoirs:* "About the first thing that Mr. Lincoln said to me, after warm congratulations for the victory . . . was: 'Do you know, general, that I have had a sort of a sneaking idea for some days that you intended to do something like this.' Our movements having been successful up to this point, I no longer had any object in concealing from the President all my movements, and the objects I had in view. . . .

"Mr. Lincoln knew that it had been arranged for Sherman to join me at a fixed time, to co-operate in the destruction of

Lee's army. I told him that I had been very anxious to have the Eastern armies vanquish their old enemy who had so long resisted all their repeated and gallant attempts to subdue them or drive them from their capital. The Western armies had been in the main successful until they had conquered all the territory from the Mississippi River to the State of North Carolina, and were now almost ready to knock at the back door of Richmond. . . . I said to him that if the Western armies should be even upon the field, operating against Richmond and Lee, the credit would be given to them for the capture, by politicians and non-combatants from the section of country which those troops hailed from. It might lead to disagreeable bickerings between members of Congress of the East and those of the West. . . . Western members might be throwing it up to the members of the East that . . . they were not able to capture an army, or to accomplish much . . . toward that end, but had to wait until the Western armies had conquered all the territory south and west of them, and then come on to help them capture the only army they had been engaged with.

"Mr. Lincoln said he saw that now, but had never thought of it before, because his anxiety was so great that he did not care where the aid came from so the work was done."

After talking for an hour and a half on the porch, where the only witnesses were the general's staff, the President's party, some cavalrymen, and a few curious townspeople, Lincoln started back to City Point, while Grant hurried after his westward-moving armies. Nothing had been heard about Richmond as yet, and news about the fate of the Confederate capital did not reach them until after they had parted.

At City Point a telegram from Stanton was waiting for the President. He read its words of caution with amusement:

> I congratulate you and the nation on the glorious news in your telegram just read. Allow me respectfully to ask you to consider whether you ought to expose the nation to the

consequence of any disaster to yourself in the pursuit of a treacherous and dangerous enemy like the rebel army. If it was a question concerning yourself only I should not presume to say a word. Commanding Generals are in the line of their duty in running such risks. But is the political head of a nation in the same condition.

To this Lincoln replied by telegram:

Thanks for your caution; but I have already been to Petersburg, staid with Gen. Grant an hour & a half and returned here. It is certain now that Richmond is in our hands, and I think I will go there to-morrow. I will take care of myself.

12

The Fall of Richmond

Sunday, April 2, and Monday, April 3

ON THE PETERSBURG FRONT, where the troops had been
in action from before dawn until after nightfall, no one had
had time to remember that April 2 was Sunday. Nor had the
fighting men noticed the glorious weather, for the fields were
covered by smoke, and the air was foul with the acrid odor of
gunpowder. But in Richmond, where the firing at the front
sounded like the echo of far-off thunder, people awakened to
a fine spring Sunday and tried to forget the war.

Rising like Rome on seven hills above a river, the city represented Virginia culture at its best. Gracious homes and walled
gardens surrounded Capitol Square, where the state Capitol
had been modeled — in accordance with Thomas Jefferson's
suggestion — after the Roman temple at Nîmes. Alongside it,
Crawford's equestrian statue of Washington was perched on top
of a sixty-foot shaft. Behind the Capitol was the small but
imposing mansion of the Governor, while in front the parklike
lawns sloped steeply downward. To the west were the Confederate governmental offices, and not far away was the White
House of the Confederacy, where President Jefferson Davis
lived. The business district of the city lay between the Capitol
and the river, while the waterfront was lined with huge mills
and tobacco warehouses crammed with the harvested crop that
the blockade had made it almost impossible to sell.

The government had long known that it might have to evacuate the city and had been making preparations accordingly. Starting in February, most of the machinery used for manufacturing ordnance had been dismantled and shipped to Danville. During the past few weeks, women and children of the wealthier families had been sent to country estates or to towns and cities farther south. Richmond was now inhabited mostly by the poor, who could not get away, or by men whose duties or business made it necessary for them to remain in the threatened capital.

On this historic Sunday, people who had to stay in the doomed city went about their usual Sabbath morning activities. Groups of men were waiting at the Post Office and the War Department, while others lounged about the streets. Carriages moved along slowly or waited in front of the churches, for regular morning services were being held. Many of the women were in mourning, and the young men attending service were in uniform or were obviously wounded. Those who listened could hear the rough growling of the guns at Petersburg, but in fashionable St. Paul's, where Dr. Charles F. E. Minnigerode was preaching his Sunday morning sermon, his clear, well-modulated voice with its Teutonic accent was loud enough to mask the faint booming of the distant guns. Mrs. Davis and the children had left the city on March 31, after selling most of the family's furniture; so the proud president of the Confederacy sat alone in his pew, his face showing none of the emotions he must have felt, for he knew how desperate the situation was. When a messenger came down the aisle to deliver Lee's fatal telegram of 10:40 A.M., announcing the necessity of evacuating the city that night, Davis got up to leave the church. Only long training in self-discipline enabled him to clamp his lips tightly together and walk with a rigidly set expression past the many questioning faces that were turned toward him. At that moment the walls of the Confederacy cracked; the crack was to widen into a deep fissure before the day was over, and in a week the entire structure would be in ruins.

No official announcement was made to the people of the city, but word spread rapidly. One of the women of Richmond, who had been in St. James's when General Samuel Cooper, Adjutant General of the Confederate Army, was called out of the church to help organize the moving of the government, told what happened when the various church congregations were let out: "Every countenance was wild with excitement. The inquiry, 'What is the matter?' ran from lip to lip. Nobody seemed to hear or to answer.... In an hour J. (who is now Professor of Mathematics in the Naval School) received orders to accompany Captain Parker to the South with the Corps of Midshipmen. Then we began to understand that the Government was moving, and that the evacuation was indeed going on. The office-holders were now making arrangements to get off. Every car was ordered to be ready to take them south. Baggage-wagons, carts, drays, and ambulances were driving about the streets; every one was going off that could go, and now there were all the indications of alarm and excitement of every kind which could attend such an awful scene. The people were rushing up and down the streets, while vehicles of all kinds were flying along, bearing goods of all sorts and people of all ages and classes...."

At Clover Station on the Richmond and Danville Railroad, nearly a hundred miles southwest of Richmond, a group of Confederate officers were sitting in the sun near the telegraph shed, waiting for any news that might come down the line. Word of one disaster after another broke upon them like a sudden storm. One of the officers, John S. Wise, son of the former Governor of Virginia, reported the messages as they were received:

"Click — click — click. 'Our lines in front of Petersburg were broken this morning. General Lee is retiring from the city.'

"Click — click — click. 'General A. P. Hill was killed.'

"Click — click — click. 'Colonel William Pegram of the artillery also killed.'

"Click — click — click. 'In the battle of Five Forks, which continued until long after dark last night, Pickett was overwhelmed by Sheridan with a greatly superior force of cavalry and infantry, and the enemy is now endeavoring to turn our right, which is retiring toward the Appomattox, to make a stand there. . . .'

"Click — click — click. 'General Lee has notified the President that he can no longer hold Richmond, and orders have been issued for the immediate evacuation of the city. The town is the scene of the utmost turmoil and confusion.' "

In Richmond, where members of the Confederate government were busy packing their most important documents and destroying all nonessential records, the price of horses rose spectacularly during the day. By late afternoon a thousand dollars — not in almost worthless Confederate paper money but in gold — was being offered for a horse. Banks were opened on that frantic Sunday afternoon so depositors could withdraw their funds before the dreaded Yankees took over the city.

Sixty young midshipmen from the training ship *Patrick Henry* were selected as a guard for the Confederate government's gold — amounting to nearly half a million dollars, which was put on the special train set aside for high government officials. This train was scheduled to leave at eight o'clock, but Davis and his cabinet sat in the office of the railroad's president, hoping for better news from Lee, which never came. At eleven o'clock they got on the train; as it pulled out of the city they glumly watched Postmaster General Reagan while he sat "whittling a stick down to the little end of nothing without ever reaching a satisfactory point." When the train crossed the railroad bridge to Manchester they had their last chance to see Richmond. Lights gleamed in many of the houses, and there was as yet no sign of the terrible disorder that was about to break out. As soon as the city was left behind, the members of the Confederate cabinet turned for solace to the plentiful supplies of old peach brandy, which George Trenholm, the wealthy Secretary of the Treasury, had been thoughtful enough to provide.

Others, not in government service, were not so fortunate. They besieged the railroad depot, willing to pay any price for a place on one of the trains, but most of them were turned away. Some people left the city by canalboat; others fled on horseback or on foot. Thousands had to stay behind, and many, especially the women, were terrified at what the Yankees might do when they entered the Confederate capital they had been trying to take for four long years.

The Negroes of the city waited in subdued silence, afraid to express themselves while their masters were still in power. Advertisements offering rewards for runaway slaves had been appearing in the Richmond papers all that week. One of the local slave dealers brought his human stock in trade in a chained coffle to the railroad station, where he was refused transportation and was told to take his slaves away on foot.

A woman who was in Richmond that night described a new terror which broke loose in the city: "A cry of dismay rang all along the streets ... and I saw a crowd of leaping, shouting demons, in parti-colored clothes, and with heads half shaven. It was the convicts from the penitentiary, who had overcome the guard, set fire to the prison, and were now at liberty. Many a heart which had kept its courage to this point quailed at the sight. Fortunately, they were too intent upon securing their freedom to do much damage."

The first thing the convicts wanted was to get rid of the prison clothes which identified them all too clearly, so they got new outfits by plundering clothing stores and private homes. Then they were able to blend more easily into the gathering crowd, which was rapidly being increased by the rabble of

Manchester who were hurrying over the bridges to get their share of the plunder.

The crowds of people who were trying to move in both directions on Mayo's Bridge were so great by this time that a solitary ambulance which had been all day getting from Petersburg to Richmond had trouble entering the city. It was after one o'clock in the morning when it finally drove up to the old Court of Appeals building on the southeast corner of Capitol Square. Two men were waiting for it there. They knew that the wagon contained the body of General A. P. Hill, who had been killed that morning. Confederate troops had temporarily recaptured the position where he had been shot and had found his body where it had fallen. The dead face was then still warm. But the two men waiting at the Court of Appeals, both of whom were members of Hill's large family, were shocked to find that the corpse had not been touched since it was picked up on the battlefield. Even the mud on the general's dead face was still there.

They told the ambulance driver to follow them and went through the ravaged streets looking for a store that stocked coffins. At last they found a likely place — an already plundered furniture shop. They tried to locate its owner, but they could not find him. Finally they decided to help themselves. The mob had had no use for coffins so there were several on hand. They put one into the ambulance and drove to a deserted office, where they did their best to prepare the body for burial. They washed the mud off the dead features and examined the corpse for the mortal wound. When they drew off the dead man's left gauntlet they found that the heavy bullet had taken off the thumb and then gone on to pierce the body through the heart and emerge from the back.

When they tried to put the stiffened corpse into the coffin they discovered that the one they had chosen was too small. But it had to do, for they were in a hurry to get away. They crammed the body into the coffin, loaded it on the ambulance, and drove to crowded Mayo's Bridge. On the other side of the river they went to a house where one of the Hill family was staying.

The defenses of Richmond were in charge of General Richard S. Ewell, known to his men as "Old Baldy." Ewell had lost a leg at Second Manassas, after which he could take part in the fighting only by being lifted up into the saddle, where he had to be strapped in place. When Ewell's horse was shot from under him at Spotsylvania, and he was badly shaken up by the fall, Lee decided that he was no longer fit for active duty and put him in command of the Richmond defenses — a post which the indomitable old soldier did not like. He had been given orders to destroy all stores which could not be removed, and had then made an inspection tour of the warehouses to determine what should be burned to keep it from falling into Union hands.

The Mayor of Richmond, Joseph Mayo, resplendent "in his white cravat and irrepressible ruffles, his spotless waistcoat and his blue, brass-buttoned coat," now called with two members of the city council to plead with Ewell not to set anything on fire inside the city limits, but he gruffly dismissed them. The tobacco warehouses and the bridges had already been marked for burning and nothing could save them — not even Secretary of War Breckinridge, who was still in Richmond and who was later blamed for not stopping the terrible destruction that went on during the night.

About three o'clock in the morning, according to Ewell, "a mob . . . of both sexes set fire to some buildings on Cary Street, and began to plunder the city. The convalescents, then stationed in the square, were ordered to repress the riot, but their commander shortly reported himself unable to do so, his force being inadequate. I then ordered all my staff and couriers who could be spared to scour the streets, so as to intimidate the mob by a show of force, and sent word to General Kershaw, who was coming up from the lines, to hurry his leading regiment into town. . . . The small bridge over the canal on Fourteenth street was burned by incendiaries, who set a canal-boat on fire and pushed it under the bridge. This was evidently done in hopes of embarrassing our retreat, and General Kershaw's division passed the bridge while on fire at a double-quick."

An eyewitness, who wrote about his experiences in the city that night, describes the blowing up of the huge supplies of ammunition which were stored in Richmond: "I was aroused by what might almost have awakened the dead. The earth seemed fairly to writhe as if in agony, the house rocked like a ship at sea, while stupendous thunders roared around. This was the blowing up of the Confederate magazine; and this was the opening gun of the august and sublime pageant of that ever-memorable day. Soon after the flames burst out from the tobacco warehouses, set on fire to prevent the tobacco from becoming spoils to the enemy, and proving the cause of the terrific conflagration which ensued. The bridges across the river — one of them the lofty Petersburg Railroad bridge, about a mile long — were speedily long lines of flame; while on the side of the city the devouring element set to work in fearful earnest. The fire had scarcely got fairly under way when the arsenal, containing, it was said, seven hundred and fifty thousand loaded shells, and the dépôts of cartridges and fixed ammunition, with the laboratory and its combustibles, began to explode."

By this time a good part of Richmond was on fire, and the city was in the hands of the mob. At 4 A.M., Colonel Walter Taylor left his midnight bride in the house on West Main Street where he had married her, and hurried off with his new brother-in-law, Colonel John S. Saunders, to Mayo's Bridge, which was still passable at that time.

General E. P. Alexander, Longstreet's artillery chief, was ordered to take part of his command out of the city on this last

remaining bridge. While waiting for his troops to cross, he
visited the nearby Danville Freight Depot where he saw
"large quantities of provisions ... which had evidently run the
blockade. ... I treated my horse to an English bridle and a felt
saddle blanket, and I hung to a ring on my saddle a magnificent
side of English bacon. ... These provisions were intended for
Lee's army, and had been sent to Amelia Court House from
Danville, the train being ordered to come onto Richmond to
take off the personnel and property of the government. Unfortunately, the officer in charge of it misunderstood his orders and
came on without unloading at Amelia. Near my station in the
street a cellar door opened in the sidewalk, and ... a solitary
Irish-woman brought many bales of blankets from the freight
depot in a wheelbarrow and tumbled them into the cellar. ...
About sunrise my last battalion passed, and I followed, taking a
farewell look at the city from the Manchester side. The whole
riverfront appeared to be in flames."

The classic Confederate account of the fall of Richmond was
written by Captain Clement Sulivane:

"Shortly before day General Ewell rode ... to my headquarters and informed me that ... my command was to hasten to
Mayo's bridge and protect it, and the one remaining foot-bridge
over the canal leading to it, until General Gary, of South Carolina, should arrive. I hurried to my command, and fifteen
minutes later occupied Mayo's bridge, at the foot of 14th Street,
and made military dispositions to protect it. ... This done, I
had nothing to do but listen for sounds and gaze on the terrible
splendor of the scene. And such a scene probably the world has
seldom witnessed. Either incendiaries, or (more probably)
fragments of bombs from the arsenals, had fired various buildings, and the two cities, Richmond and Manchester, were like
a blaze of day amid the surrounding darkness. Three high
arched bridges were in flames; beneath them the waters sparkled
and dashed and rushed on by the burning city. Every now and

then, as a magazine exploded, a column of white smoke rose up as high as the eye could reach, instantaneously followed by a deafening sound. The earth seemed to rock and tremble as with the shock of an earthquake, and immediately afterward hundreds of shells would explode in air and send their iron spray down far below the bridge. As the immense magazines of cartridges ignited, the rattle as of thousands of musketry would follow, and then all was still for the moment, except the dull roar and crackle of the fast-spreading fires. At dawn, we heard terrific explosions about 'The Rocketts,' from the unfinished iron-clads down the river.

"By daylight, on the 3d, a mob of men, women, and children, to the number of several thousands, had gathered at the corner of 14th and Cary streets . . . attracted by the vast commissary depot at that point. . . . The depot doors were forced open and a demoniacal struggle for the countless barrels of hams, bacon, whisky, flour, sugar, coffee, etc., etc., raged about the buildings among the hungry mob. The gutters ran whisky, and it was lapped as it flowed down the streets, while all fought for a share of the plunder. The flames came nearer and nearer, and at last caught in the commissariat itself.

"At daylight the approach of the Union forces could be plainly discerned. After a little came the clatter of horses' hoofs galloping up Main street. My infantry guard stood to arms, the picket across the canal was withdrawn, and the engineer officer lighted a torch of fat pine. By direction of the Engineer Department barrels of tar, surrounded by pine-knots, had been placed at intervals on the bridge, with kerosene at hand, and a lieutenant of engineers had reported for the duty of firing them at my order. The noisy train proved to be Gary's ambulances, sent forward preparatory to his final rush for the bridge. The muleteers galloped their animals about half-way down, when they were stopped by the dense mass of human beings. . . . I rode forward into the mob and cleared a lane. The ambulances were galloped down to the bridge, I retired to my post, and the mob closed in after me and resumed its wild struggle for plunder. A few minutes later a long line of cavalry in gray turned into 14th street, and sword in hand galloped straight down to the river; Gary had come. The mob scattered right and left before the armed horsemen, who reined up at the canal. Presently a single company of cavalry appeared in sight, and rode at headlong speed to the bridge. 'My rear-guard,' explained Gary. Touching his hat to me he called out, 'All over, good-bye; blow her to h–ll,' and trotted over the bridge. That was the first and last I ever saw of General Gary, of South Carolina.

"The engineer officer, Dr. Lyons, and I walked leisurely to the island, setting fire to the provided combustible matter as we passed along, and leaving the north section of Mayo's bridge wrapped in flame and smoke. We . . . saw a line of blue-coated horsemen galloping in furious haste up Main street . . . and . . . dash down 14th street to the flaming bridge. They fired a few random shots at us three on the island, and we retreated to Manchester."

While Lee's men were being moved out of the trenches around Richmond, the Confederate bands were ordered to play as loudly as they could in order to cover any noise made by the departing troops. Then some of the Union bands, as if meeting the Confederates' challenge, joined in, and martial music from both armies accompanied Lee's soldiers as they were withdrawn from the fortifications they had lived in for nearly a year.

Gary's troops had spent the earlier part of the night in trenches six miles outside the city, where they were told to keep brush fires burning in order to make the Federals believe that a large force was still opposing them.

Once Gary's men had crossed Mayo's Bridge, all the troops that had any intention of going with Lee were out of Richmond. Yet there were still many Confederate stragglers in the city,

some of them in uniform. They were loitering in the streets
when the first Union troops appeared. Those who had horses
hurriedly rode away; those who were caught were arrested and
confined in two former tobacco warehouses which the Confederate government had converted into jails for captured Union
soldiers — Libby Prison and Castle Thunder.

Two divisions of General Ord's Army of the James had been
left under the command of Major General Godfrey Weitzel to
hold the northernmost Union lines in front of Richmond.
Brigadier General Charles Devens was in charge of the 3rd
Division of the Twenty-fourth Army Corps, which was composed of white troops, while Major General August V. Kautz
commanded the 1st Division of the Twenty-fifth Army Corps,
which had Negro cavalrymen. The positions of these two divisions near Richmond determined the fact that their men were
the first to enter the city.

About 2 A.M. two deserters from the 10th Virginia Battalion
came into the Union lines with the information that Lee's
regulars were being withdrawn. This was expected, but the
Union commanders were cautious. Captain George A. Bruce,
who was in charge of the pickets of the 13th New Hampshire
Infantry, was instructed to take his men into the Confederate
works "if it could be done without too much risk or danger."
He sent a corporal and three men forward to inspect the Confederate picket line and when they reported that it was deserted,
two lines of skirmishers got ready to advance at dawn. While
they waited for the first signs of light, they heard the tremendous explosions that were taking place around Richmond and
saw the red glare of the flames above the burning city. Bruce
describes the entering of the Confederate lines:

"I rode forward toward the main works of the enemy.
Meeting a Confederate soldier on his way toward us, I turned
him about and directed him to lead us to the path used by the

enemy ... for picket duty. He conducted us to a well-beaten
track that took us safely to our goal. It passed through three
well-constructed lines of abatis and chevaux-de-frise.... To the
right and left, as far as could be seen, was a row of sticks, a few
feet apart, bearing a strip of red cloth, each indicating the
position of a buried torpedo [now called a land mine]. The
tents were all standing ... but the occupants, as we expected,
were all gone. Riding back, I directed that the men were to file
to the right and left and follow me.... One man of the Ninth
Vermont, who attempted his own pioneering, was killed by a
torpedo."

Bruce's matter-of-fact report does not convey the wild excitement which swept through the troops when they took over
the Confederate positions that had opposed them for so long.
The men rushed headlong into the abandoned works, where the
huge guns still stood in place, and jumped up to sit astride
the massive iron barrels, howling with glee while they slapped
the unresponsive cold black metal with boyish fervor. The fact
that the guns had all been spiked did not bother them; these
Confederate cannon would never fire at them again, and that
was all that mattered. Then there was a dash to explore the
tents and cabins, which had been left intact. They took much
small plunder, but most of it consisted of the pathetically poor
personal belongings that men in sudden flight are willing to
abandon.

At six o'clock orders were received for the troops to move
into Richmond. It was a pleasant morning as the marching
columns passed seemingly deserted farmhouses and suburban
dwellings. Some two hundred Confederate stragglers were
taken prisoner on the way.

On the top of a hill near the line of river defenses the troops
got their first view of Richmond. The ever observant Bruce
recorded his impressions of the scene: "The city was wrapped
in a cloud of densest smoke, through which great tongues of

flame leaped in madness to the skies. A few houses on the higher hills, a spire here and there half smothered in smoke, and the hospitals to the east, were the only buildings that could be seen. Added to the wild tumult of the flames, ten thousand shells bursting every minute in the Confederate arsenals and laboratories were making an uproar such as might arise . . . when the world's artillery joins in battle. But just on the verge of this maelstrom of smoke and fire, cattle were grazing undisturbed on the opposite hillside, and I saw a farmer ploughing in a field while cinders from the burning capital were falling at his feet."

Just below the steamship landing called Rocketts the troops met an open barouche coming toward them carrying two men with a flag of truce. These were Joseph Mayo, the Mayor of Richmond, and his brother. They had come to surrender the city and beg the invaders to bring the plundering mob under control and put out the fire.

As the troops continued their march along the shore of the James River they saw the Confederate training ship, the *Patrick Henry*, anchored in the channel. It had been set on fire and was burning briskly, but a reckless young major, William J. Ladd of General Devens' staff, wanted the Confederate flag that was still flying from the mast. He took a boat which was lying on the shore, rowed out to haul down the flag, and then got back just as the flames reached the ship's magazine. The powder stored there blew up with a tremendous blast, destroying the ship, and scattering fragments of wood and metal for hundreds of yards around.

This same adventurous young officer was also apparently the first Union soldier to enter Richmond. He had a fast horse and rode on ahead of the troops to reach Capitol Square. While he was going up Franklin Street, a Confederate sailor attacked him with a cutlass, but Ladd warded off the blow, explored the city still further, and then went back to report to General Devens.

There was a race on now to see which troops would be in Richmond first. One young officer in charge of a light battery tried to oust the infantrymen from their rightful position on the narrow road. When they refused to give way, he turned his horses into a field alongside the road, where his men dashed on with cannon and caissons bumping over rocks and stumps and flying high into the air. When he came to the end of the field, the infantry column marching there realized what he was trying to do; without orders the men broke into the double quick to prevent him from reaching the road. The infantrymen kept their ranks closed so tightly that the impatient artilleryman was not permitted to get his battery back on the road until its original place in the line came up.

Accompanying the Union troops was a young newsboy who regularly had the New York papers sent to him so he could peddle them to the soldiers. Since a fresh shipment had just reached him, he was on hand as the troops marched along the roads to Richmond. He went up and down the columns of moving men, crying, "Here is the New York *Herald,* the *Times* or the *Tribune.* What paper will you have?"

The first Union banners to fly over Richmond were two cavalry guidons that were run up on a pole on the roof of the Capitol. They did not stay there long. General George F. Shepley, who had been military governor of New Orleans, had brought north with him the American flag which had flown over that city when it was under his rule. He had made a bet that his flag would be the first to fly over Richmond, and he had entrusted it to eighteen-year-old J. Livingston De Peyster, who strapped it to his saddle and then dashed into the city with a young artillery officer, climbed up to the roof of the Capitol, contemptuously took down the two cavalry guidons, and ran Shepley's big flag up on one of the two staffs. As it unfurled in the early morning light, the two young officers, who had brought some liquor for the purpose, drank to the waving banner. But

what they did not know — and what was to provide endless
amusement to the die-hard Confederates in the city — was that
they had used the wrong flagpole, the one reserved for the state
flag of Virginia. This, the sarcastic Confederates said, sym-
bolized the triumph of centralized Federal power over states'
rights.

When the first Union infantrymen reached Main Street, all
the military bands were brought to the head of the marching
column and were told to play Northern airs. Bruce describes
the scene: "The column ... with all the regularity of a parade,
colors flying and every musician doing his best at 'Yankee
Doodle,' followed by 'Rally round the Flag,' with its refrain,
'Down with the Traitor and Up with the Stars' and the 'Battle
Cry of Freedom,' marched through various streets to Capitol
Square ... where the brigade was brought to the front and there
stacked their arms. Sweeter music never reached the human ear
than the rattling of those Union muskets as they dropped upon
the pavements of Richmond.

"The square was a scene of indescribable confusion. The
inhabitants fleeing from their burning houses — men, women
and children, white and black — had collected there for a place
of safety, bringing with them whatever was saved from the
flames. Bureaus, sofas, carpets, beds and bedding, in a word,
every conceivable article of household furniture, from baby-toys
to the most costly mirrors, were scattered promiscuously on the
green.... The sick and infirm had been hurried from the
houses, and ... were lying ... in the more secluded parts of
the yard.

"The wind, increasing with the conflagration, was blowing
like a hurricane, hurling cinders and pieces of burning wood
with long trails of flame over the houses to distant quarters of
the city. The heated air, dim with smoke and filled with ...
innumerable particles ... rendered it almost impossible to

breathe. At every gust the crowd turned to escape its fury as men turned to escape the blast of a driving snowstorm. Rising among the trees in the centre of the Square ... stood the great statue of Washington, against which firebrands thumped and rattled, little respecting the majestic form of the Father of his Country."

To the white people of Richmond this was a day of humiliation and shame, but the Negroes were thoroughly enjoying themselves. A white resident of the city tells how they behaved:

"Some of the troops had stacked their arms in the Capitol Square, and were gazing curiously around; others were marching ... through the street before us. The latter attracted much attention from the colored crowds who thronged the sidewalks. ... A large portion of them — very much the largest, I think — simply looked on, as upon any other novel and remarkable spectacle. Here and there a man waved his hat and huzzaed. The most marked demonstrations were the shaking of hands by those nearest with the passing troops, much of which was done. Some of the women courtesied and bowed at a great rate. One little weazened-faced old woman, her head crowned with a conical turban, seized a soldier's hand in both of hers, and shaking it up and down like a pump-handle, said, 'Welcum, masta! you's welcum! Glad to see you, Sah — glad to see you! Thank de Lord, dese hands do no mo' wurk!'

"The first body of colored cavalry came moving up the hill. Their appearance called forth a greeting from their brethren in the streets. ... The cavalry returned the greeting with a will, rising in their stirrups, waving their flashing sabres, their white eyes and teeth gleaming from rows of dark visages, and rending the air with wild huzzas."

The white citizens of Richmond were worried about the kind of treatment they might expect from the Yankee army of occu-

pation. Actually, they had no cause for anxiety, for the troops —
both white and black — were eager to be friendly. The soldiers
in Capitol Square gladly offered their rations to the hungry
people there and even bought food for them from sutlers' stores
which were rapidly being set up.

The troops' first job was to put out the flames. Since practically all the fire hose in the city had been deliberately hacked
to pieces, the only means of stopping the vast conflagration was
to blow up buildings to confine the fire within the area where
it was already established. This was done so well that by nightfall the flames had been brought under control. In some parts
of the city the fire continued to smolder for days, but the worst
of it had been conquered.

The Capitol was taken over as general Army headquarters;
Weitzel established himself in Jefferson Davis' house, Ripley
used the City Hall, while Devens, who had charge of the Union
troops in the city, made the Governor's mansion his headquarters. A police force was organized immediately; a printing
press was put to work turning out circulars to inform the
citizens how they were to be governed; and all troops not needed
for fire prevention or guard duty were ordered to camp outside
the city limits.

Ord sent a telegram to Weitzel, appointing him military
governor of Richmond, and instructing him to sell any available tobacco and use the money to feed the poor. Gas and water
companies were to be aided; hotels could be opened and run
by loyal men who had taken the oath, but for the time being,
no grog shops were allowed to operate.

Railroad men in the Union Army were delighted to find 28
locomotives, 44 passenger and baggage cars, and 206 freight cars
still in the yards. Evidently, more trains were not able to leave
the city on the previous hysterical evening only because there
were not enough experienced men to handle them. Work was
started to restore operation on the railroad from Richmond to

Petersburg, while hard-pressed telegraph crews were busy on the Osborn Pike running a line to army headquarters in the city. Before the day was finished, this new line was ready for use, and over it went the news that was to electrify the nation.

Some intimation of the fact that Richmond was about to be evacuated had reached Washington earlier in the day, but when the new line was ready, the Union operator at Richmond telegraphed to Fortress Monroe that the message he was sending from Weitzel to General Shepley at Norfolk should be relayed on to Washington. The operator at Fortress Monroe then called the War Department in Washington, and for the first time in nearly four years said: "Turn down for Richmond." (This meant that the Washington operator was to turn down the armature spring on his receiving instrument so it would respond to a weak signal from far away.) He did so and listened to the thrilling words being ticked out: "We took Richmond at 8:15 this morning — " The operator in Washington had heard enough; he leapt up and ran into the cipher room to break the news, while his assistant, Willie Kettles, who at fifteen was already an expert operator, took down the rest of the message. Then Willie, in his haste, upset his inkstand and knocked the telegraph instrument to the floor. He rushed the completed message to Major Thomas Eckert, who hurried to Stanton with it. Willie became the hero of the occasion. Stanton was in his shirtsleeves, but he was so excited that he picked up the boy and held him up to the open window to tell the gathering crowd outside that Richmond was at last in Union hands.

Then the War Department operators began to wire city after city to spread the news. The governors of various Northern states telegraphed their congratulations to Stanton and arranged for local celebrations to be held.

In Washington a gigantic salute of 800 guns was ordered to be fired by three artillery batteries at Fourteenth and N Streets. The guns spoke 500 times for Richmond and 300 times for Petersburg. They roared on for hours, while a 100-gun salute at the Navy Yard joined them. Church bells were ringing, and men were climbing out of windows and up on roofs to hang out flags and drape the building fronts with bunting. Every available wheeled vehicle in Washington was carrying cheering people around the city. Work was stopped in Government offices, and schools let out the children. Fire engines raced through the streets with steam whistles screaming; locomotives in the yards picked up the cry and passed it on to ships in the river, which sent it echoing wildly from shore to shore.

At the War Department an official order was issued to all the military posts and arsenals in the nation to fire salutes of 100 guns at noon. Those places beyond reach of the telegraph were to be notified by the nearest station from which a dispatch rider could be sent out. To the farthest outposts, to scattered armories and arsenals, to forts commanding the various harbors, to barracks and prison camps, as well as to the commanding officers in the larger cities, the message of victory went. And across the nation the guns boomed out in celebration of the greatest of all Union triumphs. The capital of the Confederacy had fallen, and its government was in flight!

Early on Monday morning, April 3, the train carrying Jefferson Davis and his cabinet passed Clover Station about one hundred miles south of Richmond. John S. Wise, who was at the station, recorded the train's passing: "Mr. Davis sat at a car window. The crowd at the station cheered. He smiled and acknowledged their compliment, but his expression showed physical and mental exhaustion. Near him sat General Bragg, whose shaggy eyebrows and piercing eyes made him look like a much greater man than he ever proved himself to be. In this car was my brother-in-law, Dr. Garnett, family physician to Mr. Davis. I entered, and sat with him a few minutes, to learn what I could about the home folk. His own family had been left at his Richmond residence, to the mercy of the conqueror. The presidential train was followed by many others. One bore the archives and employees of the Treasury Department, another those of the Post Office Department, another those of the War Department. I knew many in all these departments, and they told me the startling incidents of their sudden flight. I saw a government on wheels. It was the marvelous and incongruous débris of the wreck of the Confederate capital. There were very few women on these trains, but among the last in the long procession were trains bearing indiscriminate cargoes of men and things. In one car was a cage with an African parrot, and a box of tame squirrels, and a hunchback!"

That same Monday morning the men in Lee's army who had left Richmond and Petersburg during the night stopped for a brief rest just before dawn. When they started out again they are said to have felt a curious sense of elation, perhaps transmitted to them by their still optimistic commander who believed that he might yet succeed in getting through to Johnston in North Carolina. The weather was pleasant, and the troops were glad to be out of the damp earthworks where they had lived during the cold, snowy winter. All along the five different routes where the wagon trains, guns, horses, and men were stretched out for thirty miles, the army came to life as the sun rose. Behind it was the abandoned city of Richmond, but ahead lay the vast, almost empty Virginia countryside where the few scattered inhabitants could be depended upon to be friendly to the hungry, hard-driven men in the fleeing Army of Northern Virginia.

But this early-morning elation quickly wore off, especially when word was received that the approach to the southernmost of the available bridges over the Appomattox River was flooded by high water. Then it was discovered that during the hasty preparations for retreat not enough pontoon boats had been

sent ahead. A railroad bridge had to be hastily planked over
for wheeled vehicles to cross, and the unexpected concentration
of marching lines on fewer bridges than had been counted on
caused much confusion and delay. But the exhausted men,
weakened by insufficient food and rest, pushed on, while the
equally tired horses dragged the worn-out supply wagons by
harness leather so rotted out that it kept breaking and had to
be patched together.

13

Lincoln Visits Richmond

Tuesday, April 4, and Wednesday, April 5

APRIL 4 WAS Tad Lincoln's twelfth birthday. He must have felt lonely and neglected that morning, with his mother in Washington and his father endlessly busy with generals and admirals. But it was to be an important day for him, one he would always remember. Admiral Porter had persuaded his father to visit Richmond, and Tad was to go along.

Torpedo boats had worked all night to blow up the sunken hulks the Navy had placed in the James in order to block the Confederate ironclads. Then they had gone farther up the river to explode or pull out the huge floating mines that guarded the channel. The river had never been entirely closed to traffic; both Union and Confederate obstructions had narrow openings through which the small flag-of-truce boats could pass with prisoners to be exchanged.

Early in the morning, the military telegraph office at City Point learned that Weitzel's army of occupation was firmly in command of Richmond and that all the Confederate fortifications defending the upper James had been abandoned. Lincoln, Tad, and Crook started up the James in the *River Queen,* accompanied by Admiral Porter's flagship, the *Malvern,* and Barnes's gunboat, the *Bat.*

Scattered clouds moved across the sky, but the day was

pleasantly warm, and there was hardly enough wind to ruffle the broad, muddy surface of the historic river. They passed other Union ships, dressed with flags to celebrate the fall of Richmond. It was noon when they reached Aiken's Landing; an hour later they were beyond Fort Brady and what had been the most advanced Union lines. They were now running through territory which only two days before had been strongly defended by an entrenched Confederate Army. But the elaborate earthworks on both sides of the river were deserted, and the big guns mounted on them were no longer a threat.

On the way up, a careful lookout was kept for torpedoes or hulks sunk in the channel to block it; in the unfamiliar waters farther upstream the ships had to be slowed down even more, while the watch was redoubled. Occasionally, some of the giant torpedoes that had been taken up earlier that morning were seen lying on the shore like huge stranded fish. They were formidable weapons, sometimes carrying a charge of 2000 pounds of powder that could be exploded either by contact or by an electrical switch operated by an observer on shore. Floating mines like these had often taken their toll of ships and lives on this very river.

From here to Richmond the river was in dreadful condition; partly sunken ironclads, gunboats, and commercial vessels littered the channel, and the rack and ruin of war could be seen everywhere. Charred timbers from burned bridges were floating downstream, and the brown water was dotted with the bloated bodies of dead horses.

The Confederate obstruction at Fort Darling was considered too narrow to pass. At 1:40 P.M. the *Malvern* dropped anchor; then Porter came over in his barge to pick up the President, Tad, Crook, and several officers. He commandeered the naval tug *Glance* to tow the barge and his ship's third cutter up the river, and he placed a Marine guard of thirty men on the tug.

Already run aground on this same obstruction was the gun-

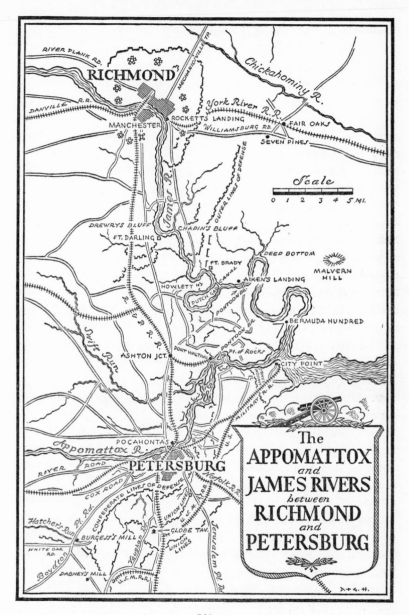

The
APPOMATTOX
and
JAMES RIVERS
between
RICHMOND
and
PETERSBURG

boat *Commodore Perry,* a converted New York ferryboat with several enormous naval cannon mounted on deck. Its captain was desperately trying to get his cumbersome vessel off by throwing part of his coal overboard and by moving the heavy guns to one side. He instructed his chief engineer to ignore all signal bells and keep moving the stranded ship back and forth until she was free. There was a very narrow stretch of deep water between the big ferryboat and the shore, through which Porter tried to take his barge. But he quickly found out that there was not enough room for his men to use their oars on both sides. The barge got out of control; the swift current suddenly caught its bow and swung the unmanageable boat toward the much larger *Perry.* At this instant the engineer of the *Perry* started to turn the ship's huge paddle wheel over. Everybody yelled, the captain of the *Perry* jangled his signal bell to the engine room, but, in accordance with orders, no one below paid any attention. It was only when the captain ran to the engine-room hatch and shouted a command to stop the paddle that the churning wheel came to a halt in a flurry of white water which nearly swamped the admiral's barge.

Porter jumped up, purple-faced and almost incoherent with rage. He ordered the captain of the luckless vessel to come to the rail. After bawling out the unhappy man, whose name was Amos Foster, the admiral said with unreasoning anger, "When you back off from here, don't you attempt to go to Richmond. Come to anchor and let the other boats go up." Captain Foster obediently said, "Aye, aye, sir," while the admiral's barge, followed by Barnes in the cutter, moved on upstream.

This was only the first of many mishaps. When they came to a bridge they saw a Confederate flag-of-truce boat, the *William Allison,* in trouble there. Since she was boldly flying the Stars and Bars, they approached cautiously, with men standing ready at arms. Then they were surprised to see a Union admiral appear on deck to wave cheerfully at Porter and greet him as an old friend. It was Admiral David Farragut, the hero of Mobile Bay and the senior officer of the United States Navy. With him was General George H. Gordon. They had come up the river during the night, and had gotten off at Aiken's Landing to ride overland to Richmond. When they heard that Porter was bringing the President up the river, they thought it would be a good joke to commandeer a rebel boat and run down to boast that they had been in Richmond first.

Admiral Porter ordered the *Glance* to go to their rescue and pull them loose. The tug promptly went aground. Porter must have felt that the humor of the occasion was wearing rather thin. He decided to go ahead under oars and enter the city without the Marine guards who were stranded helplessly on the tug. The barge started upstream, slowly followed by the cutter.

The President was more amused by his ever-diminishing fleet than Porter was. He told one of his characteristic stories, this time about an office seeker who wanted to be appointed a foreign minister. When he was refused that, the man made a more modest request. This was also turned down. Then he was willing to settle for a job as customs officer. "When he saw he couldn't get that," the President said, "he asked me for an old pair of trousers."

But Porter had little reason to be amused at the turn of events that had stripped him of ships and guards. He was the ranking officer of the expedition, personally responsible for the safety of the President of the United States, who at his suggestion was about to enter the still-burning city which had just been evacuated by the Confederate government. No one in the barge really knew what was happening in Richmond. Porter was not even aware that there were no Union troops in the southeastern part of the city, where the President's party intended to land. And he could not hope to foresee how the people in the defeated Confederate stronghold would behave when they saw the commander-in-chief of the army that had driven out their government.

Richmond lay before them now, magnificent in the grandeur of its destruction. The pillared Capitol, still intact, crowned the heights above the city, and the whole section along the nearest shore was just as it had been left by the fleeing Confederate Army. But the entire business area between the Capitol and the river was either in ruins or still aflame.

The barge headed toward Rocketts Landing. It got stuck on a rock, was pushed off, and then went on again. Confederate cannon and plundered supply wagons stood near the warehouses along the waterfront. Several dozen Negroes, who had been digging in a field, stopped work to watch the boat approach.

Some of the sailors jumped out to make the barge fast and help the President and Tad get ashore. The cutter was far behind; still farther down the river was Barnes with a few men in the gig from the *Bat*. They were rowing frantically upstream to try to overtake the Presidential party.

Twelve sailors, the President of the United States, his young son Tad, Rear Admiral David Dixon Porter, a Navy captain, an Army captain, a signal officer, and the President's bodyguard, William H. Crook, made up the party. The sailors were armed with carbines and bayonets, Crook had a Colt revolver, and the officers doubtless wore their side arms. But they still had no idea of what kind of reception to expect.

When the President stepped ashore, dressed in his long black coat and wearing his customary tall silk hat, some of the Negroes recognized him from pictures they had seen. There was a buzz of excited talk. Here, at last, was the man who had set them free; this was the long awaited Messiah whose coming had been foretold in many a secretly worded spiritual sung at nightfall on thousands of plantations throughout the South.

Here, in person, was the Father Abraham of their hopes and dreams.

A white-haired old man rushed forward to throw himself at the feet of the President, mumbling incoherently as he tried to kiss his muddied boots. The others pushed forward, shouting. Their excitement was instantly communicated to scores and then to hundreds of Negroes who sprang up from nowhere to surround the President in a wildly exultant mob.

Lincoln was embarrassed; he urged the kneeling man to get up and spoke to the others, repeatedly having to raise his voice in order to be heard above the noise of the ever-growing crowd. Porter quietly told his men to fix bayonets and form a circle around the President. More and more Negroes kept swarming over the landing, laughing, shouting, and singing as they came. Porter said later that at one time they joined together to sing a hymn.

Nothing would satisfy them but to hear from the President himself that they were really free. They kept asking him again and again to tell them so. Finally he held up his hand for silence, and those who were near enough to see the gesture quieted down. He spoke briefly, assuring them that they were no longer slaves and that they must learn to act and live like free men. Everyone cheered; then, at a nod from Porter, the sailors opened a way through the crowd, and the President started to walk toward the center of the city. His admirers had no intention of being left behind. They followed, and, as they emerged from the waterfront district, more and more people joined them, white as well as black.

During the two-mile walk through the ravaged streets of the unpoliced city, the attitude toward the lightly guarded man who was making his way slowly up the hill was simply that of curiosity, even among the whites. Most of them were poor or middle-class people, for the aristocracy had fled or were staying behind shuttered windows.

Crook said of the crowd: "The only sign of welcome I saw . . .

was from a young lady on a bridge that connected the Spots-
wood House with another hotel across the street. She had an
American flag over her shoulders." But Porter claims that a
man in shirtsleeves rushed up to greet the President with the
words "Abraham Lincoln, God bless you! You are the poor
man's friend!" Then he tried to seize Lincoln's hand, and
Porter had to push him away. The admiral also said that a
beautiful girl struggled through the crowd, "her clothes very
much disarranged in making the journey," to hand the President a bouquet and a card inscribed: "From Eva to the Libera-
tor of the slaves." Although Porter does not say so, she may
have been of mulatto birth; it seems unlikely that any white
woman then in Richmond would have dared to risk her future
with such a gesture.

Crook does not mention these two incidents. In fact, the
naturally suspicious bodyguard believed that he prevented an
attempted assassination, for he said: "The blinds of a second-
story window of a house on our left were partly opened, and a
man dressed in gray pointed something that looked like a gun
directly at the President. I dropped Tad's hand and stepped
in front of Mr. Lincoln. I was sure he meant to shoot." But
Crook admits that no one else was alarmed, including the
President. And finally he says: "It is to the everlasting glory of
the South that he was permitted to come and go in peace."

But the danger was still very real; in fact, it was increasing
every minute, for the surprise of the unexpected landing was
over. By this time, many people in Richmond knew that the
Northern President was walking through the streets of their
city with a very small guard, and it would have been easy for
one or more of them to take overt action. But no one did, and
Abraham Lincoln was permitted to pass unharmed through
the former citadel of the Confederacy.

The little group with its accompanying crowd pushed on up

the hill. The day was hot, the air was thick with the acrid odor of smoke and burning wood, and the aging President had to stop several times to rest. At last they saw their first Federal soldier, a cavalryman, sitting idly on his horse, looking on with the same curiosity as the citizens. Porter sent him to General Weitzel for a cavalry escort, which soon arrived to clear the streets. For the first time, the President was adequately guarded in the newly captured city.

Barnes and his men soon caught up with Lincoln's party, and they all went on up Capitol Hill. George A. Bruce saw them when they passed the Governor's mansion:

"Between two and three o'clock in the afternoon ... there arose from the street back of the house a great noise and tumult. ... I walked through the garden to the wall which is about twenty feet above the street. ... As I looked down, the first platoon of sailors, armed with muskets, was directly opposite to me. They were stretched out in open file and reached within a few feet of either sidewalk. In the center of the street ... was Mr. Lincoln leading his little boy. ... Farther down was the second file of sailors stretching across the street. Before, on either side, and behind were two or three hundred negroes, men, women and some children. ... This was, I believe, the wildest spectacle ever seen, and a picture of Mr. Lincoln moving wearily up this steep hill in the centre of it would be one of the most remarkable in history. ... Hats were thrown in the air, clothing pulled off and abandoned, but the most peculiar feature was the sudden throwing of themselves flat upon the ground and remaining there for some seconds, which species of demonstration or worship must have seized upon a third of the whole crowd during the short time it was in my sight. I watched Mr. Lincoln as far as my eye could follow him, and I could not see that he either turned his face or eyes to either side. After the procession passed, the street was literally covered with abandoned hats and clothing."

The little group then walked on to the house Jefferson Davis had occupied as president of the Confederacy. A number of Union officers were there to greet Lincoln. He went inside to look around curiously at the interior of the house which Davis had quit less than forty-eight hours before. Then he entered Davis' tiny office, sat down tiredly at the Confederate president's desk, and asked for a drink of water.

For the first time since he had been elected, Abraham Lincoln could now feel that he was President of the whole United States.

As he sat there at the desk of the man who had been his counterpart and his enemy, Lincoln must have thought about the four years of war. From the first fiasco at Bull Run through all the disappointments of Shiloh, the Peninsular Campaign, Second Bull Run, Fredericksburg, the bungled chances to follow up victory after Antietam and Gettysburg, and the horrible slaughter that took place in battle after battle to the north of Richmond — when Burnside, Hooker, and even Grant were successively unable to beat down Lee's incredibly competent army — the war had been one long nightmare to a man whose letters and speeches show unusual sensitivity of mind. Now the terrible bloodshed was about to end.

After resting for a short while, the President asked Weitzel's aide whether Davis' housekeeper was still on the premises. When he heard that she was not there, he got to his feet and said with almost boyish anticipation: "Come on then, let's look at the house." They went through the rooms of the three-story mansion, which wartime hardship had reduced from former elegance to a state of shabby disrepair. One living tie to the Davis family remained. A little black-and-tan dog, which had belonged to their dead son Joseph, frolicked around the visitors as they explored the house.

As the President and his guides were descending the stairs,

cavalry clattered up to the door, and General Weitzel entered, having hurried to the house as soon as he was told that the President was there. He introduced his staff officers, and the occasion was celebrated with a bottle of fine old whisky from Davis' well-furnished cellar. The President, as usual, did not drink.

Then a simple midafternoon luncheon was served, during which the state of affairs at the front was discussed. It was known that Lee was at Amelia Court House, hard pressed by his pursuers, and that his men were in desperate need of food.

Later, one of the Confederate peace commissioners, Judge John A. Campbell, who had been at the futile Hampton Roads conference in February, came to call on the President. Campbell had some ideas about reconvening the Virginia State Legislature. Lincoln was interested and made an appointment for him to call again the next morning, for he planned to stay in Richmond overnight.

George Bruce was among those asked to accompany the President on a tour of Richmond. According to him, one of the dark-colored, two-seated wagons used at corps and division headquarters was drawn up in front of the Davis house. Lincoln was seated in this with General Devens alongside him and with General Shepley, Admiral Porter, and Tad in the rear. Some twenty or thirty field and staff officers accompanied them on horseback. As they started toward the northern end of the city, General Weitzel and Crook rode close to the carriage, while the others followed in no formal order. They soon came to a private house where the funeral of a Confederate officer was being held. Bruce thought it was the ceremony for A. P. Hill, but although the Confederate general was being buried about this time, the actual interment was taking place on the other side of the James. Since the street was blocked, they drove on to Camp Lee and then went to Capitol Square, where they stopped in front of the Washington Monument. The equestrian statue of the first President faces west with the outstretched hand pointing in the general direction of Danville. Lincoln looked at the statue of his predecessor and then said without smiling: "Washington is looking at me and pointing at Jeff Davis."

At the Capitol, the Presidential party saw the upturned chairs and desks and scattered papers of the hastily departed Legislature. Negroes were bowling in the empty corridors, and vandals and souvenir hunters had already taken their toll of the furnishings. On the lawn, worthless thousand-dollar Confederate bonds were blowing across the grass. Huddled on the slopes below the building, refugees from the fire were still waiting with the few belongings they had saved.

They left Capitol Square and drove toward the river to show the President the burned district. They had trouble getting through the fallen bricks and fragments of masonry which littered the streets. Then they went on toward the waterfront, stopping to look at Libby Prison and Castle Thunder, where Confederate prisoners of war were now being held.

Somewhere along the route the party heard a 35-gun salute coming from the river. The *Malvern* had succeeded in getting through the obstructions in the James and was anchoring off Rocketts for the night. The long, tiring, exciting day was ending. It was pleasant to reach the familiar ship and have dinner on board.

When Porter arrived on his flagship he noticed that the *Commodore Perry,* despite his orders, had come up the river and was anchored nearby. He was too busy to do anything about it until after dinner; then, before he could summon Captain Foster, that officer had himself rowed over to the *Malvern* in his ship's gig. As he stepped on board, the admiral's fleet captain whispered to him: "You'll get it, old fellow, for coming up here." But Foster seemed very cool and self-assured as he waited on deck.

He was ushered into the cabin where Admiral Porter, President Lincoln, and other high officers of the nation were seated at a round table. Foster saluted and then said, "Admiral, I have the honor to report the U. S. Steamer *Commodore Perry* at Richmond."

Porter glowered at him. "I though I told you not to attempt to come up to Richmond, sir."

"I did not so understand you, sir. I understood you to say that when *I backed off*, I was not to attempt to come up the river."

"Well?" said Porter coldly.

"I did not back off. I came off bow first."

Lincoln suddenly burst out laughing. He got up and shook Foster's hand, saying, "Captain, I congratulate you on commanding the first Union ship to reach Richmond."

Porter was still angry yet there was nothing he could do but order the young captain to return to his ship. Although he threatened to review the case in the morning, before morning came he had conveniently — and sensibly — forgotten the whole matter.

Once he had the President safely on the *Malvern*, Porter realized how reckless he had been during the day in exposing him to very genuine danger. Guards were posted at the doors of his cabin, and Porter became increasingly apprehensive about his safety.

During the night several attempts were made to hail the *Malvern* from the shore, but when a boat was sent to answer the calls, no one was there. Since four men had deserted from the ship's third cutter that day, it may have been some of them trying to return to the ship. And their subsequent disappearance may have been the result of a sudden change of heart when they were faced with the prospect of the stiff punishment meted out by the Navy to wartime deserters. Porter interpreted the mysterious calls as threats of assassination. Thereafter, he later recalled, "every precaution was taken that no one should get on board the *Malvern* without full identification."

A grand illumination of Washington was ordered for the night of April 4. Not only public places but also many retail stores, banks, newspaper offices, hotels, restaurants, and even private homes were decorated with flags, bunting, lanterns, and gleaming transparencies. All the public buildings were aglow with fantastic patterns of colored light. The windows of the dome of the Capitol were brilliantly lighted, and across the pediment was displayed a huge transparency reading: "This is the Lord's doing; it is marvellous in our eyes."

On the south façade of the Patent Office, flaring gas pipes, shaped to spell the word UNION, cast a bright glow over the tall granite pillars. Below them a speaker's stand had been erected. There was a brilliant burst of rockets and fireworks, and then a band from the Harewood Hospital began to play popular national airs. A number of speakers were on hand, the most noted of whom was Vice President Johnson.

After extolling the virtues of the Constitution again, Johnson launched into an attack on slavery and on those who had rebelled against the Government. When he mentioned Jefferson Davis, the crowd cried: "Hang him!" and the Vice President cheerfully agreed by echoing: "Yes, I say hang him twenty times." He then went on to say that "signal and memorable punishment should be dealt the crafty instigators and bloody leaders." He also added that their property should be confiscated.

Since full accounts of this speech were printed in the Washington newspapers the next day, there can be no doubt that Lincoln was kept informed of what his Vice President was saying. Since their policies for the treatment of the Confederate leaders were diametrically opposed at this time, the President cannot have been pleased. Perhaps some word of his displeasure reached Johnson, for two days later he went to City Point, where he sought an interview with Lincoln.

Now that the President had risked his life by walking openly through the streets of the surrendered Confederate capital, rumors of threatened assassination came thick and fast. Colonel Edward H. Ripley of the Twenty-fourth Army Corps of the Army of the James told Porter how an empty bomb case made in imitation of a lump of coal had been found on Jefferson Davis' desk. Such bombs, mixed into a load of coal, were known to have destroyed several boats. In fact, Porter himself had had a narrow escape during the previous autumn when General Ben Butler's ship, the *Greyhound,* was blown up by bombs hidden in the coal.

Ripley came to the *Malvern* at nine o'clock in the morning of April 5, bringing with him a Confederate named Snyder who had a strange story to tell. Snyder, who had been in Rain's Torpedo Bureau, a Confederate secret service organization which specialized in explosives, had seen Lincoln walking almost unguarded through the streets of Richmond. As a result, he said, he had had a change of heart which caused him to go voluntarily to Colonel Ripley, who asked him to make a written statement. According to his statement, a man from the Torpedo Bureau had been detailed to go on a secret mission, which Snyder believed "was aimed at the head of the Yankee government."

Ripley read Snyder's statement to the President and then asked him to talk to the man. Lincoln, who had received so many threats against his life that he simply filed the written ones away in an envelope marked "Assassination," told Ripley that he saw no point in his seeing Snyder. He explained his

attitude by saying: "I must go on as I have begun in the course
laid out for me, for I cannot believe that any human being
lives who would do me any harm."

To the ship at ten o'clock came Judge John A. Campbell who
had been able to persuade only one other influential Virginian
to accompany him. This was Gustavus A. Myers, a Richmond
attorney. With them was General Weitzel, who wanted to hear
the President's views on setting up new local governments
in the Confederate States as they were taken over by Union
armies. The conference dragged on inconclusively, and no
clear-cut decision was arrived at. The subject was to be a
troublesome one in the days to come, but what happened
at Richmond that morning proved to be only a false start.
Lincoln himself apparently did not expect much from the
meeting with Campbell and Myers, for when he sent an account
of the conference to Grant he added:

> I do not think it very probable that anything will come of
> this; but I have thought best to notify you, so that if you should
> see signs, you may understand them. From your recent des-
> patches it seems that you are pretty effectually withdrawing the
> Virginia troops from opposition to the government. Nothing
> I have done, or probably shall do, is to delay, hinder, or inter-
> fere with you in your work.

Later there appeared on the scene a remarkable-looking old
man, Duff Green, who wanted to see the President. Green's
path had crossed Lincoln's many times before. They were
fellow Kentuckians from Hardin County, they were distantly
related by marriage, and both had been active in politics.
Green had taken his meals at the boardinghouse on Capitol
Hill where Lincoln had stayed when he first came to Washington in 1847 to serve in Congress. The versatile Mr. Green had
been a journalist; he had also dabbled in various kinds of trade,
in railroads, and in mining. He was an ardent secessionist who

had thrown all his efforts and his wealth into the support of the Confederacy. He had not been directly in touch with Lincoln since the beginning of the war, but he was a friend of Singleton and had not been above using that devious gentleman to intercede for him with the President when he wanted a favor.

Old Duff Green was an impressive figure as he stood on the landing carrying a heavy six-foot staff. He was dressed in tattered homespun, and he wore a broad-brimmed hat, from under which his long straight hair straggled down to his shoulders. He spoke in a commanding voice to the officer of the deck: "Tell Abraham Lincoln that Duff Green is here to see him."

Lincoln said he knew the elderly eccentric and asked that he be brought on board. Green was told to leave his wicked-looking staff behind. He was evidently in a nasty mood when he reached the deck of the *Malvern*. The President offered his hand, but Green scorned it, saying that it was stained with blood. Then he denounced Lincoln as a tyrant who had come to Richmond to gloat over the Confederacy's defeat. The welcoming smile faded from the President's face. After listening to the outburst for a few moments, he turned to Weitzel and said very quietly: "General, please give Mr. Green a pass to go to his friends."

Porter then suggested that they return to City Point, where things would be more peaceful. They steamed down the river, and by midafternoon the President was back on the *River Queen*.

14

The Confederate Retreat Begins

Tuesday, April 4, and Wednesday, April 5

THE THREAT OF RAIN hung in the air again as clouds rolled over the landscape to obscure the sun for long intervals. Under this darkening sky the troops of the retreating Confederate Army were converging by different routes on Amelia Court House, where forage for horses and 350,000 rations for men were supposed to be awaiting them. When Lee arrived there on the morning of Tuesday, April 4, he found plenty of artillery ammunition and some harness but no food. Again the unavoidable confusion of a hurried retreat had betrayed him. He had assumed that his notification to the Confederate War Department that his forces were to meet at Amelia Court House would insure rations being sent there. And last-minute telegrams giving specific instructions had reached Richmond too late to be of any use. As a result, more than 30,000 half-starved Confederates were moving toward a tiny village where there was hardly enough food for the local people.

Lee sent out wagons to scour the countryside. The drivers carried a personal message from him appealing to the farmers for supplies. But this was a poor and sparsely settled area; at the end of a long, hard winter enough food to keep a large army going just did not exist in that part of Virginia.

Amelia Court House, like Dinwiddie, owed its existence to

the presence of a court house which in this instance stood at one end of a small open square. Around it were a few houses and small one-story buildings used as law offices. Near the square was an old stage tavern which faced some fine large old oak trees. But Lee avoided the tavern and had his headquarters tent pitched in the garden behind one of the houses on the square. In this little town the high command of the Army of Northern Virginia settled down for an anxious wait, hoping against hope that rations might arrive. More troops kept coming in until "huge army trains were encamped in the suburbs of the pretty little village, and the travel-worn troops bivouacked in the fields. They were still in good spirits, and plainly had an abiding confidence in their great commander. The brigades, though thinned by their heavy losses at Petersburg, still presented a defiant front; and the long lines of veterans with bristling bayonets, led by Longstreet, Gordon, and Mahone, advanced as proudly as they had done in the hard conflicts of the past."

In order to get rations shipped to Amelia Court House, Lee sent a scout mounted on an innocent-looking mule down the railroad to try to find a place where the telegraph line might still be open to Danville. When this scout arrived at Jetersville (seven or eight miles below Amelia Court House), he encountered about two hundred cavalrymen under the direct command of General Sheridan. The man on the mule was promptly arrested and searched. Sheridan, describing the incident in his *Memoirs,* says: "There was found in his boots this telegram in duplicate, signed by Lee's Commissary-General. 'The army is at Amelia Court House, short of provisions. Send 300,000* rations quickly to Burkeville Junction.' One copy was addressed to the supply department at Danville, and the other to that at Lynchburg. I surmised that the telegraph

* In Sheridan's report on the Appomattox Campaign written on May 16, 1865, he gives this figure as 200,000.

lines north of Burkeville had been broken by Crook after the despatches were written, which would account for their being transmitted by messenger. There was thus revealed not only the important fact that Lee was concentrating at Amelia Court House, but also a trustworthy basis for estimating his troops, so I sent word to Crook to strike up the railroad toward me, and to Merritt — who ... had followed on the heels of the enemy — to leave Mackenzie there and himself close in on Jetersville. Staff-officers were also despatched to hurry up Griffin with the Fifth Corps, and his tired men redoubled their strides. My troops too were hard up for rations, for in the pursuit we could not wait for our trains, so I concluded to secure if possible these provisions intended for Lee. To this end I directed Young to send four of his best scouts to Burkeville Junction. There they were to separate, two taking the railroad toward Lynchburg and two toward Danville, and as soon as a telegraph station was reached the telegram was to be transmitted as it had been written and the provisions thus hurried forward."

The telegram was received at Danville but the Confederate authorities there were suspicious. They ordered young John S. Wise to go north on a locomotive to try to reach General Lee and find out if the message was genuine. By the time Wise returned, the situation had changed so completely that his mission no longer had any meaning.

Meanwhile, the Union scouts under command of daredevil Major Harry H. Young were at work. These picked men were described by a fellow officer as being "without the slightest air of military appearance. . . . Spreading themselves over the country in groups of two, three, or half a dozen, they cover the flanks and precede the advance of every column. They learn every road, bridge, house, church, camp, and every stable. . . . Habitually they assume the uniform — if such it can be called — of rebel soldiers, though among them you will just as frequently see men in the garb of a Virginia planter . . . in rusty homespun and broad hat, riding at a careless amble along the road.... They visited everybody, were at home in every house, and enjoyed at any hour of day or night that unreserved hospitality which they knew so well how to inspire. They conversed with every ignorant white man and every 'intelligent contraband.' They were most accurately informed of the hidden whereabouts of plate, jewelry, horses, and other concealed valuables, and knew where every road went to, and how to reach pleasant places not put down on the maps, by no road at all. Indeed these scouts were a most complete gazetteer of the country through which the cavalry marched. None could speak with more knowledge of its resources. While they led during the campaign this roving, demoralizing life, and gained much information, doubtless very interesting to themselves, they occasionally learned matters of value to their superiors. Their personal attachment to Sheridan was strong and reliable. On the march, or in action, scarcely an hour passed that they did not bring him a direct report from distant and important quarters. They visited the enemy's outposts, rode about his wagon trains, spied out his camps, and encircled the cavalry corps with a network of eyes and ears. Seldom is a general in active campaign better acquainted with the moves of his enemy than was Sheridan in this. Aside from the information which each of his generals was able to send from his own immediate vicinity, these scouts were his only secret service."

Young's scouts, dressed in gray or butternut uniforms, now rode boldly among the unsuspecting Confederates and by various ruses led them to concealed surrender centers where they were disarmed and made prisoner. Among the catch was Brigadier General Rufus Barringer, one of W. H. F. Lee's cavalry commanders.

When Lee's foragers returned at nightfall with almost empty wagons, a deep pall of gloom descended upon the hungry army.

During the night nearly one hundred extra caissons were taken to a deserted field and set on fire. One after another the ammunition in them exploded. The red flames of the burning wood and the bright flashes of the explosions lighted up the fleeing forms of deserters who had had enough of starvation and pursuit and were simply packing up and going home. During the nights of April 4 and 5 the Army of Northern Virginia started to break up. "At morning roll-calls," one Confederate commentator said with quiet understatement, "a number of men did not answer to their names."

Jetersville was "a small village on the railroad, of scarcely a dozen dwellings, a store or two, blacksmith shop, postoffice, and small railroad depot, where were found a few cars." A short way below the town Sheridan's cavalrymen set to work digging trenches across the road to block Lee's advance. When infantrymen from the Fifth Corps arrived, they helped strengthen this position, and as more and more Union troops kept coming up they soon became a formidable force. Sheridan felt that Lee had lost his last chance to get through to Burkeville because he had not attacked earlier when only a few hundred cavalrymen were blocking his way.

Confederate mounted scouts who were sent ahead on the overcast morning of April 5 to see whether the road was open were quickly driven back. Lee then personally rode out to appraise the strength of the forces opposing him and reluctantly came to the conclusion that they were too strong to be attacked. Local people were asked about other roads, but Lee finally had to rely on his maps. Orders were given for the troops to turn off to the northwest and proceed along a country lane hardly wide enough to let the wagons and artillery through. Amelia Springs, a once popular resort, was their next destination.

Union cavalry patrols had already passed through this section and had gone on to Paineville, where they heard that a Confederate wagon train made up of hundreds of vehicles and cannon was only four miles away. The Confederate wagoners were caught in a bad position in the middle of a swamp, and to make matters worse, it was beginning to rain. Before they could swing a fieldpiece into action on the narrow road, the Federal horsemen were upon them, scattering and capturing part of the mounted guard and riding up and down to set nearly two hundred of the wagons and caissons on fire. The initials C.S.A., painted on the faded canvas covers, went up in smoke as flames ate away at the wooden wagons and their contents. And being destroyed along with everything else were the manuscript records of Lee's headquarters, lost forever to history.

Confederate cavalrymen came to the aid of the wagon train, but by the time they arrived there was not much they could do. A curious little incident occurred here. When the mounted men rode along the wrecked and plundered line where caissons were still exploding and wounded horses were floundering in the mud, they saw a pretty young girl from Mississippi standing in the road accompanied by a soldier dressed in a gray jacket. She had been traveling with the ordnance train, riding in one of the ambulances. Union troopers had cut the horses loose and gone off with them, leaving her without transportation. She complained bitterly to her mounted countrymen, who listened and laughed sympathetically and then dashed on after the fast-moving Yankee raiders.

The Second and Sixth Corps were being rushed to Jetersville, which had become the temporary center of Union activity. There, too, had come General George Gordon Meade, commander of the Army of the Potomac. Meade, like Warren, had made his reputation at Gettysburg, and now, like Warren, he was learning the bitter lesson that he was no longer needed and that Sheridan and Grant were working so closely together

that he was only nominally in command. He had been seriously
ill for the past week and had to move from place to place flat
on his back in an army ambulance.

During the afternoon of April 5, Sheridan sent Grant a
message saying "I wish you were here yourself" and enclosed
a naïvely worded note written by a Confederate officer to his
mother and intercepted en route. "Dear Mamma: Our army
is ruined, I fear," the note began and then went on to say that
Lee was still at Amelia Court House.

The message was brought to Grant by one of Sheridan's
gray-uniformed scouts, a man named Campbell. He carried the
message wrapped up in tin foil and hidden in his mouth so
he could swallow it if caught. As soon as Grant read Sheridan's
words, he wrote a short dispatch alerting Ord, using his saddle
as a desk.

Grant, with Horace Porter and three other officers and
fourteen men, then started off with Campbell to ride through
the night to Sheridan's headquarters, more than fifteen miles
away. Fortunately, the sky had cleared and the moon was
nearly full, so the visibility was good. Porter said of their
journey: "After riding for nearly two hours, the enemy's campfires were seen in the distance, and it was noticed that the
fence-rails were thrown down in a number of places, indicating
that cavalry had been moving across this part of the country,
though we were certain our cavalry had not been there. Knowing that scouts are seldom trustworthy, and are often in the
employ of both sides, and feeling that the general's safety was
now entirely in the power of a comparatively unknown man,
I, for one, began to grow suspicious. Just then Campbell fell
back several paces and suddenly turned his horse into a piece
of woods which we were skirting, and seemed to be acting in
a manner that indicated either confusion or treachery. I cocked
my pistol, and rode close behind him ... determined that if
he was caught giving any suspicious signals I would at once

arrest him. The scout, however, was thoroughly loyal.... He was only looking for a short cut through the woods. About half-past ten o'clock we struck Sheridan's pickets. They could hardly be made to understand that the general-in-chief was wandering about at that hour with so small an escort, and so near to the enemy's lines. The cavalry were sleeping on their arms, and as our little party picked its way through their ranks, the troopers woke up and recognized the general in the moonlight.... Sheridan was awaiting us, feeling sure that the general would come after getting his despatch."

From Jetersville, Grant sent further instructions to Ord, telling him to move west and to watch the roads between Burkeville and Farmville. He also predicted that Lee would leave Amelia Court House during the night and said that if he was still there at dawn they would attack.

Grant and Sheridan then went to visit the ailing commander of the Army of the Potomac, George Gordon Meade, who was resting in a house about a mile and a half southeast of Jetersville. Sheridan had been annoyed because the older and more cautious Meade was unwilling to attack until the Sixth Corps came up; he evidently wanted Grant on hand to overrule Meade in person. Sheridan summarized what was almost surely a tense meeting in very few words: "Grant stated that the orders Meade had already issued would permit Lee's escape, and therefore must be changed, for it was not the aim only to follow the enemy, but to get ahead of him, remarking during the conversation that 'he had no doubt Lee was moving right then.' On this same occasion Meade expressed a desire to have in the proposed attack all the troops of the Army of the Potomac under his own command, and asked for the return of the Fifth Corps. I made no objections, and it was ordered to report to him."

The night of April 5–6 was an anxious one for both armies.

Lee was fortunate enough to have a good dinner at the home of a friend who lived near Amelia. Then he went on in the darkness to Flat Creek, where a little bridge had broken down under the pounding hoofs of the horses and the heavy weight of artillery and wagons. While Lee was waiting for his engineers to come up and make repairs, he received a message forwarded by Gordon, the general who had led the ill-fated attack on Fort Stedman. This message had been found on two young men who had been captured while wearing Confederate uniforms. They had authentic-looking passes and airtight alibis, but one of Gordon's men immediately recognized them as Union scouts. Careful search of the lining of one of their boots produced a copy of the message Grant had sent to Ord from Jetersville. When Lee read it he found out just where his pursuers were and learned that Ord would be blocking the way to Burkeville.

The formerly fashionable resort hotel at Amelia Springs was nearby. War had brought ruin to it, but it would provide temporary shelter for some of the staff. However, there was no sleeping for officers that night. Men and horses had to be urged forward through the darkness in a desperate effort to shake off Sheridan and Grant. The Union cavalry was so close that the Confederates encamped around the hotel could hear Sheridan's bands playing "Home, Sweet Home," "Annie Laurie," and other popular airs.

While the long Confederate columns moved on through the night with the men so hungry and tired that they hardly knew or cared where they were going, a strange thing happened. Just outside Amelia Court House, while one column was crossing a deep railroad cut, a sudden moment of mass hysteria seized the marching men. Some said that a runaway horse had started it; others claimed that the Yankees had crept up and were firing at them. One of the officers reported that "most of the men became panic-stricken, broke and sought cover behind trees or fences while not a few skulked disgracefully to the rear. They began to discharge their pieces at random, in many instances shooting their own comrades. ... Finally the men were induced to cease firing and partially reformed their ranks. ... Just as the line was reforming, my horse started violently at seeing Major Frank Smith's dead horse in the road, and this trifling incident caused a second disgraceful panic. ... Warned by what had happened before, the officers cried out earnestly: 'Don't shoot; don't shoot, men!' But some fifty or hundred guns were fired. With a sickening feeling, I saw in the moonlight a number of bright barrels pointed directly at me and many bullets passed close by. ... Finally, however, the firing ceased and order was restored. Valuable lives were sacrificed in this inexcusable affair. ... The whole division was disheartened ... and for some time marched on ... relapsing into gloomy silence."

Hard masters as they were, Sheridan and Grant had the important soldierly virtues of being right most of the time. When Meade's troops marched toward Amelia Court House early on April 6, they saw the rear guard of Lee's army disappearing through the woods beyond Flat Creek, over which all the bridges had just been destroyed. Union artillery was lined up along the shore to fire futilely after the vanishing Confederates. Infantrymen could wade through the water, but the guns and wagons had to wait for the bridges to be rebuilt.

Sheridan took no part in what he contemptuously called Meade's "useless advance" and was off early on his own, after having arranged with Grant to have his favorite Sixth Corps placed nearest in the line so it would be available if and when he needed infantry support.

It was raining early in the morning when Sheridan and his troopers rode toward Deatonsville, but the sun soon came out. While his men hurried off to harass the Confederate wagon

trains — which were not as vulnerable as they seemed because
they were well guarded — Sheridan rode up to the top of a
hill that overlooked the road and stayed there for half an hour
with his famous forked red and white cavalry guidon flying
briskly in the breeze. He studied the terrain carefully through
his field glasses; then he and his staff moved on for a mile
or so to another ridge, from which Captain Marcus C. Miller's
artillerymen were sent into action. Newhall said of these
gunners: "All of our horse artillery was splendid, commanded
by young and dashing fellows, whose delight was to fight with
the cavalry in an open country, where they could run a section
up to the skirmish line and second the carbines with their
whistling shells. . . . The cavalry had no better soldiers than
the battery commanders and their lieutenants . . . not very often
heard of, and not much known beyond the army, but where the
sharp fighting was they could be found; in the hardest marches
they pulled through somehow; and in camp it was pleasant
to see these swells, with their open jackets, tight trowsers with
the double crimson stripe, their gorgeous badges, their riding
whips, and their fast horses. Now, when Miller got his guns
well to work, we were not surprised to see the trains stampeded;
his first shot just clipping the fence by the roadside and glancing
on through a party of horsemen galloping by at that moment.
These we afterward learned to be General Ewell and staff, who
told us that this shell grazed the cap of one of them, the wind
of it nearly unhorsing him. Miller directed his fire at a little
opening in the woods, and soon had the range so exactly that
every shot was planted on the road, tossing the mud into the
air, damaging wagons and demoralizing teams, and the unhappy
teamsters, who, being darkeys pressed into the service, and not
paid to be shot at, and having no sympathy with the cause nor
care for the safety of the trains, objected to driving through
Miller's Gap. Some of them took out into the timber, and
some, who were arrested in the attempt, drove on only because

to refuse was certain death, while Miller might miss them."

After the Confederates got past Miller's guns they hurried on for more than two miles to Deatonsville. They went through this tiny village and then took a right fork in the road toward a valley where an insignificant and slow-moving stream named Little Sayler's Creek wanders through swampy ground to join Sayler's Creek* proper, which flows on quietly to the Appomattox River. The murky water in these obscure streams was to run red with blood on that sunny Thursday afternoon, and the swamp-bottomed valley was to be the penultimate scene of the Army of Northern Virginia's final humiliation and defeat.

* Sayler's Creek is often misspelled (especially in older Civil War books) Sailor's Creek. It was originally called Sayler's Creek after a local family and was not renamed, as was popularly supposed, after the remnants of the Confederate Navy who fought there that day.

15

From Sayler's Creek to Appomattox Station

Thursday, April 6, to Saturday, April 8

THE SUDDEN ATTACKS and counterattacks went on day and night. Some idea of what these skirmishes were like can be found in an account written by a young lieutenant in the 2nd Rhode Island Infantry who had been in the field for less than three weeks. On April 6 he and his men were trudging along a road littered with the abandoned impedimenta of the retreating Confederates. During the middle of the afternoon the lieutenant caught his first glimpse of active fighting, a battle scene which so strongly resembled the pictures in *Harper's Weekly* that there was an odd air of familiarity about it. The marching troops passed a dead cavalryman lying by the side of the road with a neat round hole through his forehead. Then they were ordered to charge the Confederate lines. The lieutenant, who wanted to see how men acted under fire, noticed "that every imaginable position was assumed, from the half-erect to an apparent attempt to tunnel the hillside.... Many of them bobbed their heads as bullets passed close to their ears. Suddenly 'whiff!' sped a ball by my right ear; involuntarily I imitated those I had been ridiculing and thereafter stooped about two inches lower."

While the bullets were flying around him, the lieutenant could not see the Confederates or even spot the flashes of their guns. His men moved forward, stopping three times to reload. When the young officer came down a hill toward a muddy creek, he felt a dull blow on his left hip. He knew he was hit and said that for no good reason "I began to laugh as the ludicrousness of the whole affair flashed upon me.... Do you want to know how it feels to be shot? Ask your brother to step in the yard some bright February day when the water is running freely in the streets, scoop up a handful of snow from the top of the nearest bank, spat it once only with his hands ... and hurl it with ordinary force from a distance of twelve feet. The dull spreading sensation will be sufficiently accurate."

The limping lieutenant, who supported himself by using his sword as a cane, managed to get to a field surgeon, who examined the wound by sticking his index finger into it, exploring for a bullet that was not there for the simple reason that it had gone on through to emerge from the other side. The surgeon then borrowed the lieutenant's silk handkerchief, moistened it with water from the creek, and placed it over the wound. This was the only dressing the mangled flesh was to get for three days. Then the wounded officer was put into an ambulance alongside a Confederate artilleryman who was also seeing his first battle and who had lost his right leg just below the knee. After a six-hour ride over bumpy corduroy roads they reached the Union field hospital at Burkeville Junction.

The chase was a harsh and unrelenting one, yet there were occasional comic incidents. One of these occurred somewhere along the route when a Maine infantry regiment discovered a large cask of syrup in a farmyard. A crowd quickly gathered, and "men pushed and fought, each endeavoring to obtain a portion of the coveted article. In Company H was a little fellow, slim and pale, not over sixteen years old, who was known as 'Sis.' On this occasion he was in the midst of the crowd, endeavoring to make his way to the syrup; the stronger men crowding against him soon raised him from his feet, and in the scramble he found himself upon their shoulders; the next moment he was thrown headlong into the half-filled cask of syrup. He was fished out but concluded that he needed no more syrup on that day."

During the morning of April 6, the retreating Confederate columns were attacked repeatedly by Sheridan's cavalry, who came after them like gadflies stinging a runaway horse. Lee and Longstreet were far ahead at Rice's Station, but the Confederate wagon trains were strung out behind them for miles. When a gap opened in the line, Union cavalry dashed through to set the wagons on fire and create general havoc. There was much confusion as the battle-weary Confederates kept moving on, trying to ignore what was happening behind them. Gordon's column, by error, had already gone astray. But worst of all was the predicament of the troops under Generals Richard Anderson and Richard S. Ewell, the one-legged commander who rode strapped into the saddle. As they came through the swamp bottom along Little Sayler's Creek, they were set upon by Union cavalry, while infantrymen from the Sixth Corps and artillery on a hilltop poured down a devastating fire. The Confederates entrenched themselves and managed to hold off a vigorous assault for a while. Then they launched a counterattack and broke the Union line in the middle, but they could not hold what they had won. Men fought back and forth across the swampy ground where the water in Little Sayler's Creek was deeper than usual. More Union fieldpieces were brought up on the hillside near the pre-Revolutionary Hillsman farmhouse, which had been turned into a field hospital. This additional artillery gave the Union forces final mastery of the situation.

The Union cannoneers on the hill had plenty of ammunition and they knew how to use it. They aimed shot after shot so accurately that a Confederate major said: "A good many had

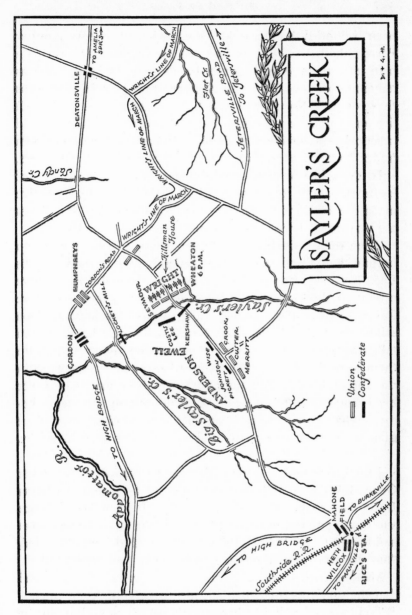

SAYLER'S CREEK

TO AMELIA SPRS
DEATONSVILLE
Sandy Cr.
WRIGHT'S LINE OF MARCH
WRIGHT'S LINE OF MARCH
WRIGHT'S LINE OF MARCH
Flat Cr.
JETERVILLE ROAD
To Jeterville
GORDON'S ROAD
Hillman House
CROCKETT'S MILL
HUMPHREYS
GORDON
SEYMOUR
WRIGHT
WHEATON 6 P.M.
Sayler's Cr.
CUSTIS LEE
KERSHAW
CROOK
EWELL
WISE
COUTLER
MERRITT
ANDERSON
JOHNSON
PICKETT
Big Sayler's Cr.
TO HIGH BRIDGE
Appomattox R.
Union
Confederate
MAHONE
FIELD
TO BURKEVILLE
HETH
WILCOX
TO FARMVILLE
RICE'S STA.
Southside R.R.
TO HIGH BRIDGE

225

been wounded and several killed when a twenty-pounder Parrott shell struck in my front on the line, nearly severing a man in twain, and hurling him bodily over my head, his arms hanging down and his hands almost slapping me in the face as they passed." No troops could be expected to withstand such fire for long, especially since the Confederates in this area had practically no artillery available. Several thousand of them under Anderson's lead managed to slip away and escape capture.

In the midst of this terrible carnage and when the tide of battle was about to overwhelm him, Ewell is reported to have made the odd and apparently irrelevant remark: "Tomatoes are very good; I wish I had some."

Then the irresistible Union forces swarmed over the swamp bottom, and Ewell, a group of generals that included Custis Lee, Kershaw, Corse, Barton, Hunton, and Du Bose, were caught in the gigantic trap with nearly 7000 men and were forced to surrender. Among those captured were some 2000 sailors from the Confederate Naval Battalion who had been taken off the ships that were destroyed on the James. With them were the artillerymen who had manned the big guns in the forts encircling Richmond. Since these men had never been taught how to take care of themselves in the rough-and-tumble fighting of an open battlefield, they suffered even more than the regular troops. Gordon, too, lost heavily that day.

Just before sunset, General Lee, accompanied by Brigadier General William Mahone, rode back to a ridge overlooking Little Sayler's Creek. Coming up out of the valley of death and disaster were the shattered remnants of the battalions that had fought there. "My God!" he is reported to have exclaimed, "has the army been dissolved?"

Mahone tried to reassure him that all was not yet lost and that the survivors could be depended upon to do their duty.

"Will you please keep those people back?" he said, using the word he habitually employed for men in the Union Army. Then, from somewhere, he obtained a Confederate battle flag and held it up as he sat slumped in the saddle watching what was left of his broken army stagger past with blind, staring eyes and wounds undressed.

The once peaceful little valley from which the Confederates were fleeing was a slaughter pit. Dead bodies lay so close together that they had to be dragged out of the way to let a horse pass. In a gulch which had been used as a rifle pit a Union general saw "a Confederate soldier apparently kneeling, his eyes open, and his hands uplifted as if in prayer. I thought he was alive and went over to him to render assistance. I found his eyes dazed in death, and beneath him in this awful ditch the bodies of his brave companions lay at least six feet deep. He was a handsome fellow, and in the general discard of all baggage had donned and looked resplendent in a bright new uniform. At the top of the hill the Confederates had destroyed their camp and garrison equipage including field desks and reserve papers. For acres the ground was white with requisitions, and an immense amount of material, doubtless of value to a future historian, was ruthlessly destroyed."

The wounded were sent to Burkeville, but there was no time to bury the dead. They were left lying on the field for days with the sun and the rain beating down on them until local people got burying parties together to shovel enough soil over them to cover the putrefying flesh.

After the battle at Sayler's Creek was over, Sheridan sent a dispatch describing the victory to Grant, who promptly forwarded it to Lincoln at City Point. It contained the famous phrase: "If the thing is pressed I think Lee will surrender." The next morning Lincoln telegraphed to Stanton, and also to Grant, saying: "Let the thing be pressed."

It must be remembered that the soldiers in the armies which were locked in a deathgrip in central Virginia were not alien foes but men of similar origins. They were Americans whose accents may have differed, but they spoke the same language, and they had much in common. This was especially true of the professional army officers, most of whom knew each other well from West Point or from having served in the Mexican War or at some small army post. Once the fighting was done they quickly forgot the hostilities of battle and got together to talk about the experiences they had shared in the past.

Newhall confirms this when he describes how the captured Confederate generals spent the night after Sayler's Creek with their former foes: "General Sheridan was sitting by his campfire . . . on top of the crest where the fighting had ended, and now he is on the broad of his back, on a blanket, with his feet to the fire, in a condition of sleepy wakefulness which can only be attained through excessive fatigue and a sense of responsibility. Clustered about are blue uniforms and gray in equal numbers, and immediately around our camp-fire are most of the Confederate generals who have just been captured. General Ewell is the principal figure in the group, and attracts, though he seems to avoid, attention. He has plainly admitted that there is no hope now for General Lee, and has begged General Sheridan to send him a flag of truce and demand his surrender, in order to save any further sacrifice, but the general has made no further response to this than to urge General Grant to push on faster. Ewell is sitting on the ground hugging his knees, with his face bent down between his arms, and if anything could add force to his words, the utter despondency of his air would do it. The others are mostly staid, middle-aged men, tired to death nearly, and in no humor for a chat; and so the party is rather a quiet one, for our fellows are about done over, too, and half starved. To this sprawling party enter Sandy

Forsyth, *aide-de-camp,* to announce that he has established headquarters in a lovely orchard, where tents are up and supper is cooking. . . . We carried the Confederate generals with us and shared our suppers and blankets with them, as we would be done by, and after a sleep of hardly an hour, took breakfast in their company and then parted . . . as we followed the general's swallow-tailed flag down the road."

Since Custer had his own Negro cook with him it may have been this colorful woman who prepared the dinner which the Union and Confederate generals shared. The next morning, when Custer rode past the Confederate officers who had been so unusually well treated as prisoners of war, he saluted them by raising his hat. This act of courtesy so delighted them that they cheered as he and his men filed by. And then, when his band, which had been playing "Bonnie Dundee," suddenly struck up the Confederate tune, "The Bonny Blue Flag," rebel yells of appreciation came from the captured generals and their fellow prisoners.

The night was cold, so cold that snow flurries were reported at Burkeville, and on the morning of April 7 it began to rain again. Fortunately, the roads were firmer in this region; anyway, Sheridan's men were too elated to mind getting wet. By three o'clock Merritt and Mackenzie's mounted troopers had reached Prince Edward Court House after "having marched nearly twenty miles since morning with that long slinging walk the horses had acquired in their numerous campaigns." Years of battle experience had turned the once clumsy city boys and mechanics into highly trained horsemen who could march in perfect order "on one road from daylight to dark and never change the gait in a single regiment."

Crook's men hurried on to Farmville where Lee and what was left of his army were concentrating because the rations which had been shipped up the Southside Railroad were

expected there. Some of the Confederates had had to fight along
the way, for Union troops had been sent toward High Bridge
where the Southside Railroad crossed the Appomattox River
on a wooden trestle near a wagon bridge. Union casualties had
been heavy in a pitched battle which had taken place on the
road, but the pursuers could afford to lose men, while the
hunted army could not. Its already depleted forces were
dwindling in number each dreadful hour. Then the Confederates had fled across the river in such a hurry that "a panic
ensued, and the bridge was a mass of wriggling humanity
wedged so tightly that moving or even breathing seemed impossible. Many were trampled underfoot, and one man [was]
forced up . . . to cling for a moment to the parapet and with a
wild scream disappear over the side."

Once the Confederates got across, they set the two bridges
on fire to prevent the Union troops from following them. But
Humphreys' Second Corps arrived just in time to save the
wagon bridge almost intact and to put out the flames on the
railroad trestle so it could be repaired and restored to use.
The men crossed over the wagon bridge under a harassing fire
and hurried after the Confederates.

Lee had slept in Farmville on the night of April 6–7, and
was up early to make sure that his troops, who were marching
toward the railroad station, received their long awaited rations.
As the Confederate regiments approached the little town, a
group of young girls standing on the porch of a local boarding
school waved gaily at the marching soldiers. Everything seemed
fine early that morning. The trains carrying rations had arrived
at last and were being unloaded while the hungry troops stood
around eagerly waiting for food to be distributed. Packages
of dried French soup done up in tin foil were handed out,
casks of meat were knocked open, and the town was soon filled
with the pleasant odor of bacon sizzling over bonfires burning

in the streets. But before the men crowding into Farmville could all be fed or even provided with rations to take with them, word came that the wagon bridge next to High Bridge had not been successfully destroyed as ordered and that Union troops were rapidly approaching. Soon sporadic rifle firing could be heard coming from the east to confirm the bad news. The ordinarily self-controlled Lee lost his temper and denounced those responsible for letting his pursuers get across the river. Action had to be taken immediately. The still unloaded food trains were sent on to Appomattox Station, where it was hoped that the troops could catch up with them. More than a hundred supply wagons had to be burned to prevent them from falling into the hands of the oncoming Federals.

Farmville was quickly evacuated, and its two bridges over the Appomattox River were successfully destroyed, but there was no way of preventing the Union troops from wading across a ford near the town. They were so close behind the Confederates that there was fighting in the streets. Lee posted his artillery on the side of a hill facing the river and dismounted his cavalrymen to form a line of battle. Shells began falling around the shore, splashing up the water and tearing up the ground. But the Union troops had artillery too, and they began to use it effectively. Cavalry attacks were made on the Confederate wagon trains, which were fiercely defended. In one of these encounters General J. Irvin Gregg of Crook's division was driven into a narrow fence corner, where he was captured by Confederate infantry. When General Gordon saw Gregg marching on foot among the prisoners he courteously offered him a horse, but Gregg declined, saying that he would rather share his men's fate.

While Union troops poured into Farmville, Grant rode into the town the Confederates had just vacated. He stopped at a long brick building which served as the local hotel and made himself at home on the porch. He remained there during the afternoon, while endless columns of blue-clad troops marched past. Bonfires were lighted from the embers of the fires the Confederates had been forced to abandon. When night came on, the fronts of the buildings lining the main street were lighted up by the dancing flames. As the soldiers passed the hotel porch where Grant was sitting "the men seized straw and pine-knots, and improvised torches; cheers arose from their throats, already hoarse with shouts of victory; bands played, banners waved, and muskets were swung in the air. A regiment now broke forth with the song of 'John Brown's Body,' and soon a whole division was shouting the swelling chorus of that popular air, which had risen to the dignity of a national anthem. The night march had become a grand review, with Grant as the reviewing officer."

At some time during the afternoon of this day Grant was visited by three of his most important commanders, Ord, Gibbon, and Wright, who wanted to suggest that perhaps the time had come for him to send a message to Lee proposing the surrender of the Army of Northern Virginia. Grant's mind had been prepared for such a move. While at Burkeville, he had talked at length with one of the recently captured prisoners of war, a Dr. Smith who had resigned from the regular army to join the Confederates. According to Dr. Smith, who was related to General Ewell, Ewell felt that the Confederate cause was already lost and that they "should make the best terms they could while they still had a right to claim concessions." Grant was also aware of the fact that Sheridan's cavalry was moving so rapidly westward that it would soon be able to seize the Confederate rations on the railroad and block Lee's advance as surely and as effectively as it had at Jetersville. He then wrote a simple note that has since become one of the key documents of American history:

> Headquarters Armies of the
> United States.
> April 7, 1865—5 P.M.

General R.E.Lee,
  Commanding C.S. Army:
General: The results of the last week must convince you of the hopelessness of further resistance on the part of the Army of Northern Virginia in this struggle. I feel that it is so, and regard it as my duty to shift from myself the responsibility of any further effusion of blood, by asking of you the surrender of that portion of the C.S. Army known as the Army of Northern Virginia.

> Very respectfully, your obedient servant,

> U.S. GRANT

> Lieutenant General,
> Commanding Armies of the United States.

He gave this note to his adjutant general, Seth Williams, with orders to get it to Lee. Williams rode off, escorted by one orderly. They were shot at as they approached the Confederate lines, and the luckless orderly was killed. The bullets missed Williams, who was then able to convince the suspicious Confederate pickets that he was there under a flag of truce. Grant's message was sent through the Confederate lines to Lee, who read it and handed it silently to General Longstreet. "Not yet," Longstreet said briefly and handed the paper back.

Lee knew that he would have to deal with a general who had earned for himself the title "Unconditional-Surrender-Grant" for his blunt statement of terms to Buckner at Fort Donelson in 1862. But Lee could not have any idea of what Lincoln had said in the private conference in the cabin of the *River Queen* only eleven days before. So the Confederate commander, who had no reason to hope for generous terms for his already beaten army, wanted to feel his way cautiously. Without consulting Longstreet he wrote to Grant for further clarification:

7th Apl '65

Genl

I have recd your note of this date. Though not entertaining the opinion you express of the hopelessness of further resistance on the part of the Army of N.Va. — I reciprocate your desire to avoid useless effusion of blood, & therefore before considering your proposition, ask the terms you will offer on condition of its surrender.

Very respy your obt. Servt
R.E.LEE
Genl

This note did not reach Grant until the early morning of April 8. He answered Lee's request for terms promptly, but at the same time urged his commanders in the field to keep up their unrelenting pressure on the disorganized Confederate Army. In his reply, he made clear to Lee that he was prepared to be generous, saying: "Peace being my great desire, there is but one condition I would insist upon, namely, that the men and officers surrendered shall be disqualified for taking up arms again against the Government of the United States until properly exchanged. I will meet you, or will designate officers to meet any officers you may name for the same purpose, at any point agreeable to you, for the purpose of arranging definitely the terms upon which the surrender of the Army of Northern Virginia will be received." Then he sent dispatches to Sheridan and Stanton predicting that Lee would surrender on this day or the next.

As the two armies rushed westward toward their final rendezvous the day was one "of uneventful marching; hardly a human being was encountered on the way. The country was enchanting; the peach orchards were blossoming in the southern spring, the fields had been peacefully ploughed for the coming crops, the buds were beginning to swell, and a touch of verdure was perceptible on the trees and along the hillsides. The atmosphere was balmy and odorous; the hamlets were unburnt, the farm-houses inhabited, the farms all tilled."

But as the exhausted Confederates stumbled on blindly through the warm spring sunshine, the fact that the end was very near was well known to the top commanders. Word had probably reached them that one of the Confederacy's last strongholds, Selma, Alabama, with its vast arsenals and supply depots, had fallen on April 2. And from nearby Lynchburg may have come news that Stoneman's army was fast approaching that city to block the roads there. A meeting of the most important Confederate generals had already been held to discuss the problem. The three possibilities they considered were reported by General Gordon:

1. To disband and allow the troops to get away as best they could, and reform at some designated point. This was abandoned because a dispersion over the country would be a dreadful infliction upon our impoverished people, and because it was most improbable that all the men would reach the rallying-point.

2. To abandon all trains, and concentrate the entire Confederate army in a compact body, and cut through Grant's lines. This proposition was in turn discarded, because without ammunition trains we could not hope to continue the struggle many days.

3. To surrender at once.

It was decided that this last course would be wisest and these devoted officers felt that they should do all in their power to relieve General Lee by giving him their moral support in taking the step.

On the afternoon of April 8, General William Nelson Pendleton, chief of artillery, went to a field where Lee had stopped to rest and was lying on the ground under a large pine tree. Pendleton later reported that "he quietly listened, and then, courteously expressing his thanks for the consideration of

his subordinates in daring to relieve him in part of the existing
burdens, spoke in about these words: 'I trust it has not come
to that; we certainly have too many brave men to think of
laying down our arms. They still fight with great spirit,
whereas the enemy does not. And besides, if I were to intimate
to General Grant that I would listen to terms, he would at
once regard it as such evidence of weakness that he would
demand unconditional surrender, and sooner than that I am
resolved to die. Indeed, we must all be determined to die at
our posts.' My reply could only be that every man would no
doubt cheerfully meet death with him in discharge of duty,
and that we were perfectly willing that he should decide the
question."

In order to consolidate the scattered and broken sections of
his diminished army Lee now reorganized it into two corps
under Longstreet and Gordon. He also relieved from command Generals Pickett, Anderson, and Bushrod Johnson.
Now, with his army stripped for action, the grim race to reach
the food-supply trains waiting on the Southside Railroad at
Appomattox Station was hurried up.

One of Sheridan's scouts had reported that the four trains
were rapidly nearing Appomattox Station. Since Sheridan
wanted the rations for his own fast-moving, lightly supplied
cavalry units, he redoubled his efforts to get to the railroad
first. Custer was within a few miles of the station when he
heard the tell-tale whistle of a locomotive sounding through
the pine woods. He sent the 1st Brigade of the 2nd New York
Cavalry Regiment ahead to capture the precious trains. This
regiment had been in more than a hundred encounters and
had some of the best-trained men in the Army. They came
tearing up to the isolated wilderness station (where supplies
were already being unloaded into wagons) and made a dash

for the locomotives. They seized the engineers at pistol point and replaced them with men who knew how to operate wood-burning locomotives. One train was set on fire; but the other three were driven down the line toward Farmville with whistles blowing, bells ringing, and their new Union crews cheering.

Custer himself was delayed by a romantic incident that took place about a mile from the station. As he rode past an isolated house, two girls came out, protesting that they were being robbed. The ever gallant general dismounted and went toward the house. He arrived there "just in time to catch a man in United States uniform running from the front door." Custer knocked the soldier down with his fist, dashed into the house, where he saw another skulker trying to make a rapid exit through the back door. He picked up an ax and hurled it after the fleeing man, hitting him in the back of the head. Then he ordered his provost marshal to leave a guard at the house while he remounted and hurried on to Appomattox Station.

The sound of shooting brought more Confederates into the conflict, for they were beginning to arrive in that area in force. North of the station, in the woods on the road to Lynchburg, was a park of sixty cannon which had been sent ahead of the army in charge of General R. L. Walker. Lee's chief of artillery, Pendleton, was with Walker when the Federals burst in upon them. They ordered three batteries arranged in a hollow circle, while the rest of the guns were hauled back to Appomattox Court House. Confederate troops came to the support of the remaining batteries and then, in the rapidly gathering twilight, "began one of the closest artillery fights in the time it lasted that occurred during the war. The guns were fought literally up to the muzzles. It was dark by this time, and at every discharge the cannon was ablaze from touch-hole to mouth. There must have been six or eight pieces at work and the small arms of some three or four hundred men packed in among the guns in a very confined space.... They [Custer's cavalry] made three distinct charges, preluding always with the bugles on the right, left, and center, confusing the point of attack, then with a cheer and up they came. It was too dark to see anything of the long dark line. They would get within thirty or forty yards of the guns and roll back under the deadly fire that was being poured upon them."

Most of the guns were limbered up and hastily drawn off down the road to Appomattox Court House, stopping on the way to fire as they went. But the narrow road was blocked by wagon trains. As a result, Custer captured more than twenty of Walker's guns.

The distant crash of artillery and rifle fire that could be heard coming from the area between Appomattox Station and the little court house village told the Confederates that their supply trains were under attack and that their last chance of getting food was gone.

The plight of the Confederate soldier during the last days of the Appomattox Campaign was truly desperate. Most of the men knew that all chance of ultimate victory was gone, and the incessant exposure to attack, the lack of sleep, and the endless marching were wearing down even the most resolute. The capture of the four trains at Appomattox Station doomed the Army of Northern Virginia. After that nothing was left. The men had already consumed everything edible, and had combed farmers' fields for last year's turnips or for anything that would serve as food.

The survivors were curiously silent about eating horse or mule meat,* but they used every scrap of beef they could get. One of them said that after slaughtering a cow, "the feet were boiled to pieces, picked clear of bones, and strained through a

* Mule meat had been officially issued as Confederate rations at Vicksburg in 1863.

rough, improvised sieve, then seasoned, mixed with flour, and fried with tallow. We thought cow hoofs were a delicacy...."

The same man described the kind of food the troops had been supplied with before they faced actual starvation at Appomattox: "The hardest piece of rations we were subjected to was a kind of meat called 'Nassau bacon' — (Nausea with a capital would have been better). It came through the blockade and we believed it was made from the hog of the tropics and cured in the brine of the ocean. More likely it was discarded ship's pork, or 'salt junk;' or, as some called it, 'salt horse.' It was a peculiarly scaly color, spotted like a half-well case of smallpox, full of rancid odor, and utterly devoid of grease. When hung up it would double its length. It could not be eaten raw, and imparted a stinking smell when boiled. It had one redeeming quality — elasticity. You could put a piece in your mouth and chew it for a long time, and the longer you chewed it the bigger it got. Then, by a desperate effort, you would gulp it down — out of sight, out of mind...."

At one time the troops came to a farmyard where, this same observer said: "We saw a large pot full of boiled turnips, corn, and shucks for cattle and hog feed. While it did not look so tempting, it smelled appetizing.... We dipped in our tin cups and drew off some of the mess. The soft corn was real good, and, stripping the turnips of the peel, we found a savory meal...."

Not only food but foot wear had given out. Apparently it had not been much good even when first issued: "Our shoes, especially those made by the Confederate department, were pitiable specimens.... Generally made of green, or at best half-cured leather, they soon took to roaming; after a week's wear the heel would be on the side at an angle to the foot, and the vamp, in turn, would try to do duty as a sole.... While hot and dry, they would shrink like parchment, and when wet they just slopped all over your feet. English-made shoes were nearly as bad. They were lined with stiff paper, and after fording a few times, they came to pieces."

Badly shod, nearly starved, and utterly exhausted, the remnants of Lee's once great army stumbled into the valley below the village of Appomattox Court House to make their hopeless last stand.

During the night women and children were evacuated from the houses near Appomattox Court House while more and more Confederates kept coming into the area. One of the townspeople testified to the fact that they "were, many of them, shirtless, hatless, and barefooted. . . . A sadder looking set of men I never saw."

Lee sent a courier to ask Pendleton to come to his headquarters. The artillery chief rode rapidly down the stage road toward Appomattox Court House and narrowly escaped being captured when a Union cavalry regiment came rushing headlong down the road after the Confederate guns that were being drawn back. The commander of this adventurous regiment, a colonel mounted on a white horse, kept going until he reached the edge of the village. There the Confederates had barricaded the road. They shot the colonel, whose body fell sprawling to the ground while his horse ran free, neighing wildly, to disappear into the night.

A sergeant from the same Union regiment had his horse shot under him while a bullet tore into his own abdomen. He lay in agony under the fallen horse, begging the townspeople to take his carbine and put a bullet through his head. He did not have long to suffer; within five minutes he was dead from the life-draining wound.

Lee did not receive Grant's note (suggesting that he was prepared to offer generous terms) until after dark. He read it by candlelight and then wrote his reply:

8th Apl '65

Genl

    I recd at a late hour your note of today. In mine of yesterday I did not intend to propose the surrender of the Army of N. Va. — but to ask the terms of your proposition. To be frank, I do not think the emergency has arisen to call for the surrender of this Army, but as the restoration of peace should be the sole object of all, I desired to know whether your proposals would lead to that and I cannot therefore meet you with a view to surrender the Army of N. Va. — but as far as your proposal may affect the C.S. forces under my command & tend to the restoration of peace, I shall be pleased to meet you at 10 A.M. tomorrow on the old stage road to Richmond between the picket lines of the two armies.

Very respy your Obt Sevt
R E L<small>EE</small>
Genl.

    While he waited for his widely scattered commanders to assemble, Lee heard the sound of the guns north of Appomattox Station, and later, as the Federal armies went into bivouac and built hundreds of campfires, the dull red glow of their leaping flames was reflected from the low-hanging clouds that were moving across the face of the nearly full moon. There was no doubt now of the position of the Union troops. They were coming up from the south and were blocking the only way he could go. If they were cavalry forces, there was at least a chance of cutting through them. But solid masses of infantry would make a barrier he could not hope to pass.

    When Fitzhugh Lee, Gordon, and Longstreet arrived, a final council of war was held around a campfire in the woods about a mile northwest of Appomattox Court House. Gordon describes the memorable scene: "There was no tent there, no table, no chairs, and no camp-stools. On blankets spread upon the ground or on saddles at the roots of the trees, we sat. . . .

No tongue or pen will ever be able to describe the unutterable anguish of Lee's commanders as they looked into the clouded face of their beloved leader and sought to draw from it some ray of hope. . . . The numbers and names of the staff officers who were present I cannot now recall; and it would be as impossible to give the words that were spoken or the suggestions that were made as it would to photograph the thoughts and emotions of that soldier group gathered at Lee's last bivouac. The letters of General Grant asking surrender, and the replies thereto, evoked a discussion as to the fate of the Southern people and the condition in which the failure of our cause would leave them. There was also some discussion as to the possibility of forcing a passage through Grant's lines and saving a small portion of the army, and continuing a desultory warfare until the government at Washington should grow weary and grant to our people peace, and the safeguards of local self-government. If all that was said and felt at that meeting could be given it would make a volume of measureless pathos. In no hour of the great war did General Lee's masterful characteristics appear to me so conspicuous as they did in that last council. We knew by our own aching hearts that his was breaking. Yet he commanded himself, and stood calmly facing and discussing the long-dreaded inevitable. It was finally determined that with Fitz Lee's cavalry, my infantry, and Long's artillery, under Colonel Thomas H. Carter, we should attempt at daylight the next morning to cut through Grant's lines. Longstreet was to follow in support of the movement. The utmost that could be hoped for was that we might reach the mountains of Virginia and Tennessee with a remnant of the army, and ultimately join General Johnston."

LINCOLN'S SECOND INAUGURATION, MARCH 4, 1865

Mrs. Lincoln
wearing one of
the elaborate costumes
for which she ran up
enormous debts
without her husband's
knowledge

National Archives

MR. AND MRS. LINCOLN

One of the last
four photographs made
of the living Lincoln.
Taken in Washington
by Alexander Gardner
on April 10, 1865.

*National
Archives*

TWO OF THE
EASY-MONEY BOYS

Orville Hickman Browning
and
James Washington Singleton

ABOVE: THE RIVER QUEEN. BELOW: THE MALVERN

Winslow Homer's sketch of Lincoln, Tad, and Grant at City Point.

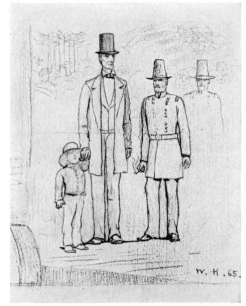

City Point and the *Monohansett,* which took Mrs. Lincoln to Washington.

THE PEACEMAKERS

G. P. A. Healy's painting of the conference in the cabin of the *River Queen*, portraying Sherman, Grant, Lincoln, and Admiral Porter. The original now hangs in the White House.

The Two
Great Adversaries

Ulysses S. Grant, U.S.A.
Robert E. Lee, C.S.A.

Union weapons neatly stacked on the streets of Petersburg,
April 2, 1865.

AN END TO VALOR

Confederate weapons — not so neatly arranged — in a trench
outside the town.

THE WAR AS SEEN BY AN ARTIST
Two pencil sketches made by A. R. Waud, one
of the roving illustrators for *Harper's Weekly*.

Above: The burned-out ruins of the Turnbull house, Lee's headquarters
west of Petersburg. Below: Custer receiving the flag of truce on the field
at Appomattox Court House, April 9, 1865.

The burning of Richmond and the flight across Mayo's Bridge.

The former tobacco warehouse that became Libby Prison.

Wilmer McLean's private residence at Appomattox Court House.

THE COUNTRY VILLAGE THAT HISTORY MADE IMMORTAL

The court house surrounded by Union troops and townspeople.

Library
of Congress

The Lincoln funeral procession on Pennsylvania Avenue, Washington.

No More Parades

The decorated stand in front of the White House for the grand review.

Library of Congress

16

Appomattox Court House

Sunday, April 9

T H E o b s c u r e Virginia village toward which more than a
hundred thousand men were rapidly converging had been
founded in 1819 when a brick tavern was built to serve as a
stagecoach stop on the road from Richmond to Lynchburg.
Since this tavern was called Clover Hill, the tiny village that
grew up around it also bore that name until a court house was
constructed there in 1846 in the newly established county of Appomattox. The two-story brick court house standing in a central square, a jail across the way from it, the tavern, and a few
scattered houses made up the village when the two armies
marched toward it. Traffic was ordinarily so light that the single
street had been boarded up to keep out stray cows.

But in this isolated and otherwise utterly undistinguished
hamlet one of the most remarkable coincidences of the entire
Civil War was about to occur. The first major battle of the war
had taken place on July 21, 1861, at Bull Run, where a family
named McLean owned a 1400-acre plantation along both sides
of that historic creek. Three days before the battle, one of the
Union batteries sent a shell crashing through the McLean house.
And then the newly recruited armies fought across the little
stream that ran through the McLean plantation. The dead lay
everywhere, and the wounded were brought into the house to

scream with pain and die. The McLeans had had enough of war; they moved several times, and in 1863 the head of the household, Wilmer McLean, told his family that he was going to take them far back into the Virginia hill country "where the sound of battle would never reach them." They settled in the village of Appomattox Court House, which was several miles away from the railroad so it was obviously of no military importance whatever. There they occupied a comfortable, two-story brick house with a porch running its entire length. This pleasant home was only a short distance from the central square, and it was the best of the few widely separated middle-class dwellings near the village. In this private residence, on the night of April 8–9, 1865, Wilmer McLean, with his wife and children, waited while destiny tramped toward them on inexorable feet.

Union infantry was being brought up to the Appomattox area by forced night marches. The men, who were now overtired and hungry, were in a sullen mood. Part of the Fifth Corps had been marched for twenty-nine miles on the heels of the Twenty-fourth Corps until late on the night of April 8, when they came to a road running through a dense forest. There "it was everyone for himself," as one young infantryman from Maine said. "The artillery, each gun and caisson being drawn by six horses, crashed and thundered along a narrow road, and by the right of superior strength claimed the right of way. We marched on as best we could, tired, hungry and mad. If the artillery horses came too near, we would hammer them over the heads with our guns. This of course would enrage their riders, and in the midst of all the uproar there was a fierce warfare of words and oaths and threats. We were descending a hill, when a gun came crashing down upon us; it was almost a case of life or death; one of our boys brought the heavy stock of his rifle down upon the head of one of the leading

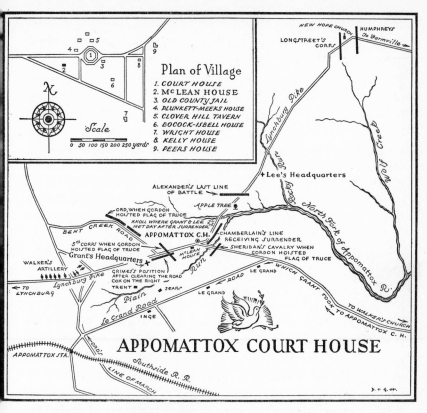

Plan of Village

1. COURT HOUSE
2. McLEAN HOUSE
3. OLD COUNTY JAIL
4. PLUNKETT-MEEKS HOUSE
5. CLOVER HILL TAVERN
6. BOCOCK-ISBELL HOUSE
7. WRIGHT HOUSE
8. KELLY HOUSE
9. PEERS HOUSE

Scale

0 50 100 150 200 250 yards

NEW HOPE CHURCH
HUMPHREYS
To Farmville
LONGSTREET'S CORPS

Lynchburg Pike

Wolf Creek

Lee's Headquarters

ALEXANDER'S LAST LINE OF BATTLE

APPLE TREE

ORD, WHEN GORDON HOISTED FLAG OF TRUCE
KNOLL WHERE GRANT & LEE MET DAY AFTER SURRENDER

BENT CREEK ROAD

APPOMATTOX C.H.

CHAMBERLAIN'S LINE RECEIVING SURRENDER
SHERIDAN'S CAVALRY WHEN GORDON HOISTED FLAG OF TRUCE

5th CORPS WHEN GORDON HOISTED FLAG OF TRUCE
Grant's Headquarters

McLEAN HOUSE

North Fork of Appomattox R.

WALKER'S ARTILLERY

GRIMES'S POSITION AFTER CLEARING THE ROAD COX ON THE RIGHT

TO LYNCHBURG
Lynchburg Pike

TRENT

SEARS

LE GRAND

ROAD

LE GRAND

ROAD WHICH GRANT TOOK TO APPOMATTOX C.H.

TO WALKER'S CHURCH

TO APPOMATTOX C.H.

Plain

Le Grand Road

INGE

LE GRAND

APPOMATTOX COURT HOUSE

APPOMATTOX STA.

Southside R. R.

LINE OF MARCH

D. + G. H.

horses, and the animal staggered and fell. The sergeant who had command of the gun rode up to a lieutenant commanding a company, and ordered the man's arrest; the officer chanced to have a rifle in his hands . . . and with a half-muttered exclamation he dealt the sergeant's horse such a blow that horse and rider went down together and we rushed on our way."

The exhausted troops were allowed to have a short rest at 2 A.M., but there was no food for them. Then, at 4 A.M., they were routed out to be driven on toward Appomattox to help Sheridan.

The early morning of Palm Sunday, April 9, was foggy, so it was difficult for Sheridan's troopers to see what the Confederates in the valley beyond the court house were doing. They did not have long to wait, however, for shortly after daybreak Fitzhugh Lee's cavalry came charging around the western end of the Union line, while Gordon's infantry hit the center. Confederate artillery banged away, and shells whistled through the trees on the ridge occupied by the Union forces. At first, the attack was remarkably successful. It drove back Sheridan's cavalrymen, who at that time were the only Union troops on the field, and overran the area so quickly that two brass Napoleons were captured with their caissons, horses, and crews intact. These were brought into the Confederate lines, where a young artilleryman who had been separated from his gun during the retreat volunteered to round up a trained crew to turn the field-pieces against the Yankees.

Wagons went behind the infantry line, dropping off boxes of cartridges so each man could fill his pockets with forty rounds of ammunition. These infantrymen were urged forward by their officers in an effort to cut through Sheridan's cavalry and make a path for the army. Skirmishers went ahead, passing quickly through woods and open fields to exchange shots with the hard-pressed Union troops. Since the Confederates had single-shot muzzle-loaders, they dragged the butts of their long weapons on the ground behind them so they could load while they kept advancing.

And then, as if it had been arranged by some skillful stage manager, the whole panorama suddenly changed. Sheridan's cavalrymen parted and moved away from the center of the field. Behind them stood the serried ranks of thousands of blue-clad infantrymen — among them some Negro troops — all of whom had been rushed to the front during the night. The Union line was two miles wide; when it began to close in like an enormous pincers the stunned Confederates paused and then began to fall back to Appomattox Court House and the country beyond it. After them came a rapidly moving line of

Union skirmishers, who took prisoners as they went. They soon recaptured the two brass Napoleons; then they swept on with irresistible force.

When one of the Napoleons was retaken, its crew found everything just as they had left it — except that in place of their fine well-fed horses were six bony, half-starved nags, the dregs of whatever the Confederates had left. But there was no chance of identifying their own artillery horses in the confusion that was going on around them. The men swore angrily at the substitution, and took back their gun with its sorry-looking horses.

Fitzhugh Lee had asked Gordon to notify him if Union infantry as well as cavalry was ahead of them. Immediately upon receiving word from Gordon that it was, he rode off down the Lynchburg Pike with part of W. H. F. Lee's cavalry division and with all of Rosser's and Munford's horsemen in an effort to save as much of the cavalry as he could.

These were not the only Confederates who were determined not to surrender. The men of such elite units as the Washington Artillery of New Orleans and the Richmond Howitzers destroyed their gun carriages and caissons when they saw that the end was at hand. Then they buried the gun barrels and took to the mountains. Hundreds of other less distinguished fighting men simply threw away their arms and vanished into the sparsely settled countryside. And many of those who did surrender refused to give up their honored battle flags. In some cases they burned them; in others they cut them into small pieces and distributed the tiny strips to the men of the regiment to take home.

Thousands of men were involved in a battle area several miles long. Everywhere little encounters were taking place on various parts of the field. One Confederate lieutenant, with a sword in one hand and a revolver in the other, backed himself up against a farmer's corncrib and refused to retreat while his fellow soldiers streamed past. They left him there, a one-man outpost of resistance that stood no more chance of stopping the relentless Union wave than a pebble on a beach. The retreating Confederates passed through a farmyard where some of their dead and dying had been thrown on a manure pile. There was no time to sort the living from the dead; there was no choice but to fall back or to be killed by the quick-firing Spencer repeating rifles with which some of the Union infantrymen and practically all the Union cavalrymen were equipped.

Three unarmed Confederate surgeons, caught in the swirling tide of battle, were having a bad time. They had come upon a Yankee cavalry sergeant who drew his revolver, took them prisoner, and ordered them to walk toward the Union rear. They could not convince their captor that they had no weapons. He kept the point of his revolver close to the head of one of them as he rode along, herding them like sheep. The unfortunate surgeon, afraid that the revolver might go off, argued in vain with his captor to lower his weapon. Seeing that he was getting nowhere, he changed his tactics.

"Sergeant," he said, "those are rather poor spurs you're wearing. Now I have in my pocket — if you'll let me get at them — a beautiful pair of spurs made from copper taken from the hull of your famous old *Merrimac*. I'd like to make you a present of them." The trooper agreed to the bargain. He put his revolver away and marched his three prisoners to his commanding officer, who received them courteously, offered them coffee, and asked them the question that was uppermost in everyone's mind: "Why doesn't General Lee surrender?"

The word surrender hung in the air that morning, but Union soldiers who were premature in demanding it met with jeers or rifle shots. One overbold cavalry officer, coatless and with a revolver in his hand, came dashing out of the woods to call upon a body of almost surrounded Confederates to give up. Before he could fire, they shot him down, and his body slumped to the ground, a useless sacrifice.

Lee had got up before dawn and, sensing that he might end the day as Grant's prisoner, had put on his best uniform. He also buckled on a fine presentation sword and tied a silk sash around his waist. While he waited at his headquarters on the Lynchburg Pike just north of the narrow upper stretches of the Appomattox River, he could hear the firing at the front, but he could not see the last desperate battle that was being fought in the morning mist.

Soon after the Union infantry had driven the Confederate cavalry from the field and beaten back Gordon's finely trained fighting men, word of what had happened was brought to Lee. Gordon, on whom he had always depended, sent the despairing message: "I have fought my corps to a frazzle . . . and can do nothing unless I am heavily supported by Longstreet's corps." But Longstreet's weary veterans could not go to his support: they were in trouble themselves. The game was up; there was no possible escape for the Army of Northern Virginia. There was nothing for Lee to do but go to Grant and reluctantly surrender, feeling, as he told his subordinates, that he would "rather die a thousand deaths."

Longstreet, Mahone, and Alexander were summoned for an emergency conference. Alexander was all for letting the troops take to the woods to try to break through as individuals. Lee listened to his proposal and then said that if that were done his men "would be compelled to rob and steal in order to live. They would become mere bands of marauders, and the enemy's cavalry would pursue them and overrun many sections they may never have occasion to visit. We would bring on a state of affairs it would take the country years to recover from. And, as for myself, you young fellows might go to bushwhacking, but the only dignified course for me would be to go to General Grant and surrender myself and take the consequences of my acts . . . Grant will not demand an unconditional surrender. He will give us as good terms as this army has the right to demand, and I am going to meet him in the rear at 10 A.M. and surrender the army on the condition of not fighting again until exchanged."

He then asked his adjutant general, Walter Taylor, the young officer who had gone to Richmond to get married on the night the city fell, to accompany him. And with him also went his military secretary, Colonel Charles Marshall. As orderly and bearer of the flag of truce, he took Sergeant G. W. Tucker, the man who had accompanied A. P. Hill on his last ride at Petersburg. They rode together up the long hill that leads to the village of Appomattox Court House.

Several flags of truce had been sent out to stop the firing that morning, and all sorts of half-true and half-legendary anecdotes have been told about them. The rarest thing in the Confederate Army at this time was a clean white piece of cloth, so various kinds of improvisations had to be made. One of the most interesting of the many flag-of-truce stories is one told shortly after the war by Captain R. M. Sims of Longstreet's staff. He said that he used a new red-bordered white towel which he had bought in Richmond a few days before at the inflated price of $20. He had to ride past a field where Gary's South Carolina cavalrymen were waiting, but they did not know what he was about to do, because he did not display the flag until he got close to the Union lines. Then he held it up and rode forward at a gallop. He was received by a Lieutenant Colonel Whitaker, who took him to Custer. Sims told Custer that he had come to ask him "for a suspension of hostilities until General Lee can be heard from" and that Lee was already on his way to meet Grant. Custer let Sims return to the Confederate lines with Whitaker and an unnamed major accompanying him. On the way, Whitaker asked for the towel as a souvenir of the war. Sims turned on him angrily, saying: "I'll see you in hell first; it is humiliating enough to have had to carry it and exhibit it, but I'm not going to let you preserve it as a monument of our defeat."

This same towel was used again when another officer was sent out to stop the firing in a different part of the field. It eventually wound up as a Union war souvenir anyway, and came into the possession of Mrs. Custer.

Sheridan, accompanied by his color-bearer, rode along a narrow ridge toward Appomattox Court House. On the way some Confederates fired at them, and they had to take shelter behind the ridge. As they rode into the village, other Confederates leveled their guns at them. Then one of the Confederates made an attempt to seize Sheridan's battle flag and was about to have his head split open by the enraged standard-bearer when Sheridan intervened and told his would-be captors what was happening. Sheridan then decided to be sensible and wait in the village until a staff officer who had been sent to Gordon returned. When he came back, Sheridan, with a large escort rode down to meet Gordon. While they were talking, they heard rifle fire start up again. Gordon felt that there must be some mistake, but Sheridan asked him to send one of his officers to stop the shooting. Gordon had no staff officers left, so a Union officer, accompanied by a ragged Confederate private, went toward the area from which the sound of firing was coming.

The shooting had been done by Gary's South Carolina Cavalry, the unit which had been the last to leave Richmond. They had been waiting quietly on the edge of a field, where some of the men had cooked breakfast in improvised utensils and had even gone to sleep. (Every soldier anywhere near Appomattox was desperately in need of sleep by this time.) Then their belligerent commander noticed some Union cavalrymen standing in the yard of a large white house. Gary immediately gave the order to charge the dismounted troopers. One of Gary's officers tells what happened:

"The party in the yard were taken by surprise.... We drove them through the yard, taking one or two prisoners.... We followed and were having it, as we thought, all our own way, when ... behind the brown oaks and moving at a close and steady tramp was a long line of cavalry, Custer's division.... An order was instantly given to move by the left flank ... [while] the enemy kept his line unbroken, pressing slowly forward, firing no volley but dropping shots from a line of scattered skirmishers in front.... We fell back to a battery ... behind us supported by a brigade of North Carolina infantry. We moved slowly, and the enemy's skirmishers got closer. Then one of our couriers bareheaded and mounted on a fine black horse, dashed between the two lines with a handkerchief tied up on a switch.... Everything came to a standstill. An officer who had been with the party in the yard rode up to Gary and with a good deal of heat and with his saber drawn wanted to know what Gary meant by keeping up the fight after there had been a surrender. 'Surrender?' said Gary. 'I have heard of no surrender. We are South Carolinians and don't surrender. Besides, sir, I take command from no officer but my own....' Sabers were out and trouble was very near when an officer of General Custer's staff ... rode up and said: 'General, I appreciate your feelings in the matter, but there has been a suspension of hostilities pending negotiations and General Lee and General Grant are in conference on the matter at this time.' His manner had its effect on Gary, who at once sheathed his saber, saying, 'Do not suppose, sir, I have any doubt of the truth of your statement, but you must allow that under the circumstances I can only receive orders from my own officers. But I am perfectly willing to accept your statement and wait for those orders.' Almost on the instant, Colonel Blackford of the Engineers, rode up sent by General Gordon with a Federal officer carrying orders to that effect. We drew back to the artillery and infantry and formed our battered fragments into regiments. Desperate as we knew our condition to be, the idea of a complete surrender, which we now began to see was inevitable, came as an awful shock.... Gary, true to the doctrine that South Carolinians do not surrender, turned his horse's head, and with ... one or two others managed to get through the cordon drawn around us and succeeded in reaching Charlotte, North Carolina."

When Sheridan went to meet Gordon he just missed being killed by a sharpshooter's bullet. If he had been slain at that moment, when he was at the top of his popularity and was entering the Confederate lines under a flag of truce, there is a good chance that his outraged followers might have fallen upon the Confederates and massacred them. Gordon tells the story: "As General Sheridan and his escort came within easy range of the rifles, a half-witted fellow raised his gun as if to fire. I ordered him to lower his gun, and explained that he must not fire on a flag of truce. He did not obey my order cheerfully, but held his rifle in position to be quickly thrown to his shoulder. In fact, he was again in the act of raising his gun to fire at Sheridan, when I caught the gun and said to him, with emphasis, that he must not shoot men under flag of truce. ... I did not tell General Sheridan of his narrow escape ... [but] this weak-minded Confederate private was one of the deadliest of marksmen."

Grant had spent the night near Curdsville in a farmhouse, nursing a sick headache which he treated by bathing his feet in a hot mustard bath while he applied mustard plasters to the back of his neck and wrists. Lee's dispatch arrived early in the morning of April 9, and Rawlins, Grant's chief of staff, read the message so loudly that a newspaper correspondent who was supposed to be asleep in the house heard every word of it. Rawlins was angry at the Confederate commander's attitude. He felt that Lee was stalling for time, and he said so in his usual forthright way. Grant, with Lincoln's gentle words of advice still fresh in his mind, tried to pacify him. He explained that Lee was "only trying to be let down easily." Then he went on to say that they would meet as Lee had requested and "settle the whole business in an hour."

But Rawlins was hard to convince. He was a lawyer by profession, and he told Grant that he had no legal right to arrange peace terms, since that was a matter which only the President and the Senate could negotiate. He also reminded Grant of the telegram of March 3, in which Stanton (signing his name to Lincoln's words) had forbidden him to hold a conference with Lee on any subject that might have political bearing. But Grant remembered Lincoln's words in the cabin of the *River Queen,* and he also knew that the telegram of March 3 permitted him to deal with Lee on the surrender of his army. He overruled Rawlins and sent the following message to Lee:

> Headquarters Armies of the
> United States
> April 9, 1865.

General R. E. Lee,
    Commanding C.S. Armies:
General: Your note of yesterday is received. As I have no authority to treat on the subject of peace the meeting proposed for 10 A.M. today could lead to no good. I will state, however, General, that I am equally anxious for peace with yourself, and the whole North entertain the same feeling. The terms upon which peace can be had are well understood. By the South laying down their arms they will hasten that most desirable event, save thousands of human lives, and hundreds of millions of property

not yet destroyed. Sincerely hoping that all our difficulties may be settled without the loss of another life, I subscribe myself,
Very respectfully, your obedient servant,
U.S. GRANT
Lieutenant-General U.S. Army.

It was suggested to the ailing commander that he use a covered ambulance that day, but Grant, stubborn as always, insisted on riding to the front. The headquarters party had to circle around part of the Confederate Army to reach Appomattox Court House. Some five or six miles short of their destination they were met by an officer bearing Lee's reply, which Longstreet had shown to Sheridan and Ord before sending it on. It read:

April 9th, 1865

General,
I received your note of this morning on the picket line whither I had come to meet you and ascertain definitely what terms were embraced in your proposal of yesterday with reference to the surrender of this army. I now request an interview in accordance with the offer contained in your letter of yesterday for that purpose.
Very respectfully
Your obt. servt
R.E.LEE

Grant and his party hurried on toward Appomattox Court House, but they were delayed by getting lost in the woods and just escaped being captured by the disorganized Confederates who were roaming around in that area. But Grant's headache had vanished. He said that it disappeared the moment he read Lee's message, and he rode on eagerly to meet the almost legendary commander of the Army of Northern Virginia, whom he had not seen since the Mexican War.

Lieutenant Colonel Orville E. Babcock was sent ahead with Grant's reply, which simply told Lee that he was on the way and wanted to know where the meeting was to take place. When

Babcock arrived inside the Confederate lines, he learned that still another note had gone from Lee to Grant asking for "a suspension of hosilities pending the interview of the terms of the surrender," and that Meade, and Ord, together with various Confederate commanders, were trying to bring the cumbersome war machine to a halt. But a few shells were still being fired, and one of them mortally wounded private William Montgomery, a teen-age boy from Pittsburgh, Pennsylvania. He was borne off the field and was believed to be the last battle casualty in the Army of the Potomac.

Babcock found Lee in an orchard, lying under an apple tree on some artillery blankets which had been stretched out on a pile of fence rails. The aging Confederate commander rose from his improvised couch to bow courteously and receive Grant's reply. Then, accompanied by Babcock and his orderly, his own scholarly-looking and bespectacled military secretary, Colonel Charles Marshall, and the ubiquitous Confederate orderly, Sergeant G. W. Tucker, he wearily mounted Traveller and again rode up the hill toward Appomattox to hear about the fate of his defeated army.

Lee asked Marshall to go into the village and select a suitable building for the conference. Why the substantially built court house or even the old brick tavern were not used has never been made clear. Marshall met Wilmer McLean, the man who had vainly tried to move his family out of the way of the clashing armies, and asked him for a suitable building. McLean first showed Marshall a dilapidated house with no furniture in it, which Marshall immediately decided was not good enough for the historic meeting. Then McLean offered the use of his own home. Marshall sent the Confederate orderly back to guide Lee and Babcock to the McLean house. A few moments later they arrived, dismounted, went up the seven broad white steps, and entered the well-lighted, medium-sized parlor on the left side of the first floor, and sat down to wait for Grant.

17

History Is Made in a Country Parlor

Sunday, April 9

LEE, MARSHALL, AND BABCOCK waited in the McLean parlor, which was a pleasant, simple room furnished with chairs, sofas, and ornaments of the early Victorian period. There were large windows on the north and south walls, a fireplace in the center of the east wall, a tall secretary with glass doors, a sofa, several chairs, and two small tables. Ordinarily the room would have been very quiet on a Sunday morning, but no place surrounded by thousands of horses and hordes of anxiously waiting men with jangling metallic accoutrements can ever be still. Muffled voices, the tramp of many feet, and the noises made by the horses as they impatiently pawed the ground or occasionally whinnied or neighed must have drifted in through the high windows, which were open to let in the warm spring air.

It was after one o'clock when Grant finally arrived. The commotion outside told the three men in the parlor that the decisive moment had come. Lee and Marshall rose to their feet, while Babcock went to open the door for his chief. Grant came in and shook hands with Lee. Then he whispered to Babcock to bring in his staff officers. According to Forsyth, who tried to keep a record of all those who entered the surrender room, these were John Rawlins, Grant's chief of staff,

Seth Williams, his adjutant general, Rufus Ingalls, his quarter-master general, and Horace Porter. A little later Sheridan, Lieutenant Colonel Ely Parker, Grant's full-blooded Indian military secretary, M. R. Morgan, his commissary general, and Lieutenant Colonel T. W. Bowers, assistant adjutant general, were ushered in. Still later Adam Badeau, Grant's other military secretary, was summoned. There may have been still others; both Porter and Sheridan say that Ord was present, but Meade, commander of the Army of the Potomac, was not there, nor was he asked to attend. The session began with some innocuous personal conversation during which Grant reminded Lee that they had met during the Mexican war. Since Lee had then been much higher in rank than Grant, he had paid little attention to his younger subordinate and hardly remembered what he looked like.

What went on during the next few hours has been described so often that any attempt to give a minute-by-minute account of it would be superfluous. Marshall was the only Confederate to write his impressions of those history-making moments, but among the Union officers, Horace Porter, Parker, Badeau, Sheridan, and Grant recorded the event. According to Badeau, Grant alone was responsible for the generous terms offered to the Confederates, although Badeau qualified this statement by saying that Grant "knew the general magnanimity of the President's views and his disposition toward clemency." Grant wrote the first draft of the celebrated surrender letter with his own hand:

Ap'l 9th, 1865.

Gen. R.E.LEE, Comd'g C.S.A.

GEN.: In accordance with the substance of my letter to you of the 8th inst., I propose to receive the surrender of the Army of N. Va. on the following terms, to-wit: Rolls of all the officers and men to be made in duplicate. One copy to be given to an officer designated by me, the other to be retained by such officer or officers as you may designate. The officers to give their individual paroles not to take up arms against the Government of the United States until properly exchanged, and each company or regimental commander sign a like parole for the men of their commands. The arms, artillery and public property to be parked and stacked, and turned over to the officer appointed by me to receive them. This will not embrace the side arms of the officers, nor their private horses or baggage. This done, each officer and man will be allowed to return to their homes, not to be disturbed by United States authority so long as they observe their paroles and the laws in force where they may reside.

Very respectfully,

U.S. GRANT,

Lt. Gl.

Grant said later that the Confederate officers' horses and effects were important to them but of no value to the United States Government, so he decided on the spur of the moment to let them keep them. He also felt that "it would be an unnecessary humiliation" to make them surrender their side arms.*

In his description of the surrender scene Grant said that: "No conversation . . . passed between General Lee and myself, either about private property, side arms, or kindred subjects. He appeared to have no objections to the terms first proposed; or if he had a point to make against them he wished to wait until they were in writing to make it. When he read over that part of the terms about side arms, horses and private property of the officers, he remarked, with some feeling, I thought, that this would have a happy effect upon his army.

"Then, after a little further conversation, General Lee remarked to me again that their army was organized a little differently from the army of the United States (still maintaining by implication that we were two countries); that in their army

---

* Grant had been in Vera Cruz in 1847 when 5000 men in the Mexican Army surrendered to General Winfield Scott. Scott, whom Grant admired, had permitted the Mexican officers to retain their horses, side arms, and private effects.

the cavalrymen and artillerists owned their own horses; and he asked if he was to understand that the men who so owned their horses were to be permitted to retain them. I told him that as the terms were written they would not; that only the officers were permitted to take their private property. He then, after reading over the terms a second time, remarked that that was clear. . . .

"I said further I took it that most of the men in the ranks were small farmers. The whole country had been so raided by the two armies that it was doubtful whether they would be able to put in a crop to carry themselves and their families through the next winter without the aid of the horses they were then riding. The United States did not want them and I would, therefore, instruct the officers I left behind to receive the paroles of his troops to let every man of the Confederate army who claimed to own a horse or mule take the animal to his home. Lee remarked again that this would have a happy effect."

Lee wrote out a brief letter of acceptance; then the military secretaries, Parker and Marshall, began making copies. While they were so occupied, the Union officers present were formally presented to Lee. After all the business of the day was over, Lee told Grant that his army was in desperate straits and that he would have to ask for rations and forage. Grant promised him rations for 25,000 men but said that he had no forage even for his own horses and mules — they had been living off the country. Three Union and three Confederate generals were then appointed to arrange the details of paroling the men and handling the surrender of the conquered army's weapons and battle flags.

What happened in Mr. McLean's parlor that Sunday afternoon was more than the conquest of an army; it was the end of an era, the finish of the way of life which Thomas Jefferson and his contemporaries had foreseen for the nation they had founded. One man more than any other had helped to bring this about. This was Eli Whitney, whose invention of the cotton gin in 1793 had made the dying system of slavery suddenly profitable. His other work, although less well known, was even more important, for his idea of using interchangeable parts in manufacturing was the key to mass-production methods. Whitney was the catalyst whose inventions had set both the South and the North aflame and had caused their armies to march against each other. There were many other issues involved, but they were all tied up in the diametrically opposed interests of the South, which wanted to preserve its patriarchal, aristocratic, easygoing agrarian way of life, while the North wanted to be up and doing — to build new railroads (especially to the Pacific), and to grow or manufacture large quantities of goods that would make their producers rich.

The men gathered in the McLean house stood for these two very different kinds of cultures, and one of those cultures — that which Robert E. Lee represented — was nearing its end that day. Lee was related by marriage to George Washington's family, and he was connected with many other prominent families of the South. He had never been in favor of slavery or the breakup of the Union, but because he had been brought up in Virginia's traditional ways he had chosen to stand with his native state against the nation. Now the nation, which had been tried in the dreadful ordeal of battle, had become supreme, while Virginia was reduced to being a local government with limited powers. The pleasant life which he and his peers had enjoyed for more than a century was outmoded. And the price for all this luxury and ease at last had to be paid. The enslavement of human beings could no longer be tolerated in a progressive world.

The others, the men in blue, differed among themselves as to what they believed the war had been fought for. Some of them perhaps still felt that the conflict which was now ending had been a holy crusade to free the slaves and preserve the integrity of the Union. Certainly many of the soldiers who had died in battle had gone to their deaths believing that. But perhaps too many such idealistic Northern men had been killed on the battlefield; a new breed was rising among the survivors and the civilians — a tough, hard, ruthless lot of men who wanted only power and wealth.

Yet the two sections, the two antagonistic cultures, had common roots in the stern and forthright moral ideas of the men who had settled the American wilderness. On Christmas Day, 1862, just after the victory at Fredericksburg, when the Confederacy seemed most sure of gaining its independence, Lee wrote to his wife a letter that could have been phrased by a seventeenth-century New England divine:

> I will commence this holy day by writing to you. My heart is filled with gratitude to Almighty God for His unspeakable mercies with which He has blessed us in this day, for those He has granted us from the beginning of life, and particularly for those He has vouchsafed us during the past year. What should have become of us without His crowning help and protection? Oh, if our people would only recognize it and cease from vain self-boasting and adulation, how strong would be my belief in final success and happiness to our country! But what a cruel thing is war; to separate and destroy families and friends, and mar the purest joys and happiness God has granted us in this world; to fill our hearts with hatred instead of love for our neighbours, and to devastate the fair face of this beautiful world!

But such earnest, devout fervor was becoming increasingly rare in both the South and the North. Lee's simple humility would have been scoffed at in the coming years when idealism was about to be thrown into the discard, as an examination of the postwar careers of some of the officers gathered in the McLean parlor will show. These men could not, of course, foresee the result of their actions. The intentions of the Union officers were generous that day; their instincts on this occasion were not only kind but noble. Yet the years ahead were to be filled with chaos and corruption, and some of the men in the parlor were to share in making the country for which they had fought into a nation that was to be regarded with shame for a generation to come.

Lee was fifty-eight at the time of the surrender and was not likely to change. He retired from public life to become the president of Washington College in Lexington, Virginia. He had had enough of war; for the five remaining years of his life his influence upon the South was beneficent but remote from the bitter struggle that was taking place around him. And his gentle-mannered aide, Colonel Charles Marshall, whose grand-uncle had been the illustrious John Marshall, the most notable of our Chief Justices of the Supreme Court, also retired from governmental service. He practiced law in Baltimore, and spent many years gathering material about the Confederate command with which he had been so intimately connected.

Other Confederate leaders went into various businesses and professions; many practiced law, and some were eventually permitted to represent their states in Congress. A few joined the United States Army to fight in the Indian campaigns and the Spanish-American War. But generally speaking, the people of the South were a conquered lot who were treated like the inhabitants of a vanquished nation for many years. They had gambled on being strong enough to establish their independence and had lost. Now they had to pay the price every loser must pay. They either withdrew from the mainstream of national life or were pushed out of it. Certainly they were to have very little to say about the management of American affairs for the next ten years.

This does not mean that all the Confederate officers who retired from the national scene led honorable lives. The South, supposedly freed from the backwardness of slavery, became a miasma-haunted section where the wrecks of ancient glory slowly fell into decay while a new class of rapacious men took over. These men were not all Northern Carpetbaggers; there were Southern Carpetbaggers as well, and some of them were former Confederate officers. And many of the weapons used by the white-sheeted terrorists of the Ku Klux Klan had been carried by their owners when they served in the Confederate Army. The corruption and the bitter violence that character-ized the next ten years were not sectional. The North had its unholy alliance between business and politics; the South had its "Redeemers," who were grimly determined to re-establish the control of the wealthy conservatives over the former Con-federate states at any price; while the still unsettled West was the stamping ground for disgruntled veterans from both armies who could settle their private grudges at the point of a gun.

Clustered around Ulysses Simpson ("U.S.") Grant, the vic-torious Union general whose spectacular rise from obscurity during the past four years was in accordance with the best American tradition, was a group of men who were to become nationally important when their leader was elected to the Presi-dency in 1868. Several of them were destined to die before that happened. Colonel Theodore Bowers, "gallant little Bowers," as he was called, was to be killed in less than a year, when he accompanied his beloved chief on a trip to West Point and accidentally fell under the wheels of the moving train. Another equally devoted follower did not have long to live. This was Seth Williams, Grant's adjutant general, who was to die of an "inflammation of the brain" in March 1866.

And Grant's closest associate, his fellow townsman from Galena, John Rawlins, was also doomed. During the Appomat-tox Campaign, Rawlins was afflicted with dreadful coughing spells. As soon as Grant was elected, he made Rawlins his Secretary of War. Five months later the newly appointed Secretary was dead, killed by the tuberculosis that was racking his body. Perhaps it was just as well, for anyone who occupied the post of Secretary of War during the Grant administration was in a dangerous and exposed position, as the career of Rawlins' successor, the notorious William W. Belknap,* shows. Even during Rawlins' brief career in the Cabinet, the "honest" general showed signs of coming under the influence of men who were using the Grant administration for their own selfish ends. They won him over to violently expansionist views on Cuba which might have brought on a war with Spain thirty years before it came or have involved the United States in an even more serious conflict with England.

Three of the Union officers in the surrender room were to die soon; two others were content to remain obscure. These were M. R. Morgan and Rufus Ingalls, who stayed in the Army in relatively minor posts and so kept out of trouble.

At least one honest man in that parlor was to have his heart broken because his good friend Grant tried to do him a favor. This was Ely Parker, the Seneca chieftain whom Grant made Commissioner of Indian Affairs in 1869. Parker, who had already suffered snubs at the hands of the white men (he had

---

* Belknap, a general who had made a good record for himself with Sherman, achieved the odd distinction of becoming the most corrupt major Government official in an era when corruption was almost universal. He and his greedy wife sold profitable Army trading posts so openly that he was impeached by the House. He then went to Grant and persuaded him to accept his resignation before the Senate could take action. Once Belknap had resigned, the Senate's jurisdiction became a matter of dispute, and the necessary two-thirds majority vote could not be obtained. Custer's career was damaged because he was remotely connected with the Belknap impeachment trial. He was summoned from the West to testify about the selling of Army trading posts, and even though he had very little to say about the subject, he incurred Grant's disfavor, for Grant was very protective about his venal Secretary of War. It was under the shadow of this disfavor that the ordinarily lighthearted and outgoing Custer went to his death at Little Big Horn in an atmosphere of deep depression and uncertainty. It has even been said that he was unconsciously seeking suicide.

studied law but was not admitted to the bar because he was
not a citizen, and he had had trouble getting a commission in
the Army because of his racial origin), was then to undergo
the crowning indignity of his life. As Commissioner of Indian
Affairs he tried to improve the lot of his fellow Indians and
necessarily interfered with one of the shabbiest but most profitable areas of corruption in a nation that had gone money
mad. He was brought before the House of Representatives on
trumped-up charges, and although found innocent, he resigned
and severed all official connection with the Government that
had treated him so badly.

Horace Porter took an active part in the Grant administration but he managed to keep clear of its scandals. Like many
other former Union officers, he became a railroad man and
allied himself with the Vanderbilt interests; he also was vice
president of the Pullman Company.

Adam Badeau was to spend many years working for Grant
as his personal historian. He claimed that only he and Rawlins
really understood the enigmatic general and once told Henry
Adams that Grant was "an intermittent energy, immensely
powerful when awake, but passive and plastic in repose." He
also said that he and Rawlins did not know why Grant succeeded, but that they believed in him simply because he did
succeed.

Perhaps that was why the American people believed in Grant
long enough to elect him to a second term. It was during this
second term that the gigantic frauds, which had been kept fairly
well hidden from the public during Grant's first term of office,
began coming to light in one shocking exposure after another.
Grant himself was not connected with his friends' dishonesty,
although members of his family and of his wife's family bene-
fited from some of the unsavory deals. Grant's reputation
shrank so badly that public esteem for him was not revived
until he struggled courageously to finish the writing of his

Memoirs before cancer ended his life in 1885. Like many others who strive for power, Grant was at his best while fighting for his spurs; once he had won them, he became arbitrary in his judgment and sometimes unreasonable in his dealings with people.

Nor was Grant the only top Union commander in the McLean parlor whose postwar career proved to be a letdown. Sheridan, the fighting cavalry leader who was so superb in battle, turned out to be as inept as Grant at handling civilian affairs and had to be removed from the administration of the troubled military district comprising Louisiana and Texas. It was only when he was sent to the West with the Indian-fighting cavalry that Sheridan again became his former soldierly self. And then, as he grew older, the hard-riding cavalry general became gross and corpulent from indulging in too much rich food. He died at fifty-seven of a heart attack.

There remains only one other figure, an officer whose career has thus far been so insignificant that his chief duty was to act as a messenger for Grant. This was Lieutenant Colonel Orville E. Babcock, the man who had carried the instructions from Grant to Sheridan that broke Warren at the Battle of Five Forks and who had also delivered Grant's last letter of April 9 to Lee and had then accompanied the Confederate commander to the McLean house. This hitherto obscure creature was to become the Cerberus of the Grant administration. To win a favor, to make a deal, to get a hearing, or to have something quashed, one needed Babcock, because he had Grant's ear and knew all the devious ins and outs of the national Government. Grant made him a general, sent him abroad on confidential missions, and put him in charge of the administration of Washington's public grounds and buildings at a time when the city was rich for plunder because it was then being extensively rebuilt. Everything Babcock did brought him money until he became such a well-known conniver that Grant, after making a desperate attempt to save his faithless follower's skin, reluctantly had to get rid of him.

These, then, were the victors at Appomattox. To them, according to the cynical precept which had been proclaimed on the floor of the Senate in 1832, belonged the spoils. Into the hands of these military men, American destiny was to be placed for a generation to come. How they and their civilian backers robbed the nation, ravaged its natural resources, tried to exterminate its original inhabitants, the Indians, by slaughtering the vast buffalo herds, and out of the waste and wreckage of a continent managed to make personal fortunes for themselves is a familiar story to Americans who know anything about the history of their own country. These men left us a heritage of evil that still runs like a dark and muddied stream below the surface of American life. Fortunately, the only physical relics of theirs which we still have to live with are some of the ugliest public buildings ever constructed anywhere in the world.

Oddly enough, none of the Union officers in the McLean house ever became very rich. As soon as they accumulated some wealth they lost it to the same kind of civilian advisers who had helped them gain it. They were only pawns; in the final game for the really big stakes military rank did not count.

On that quiet Sunday afternoon at Appomattox, power was being taken from the former slaveholders to be handed over to the shrewd, greedy men who had been waiting in the financial sections of various Northern cities for just such a chance. The slaveholders had built their unsteady structure of wealth and power on the exploitation of Negroes whom they owned outright, and whom they had to support when illness or old age rendered them useless. The new rulers were smarter; they exploited all kinds of labor, black, white, or yellow, and assumed no responsibility for the worn-out hulks of men whose lives, like raw materials, were used up in the process. The valor displayed on the battlefield was now to be replaced by naked greed. The day of the bitch-goddess had come.

Even the outrageously fraudulent Hayes-Tilden election of 1876 did not unduly disturb the American people, who by this time had grown completely cynical about corruption. But that election marked the real end of the Civil War. The Republicans maneuvered Hayes into office by a single electoral vote, which was obtained by shamelessly reshuffling the votes of three "reconstructed" Southern states until the necessary majority was gained. In order to persuade the Democrats to agree to this highhanded procedure, the Republicans had to give back control of the South to its former masters, thus abandoning the central principle for which the war had been fought.

This was to be the price of victory, this was the blind deal that was made at Appomattox. During the conference with Lee and Marshall, Grant and his staff had offered generous terms and had behaved exceedingly well. But these Union officers were going to be manipulated by men of wealth and power who stood ready to sack a continent.

On the night of April 9, these grotesque creatures were far from the battlefront, waiting in rooms more elaborately furnished than Mr. McLean's simple parlor to hear that the business at Appomattox was done. Then they would drink loud and boisterous toasts to the soldiers who had done the fighting and wanted only to be finished with killing or being killed.

Sunday, April 9, 1865, marked a beginning as well as an end. On that night in Vienna, Austria, in an experimental shop at 107 Mariahilferstrasse, a young inventor named Siegfried Marcus was about to set in motion a mechanical device that was to change the world in less than two generations. He wheeled out a clumsy-looking vehicle powered by a homemade internal-combustion engine, which he started by rapidly revolving one of the rear wheels. The machine sputtered and roared and then rolled down the street. At that moment the age of the automobile began.

18

The End of the Army of Northern Virginia

Sunday, April 9, to Thursday, April 13

WHILE THE FATE of the nation was being settled in Mr. McLean's parlor, the soldiers of both armies waited anxiously along the Lynchburg Pike. Sentinels had been posted to stop the Union troops from straying into the Confederate lines, but no one had said anything about keeping the Confederates out. They wandered across the road, eager to swap trinkets, souvenirs, and almost anything they owned for the food they needed so badly. They were served real coffee with condensed milk and sugar. One Union soldier had managed to obtain a little butter from a farmhouse somewhere along the road. The Confederates looked at this admiringly, taking it for granted that such a luxury was a regular part of the obviously well-fed Union Army's daily issue of rations. And while the men fraternized, they exchanged stories about what had really happened at various places along the retreat route.

Their officers talked too. Many of them knew each other well. Some preserved the formalities of the occasion; others forgot their military manners and spoke fondly about the old days when their wives and families had moved in the same intimate circle of United States Army life.

General John Gibbon, commander of the Twenty-fourth Corps of the Army of the James, was talking to Longstreet and

Harry Heth when General Cadmus M. Wilcox rode up on a sorry-looking old horse. It was a warm day, but the Confederate general was wearing a long gray overcoat. He dismounted and shook hands with everybody. Then one of the Union officers asked him if he was cold. He shook his head and said, "This coat is all I have. Sheridan got our baggage." He opened the coat to show them that a tattered shirt was the only garment he wore underneath it.

In front of the McLean house the three most famous horses of the war were cropping the tender spring grass. Here was Lee's beloved Traveller, veteran of countless battles. Near him were Grant's Cincinnati and Sheridan's immortal Rienzi. The horses moved slowly across the lawn, seeking fresh grass while their owners' orderlies kept close watch over them.

On the broad wooden steps of the house, some Union officers waited for the business going on inside to end. The sound of chairs being shoved back on the floor of the McLean parlor gave them their signal. They stood up and waited expectantly. Forsyth, of Sheridan's command, closed a notebook in which he had been writing and took up a position to the left of the entrance door where he could lean against the railing and watch the top officers come out. He wrote a detailed account of what happened during the next few minutes: "The inner door slowly opened, and General Lee stood before me. . . . This is what I saw: A finely formed man, apparently about sixty years of age, well above the average height, with a clear, ruddy complexion — just then suffused by a deep crimson flush, that rising from his neck overspread his face and even slightly tinged his broad forehead, which, bronzed where it had been exposed to the weather, was clear and beautifully white where it had been shielded by his hat — deep brown eyes, a firm but well-shaped Roman nose, abundant gray hair, silky and fine in texture, with a full gray beard and mustache, neatly trimmed and not over-long, but which, nevertheless, almost completely concealed his mouth. A splendid uniform of Confederate gray cloth, that had evidently seen but little service, was closely buttoned about him, and fitted him to perfection. An exquisitely mounted sword, attached to a gold-embroidered Russia-leather belt, trailed loosely on the floor at his side, and in his right hand he carried a broad-brimmed, soft, gray felt hat, encircled by a golden cord, while in his left he held a pair of buckskin gauntlets. Booted and spurred, still vigorous and erect, he stood bareheaded, looking out of the open doorway, sad-faced and weary: a soldier and a gentleman, bearing himself in defeat with an all-unconscious dignity that sat well upon him. . . . As General Lee stepped out onto the porch, every hand was raised in military salute. Placing his hat on his head, he mechanically but courteously returned it, and slowly crossed the porch to the head of the steps leading down to the yard, meanwhile keeping his eyes intently fixed in the direction of the little valley over beyond the Court-house, in which his army lay. Here he paused, and slowly drew on his gauntlets, smiting his gloved hands into each other several times after doing so, evidently utterly oblivious of his surroundings. Then, apparently recalling his thoughts, he glanced deliberately right and left, and not seeing his horse, he called, in a hoarse, half-choked voice, 'Orderly! Orderly!' 'Here, General, here,' was the quick response. The alert young soldier was holding the General's horse near the side of the house. . . .

"Descending the steps, the General passed to the left of the house, and stood in front of his horse's head while he was being bridled. As the orderly was buckling the throat-latch, the General reached up and drew the forelock out from under the brow-band, parted and smoothed it, and then gently patted the gray charger's forehead in an absent-minded way, as one who loves horses, but whose thoughts are far away, might all unwittingly do. Then, as the orderly stepped aside, he caught up the bridle-reins in his left hand, and seizing the pommel of the saddle with the same hand, he caught up the slack of the reins in his right hand, and placing it on the cantle he put his foot in the stirrup, and swung himself slowly and wearily, but nevertheless firmly, into the saddle (the old dragoon mount), letting his right hand rest for an instant or two on the pommel as he settled into his seat, and as he did so there broke unguardedly from his lips a long, low, deep sigh, almost a groan in its intensity, while the flush on his neck and face seemed, if possible, to take on a still deeper hue. . . . As soon as the Colonel [Marshall] had mounted, General Lee drew up his reins, and, with the Colonel riding on his left, and followed by the orderly, moved at a slow walk across the yard towards the gate.

"Just as they started, General Grant came out of the house, crossed the porch, and passed down the steps into the yard. At this time he was nearly forty-two years of age, of middle height, not over-weighted with flesh, but, nevertheless stockily and sturdily built, light complexion, mild, gray-blue eyes, finely formed Grecian nose, an iron-willed mouth, brown hair, full brown beard with a tendency toward red rather than black, and in his manner and all his movements there was a strength of purpose, a personal poise, and a cool, quiet air of dignity, decision, and soldierly confidence that were very good to see. On this occasion he wore a plain blue army blouse, with shoulder-straps set with three silver stars equi-distant, designating his rank as Lieutenant-General commanding the armies of the United States; it was unbuttoned, showing a blue military vest, over which and under his blouse was buckled a belt, but he was without a sword. His trousers were dark blue and tucked into top-boots, which were without spurs, but heavily splashed with mud, for once he knew that General Lee was waiting for him at Appomattox Court-house, he had ridden rapidly across country, over road and field and through woods, to meet him. He wore a peculiar stiff-brimmed, sugar-loaf-crowned, campaign hat of black felt, and his uniform was partly covered by a light-weight, dark blue, water-proof, semi-military overcoat, with a full cape, unbuttoned and thrown back, showing the front of his uniform, for while the day had developed into warm, bright, and beautifully sunny weather, the early morning had been damp, slightly foggy, and presaged rain.

"As he reached the foot of the steps and started across the yard to the fence, where, inside the gate, the orderlies were holding his horse and those of several of his staff-officers, General Lee, on his way to the gate, rode across his path. Stopping suddenly, General Grant looked up, and both generals simultaneously raised their hands in military salute. After General Lee had passed, General Grant crossed the yard and sprang lightly and quickly into his saddle."

As soon as Lee and Grant had left McLean's front yard, "relic-hunters charged down upon the manor-house, and began to bargain for the numerous pieces of furniture. Sheridan paid the proprietor twenty dollars in gold for the table on which General Grant wrote the terms of surrender, for the purpose of presenting it to Mrs. Custer, and handed it over to her dashing husband, who galloped off to camp bearing it upon his shoulder. Ord paid forty dollars for the table at which Lee sat, and afterward presented it to Mrs. Grant, who modestly declined it, and insisted that Mrs. Ord should become its possessor. General Sharpe paid ten dollars for the pair of brass candlesticks; Colonel Sheridan, the general's brother, secured the stone inkstand; and General Capehart the chair in which Grant sat.... Captain O'Farrell of Hartford became the possessor of the chair in which Lee sat. A child's doll was found in the room, which the young officers tossed from one to the other, and called the 'silent witness. . . .' Bargains were at once struck for nearly all the articles in the room; and it is even said that some mementos were carried off for which no coin of the republic was ever exchanged."

McLean did not want to sell his household possessions which had suddenly taken on historic significance and is said to have flung the proffered money down on the floor in disdain. This gesture, however, had no effect on the eager souvenir seekers. They not only took possession of the more important articles of furniture but even cut upholstery fabric and chair caning to fragments so they could carry away something from the famous surrender house. And the rank and file, who were not permitted to enter, overran the garden and stripped it of flowers to press and send home.

Many of the Union soldiers who were not allowed to approach the McLean house decided that bits of wood from the apple tree under which Lee had rested would make good souvenirs. They began by cutting off snippets from the branches, "then one of them, a lusty Maine fellow, seized an ax and within ten minutes every bit of the wood was cut up into convenient pieces for mementos. Not satisfied with this they dug up the roots and tendrils, and within an hour all that was left to mark the spot was a hole in the ground deep enough to bury a horse."

Meanwhile, active trading was going on between the men who had been shooting at each other only a few hours before. The Confederates needed money to get home, and some of the officers who still owned a fine horse (fine even though it was somewhat gaunt and bony), were willing to sell their last valuable possession in order to reach the nearest railroad or steamship connection as quickly as possible. They knew they could go there on foot or on a poorer mount and then hurry home. Presentation swords and elaborately chased revolvers or imported sharpshooter's rifles also brought good prices. And sometimes the buyer knowingly or unknowingly acquired a horse or a weapon that had originally come from the North.

The sound of artillery fire came from somewhere in the distance. At first everyone was afraid the fighting had started again, but experienced officers examined their watches and soon noted that the guns were being discharged at regularly timed intervals, which meant that someone was firing an un-authorized salute in celebration of the victory. Then there was a burst of rifle shots from a point nearer at hand where the colored troops were joyously shooting off their guns to welcome the long awaited day of jubilee. Grant was opposed to all such unauthorized firing of weapons, fearing that the warlike noise might cause trouble, so he sent couriers to silence all the guns, and the fields around Appomattox at last became quiet.

The indefatigable telegraph corps was busy stringing wires on temporary poles to connect Appomattox Court House with the main line along the Southside Railroad, where train service had already been restored as far west as Burkeville. On his way back to his headquarters tent, which had been pitched near the Lynchburg Pike west of the village, Grant was reminded that he had not yet officially notified the War Department of Lee's surrender. He got off his horse, sat down on a stone by the side of the road, and wrote out the words which were soon to be flashed all over the United States:

> HEADQUARTERS ARMIES OF THE UNITED STATES
> April 9, 1865 — 4:30 p.m.
>
> Hon. E. M. STANTON
>   Secretary of War:
> General Lee surrendered the Army of Northern Virginia this afternoon upon terms proposed by myself. The accompanying additional correspondence will show the conditions fully.
>
>   U.S. GRANT,
>   Lieutenant-General

Then he rode through a light April shower to his tent. There his staff and his leading commanders gathered around

him, eager to hear what he might have to say about the surrender. But he did not even mention it and began to talk with
Ingalls, who had been with him in the Mexican War, about an
old white mule that had behaved badly when they went on a
sight-seeing trip to Popocatepetl.

As Lee rode through the ranks of his vanquished army, the
men reacted in various ways to the dreaded news of surrender.
Some cursed at the Yankees, others wept openly, and still others,
knowing that the job was done and over with, took the announcement stoically and began to talk about the quickest way
of getting home. No one blamed Lee for what had happened;
he took on even greater stature in the eyes of the men who had
fought with him.

But Lee himself was depressed, and he was in what one of
his engineers called "a savage mood." He did what he had to
do for the rest of the day, and he reluctantly received a few
Union Army officers who asked to be presented to him. Finally
he went into his headquarters tent, wanting only to be alone.

A file of men carrying boxes of hardtack, followed by army
wagons filled with all kinds of rations, entered the Confederate
lines. With them came beef cattle from the Union herd, which
were slaughtered on the spot and cut up into strips of meat
that were still blood-warm when distributed. Campfires blazed
on the surrounding hills, and the odor of roasting meat filled
the valley. Then the men of both armies prepared to sleep.
Custer, to whom an old Army friend was still a friend no matter
what color uniform he wore, put up a number of Confederate
officers for the night.

Clouds again rolled across the sky, and the smell of rain
hung heavily in the warm spring air. One of the men who was
there described the night when the armies had ceased fighting
for the first time in four years: "The fires are burning low,

and only here and there can we see a man with clasped knees still looking into the failing blaze. Hark! the first bugle is sounding 'taps,' and ... if you have never heard it blown on the field, you will not realize the depth of its moving tones; that call, to be at its best, must be heard on the edge of a battlefield and in the presence of an enemy. Then the night-enveloped neighboring fields and woods, and the vaulted skies seem to lend each note some of their own subdued, sweetly-lamenting loneliness. One by one, camp after camp, battery after battery, is sounding the call, and now the last one — oh, trumpeter, you nor any other will ever blow its like again — is dying away, dying over the field of Appomattox — its last note lingers as if reluctant to go, it is fading, it is gone."

And then, after the last bugle note had died away, and the rain began to fall gently on the open fields, one of Sheridan's bands began to play very softly the plaintive notes of "Home, Sweet Home."

It was still raining the next morning when Grant and Lee met again. Lee had asked Marshall to draft a final order to the Army of Northern Virginia, an order in which he would thank the troops for their services and bid them farewell. This was not easy to write, and Marshall had understandably delayed putting the words down on paper. Before Lee rode off to keep his appointment with Grant, he told Marshall to get into his headquarters ambulance and stay there until he had the message prepared. Then he posted an orderly at the door of the ambulance to make sure Marshall was not disturbed.

Lee found Grant waiting for him just outside the village on a little hill from which one could look down over the North Fork of the Appomattox River and see the Confederates who were camping in the valley around it. A good many Union officers had come to the hillside to get a good look at their celebrated opponent, but they were ordered to stand back while the two top generals sat on their horses, talking together in the rain. Grant left an account of the conference: "We had ... a very pleasant conversation of over half an hour, in the course of which Lee said to me that the South was a big country and that we might have to march over it three or four times before the war entirely ended, but that we would now be able to do it as they could no longer resist us. He expressed it as his earnest hope, however, that we would not be called upon to cause more loss and sacrifice of life; but he could not foretell the result. I then suggested to General Lee that there was not a man in the Confederacy whose influence with the soldiery and the whole people was as great as his, and that if he would now advise the surrender of all the armies I had no doubt his advice would be followed with alacrity. But Lee said, that he could not do that without consulting the President first. I knew there was no use to urge him to do anything against his ideas of what was right."

Then some of Grant's officers asked permission to enter the Confederate lines in order to see some of their old friends. There was much fraternizing among the officers of both armies that morning. Some of the Confederates were brought to the McLean house to be presented to Grant, who sat for a while on the porch. Later he rode off with his staff to Burkeville to get a train to City Point so he could return to Washington, for he wanted to cut down army expenses, which were then running about four million dollars a day.

The railroad line from Burkeville to City Point had been repaired, but the work had been done so hastily that Grant's train ran off the track three times, and there were so many delays that he did not reach the end of the line until 5 A.M. on April 12. A newspaper correspondent at City Point told how the victorious general arrived there in the early dawn: "While standing on the platform in the dim light, I saw General Grant emerge from a car.... He had a dusty, dingy look. His high boots were covered with mud, and he had a quiet, unconcerned look about him. He presented anything but the appearance of a great conqueror. He was smoking a cigar, and as he strolled along the platform, he had his hands in his trousers pockets, and he bent forward as he walked carelessly along. I noticed him glance back at the rear car, and turning to one of his staff, he remarked: 'I suppose those men know enough to take care of the horses?' "

Upon being assured that everything would be all right, Grant "shambled along the platform" to rejoin his wife. She and some of the wives of staff officers had prepared a festive meal for him and had tried to stay up until he arrived. But they had fallen asleep before dawn and had to be awakened. The food was served for breakfast, and with the eating of it, Grant's part in the great Appomattox Campaign came to an end.

Throughout the North, where the fall of Richmond was still being celebrated, the even greater news of the surrender of General Lee's long feared Army of Northern Virginia caused a fresh outburst of public rejoicing. Still more thunderous artillery salutes were fired, bands played martial music, and people thronged the streets day and night, feeling certain that the other Confederate armies must surrender soon and that Jefferson Davis and his fleeing cabinet members would be captured, imprisoned, and perhaps hanged. But nowhere through the United States was word from Appomattox received with more enthusiasm than in the Union armies in the field.

The Twenty-third Army Corps was on its way to Raleigh in the campaign against Johnston. The men had already heard that Richmond had fallen and that Lee was in full retreat somewhere in western Virginia. An orderly from Sherman's headquarters rode up to the commanding general, who was proceeding quietly along the road at the head of a long column of marching troops. A captain who was riding with the general tells how the message was received: "General Cox opened [the dispatch] and read it over as he would have done an ordinary official communication. There was nothing in the manner of the messenger to indicate that he was the bearer of any unusual or important news, and he sat listlessly on his horse while a receipt was being written. . . . In great excitement he [the general] turned and directed that his escort and staff be drawn up in line that he might read to them a message from General Sherman. It was done in a hurry, and with head uncovered he read a brief dispatch. . . . It was the message long looked for, long fought for, and although it came to us on the roadside so unexpectedly, its full significance was at once appreciated. It meant home and wife and children and happy meetings throughout the land. Such cheers as rang through that North Carolina pine thicket . . . were never heard before or since. . . . My horse became frightened, and quick as a flash he whirled around . . . at full speed toward the approaching column. I had hardly checked his rapid stride when the thought flashed upon me that it would be a glorious thing to carry the news to the twenty thousand men of the Twenty-fifth Army Corps, who were all marching on the broad road before me, all unconscious of the glad tidings that awaited them. . . . Spurring up and giving free rein to the excited horse, he flew over the ground. . . . Soon I came in sight of the first column. . . . They had heard our cheers, and as they saw me coming down the road at full speed, with hat off, waving for a clear road by which to pass, they opened ranks to the right and left. . . . As soon as I was within shouting distance I cried out, 'Lee with his whole army has surrendered to Grant; make way for the bearer of the glorious news!' Then their wild cheers rang out. . . . Onward I pressed my way through the surging ranks, before me an open road, on each side anxious men leaning forward to catch the first sound of the good news . . . behind me a crowd of men suddenly transformed into lunatics . . . pounding each other with knapsacks, waving blankets on the points of their bayonets, pounding canteens with belt buckles, and making a pandemonium of sounds. . . . One of the soldiers said: 'Great God, you're the man I've been looking for for the last four years!' "

The formalities of surrender had been complied with at the McLean house on the afternoon of April 9, but Grant insisted that the weapons and battle flags of the Army of Northern Virginia be officially given up. The three generals from each army who were in charge of this and of the issuing of paroles went into conference. It was agreed among them that parole blanks could be printed on a portable press which General John Gibbon had with him in one of the wagons belonging to the Twenty-fourth Corps. General Joshua Chamberlain was ordered to supervise the surrender of the Confederate arms, and the ceremony was scheduled to take place early on April 12. Chamberlain wrote a graphic account of what must have been one of the most spectacular and moving scenes in American history:

"I had been ordered to have my lines formed for the ceremony at sunrise. It was a chill gray morning, depressing to the senses. . . . We formed along the principal street, from the bluff bank of the stream to near the Court House on the left, to face the last line of battle, and receive the last remnant of the arms and colors of that great army which ours had been created to confront. . . . We were remnants also: Massachusetts, Maine, Michigan, Maryland, Pennsylvania, New York; veterans, and replaced veterans; cut to pieces, cut down, consolidated, divisions into brigades, regiments into one. . . .

"Our earnest eyes scan the busy groups on the opposite slopes, breaking camp for the last time, taking down their little shelter-tents and folding them carefully as precious things, then slowly forming ranks as for unwelcome duty. And now they move. The dusky swarms forge forward into gray columns of march. On they come, with the old swinging route step and swaying battleflags. In the van, the proud Confederate ensign — the great field of white with canton of star-strewn cross of blue on a field of red, the regimental battle-flags with the same escutcheon following on, crowded so thick, by thinning out of men, that the whole column seemed crowned with red. At the right of our line our little group mounted beneath our flags, the red Maltese cross on a field of white. . . .

"The momentous meaning of this occasion impressed me deeply. I resolved to mark it by some token of recognition, which could be no other than a salute of arms. . . . Instructions had been given; and when the head of each division column comes opposite our group, our bugle sounds the signal and instantly our whole line from right to left, regiment by regiment in succession, gives the soldier's salutation, from the 'order arms' to the old 'carry' — the marching salute. Gordon at the head of the column, riding with heavy spirit and downcast face, catches the sound of shifting arms, looks up, and, taking the meaning, wheels superbly, making with himself and his horse one uplifted figure, with profound salutation as he drops the point of his sword to the boot toe; then facing to his own command, gives word for his successive brigades to pass us with the same position of the manual, honor answering honor. On our part not a sound of trumpet more, nor roll of drum; not a cheer, nor word nor whisper of vainglorying, nor motion of man standing again at the order, but an awed stillness rather, and breath-holding, as if it were the passing of the dead! As each successive division masks our own, it halts, the men face inward towards us across the road, twelve feet away; then carefully dress their line, each captain taking pains for the good appearance of his company, worn and half-starved, as they were. The field and staff take their positions in the intervals of regiments; generals in rear of their commands. They fix bayonets, stack arms; then, hesitatingly, remove cartridge-boxes and lay them down. Lastly — reluctantly, with agony of expression — they tenderly fold their flags, battle-worn and torn, blood-stained, heart-holding colors, and lay them down; some frenziedly rushing from the ranks, kneeling over them, clinging to them, pressing them to their lips with burning tears. And only the Flag of the Union greets the sky!

"What visions thronged as we looked into each other's eyes! Here pass the men of Antietam, the Bloody Lane, the Sunken Road, the Cornfield, the Burnside-Bridge; the men whom Stonewall Jackson on the second night at Fredericksburg begged Lee to let him take and crush the two corps of the Army of the Potomac huddled in the streets in darkness and confusion; the men who swept away the Eleventh Corps at Chancellorsville; who left six thousand of their companions around the bases of Culp's and Cemetery Hills at Gettysburg; these survivors of the terrible Wilderness, the Bloody-Angle at Spotsylvania, the slaughter pen of Cold Harbor, the whirlpool of Bethesda Church!

"Here comes Cobb's Georgia Legion, which held the stone wall on Marye's Heights at Fredericksburg, close before which we piled our dead for breastworks so that the living might stay alive.

"Here too come Gordon's Georgians and Hoke's North Carolinians, who stood before the terrific mine explosion at Petersburg, and advancing retook the smoking crater and the dismal heaps of dead — ours more than theirs — huddled in the ghastly chasm.

"Here are the men ... who broke the Fifth Corps lines on the White Oak Road, and were so desperately driven back on that forlorn night of March 31st by my thrice-decimated brigade. . . . Here passes the proud remnant of Ransom's North Carolinians which we swept through Five Forks ten days ago,

and all the little that was left of this division in the sharp
passages at Sailor's Creek five days thereafter.

"Now makes its last front A. P. Hill's old Corps, Heth now
at the head, since Hill had gone too far forward ever to return:
the men who poured destruction into our division at Shepards-
town Ford, Antietam, in 1862, when Hill reported the Potomac
running blue with our bodies; the men who opened the desperate first day's fight at Gettysburg. . . .

"Now the sad great pageant — Longstreet and his men! What
shall we give them for greeting that has not already been spoken
in volleys of thunder and written in lines of fire on all the
riverbanks of Virginia?

"Now comes the sinewy remnant of fierce Hood's Division,
which at Gettysburg we saw pouring through the Devil's Den,
and the Plum Run gorge; turning again by the left our stubborn Third Corps, then swarming up the rocky bastions of
Round Top, to be met there by equal valor, which changed
Lee's whole plan of battle and perhaps the story of Gettysburg.

"Is this Pickett's Division? — this little group left of those
who on the lurid last day of Gettysburg breasted level cross-fire
and thunderbolts of storm, to be strewn back drifting wrecks,
where after that awful, futile, pitiful charge we buried them
in graves a furlong wide, with names unknown!

"Met again in the terrible cyclone-sweep over the breastworks at Five Forks; met now, so thin, so pale, purged of the
mortal — as if knowing pain or joy no more. . . .

"Thus, all day long, division after division comes and goes,
surrendered arms being removed by our wagons in the intervals, the cartridge-boxes emptied in the street. . . .

"The last flag . . . came in borne by a little remnant of a
regiment. . . . The poor fellows . . . clung to the old flag, battle-
smoked and blood-stained as if it were dearer than life to
them. . . . As the color-bearer delivered up the flag he burst
into tears and said: 'Boys, this is not the first time you have

seen that flag. I have borne it in the front of the battle on many victorious fields, and I had rather die than surrender it now. . . .'

"When all is over, in the dusk of evening, the long lines of scattered cartridges are set on fire, and the lurid flames wreathing the blackness of earthly shadows give an unearthly border to our parting."

The fires burning on the hills around Appomattox Court House died down, and soon the paroled Confederates, each bearing a signed slip of paper that entitled him to pass any Union troops he might encounter, started out singly or in groups on the long journeys to their widely scattered homes. And the Union regiments, all still in active service, began to be withdrawn in marching order in the general direction of Petersburg.

At Burkeville Junction a vast field hospital had been temporarily set up to receive the wounded who were being brought in from the various farmhouses, churches, and schools to which they had been taken. Most of the Confederate wounded had been sent to Farmville, where their own surgeons were in charge. Some of them — especially the more illiterate soldiers, were surprised when their opponents did not shoot them. "What will you 'uns do with we 'uns now?" was the pathetic question asked by mountain boys whose only contact with the Yankees had been across the sights of their guns.

For many days and nights after Appomattox, at the Burkeville field hospital "wagons came creeping over the hills as if to soften the agony of such transportation. . . . The men were laid upon the ground under the shelter of brush, in freight depots, in the open air under extemporized roofs of rubber blankets. . . . There were but few surgeons, and these were overworked at the operating tables, while three thousand men were lying in this squalid suffering. . . . In one row were five men lying on a hard floor, all thigh amputations, and all dying.

Two of them were conscious and were able to gasp out some last words for wife or mother which were written quickly down. . . . In a small room partitioned off from the main shed, were three hopeless cases, placed there that they might breathe their last in peace apart from the noise and excitement of this overcrowded shed — one with a shell wound through both hips, another with an arm and shoulder carried away, and the other with his jaw and face terribly shattered and his tongue half gone."

A thousand of the wounded men were placed in railroad cars that were supposed to start for City Point before dark. But when night came on, the train had not moved because the surgeon in charge of it could not be found. He was finally located at midnight in a house about half a mile away where he had gone to play cards. The men in the cars had had nothing to eat for twelve hours. Some of them were in great suffering, which could be only slightly alleviated by attendants who went from car to car with buckets of cool water to moisten the fast-drying, fevered wounds. The train did not leave Burkeville until 2 A.M., when a new convoy of wagons bearing still more wounded arrived.

Candles and medical supplies gave out, and the rain poured down upon the wounded, the exhausted hospital attendants, and the blood-covered surgeons, who were so tired that they could hardly stand on their feet. Thus was the price for Appomattox paid, and while the civilians in the Northern cities caroused in wild celebration, those who had been hurt in the fighting lay suffering in the darkness and the rain.

19

The Lincolns Return to Washington

Wednesday, April 5, to Sunday, April 9

ON APRIL 5, while Grant and Sheridan were still pursuing Lee's retreating army, Mrs. Lincoln led a number of distinguished guests to the wharf in Washington, where their ship left for City Point at 11 A.M. The party included her good friend Senator Charles Sumner, Senator and Mrs. James Harlan and their daughter Mary, who was to marry Robert Lincoln, the Marquis de Chambrun, a liberal young French nobleman who favored the Union cause, and Elizabeth Keckley, Mrs. Lincoln's Negro dressmaker and confidante, who wanted to revisit Petersburg, where she had been born.

Seward, who had returned to Washington only a few days before from a brief visit to City Point to confer with the President, sent this telegram to Lincoln:

> We need your personal sanction to several matters here which are important and urgent in conducting the Government but not at all critical or serious. Are you coming up or shall I go down to you with the papers. The public interest will not suffer by you remaining where you are.

As soon as Lincoln returned to City Point from Richmond he wired to Seward, saying that he did not expect to stay away from Washington for more than two days. The eventful holiday — the only one the President had had during four years of war — was ending. The scene of action had shifted from City Point to western Virginia, where the two armies were facing each other in a running battle that could have only one outcome. But the President had to view the military scene from a distance anyway, and he could do it just as well in Washington — where he was needed — as at City Point.

During the afternoon Seward left the State Department to go to his home on Lafayette Square. It was a mild, cloudy day with an overcast sky that threatened rain, but the overworked Secretary of State wanted to take his daughter Fannie and his son Frederick for a drive in the family carriage. They stopped on Vermont Avenue to pick up one of the young people's friends, a Miss Titus. The coachman got down to close the door for her and, knowing that he had a skittish team, he kept a firm grip on the reins. But something caused the horses to rear, and Frederick Seward, in an effort to help the driver, grabbed at the reins. The sudden gesture frightened the horses even more. Still wanting to be helpful, young Seward tried to get out of the carriage so he could run forward and catch the horses' bridles. They made a movement which was so sudden that it threw him off balance, and he fell to the street. The horses, startled by what was happening behind them, broke away and dashed madly along the avenue. Secretary Seward tried to get the reins. As he stood up, the runaway team turned quickly into a side street, throwing Seward violently out of the wildly careening vehicle. The horses kept going until they were almost at their stable, but they entered the driveway so fast that one of them stumbled and fell. The terrified girls were then able to climb out of the carriage unhurt.

People gathered around the unconscious form of the Secretary of State as it lay in the street. He was taken to his home, where three doctors examined him and found that he had a broken jaw and a badly smashed shoulder. The jaw was difficult and painful to set. In order to keep the shattered bones firmly in place, a steel collar had to be placed around the injured man's neck.

Telegrams about Seward's accident went to the President at City Point and from him to Grant in the field. A message for Mrs. Lincoln was delivered when her ship stopped at Fortress Monroe. It was then three o'clock in the morning, and the easily disturbed woman, who saw her plans for a pleasant jaunt to Richmond endangered, wired frantically to Stanton: "If it is ascertained that Mr S— is not *fatally* injured, I know that Mr. Lincoln would prefer remaining to meet us — and it does not appear to me, to be a necessity for our returning. Mr. L— will of course use his own discretion about remaining at C — Pt."

Stanton replied reassuringly that the injury was not fatal and told her that he had notified the President that there could be no objection to his remaining at City Point until she arrived. When the ship carrying his wife's party pulled up to the wharf, Lincoln received them graciously on the *River Queen*. He explained that the after-cabin had recently been the scene of two historic conferences (Hampton Roads on February 3 and the meeting with Grant, Sherman, and Porter on March 27 and 28). He then took out his maps and showed them where Grant expected the soon-to-be trapped Confederates to surrender.

Mrs. Lincoln was put out that her husband had already visited Richmond and that he had no intention of going there again, but she had to make the best of it. She took her party up the James on the *River Queen* that afternoon (April 6) while Lincoln returned to the *Malvern* for the night.

At some time during this day Vice President Johnson and his friend, former Senator Preston King of New York, arrived at City Point on their way to visit Richmond. Johnson wanted to talk to the President, but both Porter and Crook state in no uncertain terms that Lincoln refused to see his Vice President and let him go on to Richmond without granting him an interview.

At nine o'clock on Friday, April 7, the *River Queen* returned to City Point from Richmond. Lincoln was at the dock to tell Mrs. Lincoln and her guests that an expedition to Petersburg had been arranged for them. De Chambrun tells how they traveled:

"Our car was an ordinary American car, and we took seats in its centre, grouping ourselves around Mr. Lincoln. In spite of the car's being devoted to Mr. Lincoln's special use, several officers also took their places in it without attracting any remark. Curiosity, it seems, also had induced the negro waiters of the *River Queen* to accompany us. The President, who was blinded by no prejudices against race or color, and who had not what can be termed false dignity, allowed them to sit quietly with us.

"For several miles the train followed the outer line of Federal fortifications. . . . Farther on we crossed the Confederate lines of defence that had protected Petersburg eight days ago; the guns were yet on their mountings, but no human sound troubled . . . that solitude. . . .

"Arrived at Petersburg . . . everything bespoke desolation. All the houses were closed, the shops abandoned or pillaged; crowds of darkies were in the streets greeting and cheering loudly the author of their independence. Every now and then a white man could be seen hastening to take refuge in some house, in order to escape the sight of his conqueror. . . .

"The headquarters were located at the other end of the town; we drove over to them. They occupied a pretty house, around which the vegetation of spring was already luxuriantly developing in this Southern climate. While Mr. Lincoln was in conference with the generals commanding the garrison, we visited this house. . . .

"Soon after we regained our carriages. While we were on
the road . . . to the train, Mr. Lincoln noticed on the roadside
a very tall and beautiful tree. He gave orders to stop the carriage, looked a while at the tree with particular attention, and
then applied himself to defining its peculiar beauty. He
admired the strength of its trunk, the vigorous development of
branches, reminding one of the tall trees of Western forests,
compared it to the great oaks in the shadow of which he had
spent his youth, and strove to make us understand the dis-
tinctive character of these different types. The observations
thus set forth were evidently not those of an artist who seeks
to idealize nature, but of a man who seeks to see it as it really
is; in short, that dissertation about a tree did not reveal an
effort of imagination, but a remarkable precision of mind. . . .

"In the . . . vast plains where the encampments were located
a large area had been reserved for ambulances [temporary field
hospital buildings]. . . . Each army corps had its separate ambulance space. This consisted of a large rectangle of ground
divided by open corridors placed at equal distances from one
another. Between these corridors stood a row of tents or of
frame huts, each of which was capable of containing about
twenty wounded. One side of these corridors was given up to
officers, the other to privates. At the centre . . . was located a
pharmacy, a kitchen, and that which Americans consider as
always essential — a post-office. . . . A Bible and newspapers were
to be found on nearly every bed. . . .

"Our visit began with the hospitals of the Fifth Corps. Mr.
Lincoln went from one bed to another, saying a friendly word
to each wounded man, or at least giving him a handshake. . . .
Following Mr. Lincoln . . . we reached a bed on which lay a
dying man; he was a captain, aged twenty-four years, who had
been noticed for his bravery. Two of his friends were near
him; one held his hand, while the other read a passage from
the Bible in a low voice. Mr. Lincoln walked over to him
and took hold of his other hand, which rested on the bed.

We formed a circle around him, and every one of us remained silent. Presently the dying man half-opened his eyes; a faint smile passed over his lips. It was then that his pulse ceased beating."

They returned to City Point by train and had dinner on the *River Queen*. Mrs. Keckley tells how Mrs. Lincoln behaved that evening: "One of the guests was a young officer attached to the Sanitary Commission. He was seated near Mrs. Lincoln, and, by way of a pleasantry, remarked: 'Mrs. Lincoln, you should have seen the President the other day on his triumphal entry into Richmond. He was the cynosure of all eyes. The ladies kissed their hands to him and greeted him with a waving of handkerchiefs. He is quite a hero when surrounded by pretty young ladies.'

"The young officer suddenly paused with a look of embarrassment. Mrs. Lincoln turned to him with flashing eyes, with the remark that his familiarity was offensive to her. Quite a scene followed, and I do not think that the Captain, who incurred Mrs. Lincoln's displeasure, will ever forget that memorable evening. . . ."

The President's holiday was over, and the *River Queen* was being made ready to return to Washington. After the unthinking exposure of the President to the possibility of assassination in Richmond, the men around him now began to smell danger. Barnes's gunboat, the *Bat,* was to act as an escort again, and Admiral Porter put an extra guard on the President's ship. He suddenly became suspicious of its crew and had their records examined for loyalty.

The Secret Service kept itself well posted on rebel plots. One of its agents, William P. Wood, who was also superintendent of the Old Capitol Prison, was using counterspies so he could intercept and copy underground Confederate dispatches before they were sent on to the South. The Government knew about the plot to kidnap the President which John Wilkes Booth and his comic-opera conspirators had bungled in March. It knew also that Booth's most intelligent associate, John Harrison Surratt, had arrived in Washington from Richmond on April 3 and had gone on to Montreal. And anyone who wanted to examine the register of the National Hotel on Saturday, April 8, could have seen entered on one of its pages the bold signature of John Wilkes Booth, who had returned to Washington after an absence of more than a week.

Now the threads of human destiny were beginning to be woven into a dark and tragic pattern. The archconspirator was in Washington; Grant and Lee were approaching an obscure Virginia village named Appomattox Court House; and Abraham Lincoln and his mentally ailing wife were about to leave City Point, where the fifty-six-year-old President, in the midst of battle and turmoil, and burdened with momentous decisions and domestic discord, had been able to forget most of his troubles for a few days.

A military band came on board the *River Queen* to serenade the President. In honor of De Chambrun, Lincoln asked the musicians to play the "Marseillaise," telling his guest that he had to come to America to hear it, for Napoleon III would not permit that revolutionary anthem to be played in France. Then he said that he was going to have the musicians play a tune which he felt could now rightfully be considered to have been recaptured from the rebels. The band struck up "Dixie," and it was to the strains of that celebrated Southern melody of Northern origin that the ship got ready to steam down the river.

They were late in getting away, and it was not until eleven o'clock in the evening that the *River Queen* left City Point and went down the winding river toward the sea. Fifteen

minutes later their escort, the *Bat,* joined them. It was the
night before the full moon, so the way was well lighted. They
reached Hampton Roads before dawn, paused just long enough
to pick up a pilot, and were off again a few minutes before
sunrise. The eastern sky was unusually red that morning, but
the sunlight did not last long, for clouds soon rolled in, driven
from the sea by an east wind that would bring in rain before
night came.

It was April 9, the day of Appomattox, but on the broad
reaches of Chesapeake Bay no one could have any idea of what
was happening 150 miles to the west. The party on the *River
Queen* spent a quiet and restful Sunday. According to De
Chambrun, the conversation was mostly about literary subjects.
Lincoln read passages from Shakespeare aloud. He seemed
especially interested in *Macbeth* and paused after the famous
passage:

> Duncan is in his grave;
> After life's fitful fever he sleeps well;
> Treason has done his worst; nor steel, nor poison,
> Malice domestic, foreign levy, nothing
> Can touch him further.

Then, De Chambrun said, the President was apparently so
impressed by the dark import of the words — which were to
have their dire prophecy realized before the week was over —
that he read them again.

Shortly after three o'clock the water in the *Bat*'s troublesome
boilers began to foam, and the gunboat had to fall behind. The
River Queen slowed down to let Barnes try to catch up, but it
soon became evident that his ship could not keep up the pace.
The *River Queen* went on alone and unguarded. It was still
light when they passed Mount Vernon, where Washington's
imposing mansion faces the river. De Chambrun told the President that he thought Springfield would someday be equally

honored. Lincoln smiled and said that he would be happy to return there in four years so he could live in his home town in peace.

The ship sailed on up the darkening river, bearing its sacrificial victim to the appointed place. No sun could be seen in the clouded sky, but it was time for it to set, and flags were being hauled down in the forts and camps around Washington. The long sad notes of bugles drifted out over the quiet water, and the faint booming of faraway sunset guns could be heard. As they approached the wharf, rain began to fall from the lowering clouds. The streets were wet as the President's carriage drove to the White House, and everything was very quiet, for it was Sabbath and the great news from Appomattox had not yet come.

Despite the night and the rain, the tall form of the President could be seen mounting the steps of Seward's house on Lafayette Square, across the street from the White House. The injured man was in great pain and could hardly talk, but he could listen. Lincoln spent half an hour with him, telling him about City Point and Richmond. Then the Secretary of State sank down into the drug-induced sleep that temporarily wipes out pain, and the President went home.

20

Victory Week

Monday, April 10, to Thursday, April 13

WORD FROM APPOMATTOX reached Washington so late on Sunday night that only a few newspaper men were on hand to hear the news of victory. Among them was Lincoln's friend, young Noah Brooks, who was to replace John Hay as one of the President's secretaries. The rollicking correspondents sent out telegrams from Maine to California and then proceeded to get grandly and gloriously drunk. The city was awakened in a gray and rainy dawn by a tremendous salute of five hundred guns, which were fired one after the other until they had aroused everyone in Washington. Then the muddy streets, Brooks said, "were all alive with people singing and cheering, carrying flags, and saluting everybody, hungering and thirsting for speeches. General Butler was called out, among others, and he made a speech full of surprising liberality and generosity toward the enemy. The departments gave another holiday to their clerks; so did many business firms; and the Treasury employees assembled in the great corridor of their building and sang 'Old Hundredth' with thrilling, even tear-compelling effect. Then they marched in a body across the grounds to the White House, where the President was at breakfast, and serenaded him with 'The Star-Spangled Banner.'

"As the forenoon wore on, an impromptu procession came

up from the navy-yard, dragging six boat-howitzers, which were fired through the streets as they rolled on. This crowd, rein-forced by the hurrahing legions along the route, speedily swelled to enormous proportions, and filled the whole area in front of the White House, where guns were fired and bands played while the multitude waited for a speech. The young hope of the house of Lincoln — Tad — made his appearance at the well-known window from which the President always spoke, and was received with great shouts of applause, whereupon he waved a captured rebel flag, to the uproarious delight of the sovereign people below. When Lincoln came to the window shortly after, the scene before him was one of the wildest confu-sion. It seemed impossible for men adequately to express their feelings. They fairly yelled with delight, threw up their hats again and again, or threw up one another's hats, and screamed like mad. From the windows of the White House the surface of that crowd looked like an agitated sea of hats, faces, and arms. Quiet being restored, the President briefly congratulated the people on the occasion which called out such unrestrained enthusiasm, and said that, as arrangements were being made for a more formal celebration, he would defer his remarks until that occasion; 'for,' said he, 'I shall have nothing to say then if it is all dribbled out of me now.' He said that as the good old tune of 'Dixie' had been captured on the 9th of April, he had submitted the question of its ownership to the Attorney-General, who had decided that that tune was now our lawful property; and he asked that the band should play it, which was done with a will, 'Yankee Doodle' following. Then the President proposed three cheers for General Grant and the officers and men under him, then three cheers for the navy, all of which were given heartily, the President leading off, wav-ing his hand; and the laughing, joyous crowd dispersed."

About five o'clock in the afternoon another crowd assembled on the White House lawn under the mistaken impression that the President had promised to speak to them at that time. He told them briefly that he wanted to prepare his words carefully before he made a formal public address on the crucial issues that were facing the country as a result of the surrender. Then he said he would be ready to present his views on the following evening.

That first day back in Washington had been a busy one for the President. Among other things he had gone with Tad to Alexander Gardner's studio at Seventh and D Streets to have several photographic portraits made. (They were the last ever taken.) And he had found time to write two letters for Tad — one to Stanton asking for some flags and the other to Gideon Welles requesting a Navy sword.

The week following the surrender at Appomattox was one of intermittent rain, during which the sun was seldom seen. Monday, April 10, was the night of the paschal full moon, and by a strange coincidence a partial eclipse was taking place at the very time the brightening satellite was reaching its peak of fullness. But no one in Virginia or Washington saw the gradually darkening shadow creep over the face of the moon at so significant a moment (which would have been an ominous portent to the ancient seers) because the sky was covered with clouds. So if the moon that evening "was sick almost to doomsday with eclipse," the people who were to be involved in the disaster that was being predicted in the shrouded sky were mercifully spared from knowing anything about it. They went about their business as usual, glad that the war seemed so near an end, and there was much coming and going in the whole area between Washington and Appomattox. Everyone was talking about the impending surrender of Johnston to Sherman and wondering what was happening to Jefferson Davis and members of his cabinet, all of whom had apparently disappeared somewhere in the South.

There was much discussion, too, about Kirby Smith, who was in command of all the Confederate forces west of the Mississippi. He was occupying a potentially dangerous area, for it was known that last-minute plans were being made to consolidate Texas, Louisiana, Mississippi, and Arkansas into a new confederacy which might be affiliated in some way with Maximilian's French-supported regime in Mexico. Many people believed that Davis was heading toward this part of the country to take over the reins of government there. And uppermost in everyone's mind was the problem of what was to be done with the former Confederate States that were already under the control of Union armies.

Lincoln's good friend and trusted companion, Ward Hill Lamon, had been approached by a group of speculators who told him that they could get possession of three Confederate steamboats and their cargoes (probably cotton) and bring them through the lines to be sold for a large profit. They had asked him to intercede in their behalf with the President, and on March 23 he had written to Lincoln, saying that the enterprise seemed such a worthy one to him (because the loss of the ships would damage the rebels) that he was willing to supervise the transaction himself. It has never been definitely shown that this venture was the reason for Lamon's applying on April 11 to Lincoln for a pass to go to Richmond with a friend whose name remains unknown. But he did apply, and Lincoln dutifully wrote out the pass. According to Lamon, he was being sent to the former Confederate capital "on business for Mr. Lincoln connected with the call of a convention for reconstruction, about which there had risen some complications." But whatever the reason for Lamon's going, his departure from Washington deprived the President of the services of a physically powerful and personally loyal man who had acted as Lincoln's watchdog all through the war. Just before he left,

Lamon persuaded John P. Usher, Secretary of the Interior, to go with him to the White House to try to make the President promise not to go out at night, "particularly to the theatre."

Lamon reported Lincoln's reply in these words: " 'Usher, this boy is a monomaniac on the subject of my safety. I can hear him or hear of his being around, at all times of the night, to prevent somebody from murdering me. He thinks I shall be killed; and we think he is going crazy.' " He then added: " 'What does any one want to assassinate me for? If any one wants to do so, he can do it any day or night, if he is ready to give his life for mine.' "

So Lamon went off to Richmond. He was never again to see his friend Abraham Lincoln alive.

April 11 was another busy day for the President, because he had to confer with the State Department about the blockade and other maritime matters involving foreign nations. Yet even though he was occupied with major affairs of state, the President still found time to consider the case of a half-breed Indian who had been charged with stealing cattle. An Indian agent had put in a plea for the man, saying that he was badly needed as an interpreter for his tribe, so the ever merciful pen wrote out the words "Pardon & send to tribe."

That night the people of Washington converged upon the White House to hear the President's promised speech on reconstruction. Mrs. Lincoln had written to Sumner and the Marquis de Chambrun, inviting them to come to the White House as her guests. She also had present Miss Clara Harris, the young daughter of Senator Ira Harris of New York.

Noah Brooks describes the President's last public address. "The night was misty, and the exhibition was a splendid one. The reflection of the illuminated dome of the Capitol on the moist air above was remarked as being especially fine; it was seen many miles away. Arlington House, across the river, the old home of Lee, was brilliantly lighted, and rockets and colored lights blazed on the lawn, where ex-slaves by the thousand sang 'The Year of Jubilee. . . .'

"An immense throng of people . . . with bands, banners, and loud huzzahs, poured into the semicircular avenue in front of the Executive Mansion. After repeated calls, loud and enthusiastic, the President appeared at the window, which was a signal for a great outburst. There was something terrible in the enthusiasm with which the beloved Chief Magistrate was received. Cheers upon cheers, wave after wave of applause, rolled up, the President patiently standing quiet until it was over. . . . It began with the words, now classic, 'We meet this evening, not in sorrow, but in gladness of heart. The evacuation of Petersburg and Richmond, and the surrender of the principal insurgent army, give hope of a righteous and speedy peace, whose joyous expression cannot be restrained. . . .'

"While the crowd was assembling in front of the house, and before the President went up-stairs to the window from which he was to speak, I was with him, and noticed that his speech was written out, and that he carried a roll of manuscript in his hand. He explained that this was a precaution to prevent a repetition of the criticisms which had sometimes been made . . . upon his offhand addresses. . . . From a point of concealment behind the window drapery I held a light while he read, dropping the pages of his written speech one by one upon the floor as he finished them. Little Tad . . . scrambled around on the floor, importuning his father to give him 'another,' as he collected the sheets of paper fluttering from the President's hand. Outside was a vast sea of faces, illuminated by the lights that burned in the festal array of the White House, and stretching far out into the misty darkness. It was a silent, intent, and perhaps surprised, multitude. Within stood the tall, gaunt figure of the President, deeply thoughtful, intent upon the elucidation of the generous policy which should be pursued toward the South. That this was not the sort of speech which the multitude had expected is tolerably certain. In the hour of his triumph as the patriotic chief magistrate of a great people, Lincoln appeared to think only of the great problem which would demand the highest statesmanship, the greatest wisdom, and the firmest generosity."

Standing in the crowd on the White House grounds were two sinister figures who went almost unnoticed in the dense throng. They were the handsome young actor, John Wilkes Booth, and the only one of his ill-assorted gang of conspirators who was to strike fiercely and unafraid. This was the giant former Confederate soldier, Lewis Paine, who later told Major Thomas T. Eckert that Booth, after seeing the man he hated most, had said: "That is the last speech he will ever make." It was at this time that Booth is believed to have changed his plot to abduct the President to a plot to kill.

Elihu Washburne, Grant's good friend from Galena and his sponsor in Congress, had come down to visit Appomattox. While he was riding to Burkeville to get a train to Washington, he was accompanied by a mixed group of Union and Confederate officers. Among them was Lee's artillery commander, General E. P. Alexander, who was on his way to Washington to ask the Brazilian minister to help him obtain a job in his far-off country. Alexander asked Washburne if he had any idea of what Lincoln was going to do about the reconstruction of the Southern states. Washburne said that he had discussed the matter recently with the President and that his ideas on the subject would "not only astonish the South but ... Europe and foreign nations as well." He predicted that within a year Lincoln would be as popular in the South as he was in the North; he also hinted that some kind of plan for compensating the slaveowners for the loss of their property was under consideration.

Perhaps the future of the South could not have been settled as easily as Washburne thought. Another party of Congressmen, the little group of grim investigators who made up the Joint Committee on the Conduct of the War, were visiting Richmond, traveling on the steamer *Baltimore*. They had invited B. B. French, Commissioner of Public Buildings in Washington, to be their guest. On the morning of April 12, French went ashore to get the newspapers. Among those he brought back to the ship was a copy of that day's Richmond *Whig*, which contained an address to the people of Virginia signed by members of the new Virginia State Legislature which Judge Campbell was trying to assemble. The address was endorsed by General Weitzel, which seemed to give it more official standing than it actually deserved, for later in the day Lincoln telegraphed Weitzel withdrawing his endorsement of the proposed Legislature. When Ben Wade of Ohio, one of the most extreme radical Republicans in the Senate, heard the newspaper story read aloud, he made a statement which impressed French so strongly that he wrote it down. He reported that "Mr. Wade said in substance, if not in exact words, that there had been much talk of the *assassination* of Lincoln — that if he authorized the approval of that paper . . . by God, the sooner he was assassinated the better!" None of the others seemed shocked by this denunciation, French said, and added that Senator Zachariah Chandler of Michigan "was also exceedingly harsh in his remarks."

On April 11, Jefferson Davis and his entourage reached Greensboro, North Carolina, after having left Danville, Virginia, in a great hurry the night before. Grant's men were close behind them, while Sherman's army was between them and the sea. They received a rather poor reception in the piedmont town where Union sentiment had been unusually strong, and only George Trenholm, Secretary of the Confederate Treasury, was given first-rate quarters at the home of one of the city's wealthiest residents, who hoped in this way to salvage some of the money he had sunk in Confederate bonds and currency. Word was spreading that the fleeing government had many millions of dollars worth of gold with it. The rumor was not only embarrassing but was also endangering the safety of the expedition. In order to prevent trouble, Captain William H. Parker and his sixty midshipmen were sent on to Charlotte with most of the treasure (about $425,000). Davis was put up at the home of one of his first wife's relatives, while the rest of the Confederate government made their temporary head-quarters in an old boxcar in which they slept, ate, and carried on what little official business there was left to do.

While the most important internal issue ever to face the people of the United States was being settled by force of arms, the shrewd speculators, the big plungers, and the little jackals were all trying to profit from disturbances in the violently upset economy. That indefatigable professional doer-of-favors, Orville H. Browning, was making his daily rounds of the Government departments; despite his Copperhead reputation, he still had the ear of the President. On the day the Battle of Five Forks was being fought on April 1, two Southerners were brought to him by "General" Singleton. One was W. J. Bibb of Montgomery, Alabama; the other was Benjamin F. Ficklin, who had been in Europe as an agent for the Confederate government to purchase ships for blockade running. Ficklin was reported to have been "one of the loudest talking seccessionists at the Kirkwood House" when the war began, and it was said that he had had to leave Montgomery because he had killed a man there. The two men had had to wait for the President's return and had taken quarters in a boardinghouse on Capitol Hill near Browning.

Ficklin had just come through the lines from Richmond with certain papers belonging to Mrs. Lincoln's widowed half sister,

Mrs. Emilie Todd Helm. These papers, which undoubtedly had to do with the cotton which Mrs. Helm was trying to bring out of the Confederacy, were addressed to General Singleton. Provost Marshal James R. O'Beirne, in a report written later about the activities of Ficklin and his friends, said: "It is very plain to my mind that ... Browning, Singleton, and Fickland [*sic*] had embarked in an immense cotton speculation, the whole to be consummated over the head and ostensibly for the benefit of this Mrs. Helm."

Browning got busy at once. Despite the fact that he knew the President was not feeling well and was swamped with weighty issues of war and peace, he took Bibb to the White House on April 12. Since Bibb carried a letter of introduction from Captain John L. Worden, who had been in command of the *Monitor,* Lincoln received his Confederate visitor kindly, spoke to him at length, and give him the necessary passes to return to Alabama. The President also promised Browning that he would see Singleton.

Later that day William P. Kellogg, whom Lincoln had known in Illinois, was having an interview with the President, during which Lincoln said prophetically: "Finances will rule the the country for the next fifty years." As if on cue, a messenger entered the room at that moment to present a card announcing Singleton's arrival.

No one knows what was said between the two men, but Singleton left the White House bearing a pass* allowing him to go to Richmond and return.

The little group of cotton speculators must have been in an exultant mood that night. Bibb was so encouraged by the good reception he got at the White House that he wrote letters to the President introducing Robert E. Coxe of Alabama and his new friend Ficklin. In the letter about Ficklin, Bibb rambled

---

* Since the pass, which still exists, is dated April 13 instead of April 12, Kellogg may have been mistaken about the date.

on (perhaps under the influence of liquor), giving Lincoln presumptuous advice on the reconstruction of the South and pointing out that only wealthy conservatives like himself were fit to rule.

Grant arrived in Washington by steamboat early on April 13 and drove directly to Willard's Hotel (where he had been offered a small room on the top floor hardly more than a year before when he came to the East to assume command of the Union Army). His chief interest was to get to the War Department as quickly as possible in order to see Stanton about cutting down military expenditures. But the victor of Appomattox was recognized as soon as he appeared. So large a crowd gathered around the hotel to cheer their hero that the police had to be called to clear a way through the densely packed ranks of the general's admirers.

During the afternoon a public announcement was made at the War Department that drafting and recruiting were to be stopped and that the purchase of most war material was to be curtailed. Since this showed that Grant and Stanton evidently felt that the fighting was as good as over (although several Confederate armies were still in the field), the people of the city took the announcement as another occasion to celebrate. Most of the major buildings had already been illuminated, but now men were put to work building even more elaborate transparencies, setting up still larger groups of flags, and creating ingenious lighting devices of all kinds.

Mrs. Lincoln sent a letter to Grant, saying that her husband was "indisposed with quite a severe headache," but that they would be pleased to receive him at the White House at eight o'clock and then drive around to see the illumination. The letter was addressed to Grant personally, but made no mention of his wife. Because of this he evidently felt uneasy about the awkward situation and declined the invitation even though it was practically a command. But the Grants did go to a reception at Stanton's home.

The city must have been a splendid sight that evening. The night was clear, and the moon, which was only three days past being full, rose a few minutes after nine. The Washington *Star* described the great spectacle: "The streets began to fill up at an early hour; long before night a tide of people set strongly toward the Avenue, increasing in strength until at dark the latter was a sea of life and animation, swallowing up the endless streams that poured in from adjacent streets, and making queer eddies at the corners, in which at times, a knot of distracted pedestrians would whirl as if lost altogether. There seemed to be no regular hour for lighting up, everyone applying the match as suited him best. . . . By 7 o'clock, however, the lights were all blazing. . . .

"The scene as viewed from the City Hall was of the most magnificent description. Far as the vision extended were brilliant lights, the rows of illuminated windows at a distance blending into one and presenting an unbroken wall of flame. . . . High above all towered the Capitol, glowing as if on fire. . . . Away to the right a halo hung over the roofs, rockets flashed to and fro in fiery lines, and the banners waved above the tumultuous throng, whose shouts and cheers rolled up in a dense volume from the city, and with the incense of the grand conflagration drifted away to the darkness of the surrounding hills."

At the Patent Office six thousand lights blazed in the many windows, while hotels, theaters, restaurants, and even private homes were illuminated. The names Grant, Sherman, and Sheridan appeared all over the city. Stanton's home was decorated with all kinds of flags lent by the Army, while the White House was made colorful by lights and flags from various branches of the services. A crowd gathered on the lawn, hoping that the President would make another speech, but he did not appear.

While the victory lights blazed in Washington, in Greensboro the defeated Confederate government had wound up a two-day meeting that was its last official act. Davis, the irreconcilable, had tried to persuade his cabinet and Generals Johnston and Beauregard that the already conquered Confederacy still had a chance to fight it out on the battlefield. His generals did not agree with him, and Johnston said that the Union forces now outnumbered them seventeen to one. The arrival of Secretary of War Breckinridge on the second day decided the matter. He had come from a conference with Lee just before the surrender at Appomattox, and he knew the realities of the situation. It was finally agreed that Johnston should approach Sherman to sue for peace.

21

A Darkness over the Land

Good Friday, April 14

THE APPOINTED DAY had come; within its span was the hour, and within that hour was the moment when the man who had been born in the Kentucky hill country fifty-six years before was to be struck down by a slayer he would never see. Abraham Lincoln's ever-migrating ancestors, his family, and his wife's family had blood-ties to both the North and the South, and now that the war between the two sections was nearing its end and an uneasy peace was being made, the man who had held the nation together was to be sacrificed to seal the hard-won unity with his blood.

His assassination was allegedly foreseen and foretold in many places. There are stories of mysterious men who waited anxiously in far-off telegraph stations on that destiny-laden night, asking for news momentarily expected from Washington. And wagers were made openly that "Old Abe" would be dead within a few days. Most curious of all is a series of documents in the Joseph Holt papers in the Library of Congress. According to these letters and affidavits, a soldier in a United States General Hospital in Frederick City received a letter *dated April 9* from his sister who lived in a small town north of Binghamton, New York. In it she said that she had heard that "Abraham Lincoln was shot through the head and killed." When this strange prediction became a hard reality five days later, the soldier showed the letter to an officer, and the War Department, scenting a possible conspiracy, began to investigate. A provost marshal sent to this remote place, soon found out that the prediction was only children's talk, for two little girls, ten or twelve years old, had heard the tale from a boy who had been visiting the village.

There were other signs and portents. B. B. French, whose job as Commissioner of Public Buildings took him everywhere and enabled him to see everything, wrote a few days later that Mrs. Lincoln was even "crazier than she used to be." Then he went on to say that she, whose wildly extravagant purchases of clothing were known to everybody except the President, had bought a thousand dollars worth of mourning goods before her husband was killed.

And in Homestead, Pennsylvania, there was an oil well in which John Wilkes Booth, who had speculated heavily in that area, was supposed to have invested some money. An American flag had been placed on top of the wooden derrick to celebrate the end of the war. On the night of April 14, when a violent thunderstorm swept over western Pennsylvania, a bolt of lightning struck the flag-decorated derrick and set the oil well on fire.

Another American flag figured prominently in that day's news. In Charleston Harbor a ceremony was to be held in what remained of Fort Sumter after Union guns had blasted away at it for nearly four years. There on April 14, 1861, the Federal garrison had turned the besieged island fort over to the Confederates, and the war had officially begun. Several shiploads of Northern dignitaries had gone down to Charleston to attend the ceremonies; Henry Ward Beecher, among others, was to speak. Present also was the fighting early Abolitionist, William Lloyd Garrison, who had suffered at the hands of an antislavery mob even in his native Massachusetts. General Robert Anderson was to raise the same battle-torn flag he had hauled down to signify surrender four years before. This ceremony, it was felt, even more than Appomattox, crowned the decisive victory of the North.

Promptly at twelve o'clock the military bands began to play, and General Anderson pulled on the halyards that ran the historic banner up the newly erected flagpole. The wind whipped out its folds so the stars and stripes pointed directly at the once rebellious city. Six guns mounted on the shattered parapet fired a salute which was replied to by guns in all the forts and batteries around the harbor, while naval cannon on the ships and monitors of the Union fleet roared out in a mighty chorus. Smoke from the tremendous salute drifted over the ruined and burned-out city which had known the smell of gunpowder all too well.

The ceremony was closed by a prayer and benediction read by the Reverend Dr. R. S. Storrs of Brooklyn, who asked a blessing for the Confederates when he said: "Remember those who have been our enemies, and turn their hearts from wrath and war, to love and peace. Let the desolations that have come on them suffice, and unite them with us in ties of a better brotherhood than of old; that the cities, and homes, and happiness they have lost may be more than replaced in the long prosperity they shall hereafter know."

That night the whole harbor was illuminated while bands played on the decks of the ships. An eyewitness described the scene: "At a given signal from the flag-ship, every man-of-war, transport and monitor in the harbor, became a skeleton pyramid of flame. Lanterns thickly slung to the rigging and culminating at the top of the mainmast, flashed out a starry light or line of lights, reduplicated by reflection in the water, while on the decks the most brilliant Gregorian fires of red, white, blue, green, pink, purple and gold, were lighted, whose columns of smoke, rolling lazily upward and illuminated respectively by their own peculiar flame, presented a spectacle of almost dazzling beauty. Rockets . . . screamed skyward from every deck, and bursting with a muffled sound, dissolved into various gorgeous tints, dropped gently downward, and quenched their splendor in the tide."

Then, when a signal gun was fired from the flagship, the lights were suddenly extinguished, and the fireworks ceased. Night closed in over the dark waters of the harbor and the ruins of the city where the great rebellion had begun.

The President had many visitors during the day; they came and went from early morning until after dark. Mrs. Lincoln, who was still determined to capture the great lion, General Grant, made arrangements for a small party to go to Ford's Theatre, where Laura Keene's company was to present Tom Taylor's long-successful comedy, *Our American Cousin*. A message was sent to Ford's to reserve a box. The management of the theater promptly placed advertisements in the city's newspapers featuring the fact that Grant was to be there but made no mention of his wife, although Mrs. Lincoln's name was listed.

According to Badeau, who seems to have been ubiquitous when anything concerning — and detrimental to — Mrs. Lincoln was involved, Stanton and his wife were also invited. Badeau then says: "Mrs. Stanton called on Mrs. Grant to inquire if she meant to be of the party. 'For,' said Mrs. Stanton, 'unless you accept the invitation, I shall refuse. I will not sit without you in the box with Mrs. Lincoln.' Mrs. Grant also was tired out with what she had endured, and decided not to go to the play. . . . She determined to return that night to Burlington, in New Jersey, where her children were at school, and requested the General to accompany her. Accordingly a note of apology was sent to Mrs. Lincoln, and Mrs. Stanton also declined the invitation."

A Cabinet meeting, which was to be devoted largely to the problems of reconstruction, was scheduled for eleven o'clock that morning. As a courtesy, General Grant had been asked to attend. Gideon Welles, who was present, tells how the meeting began: "Earnest inquiry was made whether any information had been received from General Sherman.... General Grant ... said he was expecting hourly to hear from Sherman, and had a good deal of anxiety on the subject.

"The President remarked that the news would come soon and come favorably, he had no doubt, for he had last night his usual dream which had preceded nearly every important event of the war. I inquired the particulars of this remarkable dream. He said ... that he seemed to be in a singular and indescribable vessel ... moving with great rapidity toward a dark and indefinite shore; that he had had this singular dream preceding the firing on Sumter, the battles of Bull Run, Antietam, Gettysburg, Stone River, Vicksburg, Wilmington, etc. General Grant remarked with some emphasis and asperity that Stone River was no victory — that a few such victories would have ruined the country, and he knew of no important results from it. The President said that perhaps he should not altogether agree with him but ... his singular dream preceded that fight. Victory did not always follow his dream, but the event and results were important. He had no doubt that a battle had taken place or was about being fought, 'and Johnston will be beaten, for I had this strange dream again last night. It must relate to Sherman; my thoughts are in that direction, and I know of no other very important event which is likely just now to occur.' "

When the ever-vexing problem of reconstruction came up, the President, according to Welles, said that he was glad the initial steps could be taken while Congress was not in session. He then went on to express his liberal views on the subject again: "He hoped there would be no persecution, no bloody work, after the war was over. None need expect he would take any part in hanging or killing those men, even the worst of them. Frighten them out of the country, open the gates, let down the bars, scare them off, said he, throwing up his hands as if scaring sheep. Enough lives have been sacrificed. We must extinguish our resentments if we expect harmony and union. There was too much of a desire on the part of some of our very good friends to be masters, to interfere with and dictate to those States, to treat the people not as fellow-citizens; there was too little respect for their rights."

When the Cabinet meeting ended, Grant received a message from his wife. After reading it he told the President that they would be unable to go to the theater. Again the doomed victim was deprived of the protection of a man sturdy and resolute enough to defend him.

During the afternoon, Andrew Johnson came to the White House and is reported to have been received cordially by the President. There were many other callers, so it was late when the President was able to get away for a promised drive in an open barouche with Mrs. Lincoln. She said later that he was in an unusually happy mood that afternoon and spoke about what they would do when his second term was over.

Although the drive lasted for hardly more than an hour, the Lincolns are said to have paid a brief visit to the Navy Yard, where they are supposed to have gone on board the monitor *Montauk,* which had been brought in for repairs to damage done at the capture of Fort Fisher. Both the *Montauk* and its sister ship, the *Saugus,* which was anchored nearby in the Potomac, were soon to serve as floating prisons for the chief conspirators when they were arrested. And on the early morning of April 27, the dead body of John Wilkes Booth was to be brought aboard the deck of the *Montauk* to be identified and have an autopsy performed upon it. But the log books of the two monitors and of the Washington Navy Yard say nothing about the President's having honored the Navy with a visit on the last day of his life.

After Mr. and Mrs. Lincoln returned to the White House, the President, accompanied by Crook, walked over to the War Department. Something had caused his high spirits to vanish. Crook said that "the President was more depressed than I had ever seen him, and his step was unusually slow." On the way they passed some men who were boisterously drunk. Their rude behavior may have put the thought into Lincoln's mind, for he told Crook, "Do you know I believe there are men who want to take my life?" Then, after a pause, he said half to himself, "And I have no doubt they will do it."

During the day John Wilkes Booth had been busy preparing everything for the night's dark work. He had bored a peephole into the inner door of the President's box and had fixed the outer door so it could be blocked shut behind him. He was very careful in arranging all the details which affected his own safety, but he was exceedingly careless about the fate of those who were in any way involved with him. He left a bundle of letters in his trunk at the National Hotel, and he hired a carriage so Mrs. Surratt could go to her tavern in southern Maryland. She had legal business of her own to do there, but he paid for the journey in return for her delivering a spyglass to the tavern for him to pick up for use during his escape. This errand connected her with Booth on the day of the assassination and led directly to her execution.

At the War Department, Stanton urged the President not to go to the theater, or, if he felt that he must go, at least to have a powerful guard accompany him. Lincoln told his Secretary of War that Major Thomas T. Eckert, chief of the War Department Telegraph Office, could break an iron poker over his arm. But Stanton said that "he had important work for Eckert that evening and could not spare him." Lincoln went into the cipher room to speak to the major. Eckert confirmed Stanton's statement that his work could not be put off. The President thereupon lost his last chance of obtaining the services of a powerfully built fighting man to be with him in the box at Ford's Theatre that night.

During their return to the White House, Crook noticed that all trace of Lincoln's depression had gone. When the President mentioned the theater party, he said, "It has been advertised that we will be there, and I cannot disappoint the people. Otherwise I would not go. I do not want to go."

This last remark surprised Crook, for he knew how fond of the theater Lincoln ordinarily was. He was even more surprised when they reached the White House, for Lincoln then said: "Good-by, Crook." This was unlike his usual way of merely saying, "Good-night, Crook"; as a result it impressed the loyal bodyguard so strongly that he remembered it. But he went home, and his duties were taken over by a man whose employment had been approved by Mrs. Lincoln during the few days she was in Washington early in April, when she also had the new guard excused from the draft. This was John F. Parker, a former member of the Metropolitan Police Force. Men were scarce in wartime, but Parker's record with the Washington police was so bad that they were probably not sorry to be rid of him.*

Visitors, wanted and unwanted, were always calling at the White House. This night was no exception. Schuyler Colfax came to say good-by before leaving for California. And cotton

* Since there were Parkers in Mrs. Lincoln's family, it is possible that the man claimed some kind of distant relationship. It would be in accordance with Mrs. Lincoln's Southern idea of family loyalty to go out of her way to try to help a relative, no matter how distant.

speculation went on as usual. George Ashmun, Republican Representative from Massachusetts, dropped in after dinner to press settlement for one of his constituents' cotton claims. It was time to leave for the theater, and Lincoln had had enough of cotton cases. Since Ashmun was politically important he could not be ignored, so the President put him off until morning, writing out a card for him that would admit the Congressman and his friend at nine o'clock. These were Lincoln's last written words.

The ever industrious Browning was also at the White House, but he was less fortunate than Ashmun. He waited upstairs until eight o'clock without getting a chance to see the President. He went home, not realizing that his hope for making a vast fortune from the wreckage of the war was to be ruined in a few hours by an assassin's bullet. And his client, the rabid secessionist, B. F. Ficklin, was denounced as a possible conspirator before the night was over, so that Browning had to spend more than two months trying to get him out of the Old Capitol Prison.

Mrs. Lincoln had decided to ask Senator Harris' daughter, Miss Clara Harris, and her fiancé, Major H. R. Rathbone* (who was also her stepbrother) to go to the play with them. It was arranged that the President's carriage was to pick up the young couple at the Harris home at Fifteenth and H Streets on the way to the theater. Major Rathbone was a brave young man, but he was lightly built, frail, and slender in comparison with tough Marshal Lamon, the mighty Eckert, or the redoubtable Grant.

The carriage drove down the curving drive and entered the dimly lighted streets of Washington shortly after eight o'clock. It called for the young couple and reached Ford's Theatre

---

* Everyone in the theater box that night was marked for disaster. Major Rathbone married Miss Harris; they went to Germany, where he became insane, murdered his wife, and was confined in an asylum for the rest of his life.

about eight-thirty, after the play had already begun. A gas lamp mounted on a post lighted up the high, red-brick façade of the new theater building with its five arched doorways and double-tiered windows. There was a wooden platform to enable passengers to get out of their carriages without having to step into the mud of the unpaved street. Parker and the footman, Forbes, went ahead of the President, while the driver moved his carriage a few feet away to clear the entrance for others. When the Presidential party entered the theater, William Withers, who had been one of the conductors at the inaugural ball in the Patent Office, ordered the orchestra to play "Hail to the Chief." As soon as the President reached the upper stage box he came forward and bowed to Withers and the applauding audience. Then he sat down in the big comfortable rocking chair which had been provided for him. Parker was supposed to occupy a small chair just outside the door leading to the President's box, but he could not see the play from there, so he moved into the dress circle, leaving the door unguarded.

At the opposite end of the block of buildings in which the theater was located, stood a second-rate hotel known as the Herndon House. There, in a corner room on the third floor, the conspirators were making their last-minute plans. Booth had decided to have his one strong and trusted lieutenant, Lewis Paine, strike at the disabled Seward. And because the tiger-like giant did not know the city well, David Herold was to conduct him to Seward's home on Lafayette Square. Atzerodt, the ignorant and cowardly German carriage-maker from Port Tobacco, was supposed to go to the Kirkwood House to take Vice President Johnson's life. And Booth, knowing that Grant had left the city, would enter the passageway leading to the President's box alone and unaided just after ten o'clock.

And now the fates were readying the final knot in the dark cord that was to tie together the names of John Wilkes Booth and Abraham Lincoln for all time to come. And this, as Lloyd Lewis has pointed out, "was according to a pattern of antiquity. Most of the gods who had died for Man had taken their betrayers with them into the realm of legend. Worshiping multitudes in ancient and mediaeval days awarded immortality to the slayers of their gods as well as to the gods themselves. Osiris shared his myth-heights with his slayer, an evil brother Set; Adonis, the radiant, was believed to have been doomed by the swart and jealous Ares, who could not therefore be forgotten; Balder the Beautiful lifted his envious assassin Loki into the superstitions of the Germanic peoples; Dionysus gave an added demon-stature to his killers, the grimy Titans, themselves already gods; Britons remembered with fond hatred Sir Modred, the dark knight who had taken from them their bright-browed King Arthur. And Judas Iscariot, in the eyes of Christians, most terrible of all, had won eternal infamy by his betrayal of Jesus."

22

Aftermath

Saturday, April 15, to Monday, May 22

THE ASSASSINATION of Abraham Lincoln hit the United States like a tidal wave. The first shock gave rise to astonishment and disbelief, which was quickly followed by fear that the Confederates were trying to disrupt the Northern government by a series of carefully planned assassinations. And there were also ugly rumors that the whole confusing affair was a Northern plot, a *coup d'état* to prepare the way for a military or political junta to take over the country and rule it by dictatorship.*

France, Maximilian in Mexico, and, because of its connection with these foreign powers, the Catholic Church were also suspected, but the real truth was that no one — except those who were part of the conspiracy — had any idea of what people or what powers were behind the overt act. Even so knowing a person as Browning, who had many sources of private information, wrote in his diary on the night of the assassination: "I am at a loss as to the class of persons who instigated the crime — whether it was the rebel leaders — the copperheads in conjunc-

---

* This fear of a national military dictatorship was even greater in the South at this time than in the North. When General Joseph E. Johnston telegraphed to Jefferson Davis that Lincoln had been assassinated, he closed the message with the statement: "Grant has marched his army back to Washington to declare himself military dictator."

tion with foreign emissaries, gold speculators, or the friends and accomplices of Bealle." ("Bealle" was John Yates Beall, a Southern agent who was executed for trying to capture the United States steamer *Michigan* on Lake Erie and use it to set free the Confederate prisoners of war confined on Johnson's Island. He was arrested after making an equally unsuccessful attempt to wreck an Erie Railroad train near Buffalo. Some people thought he was a friend of John Wilkes Booth, but this was not so.)

This first wave of astonishment, disbelief, and fear was followed by an even greater burst of grief and anger. Most of the people of the North, even those who had opposed Lincoln, were outraged at his assassination. And even though there were some very young, very ignorant, or very recalcitrant Southerners who rejoiced openly when they heard that Lincoln had been slain, the more intelligent people realized that the South had lost an influential friend at the very moment when she was most in need of such a person in Washington.

Simultaneously with the nationwide man hunt for the conspirators, the elaborate funeral ceremonies went on. Hundreds of thousands of people came to see the dead face of Abraham Lincoln as he lay in state in the White House, in the rotunda of the Capitol, in the City Hall of New York, and in various public buildings in numerous cities along the railroad route from Washington to Springfield. The violence stirred up by his killing undid all the good he had been trying to do. His ideas for a reasonable treatment of the South were forgotten while the forces demanding vengeance took command. In the Union Army, the officers had to break the news carefully to their men lest they go on a murderous rampage against the people of the South or the prisoners of war whose lives were in their hands.

Johnston, following the decision of the Confederate cabinet, but not knowing that Lincoln had been killed, asked Sherman for peace. At eight o'clock in the morning of April 17, Sherman was ready to leave Raleigh to go to a point midway between Durham and Hillsboro, where Johnston was to meet him. Sherman tells what happened: "Just as we were entering the car, the telegraph-operator ... ran down to me and said that he was ... receiving a most important dispatch in cipher ... which I ought to see. I held the train for nearly half an hour, when he returned with the message translated and written out. It was from Mr. Stanton."

The telegram had been sent from Washington at 12:10 P.M. on April 15. It read:

> President Lincoln was murdered about 10 o'clock last night in his private box at Ford's Theatre in this city, by an assassin who shot him through the head by a pistol ball. About the same hour Mr. Seward's house was entered by another assassin who stabbed the Secretary in several places, but it is thought he may possibly recover. . . . The assassin of the President leaped from the box brandishing a dagger, exclaiming, "Sic semper tyrannis!" and that now Virginia was revenged.
>
> Mr. Lincoln fell senseless from his seat and continued in that state until twenty-two minutes after 7 o'clock at which time he breathed his last. General Grant was published to be at the theatre, but fortunately did not go. Vice-President Johnson now becomes President, and will take the oath of office and assume the duties today. I have no time to add more than to say that I find evidence that an assassin is also on your track, and I beseech you to be more heedful than Mr. Lincoln was of such knowledge.

Sherman ordered the telegraph operator not to reveal the news until he returned. Then he hurried on to meet Johnston. They went to a small, roughly built farmhouse which they entered, at Sherman's request, without their staff officers. Sherman recorded the story of their meeting: "As soon as we were alone together I showed him the dispatch announcing Mr. Lincoln's assassination, and watched him closely. The perspiration came out in large drops on his forehead, and he did not attempt to conceal his distress. He denounced the act as a disgrace to the age, and hoped I did not charge it to the Confederate Government. I told him I could not believe that he or General Lee, or the officers of the Confederate army, could possibly be privy to acts of assassination; but I would not say as much for Jeff. Davis, George Sanders, and men of that stripe. We talked about the effect of this act on the country at large and on the armies, and he realized that it made my situation extremely delicate. I explained to him that I had not yet revealed the news to my own personal staff or to the army, and that I dreaded the effect when made known in Raleigh. Mr. Lincoln was peculiarly endeared to the soldiers, and I feared that some foolish woman or man in Raleigh might say something or do something that would madden our men, and that a fate worse than that of Columbia would befall the place.

"I then told Johnston that he must be convinced that he could not oppose my army, and that, since Lee had surrendered, he could do the same with honor and propriety. He plainly and repeatedly admitted this, and added that any further fighting would be 'murder;' but he thought that, instead of surrendering piecemeal, we might arrange terms that would embrace *all* the Confederate armies. I asked him if he could control other armies than his own; he said, not then, but intimated that he could procure authority from Mr. Davis. I then told him that I had recently had an interview with General Grant and President Lincoln, and that I was possessed of their views; that with them and the people North there seemed to be no vindictive feeling against the Confederate armies, but there was against Davis and his political adherents; and that the terms that General Grant had given to General Lee's army were certainly most generous and liberal. All this he admitted, but always recurred to the idea of a universal surrender."

When Sherman returned to Raleigh he formally announced

the news of the assassination to the men in his army. They took
it badly but fortunately made no attempt at retaliation. He
met again the next day with Johnston to settle the final terms
of surrender with him, his staff, and with John C. Breckinridge,
who was admitted to the conference as a Confederate general
but not as the Confederacy's Secretary of War.

Johnston, many years later, told how Breckinridge and
Sherman got along on that occasion: "For several days, Breckinridge had found it difficult, if not impossible, to procure liquor.
He showed the effect of his enforced abstinence. He was rather
dull and heavy that morning. Somebody in Danville had given
him a plug of very fine chewing tobacco, and he chewed vigorously while we were awaiting Sherman's coming. After a while,
the latter arrived. He bustled in with a pair of saddlebags over
his arm, and apologized for being late. He placed the saddlebags carefully upon a chair. Introductions followed, and for a
while General Sherman made himself exceedingly agreeable.
Finally, some one suggested that we had better take up the
matter in hand.

" 'Yes,' said Sherman; 'but gentlemen, it occurred to me that
perhaps you were not overstocked with liquor, and I procured
some medical stores on my way over. Will you join me before
we begin work?'

"The expression of Breckinridge at this announcement . . .
was beatific. Tossing his quid into the fire, he rinsed his mouth,
and when the bottle and the glass were passed to him, he
poured out a tremendous drink, which he swallowed with great
satisfaction. With an air of content, he stroked his mustache
and took a fresh chew of tobacco.

"Then they settled down to business, and Breckinridge never
shone more brilliantly than he did in the discussions which
followed. He seemed to have at his tongue's end every rule
and maxim of international and constitutional law, and of the
laws of war — international wars, civil wars, and wars of re-

bellion. In fact, he was so resourceful, cogent, persuasive, learned, that, at one stage of the proceedings, General Sherman, when confronted by the authority, but not convinced by the eloquence or learning of Breckinridge, pushed back his chair and exclaimed: 'See here, gentlemen, who is doing this surrendering anyhow? If this thing goes on, you'll have me sending a letter of apology to Jeff Davis.'

"Afterward, when they were nearing the close of the conference, Sherman sat for some time absorbed in deep thought. Then he arose, went to the saddlebags, and fumbled for the bottle. Breckinridge saw the movement. Again he took his quid from his mouth and tossed it into the fireplace. His eye brightened, and he gave every evidence of intense interest in what Sherman seemed about to do.

"The latter, preoccupied, perhaps unconscious of his action, poured out some liquor, shoved the bottle back into the saddle-pocket, walked to the window, and stood there, looking out abstractedly, while he sipped his grog.

"From pleasant hope and expectation the expression on Breckinridge's face changed successively to uncertainty, disgust, and deep depression. At last his hand sought the plug of tobacco, and, with an injured, sorrowful look, he cut off another chew. Upon this he ruminated during the remainder of the interview, taking little part in what was said.

"After silent reflections at the window, General Sherman bustled back, gathered up his papers, and said: 'These terms are too generous, but I must hurry away before you make me sign a capitulation. I will submit them to the authorities at Washington, and let you hear how they are received.' With that he bade the assembled officers adieu, took his saddlebags upon his arm, and went off as he had come. . . .

" 'Sherman is a bright man, and a man of great force,' said Breckinridge, speaking with deliberation, 'but,' raising his voice and with a look of great intensity, 'General Johnston,

General Sherman is a hog. Yes, sir, a *hog*. Did you see him take that drink by himself? No Kentucky gentleman would ever have taken away that bottle. He knew we needed it, and needed it badly.' "

It was agreed that the two armies were to remain immobilized until Sherman got approval — or at least instructions — from Washington. He sent Major Henry Hitchcock there by rail and steamer, urging him to make all possible speed. Hitchcock returned at 6 A.M. on April 24, accompanied by General Grant, who told Sherman that his proposed terms had been disapproved by Stanton and the new administration. The assassination had changed everything, and all intention of acting generously to the already defeated Confederacy had been swept away in a wave of hatred. Grant had been present at the Cabinet meeting which decided the matter, and he knew that Government policy had gone back to the kind of thinking that existed on March 3, when he had been sent the joint Lincoln-Stanton telegram ordering him to have no dealings with the Confederates on political or civil matters. (Sherman, of course, had never received this important message.) Grant also knew that the Cabinet wanted Sherman to "press on and crush out the Rebels."

It was fortunate that Grant was there to restrain Sherman, who was easily hurt and easily angered. Grant took no part in the negotiations, nor did he appear publicly. But he persuaded Sherman to go back to Johnston and rearrange the surrender terms so they applied only to the troops directly under his own command and were identical with those given to Lee at Appomattox. Johnston, under the circumstances, had no choice but to accept, which he did on April 26.

Grant left the next day; then on the 28th, Sherman got hold of a copy of the *New York Times* for April 24. This contained garbled information released by Stanton and a misquotation from General H. W. Halleck, all of which cast suspicion upon Sherman's good sense and even upon his honesty. The proud commander was so offended by this that ten years later, when he wrote his *Memoirs,* he said: "I regarded this bulletin of Mr. Stanton's as a personal and official insult." When he passed through Richmond he refused to meet Halleck and countermanded orders which that commander had given for holding a review of one of Sherman's corps. The doughty redheaded general, whose fiery energy had cut the Confederacy in half, was getting his fill of politics. In a private letter written to a member of his family on May 8 he said bitterly: "Washington is corrupt as Hell, made so by the looseness and extravagance of war. I will avoid it as a pest house."

Literally hundreds of people were arrested for suspected complicity in the assassination plot; some were interrogated and quickly let go, but many were thrown into the Old Capitol Prison until its ancient rooms were overcrowded with prisoners who did not even know what charges were to be made against them. Once a person was incarcerated there, it was almost impossible to get him out. And the huge dragnet brought up all sorts of strange fish — among them four men who had been picked up in Washington dressed in women's clothing.

Rumors that Booth had been seen in various places began to circulate, made a great stir for a day or two, and then turned out to be untrue. There was a riot in Washington on April 17 when someone thought the assassin was in a group of Confederate prisoners who were being led through the streets of the city. Several people, including some of the Union soldiers guarding the prisoners, were wounded before the unruly mob was satisfied that Booth was not in the marching column. These false Booths were especially prevalent in Pennsylvania, perhaps because of the archconspirator's association with the oil regions there. The people and the police of Tamaqua were convinced for a few days that the notorious assassin was in their town. But this also proved to be a myth. It was not until April 27, when the real Booth's body was brought to Washington and the news of his capture was released, that the hysteria connected with the greatest man hunt in the nation's history died down.

Most public reaction in the South went strongly against Booth. Twenty-two thousand Confederate prisoners of war confined at Camp Lookout passed a resolution to be forwarded to the War Department, in which they expressed "their abhorrence of the assassination of the late President." And on April 20, when General Lee, who had quietly returned to his home in Richmond five days before, was told about Lincoln's death, he said that at Appomattox he had surrendered as much to the President's "goodness as to Grant's artillery."

During the night of April 27, while Booth's body was being brought by steamship to Washington to be dumped on board the deck of the *Montauk* at one-thirty in the morning, the Mississippi steamboat *Sultana* was leaving Memphis, bound up the river. Although she was supposed to carry only 376 passengers, the captain had been persuaded to take on board about 2000 men who had made their way overland to Vicksburg from the horrors of Andersonville, Salisbury, and other Southern prison camps. The men were in bad condition, and they wanted desperately to reach their homes in the Middle West. The incredibly overloaded boat was slow and sluggish in the rapidly flowing current, and her four boilers had to be pressed to the limit to keep her moving. Shortly after 2 A.M., one of the boilers blew up with a terrific blast, setting the steamboat on fire. Many of the sleeping soldiers were killed outright; others were burned to death or drowned. Since some of the bodies were probably never recovered, no one knew the exact toll, but as many as 1800 men may have lost their lives in the most terrible maritime disaster in history. The Chicago

Tribune commented bitterly that "more lives were sacrificed to a patched boiler and a captain's criminal cupidity than it cost us ... to capture Lee's army and terminate the rebellion."

Once the seven men and one woman* who were to be tried for the assassination had been arrested, orders were issued by the President on May 1 to appoint a Military Commission of nine officers to hear the testimony. There was considerable doubt as to whether such a court had proper jurisdiction over the lives of civilians, but the Commission went grimly ahead with its work. The very next day a new sensation was created when President Johnson issued a proclamation charging Jefferson Davis and the Confederate commissioners in Canada of being directly implicated in the conspiracy to kill Lincoln and Seward. Enormous rewards were offered for their arrest — $100,000 for Davis and from $10,000 to $25,000 for the others.

One of the Confederates in Canada, George N. Sanders, promptly struck back by issuing a statement bluntly accusing Andrew Johnson of murdering the President, while his associate, Beverly Tucker, said in a letter to a newspaper that circumstantial evidence pointed more directly to Johnson than it did to the Confederate commissioners. Both men wrote to Johnson on May 4, offering to enter the United States at Rouse's Point, New York, to be tried at the United States fort

---

* They were David E. Herold, Lewis Paine, George Atzerodt, Mrs. Mary E. Surratt, Michael O'Laughlin, Samuel Arnold, Dr. Samuel A. Mudd, and Edward Spangler. The first four were hanged on July 7, 1865. Spangler, who worked backstage at Ford's, got a six-year sentence for allegedly helping Booth escape from the theater. O'Laughlin and Arnold, who were involved in the plot to kidnap but not in the plot to kill, were sentenced to life imprisonment at hard labor. So was Dr. Mudd, for giving medical assistance to Booth after he had broken his leg. Many people who had done much more to help Booth escape were arrested but for some strange reason were never brought to trial. Mrs. Surratt was hanged because the authorities could not get their hands on her son, John Harrison Surratt, who was believed to be the key to the case. He had fled to Canada and then to Europe. He was arrested and tried in 1867, but the case was nol-prossed, and he went free.

there by a court-martial of nine generals who were to be chosen from a list of twenty-five of the top-ranking commanders of the Union Army — whom they named, with Grant and Sherman among them. No attention was paid to their offer, perhaps because they wanted the Government to pay all the expenses of the trial.

Close upon these charges and countercharges came word from Irwinville, Georgia, that Jefferson Davis had been captured there on May 10. The story immediately began to spread that he had been taken while trying to elude his captors by dressing in women's clothes. All through the war the cry had been "Hang Jeff Davis to a sour apple tree," and much of the North's hatred had been focused on the president of the Confederacy. Now he was made an object of ridicule. Cartoons and drawings of him wearing women's clothing appeared in Northern newspapers, and the stiff, unbending man who had been a professional soldier and United States Secretary of War before he became the head of the Confederate government was the butt of jokes, some of them obscene.

What actually occurred was dramatic enough. Two troops of U. S. cavalry, hot on the trail of the man for whose capture the huge reward had been offered, collided with each other in the dark, began firing, and killed two of their own men. When they reached the camp where the Confederate president and his wife (who had joined him only three days before) were asleep in a tent, some strange things happened. According to Davis: "As it was quite dark in the tent, I picked up what was supposed to be my raglan, a waterproof, light overcoat, without sleeves; it was subsequently found to be my wife's, so very like my own as to be mistaken for it; as I started, my wife thoughtfully threw over my head and shoulders a shawl.

"I had gone perhaps fifteen or twenty yards when a trooper galloped up and ordered me to halt and surrender, to which I gave a defiant answer, and dropping the shawl and raglan from my shoulders, advanced toward him; he leveled his carbine at me, but I expected, if he fired, he would miss me, and my intention was in that event to put my hand under his foot, tumble him off on the other side, spring into the saddle, and attempt to escape. My wife, who had been watching, ran forward and threw her arms around me. Success depended on instantaneous action, and, recognizing that the opportunity had been lost, I turned back. . . ."

His wife's raglan and shawl, of course, were what gave rise to the rumors that Davis was trying to escape while disguised as a woman. The rumors got further impetus when one of the troopers, who was trying to pry open Mrs. Davis' locked trunk with a loaded musket, shot off his own hand. When the trunk was finally broken into, it was found to contain a hoop skirt. The soldiers, angered by their own self-inflicted losses, are then supposed to have given out the statement that Davis was wearing not only his wife's raglan and shawl but her skirt as well. When this story reached Washington, Halleck gleefully recommended to Stanton that "if Jefferson Davis was captured in his wife's clothes, I respectfully suggest that he be sent north in the same habiliments."

Davis was imprisoned in Fortress Monroe, where he was held for two years without being brought to trial, and was finally let go.

The eight conspirators were tried in a building on the grounds of the Washington Arsenal. To this isolated place the necessary witnesses were brought each day, and a few privileged spectators were allowed to be present when provided with properly signed passes. Since Lewis Paine had tried to beat his brains out against the iron sides of the monitor in which he was first confined, an order was issued that the prisoners were not only to be manacled with iron bars and chained to heavy weights but were to have their heads covered with padded canvas hoods that left only an opening for the mouth. Only Mrs. Surratt, as a woman, was excepted, and even she was kept in irons for the first few days.

On the morning of May 16, one month and two days after the assassination, the members of the Military Commission went in army ambulances to inspect Ford's Theatre so they could get a better understanding of the complicated and unfamiliar layout of the backstage area which had played a part in the assassination. According to the Washington *Star,* they found the building, which soldiers were still guarding day and night, curiously unchanged. "The stage is almost precisely in the condition it was at the moment of the assassination. The scene, third act of *American Cousin,* is set as at that moment with a red curtained recess in the centre.... The box used by Mr. Lincoln bears the same picture of Washington at its front and a couple of flags are draped over the boxes, but not the Treasury Guards' flag, which caught Booth's spur on that occasion. The green baize stagecloth has a long rent where Booth struck the stage.... The box was in much the same condition as when the assassination took place with the exception of the rocking chair used by Mr. Lincoln [which] has been removed.... The seats in the theatre were covered by a heavy coat of dust, adding something to the general feeling of unpleasantness about the sombre, dimly lit interior of any theatre by day."

The generals and colonels of the Military Commission explored the interior of the building and then went out to examine the rear alley from which Booth had made his escape on horseback. Still standing against the back wall was the long wooden bench on which the theater's innocent peanut vendor had sat while he held Booth's horse during the assassination. Some of the guards were lounging on this, whittling souvenirs from wood they had stripped from the interior of the building.

Because Mrs. Lincoln's reactions to her husband's assassination were so violent that she had to be confined to bed for five weeks (during which time she could be seen only by her physicians and a few close friends) the White House also remained relatively unchanged. George Alfred Townsend, the New York *World*'s enterprising reporter, visited the house just one month after the assassination. He sat in the dead President's chair and wrote a description of the historic building as it had been in Lincoln's time: "I am sitting in the President's office. . . . A bright-faced boy runs in and out, darkly attired, so that his fob-chain of gold is the only relief to his mourning garb. This is little Tad, the pet of the White House. That great death, with which the world rings, had made upon him only the light impression which all things make on childhood.

"The room is long and high, and so thickly hung with maps that the color of the wall can not be discerned. The President's table, at which I am seated, adjoins a window at the farthest corner; and to the left of my chair . . . there is a longer table before an empty grate, around which there are many chairs, where the Cabinet used to assemble. The carpet is trodden thin, and the brilliance of its dyes is lost. The furniture is of the formal cabinet class, stately and semi-comfortable. . . . They are taking away Mr. Lincoln's private effects . . . and the emptiness of the place, on this sunny Sunday, revives that feeling of desolation from which the land has scarce recovered. I rise from my seat and examine the maps; they are from the coast survey and the engineer departments, and exhibit all the contested ground of the war; there are pencil lines upon them where some one has traced the route of armies, and planned the strategic circumferences of campaigns. . . .

"I see some books on the table; perhaps they have lain there undisturbed since the reader's dimming eyes grew nerveless. A parliamentary manual, a thesaurus, and two books of humor, 'Orpheus C. Kerr,' and 'Artemus Ward.' These last were read by Mr. Lincoln in the pauses of his hard day's labor. Their tenure here bears out the popular verdict of his partiality for a good joke; and, through the window, from this seat of Mr. Lincoln, I see across the grassy grounds of the Capitol, the broken shaft of the Washington Monument, the Long Bridge and the fort-tipped Heights of Arlington, reaching down to the shining river side. . . .

"Outside of this room there is an office, where his secretaries sat — a room more narrow but as long — and opposite this adjunct office a second door, directly behind Mr. Lincoln's chair, leads by a private passage to his family quarters. This passage is his only monument in the building; he added or subtracted nothing else; it tells a long story of duns and loiterers, contract-hunters and seekers for commissions, garrulous parents on paltry errands, toadies without measure, and talkers without conscience. They pressed upon him through a great door opposite his window, and hat in hand, came courtesying to his chair, with an obsequious 'Mr. President!'

"If he dared . . . to go out by the great door, these vampires leaped upon him . . . and barred his walk to his hearthside. He could not insult them, since it was not in his nature . . . so he called up the carpenter and ordered the strategic route cut from his office to his hearth. . . .

"So dwelt the citizen who is gone — a model in character, if not in ceremony. . . . I am glad to sit here in his chair, where he has bent so often . . . inditing at his table the goodness of his life and the eternity of his memory."

Mrs. Lincoln's long stay in bed greatly inconvenienced President Johnson, who was put up by friends for some time and then used the Kirkwood House as his headquarters. Mrs. Keckley said that after she had gone to see Lincoln's body as it lay in a coffin in the White House she returned to his widow's darkened room to find her "in a new paroxysm of grief. Robert was bending over his mother with tender affection, and little Tad was crouched at the foot of the bed with a world of agony in his young face. I shall never forget the scene — the wails of a broken heart, the unearthly shrieks, the terrible convulsions, the wild, tempestuous outbursts of grief. . . ."

The ailing woman was in no condition to attend the elaborate funeral procession that had been held in Washington for her husband on April 19, so the impressive cortege moved away from the White House without her. Seward also was too ill to leave his home, but he was well enough by this time to be put in a chair near a window from which he could look out at the procession. But he was still so weak from his wounds that he said later the great occasion was as hard for him to recall as the elusive images seen in a dimly remembered dream.

The President's seriously disturbed widow did not vacate the White House until May 22, when she took a train to Chicago. With her went Robert, Tad, Mrs. Keckley, and Dr. Anson G. Henry. As their carriage drove to the railroad station at the foot of Capitol Hill it passed through a city that was rapidly filling up with people arriving to see the greatest spectacle of the postwar era, the grand review of the victorious Union Armies on the wide main street that belongs to the entire nation — Pennsylvania Avenue.

23

An End to Valor

Tuesday, May 23, and Wednesday, May 24

ORDERS HAD GONE OUT for the troops of the various commands to come to Washington for a final two-day review. Tens of thousands of men began streaming toward the city; some traveled by rail or ship but most of them came the way they had moved during the war — on foot. Sherman proudly boasted that his army had marched nearly two thousand miles through hostile country since it began its last campaign.

Hardly more than half of the troops still in the Union ranks were allowed to go to Washington — about 150,000 men. Others had to remain at their posts to do guard duty in the recently conquered and still resentful Southern states. And, by some quirk of military thinking, the North's great hero, Sheridan, was not at the review, for he was being sent to New Orleans to guard the Rio Grande against Maximilian's government in Mexico and also to force the surrender of Kirby Smith, who was still holding out with a large force west of the Mississippi. Sheridan, who loved parades, was heartbroken, especially since his orders called for his missing the elaborate ceremony only by a day or two. He called on Grant to plead for a brief stay, but the general was adamant, and the victorious cavalry leader was deprived of the chance of riding down Pennsylvania Avenue at the head of his mounted men.

As the soldiers marched northward they were eager to revisit the battlefields on which they had fought, or, as was the case with Sherman and his men, to see the celebrated places they had only heard about. They sometimes went out of their way to inspect the more important battle areas, and since the fighting was hardly over, they found the scars of war still deep upon the land. At Petersburg the trenches were practically intact, but the local people were cutting up the abatis and chevaux-de-frise for firewood. And a thriving business was being done in collecting scrap metal from fought-over ground. (The lead pipes of the next generation were to contain a large proportion of metal from salvaged bullets.)

General Warren was in Petersburg when the Fifth Corps, which he had commanded until that fatal hour at Five Forks, came through the town. His men felt that he had been unjustly removed from command, so they gave him a tremendous ovation as they marched past the hotel he was using as his headquarters.

The troops were strung out for miles on all the roads that led north to Washington. Each night a new camp was made; each morning it was broken up. Tents were struck, baggage was packed, and horses were hitched to thousands of wagons and fieldpieces. Everywhere tokens of mourning for the slain President were displayed. The officers had crape on their tents and scabbards, while the men wore black bands on their arms.

The cavalry, of course, were better off than the infantry because they could ride instead of having to plod along the badly cut up roads. Custer's beautiful young wife was the first woman to use the Southside Railroad. She hurried toward Appomattox by rail and horse to join her dashing husband, whom she adored. Then, with Colonel Pennington's wife, she rode at the head of the cavalry column day after day until the troops reached Washington.

Chamberlain, while marching with the Fifth Corps, tells how the relics of battle were still strewn across the war-torn earth. One night he heard his horse, which had been tethered in a nearby pine grove, stir uneasily. Fearing that someone might be stealing his much prized animal, which had been shot from under him three times but which had recovered from its wounds, the good Maine general did not bother to send a guard but went to see what was wrong. "Before I reached him," he said, "my foot crushed through the breast-bones of a body half buried by the fallen pinecones and needles. . . . I found that the horse, pawing the earth within the scope of his picket-rope, had rolled out two skulls and scattered the bones of bodies he had unearthed, and was gazing at the white skulls as if lost in doubt; now and then snorting to call others to solve the mystery, or swaying at his tether as if to get away himself. It was a weird, uncanny scene: the straggling, uncompanionable pines; the night brooding still and chill; black lowering clouds, now massing, now rifting, disclosing, then shutting out of sight, the white skulls mocking life. The horse was not easily pacified — not until I had gathered up the menacing skulls and the outlying limbs . . . and showed him that I was not afraid.

"In the morning the men got to looking around among the bodies and relics, and by initials cut into the breast-plates or other marks or tokens identified the remnants of bodies of comrades long left among the missing. . . . They asked permission to gather up these mournful remnants and pack them in empty cracker-boxes . . . to be sent to friends who would gladly cherish such tokens. . . . I was glad to grant this and to instruct the wagoners to take especial care of these relics. . . . And so the strange column set forth, bearing in its train that burden of unlost belongings. . . ."

The great trek to Washington was hard work for men who

were exhausted by years of fighting; the marches were long, averaging about twenty miles a day with full equipment. And all the nervous energy bred by active combat was gone. It was just a matter of getting to Washington and then going home.

The weather was becoming hotter each day, and the heat sometimes produced freak storms of sudden violence. Chamberlain describes one that burst upon his long columns of marching men on May 11: "I chanced to be ... on the summit of a very high hill, from which I could see the whole corps winding its caravan with dromedary patience. The first lightning bolt nearly stunned me. I saw its forerunner flashing along the cannon far ahead and illuminating Crawford's column with unearthly glare; and turning quickly toward my own I could see the whole black column struggling on ... when this ever-recurrent pulse of flame leaped along the writhing column like a river of fire. It looked to me as if the men had bayonets fixed, the points of light flew so sharp from the muzzles sloping above the shoulders. Suddenly an explosion like a battery of shrapnel fell right between our divisions. An orderly came galloping up to me, with word that one of the ambulances was struck, killing the horses and driver, and stunning the poor fellows who, unable to keep up with the rushing column, had sought this friendly aid.... I sent instructions for the stricken men to be cared for, and for the forage trains to take along the disabled ambulance. We were bringing one dead body already, besides the strange freight of rescued fragments packed in the bread-boxes."

A few days before the grand review the hills around Washington were white with tents and wagon covers. Those who were lucky enough to be allotted camping space on Arlington Heights near Lee's former home could look down upon the capital city of the nation they had fought for. Many of the boys from country towns and the West got their first view of the white dome of the Capitol as it stood proudly on a hill on the other side of the river. The White House, the Patent Office, and the half-completed shaft of the Washington Monument were pointed out to them. To the right stood the red sandstone battlements of the Smithsonian Institution, which had been damaged by fire earlier in the year. And all around the city, encircling it protectively, was the ring of earthwork forts where the big black guns were still in place.

There was much visiting back and forth among the officers, and there was a great deal of horseplay and occasional fighting among the men, especially between those in the rival Eastern and Western armies. Friends and relatives who had come to Washington to view the widely publicized spectacle invaded the camps, and the usually all-male tent cities for once had plenty of feminine visitors. By day the vast encampments were centers of activity while all kinds of equipment needed in the review were cleaned and polished; at night, when thousands of campfires, candles, and oil lamps burned in or around the tents, Washington was surrounded by a glowing halo that far outshone the pale crescent of the waning moon.

From Thursday, May 18 until Monday, May 22, there was some intermittent rain. Then, on Monday a three-day spell of magnificently fine weather began. The sun shone brightly, but the temperature remained in the comfortable seventies, and everyone felt that the glorious weather had been sent by Heaven as a special reward to the Union armies for all the hard fighting they had done.

On Sunday the cavalry rode into the city and camped on vacant land east of the Capitol. On Monday night the Ninth Corps moved in, followed at four o'clock in the morning by the Fifth Corps. As the troops marched through the streets of the city they found barrels of drinking water placed on the sidewalks for them, and everywhere flags and bunting were displayed. Over the front door of the Capitol, Commissioner French had placed a large gilded eagle, and on the north end, where the procession was to start, he had mounted a long banner proclaiming the words: "The only national debt we can never pay is the debt we owe to the victorious Union soldiers."

It was impossible to keep liquor away from "the victorious Union soldiers" once they got into the city. There was much drinking and hell-raising, but everyone's mood was merry, and the guards and officers overlooked many breaches of discipline they would never have tolerated in the field.

A covered reviewing stand for the highest officials of the Government had been erected on Pennsylvania Avenue in front of the White House. Across the street was another stand for Congressional and state officials, members of the Supreme Court, the diplomatic corps, the press, and distinguished guests. Near it was a platform which had been built by private funds donated by a wealthy Bostonian to provide a place where wounded and permanently disabled veterans from the Washington hospitals could sit and watch the parade.

The troops gathered at the Capitol, and there, in the shadow of that symbol of centralized government, the grand review began promptly at nine o'clock on Tuesday morning when a signal gun was fired. The District's twenty-five hundred school children had been given a holiday, and dense masses of them, the girls clad in white dresses and the boys in white trousers and blue jackets, stood on Capitol Hill to wave miniature flags and to sing the songs the war had made popular. Bugles blew, drums rolled, the military bands began to play, and the wide column marched around the Capitol and down the long slope to Pennsylvania Avenue, led by General Meade, head of the Army of the Potomac, followed by his staff officers. Then came the cavalry, Sheridan's famous cavalry, but now under the command of Wesley Merritt, while Sheridan was away. As the seemingly endless column of horses clattered along the Avenue, people lining the streets, perched in trees, standing on rooftops, or crowding all the windows, cheered this favorite — and favored — branch of the services. Meade reached the White House reviewing stand before the President and his party got there. Grant came to the stand on foot, walking over from the nearby War Department. He was greeted with enthusiasm, but the general the crowd really wanted to see was Sherman, about whom they had heard so much but who was a stranger to them. As each chief commander taking part in the parade reached the main stand, he saluted the President, Grant, and Sherman, and then dismounted so he could go up on the platform to be received by the dignitaries there and stand at attention while his men marched past.

Several officers had trouble managing their horses when overenthusiastic girls threw bouquets or floral wreaths at them. When Custer approached, riding a stallion captured from the Confederates a few days before Appomattox, about three hundred teen-age girls dressed in white began to sing "Hail to the Chief" and literally bombarded their hero with flowers. This sudden movement frightened the horse, and the skittish animal dashed down the Avenue past the White House stand. Custer, far ahead of his troops, tried to salute the President with his sword. Its point caught his wide-brimmed hat, and hat and sword fell to the street. An orderly quickly picked them up and handed them to the cavalry commander, who jammed his hat on his head, took his sword, brought his nervous horse under control by skill and sheer force, and then galloped back to rejoin his men. He was at their head when his subdued horse went meekly past the reviewing stand at a proper walk.

After the cavalry came the Provost Marshal's Brigade, the Engineers with their pontoon boats on wagons, and then the infantry and artillery, miles and miles of troops that took six hours to pass the White House. The Ninth Corps, the Fifth Corps, and the Second Corps, all of which had been active in the Appomattox Campaign, filed by with bands playing and flags flying. Only those who had taken part in actual battle were allowed in the parade, so some of the regiments which had recently been brought to full strength by heavy replacements appeared on the Avenue represented only by a small group of veterans who had faced the Confederates' guns year after year and yet had somehow managed to survive. The more battle-torn and bloodstained their flags were, the prouder the men were of them.

Down Pennsylvania Avenue the troops came by the thousands, twenty abreast, with horse-drawn artillery and ambulances rumbling along behind each solid phalanx of foot soldiers. Here were the men who had fought in the terrible battles around Washington and Richmond. These were the veterans of every major or minor engagement from Bull Run to Appomattox. And as they went by in this last great review, those who knew them remembered the early defeats of the Army of the Potomac and its never-ceasing struggles against the Army of Northern Virginia. With the passing of these men went the dark and bloody memories of the Peninsular Campaign, Fredericksburg, Chancellorsville, Antietam, Gettysburg, the Wilderness, Spotsylvania, Cold Harbor, Petersburg, and the long running fight westward to Appomattox. Here were the remnants of the famous Iron Brigade, the decimated veterans of what had once been Phil Kearney's command still wearing their red diamonds, and the devil-may-care swaggerers of the Irish Brigade, each man with a sprig of green boxwood stuck into his cap. Here were the army badges that had been made famous — the scarlet trefoil of the Second Corps, the maltese cross of the Fifth, the anchor and cannon of the Ninth, and the crossed red swords of the cavalry. All kinds of banners and guidons dressed the ever-moving blue columns with bright colors, but nothing anywhere along the way got as much attention as the flag of the Treasury Guards, which had never seen battle. It hung from a portico of the Treasury Building, and every man among all those thousands knew what it meant as he marched by, for in one corner of it was a long tear which had been made by the spur of the assassin as he leapt to the stage in Ford's Theatre after having mortally wounded the man who had led this great army through four years of war. Except for the mourning bands on the soldiers' arms, this was the last reminder of the dead President, for even the flag, which had been half-masted at the White House ever since his death, had been run up to the top of the tall white pole for the first time since April 15 to honor the passing of the armies.

The trial of the Lincoln assassination conspirators, which was going on at the Old Arsenal Grounds, was delayed during the day because witnesses could not cross Pennsylvania Avenue to get to the isolated military court on the Old Arsenal Grounds near the Potomac. Snatches of band music occasionally reached the trial room when the breeze blew from the Avenue, and the two prisoners seated nearest the window once dared to stand up to look out. They were sternly ordered to sit down and not get up again.

Because few witnesses were present, the trial moved so slowly that the court finally decided to adjourn until Thursday morning, when the two-day review would be over.

And now, on Wednesday, May 24, Sherman's Army of the Tennessee and the Army of Georgia were to march down the wide Avenue. The Army of the Potomac had so many commanders — most of them unsuccessful — that it was not identified with any one of them. Even Meade, who had been in nominal command ever since Gettysburg, was not so closely associated with his army in the public's mind as Sherman was with the Western troops. Although the great majority of the men in the Army of the Potomac came from the Northeastern states there were also several regiments from Michigan and Minnesota. And in Sherman's army, which was composed largely of troops from Middle-Western and border states, there were many regiments from New York, Pennsylvania, Massachusetts, and New Jersey. The high command at Washington, like a master chess player, had moved its men from place to place as they were needed. But Sherman's armies had fought with amazing success in the West and in the deep South; from them had come Grant and Sheridan to fill posts of high responsibility in the East, and there was no doubt that Sherman's men thought very highly of themselves. They had good reason to: unlike the soldiers of the Eastern armies, they had had very few defeats, and they had just finished a triumphant sweeping march through the heart of the Confederacy. Theirs had been a scorched-earth policy, a policy which their disciple, Sheridan, had applied to the Shenandoah Valley until it was said that a crow flying over that once fertile garden spot would have to carry its own rations.

The second day's review also began at nine o'clock, and since everyone was curious to see the celebrated Western fighting men, the crowds were just as large as they had been the day before. Sherman rode proudly at the head of his armies accompanied by General O. O. Howard, who had lost an arm in the war. Noah Brooks said of the troops: "Comparisons between the Eastern and the Western men were made at once. It was observed that the Western men wore a more free-and-easy uniform, generally adopting the loose blue blouse and the sugar-loaf-shaped felt hat, rather than the close-fitting coat and natty French kepi of the Eastern soldiers. . . . But nothing could be more perfect than their marching order, each rank stepping out as one man. As a rule, the Westerners were of larger build than their brothers in the Army of the Potomac."

When the head of the column approached the White House reviewing stand, the band struck up the tune which Sherman had made famous, "Marching Through Georgia," and he got more applause than any other commander who had led troops down the Avenue. After they passed the platform, Sherman and Howard dismounted and went up to be received by the President and review their marching columns from that honored place. There then occurred an incident which caused more talk than anything else that happened during those eventful two days. Sherman was still angry at Stanton for the way the untactful Secretary of War had repudiated the terms of peace he had offered to Johnston. (Halleck, fortunately for him, was at Fortress Monroe, supervising the arrangements for imprisoning Jefferson Davis there.) Grant had sent a message to Sherman on May 18, saying that he wanted "to talk about matters on which you feel sore," but no matter what his friend and superior officer may have advised, Sherman was still nursing a grudge, and he was not the kind to conceal his feelings.

Noah Brooks, who was seated in the stand across the street, describes what he saw from there: "I sat ... between Senator Conness of California and Senator Wilson of Massachusetts; and when Sherman, removing his hat, emerged upon the platform from the crowd near the President, Senator Wilson excitedly said: 'Now let us watch Sherman; people think he will affront Stanton, whom he hasn't met yet.' We trained our field-glasses on the group and saw Stanton extend his hand to Sherman, who, after saluting the President, approached the Secretary of War. At our distance from the party in the grand stand, we could not hear whether any words were spoken; but we could see that Sherman, declining Stanton's greeting, firmly placed his right hand by his side with a very slight gesture.

Stanton's face, never very expressive, remained immobile. Sherman, as he turned his attention to the troops passing by, looked grimmer than ever, and a dark-red scar, the mark of a recent slight accident, imparted to his visage a certain sinister expression which rather heightened the effect of this little episode. Some have said that Sherman put his hands behind him, and at the same time made a curt remark as he put aside the greeting proffered by Stanton."

Ben: Perley Poore, the popular gossip columnist of Washington, claims that Sherman told Stanton "I do not care to shake hands with clerks," but Sherman in his *Memoirs* merely said: "I shook hands with the President, General Grant, and each member of the cabinet. As I approached Mr. Stanton, he offered me his hand, but I declined it publicly, and the fact was universally noticed."

Brooks described Sherman as he saw him watching his troops march past for six and a half hours. "In the group of notable men on the grand stand, Sherman was certainly the most notable in appearance. His head was high and narrow, his hair and whiskers were sandy in hue, his moustache stiff and bristling, and his eyes keen and piercing. He was very tall, walked with an immense stride, talked rapidly and nervously, and would be picked out in any assemblage as a man of distinction. All eyes were fastened upon his striking countenance, the vast multitude gazing with a certain rapture at the famous man whom they now saw for the first time."

Sherman had been afraid that his Westerners might not make as good an appearance as the better-clad Eastern troops, but he was a clever showman so he placed special emphasis upon aspects that were peculiar to his armies. Horace Porter describes the Negro soldiers and the "bummers" whom Sherman had put into the procession along with his crack outfits: "Each division was preceded by a pioneer corps of negroes, marching in double ranks, with picks, spades, and axes slung across their brawny shoulders, their stalwart forms conspicuous by their height. But the impedimenta were the novel feature of the march. Six ambulances followed each division to represent its baggage-train; and then came the amusing spectacle of 'Sherman's bummers,' bearing with them the 'spoils of war. . . .' The trophies . . . which appeared in the review consisted of pack-mules loaded with turkeys, geese, chickens, and bacon, and here and there a chicken-coop strapped on to the saddle with a cackling brood peering out through the slats. Then came cows, goats, sheep, donkeys, crowing roosters, and in one instance a chattering monkey. Mixed with these was a procession of fugitive blacks — old men, stalwart women, and grinning piccaninnies of all sizes, and ranging in color from a raven's wing to a new saddle. This portion of the column called forth shouts of laughter and continuous rounds of applause."

At half-past three, the last brigade, one of artillery, came down the Avenue. Its ten-pound black iron Parrots with their big breech-bands looked somber as they rolled along the street, but the barrels and fittings of the twelve-pound brass Napoleons had been polished so they gleamed brightly in the sunlight as they rolled past the reviewing stand. And then the great armies which had fought at Shiloh, Vicksburg, Missionary Ridge, and had swept through Georgia to the sea, passed into history. The Grand Review was over. One of the generals who had watched the troops march by for two days, said of those winnowed ranks: "Had the eye of the spirit been opened . . . the spectator would have seen by the side of each man who moved firmly and proudly in the victorious column three wounded and crippled men, limping and stumbling in their eager desire to keep up with their more fortunate comrades, while with the four stalked one pale ghost."

And now there remained only the herculean task for the

street cleaners of Washington to do. Sherman had not brought any cavalry with him, but thousands of horses had been in Washington during the past two days, and the city smelled like an enormous stable. Shovels were not enough; steam from fire engines had to be used to get Pennsylvania Avenue back to its normally none-too-sanitary condition. But this job of cleaning the vast Augean stables was perhaps symbolic of what was to come, for now that the great years of heroism and glory were over, an era which would have made the foul stables of the King of Elis smell sweet was about to descend upon the land.

24

Beyond the End

Beautiful that war and all its deeds of carnage
must in time be utterly lost,
That the hands of the sisters Death and Night
incessantly softly wash, again and ever again,
this soiled world.

WALT WHITMAN

DOWN CAME the flags and the bunting, the field armies left Washington to be disbanded, and the city again became the reasonably quiet and orderly seat of national government it had been before the war. Yet it was to be a long while before the American Civil War was finished.

In the northern part of the Pacific Ocean the Confederate raider *Shenandoah* was still burning and sinking New England whaling vessels. The master of a ship seized on June 28 showed the raider's captain a San Francisco newspaper dated April 15 with dispatches telegraphed from Washington that described Lee's surrender and Lincoln's death. Nevertheless, the *Shenandoah*'s officers decided to continue their activities because the newspaper also said that some Confederate armies were still active. They were not convinced that the war was really over until August 2, when they hailed a British ship off the western coast of Mexico and were told that they no longer had a government and therefore did not have even the pretense of legality to justify what they were doing. They made a fast run for Liverpool and arrived there on November 6 to surrender their ship to the British authorities, who turned the famous raider over to the United States Government.

But that was still not the end of the Civil War. Fifteen months after Appomattox, a Texas corporal commanding two privates from Georgia emerged from Virginia's Dismal Swamp, where they had been posted in the spring of 1865 to keep watch over the Yankee soldiers stationed in Norfolk. Texans were bitter-enders; South Carolina had been the first Confederate state to secede, but Texas was the last to be brought back into the Union. When President Johnson officially proclaimed the nation to be at peace on April 2, 1866 (the first anniversary of the fall of Petersburg and Richmond), he specifically exempted Texas and did not proclaim peace there until August 20, 1866.

At last the martial music was stilled, and the reunited nation settled down to count the cost of the war. Two important gains had been made: slavery had been abolished and the Union had been preserved. There were other achievements. So much courage and determination had been displayed on both sides that the American fighting man took on added stature in the eyes of the world's military experts. So did American inventiveness in thinking up new weapons and new ways of fighting a war. The four years of conflict had made wooden navies obsolete; had seen fire power stepped up enormously by the adoption of the brass cartridge and the repeating arm;* and had proved that digging in was a quick, simple, effective, and inexpensive method of protecting troops from attack. A great deal had also been learned about the mass production of weapons, equipment, and clothing.

Major General J. F. C. Fuller of the British Army has summed up with professional skill the military significance of the Civil War: "The 1864–1865 campaign in Virginia was the first of the modern campaigns; it initiated a tactical epoch, and did not even resemble the wars of ten years before its date.

* This applies only to hand weapons, not to larger guns. Machine guns had been invented and improved during the Civil War but had not been factors in the fighting.

It was not a campaign of bayonets but of bullets. ... On the battlefields of the Wilderness and of Spotsylvania the Confederate ordnance officers collected for recasting more than 120,000 pounds of lead, and even if this amount represents a twentieth part of the bullets fired, then, at two ounces* apiece, the number expended was 19,000,000. When did Marlborough, or Wellington, or Napoleon face such a hail of projectiles?

"It was the bullet which created the trench and the rifle-pit; which killed the bayonet; which rendered useless the sword; which chased away guns and horsemen; which, from May 5, 1864, to April 9, 1865, held the contending forces in 'constant close contact, with rare intervals of brief comparative repose,' and which prevented the rapid decisions of the battles of preceding centuries. In 1861–1865 the rifle bullet was the lord of the battlefield as was the machine gun bullet in 1914–1918.

"This must be remembered, for otherwise it is futile to attempt to assess the generalship of Grant or Lee. Neither of them understood the tactics of the bullet, or its influences upon former tactical conceptions, morale, and tactical organization. Both were like children playing with a new and complicated toy, and seeing that, in 1914–1918, Marshal Foch understood the bullet no better, it is a remarkable fact that Grant and Lee understood it as well as they did. This lack in the appreciation of the power of the rifle bullet has constituted the supreme tragedy of modern warfare, a drama of insanity in which millions have perished for a dream — the bayonet clinch, the flash of steel, the stab, and the yell of victory."

An end to slavery, the preservation of the Union, and some technological progress were the Civil War's few benefits.

* General Fuller overweighs Civil War bullets; a Minié ball weighs just under 1¼ ounces; the average musket ball not quite an ounce. Consequently the total number of bullets fired on these two battlefields would be almost twice 19,000,000. Two factors, however, must remain uncertain — the "twentieth part" recovered and the relative number of Minié balls and musket balls fired.

Against them must be set the cost. More than 600,000 men had died in the war, while hundreds of thousands more had been wounded — some of them so badly that they were crippled for life. Whole cities had been destroyed, and thousands of homes, farmhouses, barns, factories, and public buildings had been burned. The red hand of war had fallen heavily upon the land, and its dreadful effect was to be felt by generations still unborn.

The cost of getting rid of slavery by fighting out the issue on the battlefield was enormous. It has been estimated that the direct cost of the Civil War to the United States Government was $3,400,000,000. About $8,200,000,000 was paid in later years for pensions, making a total of $11,600,000,000. And this does not take into account what was spent by the Confederate States.

Lincoln, the shrewd and practical attorney who had a keen sense of property rights and a good knowledge of the last sentence of the Fifth Amendment, which states that "private property may not be condemned or appropriated for public use unless it is fully and fairly paid for," had long been in favor of having the Federal Government compensate the slave-owners for their human property by giving them $400 for each slave. Since there were nearly four million slaves in the country in 1861, freeing them would have involved incurring a long-term debt of $1,600,000,000 — which was just ten billion dollars less than the war actually cost in terms of money alone. But no one, not even Lincoln's own Cabinet members, would listen seriously to his seemingly quixotic proposal, so emotion prevailed over reason, and billions of dollars and hundreds of thousands of lives were thrown away on the battlefields.

Yet by 1861 slavery had become an incubus that was dragging the South down into a dark and ancient mire where thought stagnated and judgment decayed. The more intelligent Southerners knew how desperate their position was; they also knew that time was working against them and in favor of the

North. There seemed to be no solution to the problem unless they broke the less-than-a-century-old compact between the various American states to strike out on their own as an independent nation. Actually, this was not so outrageous an idea as Lincoln thought it was. Compacts made by men can be amended by men, and if a peaceful separation could have been arranged all might have gone well. But this was practically impossible to do, for the two sections had long been closely integrated. Privately owned railroads and telegraph lines tied them together, and there were other important commercial connections that could not easily be broken — especially since the South was continually in debt to Northern bankers and brokers. There were other ties, invisible ties of family and friendship that play a decisive part in determining man's fate. It was an uneasy marriage for which no legal means of separation had ever been provided — or even contemplated. Such an impasse often results in an outburst of violence, as this one did.

Once the first gun had been fired at Fort Sumter the issue could no longer be solved by peaceful means. Then, as Lincoln said, "Both parties deprecated war; but one of them would make war rather than let the nation survive; and the other would accept war rather than let it perish. And the war came."

Attempts have been made to show that it would have been better if the South had been allowed to become a separate nation. Some of these attempts were serious; others, like Winston Churchill's amusing bit of speculation entitled "If Lee Had Not Won the Battle of Gettysburg,"* were intended

* This brilliant essay is one of eleven by various authors in *If, Or History Rewritten* (New York: Viking Press, 1931). In it, the man who was to be Britain's Prime Minister during the Second World War tries to show how the successful establishment of two American governments on United States soil would have led to the formation of a powerful English-Speaking Association with Great Britain — an organization that would have been strong enough to prevent the First World War.

only as entertaining essays. But this kind of speculation is merely a parlor game. There are no if's in history. The continuous cycle of cause and effect works as inevitably in human affairs as it does in everything else. The American Civil War was fought because all the antecedent action led to armed conflict and could have led to nothing else. Aeschylus knew this twenty-five hundred years ago when he said: "Things are where things are, and, as fate has willed, so shall they be fulfilled." There is no appeal from the verdict of what actually did happen.

Once the war began, the result was equally inevitable, for in any long continued struggle, the North, with its vastly greater population and resources, had to win. In fact the North gained more people during the war by immigration alone than it lost as battle casualties. The South's only chance for continued independence was to get open support from other strong world powers, and that it was never able to obtain. The Confederacy's fate was settled not on the field of battle but in the chancelleries of Europe. In England, liberal-minded people and the laboring class prevented the country from backing the Confederate States; on the Continent feudal-minded monarchs and their ministers, after long hesitation, were finally unwilling to back any nation that had had even a taste of political freedom. The miracle is that the Confederacy lasted as long as it did. But even valor on the battlefield and the brilliant use of available fighting forces cannot enable a government to hold out indefinitely against a much more powerful adversary.

What, then, was accomplished by the victory of the Northern states? What was gained by this appalling sacrifice of battle-squandered wealth and human lives? It would be pleasant to be able to say that much good was accomplished, that enormous benefits to the reunited nation were gained. It would be fitting and right if the price paid in human suffering could purchase an equivalent amount of human welfare. But that is not always the way the world runs. The lessons taught us in the nursery about rewards and punishments may seem to be just but they are not necessarily true. Actually, the period that followed the Civil War was the most grotesquely corrupt in American history. The entire country was at the mercy of ruthless moneygrubbers who controlled both local and national government. There were few legal restraints on such creatures then, so they were able to do pretty much as they pleased. The struggle for legislation to limit their almost untrammeled power went on for generations. Even today their breed is far from extinct.

The reign of the robber barons was a monstrous era when the ethics of the nation sank to a new low. These shameless plunderers emerged from a war in which the Confederates had fought bravely to defend a bad cause — slavery and the obsolescent idea that a state was more important as a unit of government than the nation — while the men of the North had fought just as bravely for a good cause, which they now forgot.

Here the bright colors of American life — the dark green of the forest age, the yellows and scarlets of Indian times, the clear ocean-blue of the clipper ship era, and the bloodstained red of all the wars — were mixed to make the dull sodden brown that results when pigments of different colors are carelessly slopped together. Out of this mixture came the brown age, the age of the brownstone front, in which venality was masked by a show of pious respectability. There was little protest; rich and poor alike reveled in the dark brown mud and manure that lay deep around the hog trough.

And so did valor end in corruption for the North and the South alike. And yet, as Lincoln said at Gettysburg, the Civil War had not been fought in vain. It was a major surgical operation which the nation had to endure — or perish. The great raw red wound has not healed entirely even now.

The ancient smoothbores and the rifled cannon are forever stilled, and their wooden carriages and caissons have rotted away. The bugle is now heard only on the parade ground, where its martial commands are more likely to come from a phonograph record than from a real instrument. The last Army mule was officially mustered out of service in December 1956, and the few remaining horses, the brave white steeds which are all that are left to represent the enormous Civil War herd, are kept chiefly for use in military funerals so they can haul a flag-covered casket to a soldier's grave. Tourists in sports clothes roam the battlefields, which have been made into attractively landscaped national parks. There, in well-tended glades or on closely cropped lawns, monuments of bronze or stone commemorate the deeds of otherwise forgotten regiments that made the name of some nearby village or crossroads forever famous. And the earthworks, which bristled with cannon and chevaux-de-frise when soldiers manned them, have become softly rounded grassy mounds on which children play. Large trees and thick undergrowth now block the vistas which artillerymen once commanded with deadly crossfire. The tangled mess, the ugly disorder, and the trampled mud in which the troops lived and struggled have long ago been cleaned up.

The land on which the Civil War battles were fought is changing and must continue to change. Eventually all trace of what went on there will be obliterated. The wind and the rain will level the earthworks, and with the passage of enough time, will even destroy the bronze and stone monuments that were intended to last forever. Someday no physical evidence will remain to tell us that tens of thousands of men fought and died on these quiet fields.

Those who survived the battles have gone to join their dead comrades. Even those who lived as children during that war are now so old that their senile recollections are misted over until they are nothing but shadowy images, uncertain and insubstantial, in which fact and fancy are hopelessly inter-mingled. Soon all living memory of the American Civil War will be gone, and we shall have only the documents, the printed records, and the pictures. These too must perish, and at some remote time the truth about the stirring events of the 1860's will pass into myth. Then the very real heroes will be trans-formed into vague legendary figures, gigantic and impressive, but very different from the hard-bitten troopers who behaved very much as any soldiers do in any war. Then the Civil War battles will seem as far away as those in which half-naked men in armor clashed and clanked on a dusty plain in the red dawn-light of a world that was still young. Finally Richmond will be one with Troy, and Appomattox and Waterloo will come equally to mean an end to long-continued conflict. If civiliza-tion has then advanced accordingly, the people of that more intelligently run world will shudder at the wanton waste and welter of all wars. But that will be another world and another time.

Except for the small area around Harpers Ferry, Antietam, and Gettysburg, the Civil War left no enduring physical marks upon the landscape of the Northern states. But the Southern states were deeply scarred, and many of the scars remain. The tortured earth around Petersburg and Richmond shows how vast and complicated the siegeworks investing those two cities were. In the back country, the route the armies followed to Appomattox can be traced, but only with difficulty, because many of the roads have been abandoned or changed. Dinwiddie is still a very small town, and the country north of it even now is so sparsely settled that Five Forks is the same lonely place where the same secondary roads come together to make an intersection that was to be world-famous for a few days and then be forgotten. Of all the important Civil War battlefields this is the one which is least visited and most neglected. There are no markers, and strangers who pass by do not know they are on historic ground.

The original Amelia Court House has been replaced by a more recent structure, but the quiet little town is very much as it was when Lee's haggard and hungry veterans arrived there seeking rations that had never been sent. The once gay resort at Amelia Springs is utterly deserted. Its smaller buildings have fallen into complete ruin, the road is washed out, and the big brick hotel is a gaunt and windowless wreck, a ghostly reminder of what its former splendor must have been.

At Jetersville, near the railroad which runs on the same right-of-way used by the old Southside, the weathered remnants of Sheridan's trenches cross the highway. Northeast of them is the now abandoned road which Lee's army took to head west toward Appomattox and certain defeat. The ground around Sayler's Creek is so densely tangled with second-growth woods and underbrush as to be almost impenetrable, but on the hill above it, where Union artillery poured its murderous fire down into the valley, the restored Hillsman house still stands. Its ancient wide-planked floors are stained with the mingled blood of the Confederate and Union wounded who were brought there after the battle.

Farmville and Appomattox, which are now on a main highway, have become highly industrialized. But only three miles from the modern town of Appomattox, the historic little surrender village still exists. The court house which gave the town its reason for being was destroyed by fire in 1892, and most of the other buildings were allowed to fall into ruin until 1940, when the National Park Service began to restore the village that saw the end of Lee's Army of Northern Virginia. Now the McLean house, completely rebuilt and refurnished, is open to the public, and the scenes associated with Grant and Lee's momentous encounter in that destiny-haunted hamlet can be visited. Nearby, in a tiny iron-fenced cemetery, are the saddest memorials of the Civil War. Eighteen plain headstones, lined up in a row, mark the graves of seventeen Confederates and one Union soldier who were among those killed in the useless fighting during the morning of the final day.

In Richmond, Jefferson Davis' official residence is now a museum where some of the most important relics and memorabilia of the Confederacy can be seen. Capitol Square, St. Paul's Church, and General Lee's home remain very much as they were. The burned-out district downtown was, of course, rebuilt soon after the war.

In Washington, Lincoln's official residence, the White House, is still the center of Presidential activity, but it is only the outer shell of the former structure, for the inside was completely replaced from 1949 to 1952. Ford's Theatre also has only its original outer walls; its interior collapsed in 1893 at the very time that the funeral of John Wilkes Booth's celebrated brother Edwin was being held in New York. The Peterson house across the street from the theater is practically unchanged, and the tiny bedroom in which Lincoln died has been refurnished to make it look as it did on that fatal night.

At the eastern end of Pennsylvania Avenue is the building that played the most important part in the Civil War and in the destiny of the nation. This is the Capitol of the United States; under its massive dome, which the people of the early 1860's saw grow to completion, the great rotunda where Lincoln's body lay in state is still the same. Far down below it is a little-known, seldom visited tomb which was intended to hold the mortal body of George Washington, but which one of his heirs refused to let the Government use for that purpose. When the tomb was offered to Mrs. Lincoln for her husband's remains, she, too, refused it. In it is kept the original catafalque on which Lincoln's body lay in state. On this bier have rested the remains of a dozen other distinguished Americans, including the Unknown Soldier of the First World War. Here, in the very heart and center of the Capitol, this dark rock chamber, this secret reliquary, ties together our historic past from Washington and Lincoln to the fighting forces that took part in our more recent wars. Across the Potomac, in Arlington National Cemetery, thousands of men from both the Union and Confederate armies are buried. And around the various battlefields and in scattered cemeteries throughout the land lie the nineteenth-century Americans who fought against each other in a war that no one could win. Perhaps the best epitaph for them was spoken by Abraham Lincoln at his first inauguration, when all that mighty host was still alive:

> We are not enemies, but friends. . . . Though passion may have strained, it must not break our bonds of affection. The mystic chords of memory, stretching from every battlefield and every patriot grave to every living heart and hearthstone in this broad land, will yet swell the chorus of the Union.

Appendix

on *Civil War Battle Statistics*

F I G U R E S for battle casualties and troops present are given
in round numbers in the text. Many works on Civil War military engagements print numbers which may seem to be exact.
Unfortunately, there are very few exact figures about Civil
War battles, despite the fact that an enormous amount of work
has been done over a period of many years to determine accurate
statistical data.

Books like *Numbers and Losses in the Civil War* by Thomas
L. Livermore (1900), *Statistical Record of the Armies of the
United States* by Frederick Phisterer (1893), *Regimental Losses
in the American Civil War* by William F. Fox (1889), *A Com-
pendium of the War of the Rebellion* by F. H. Dyer (1908),
the War Department's *List of Field Officers, Regiments, and
Battalions in the Confederate State Army,* 1861–1865 (n.d.),
as well as the statistical material contained in *Official Records,*
are all useful but their information is seldom as exact as it
appears to be.

There are a number of reasons for this: Confederate records
were never well kept and many of them were destroyed; Union
records were reasonably well kept and are still preserved, but
there was never any general agreement about the status of
men employed in the regimental, medical, and quartermaster's
departments, nor were musicians, company clerks, cooks, or

officer's servants necessarily counted as among those present at a battle. Yet some of these men were killed or wounded, and many of them died as the result of the various camp diseases that took a greater toll of lives than the actual fighting. They were true casualties of the war.

Still worse, however, than the uncertainty about these men, whose status was marginal, is the discrepancy between the figures reported by various commanders about the number of fighting men who were supposedly "present for duty" (although perhaps without arms or cavalry mounts), "present for duty equipped" (although perhaps hardly able to stand up straight), or "effective" (which is supposed to mean fully armed, adequately supplied with ammunition, and able to go into battle). Because of lack of agreement as to who should be counted, Confederate commanders (usually) and Union commanders (sometimes) excluded from their reports all officers and even the active fighting men in the artillery and cavalry units.

As a result, figures for the entire war, a major campaign, or a single battle are undependable. A good example of this occurred when Sheridan rode toward Dinwiddie Court House with a large body of cavalrymen on March 29. According to his own report (*Official Records*, Vol. 95, p. 1101) dated May 16, 1865, he had with him:

Custer and Devin	5700
Crook	3300
	9000 effectives

In his *Memoirs* (Vol. II, p. 148), he corroborates this figure; so does his adjutant general, Lieutenant Colonel F. C. Newhall, in his book *With General Sheridan in Lee's Last Campaign* (p. 52). Newhall says that as the men rode across Rowanty Run before reaching Dinwiddie the effective strength of men and horses was verified by actual count.

All this seems very definite. But *Official Records* (Vol. 97, p. 391) also has a table entitled: "Abstract from returns of the cavalry forces commanded by Maj. Gen. Philip H. Sheridan . . . for the month of March, 1865." This table gives a total of 591 officers and 12,835 men as being present for duty (but not necessarily effective, of course).

General Andrew A. Humphreys' *The Virginia Campaign of '64 and '65* (New York, 1883) has a table on page 433 about Sheridan's men headed: "Morning Report, March 31, 1865, Cavalry present for duty, not present for duty, equipped." It reads:

	Officers	*Men*
Custer	209	4355
Devin	192	3439
Crook	210	5415
	611	13,209

The Military Historical Society of Massachusetts' publication entitled *The Shenandoah Campaigns of 1862 and 1864 and the Appomattox Campaign of 1865* (Boston, 1907), Vol. VI, prints a table on page 503 which gives Sheridan's effectives as 11,412 but says that Sheridan may not have included his officers or artillerymen.

The interested reader can find still more examples of such discrepancies for Civil War military statistics by spending a little time in any well-equipped library. One reason for such wide variations is the fact that nearly all these figures were printed before the completion of the War Department's 128 volumes of *Official Records of the Union and Confederate Armies* in 1901. (The *Official Records* of the Navy were not completed until 1927.) Yet even this vast compilation is far from complete, as can be seen by examining the manuscript sources in the National Archives on which it was based. And beyond the official records are the details of the regimental books which give day-by-day reports. Muster rolls, cemeterial records, and other such documents in the National Archives and elsewhere would give a truer picture of Civil War statistics (for the Union Army at least) than anything that now exists. But to establish such data would take years of work for a trained staff.

Until such work is done it is futile to try to give anything except round figures — and even those with caution. In a letter to the author regarding this problem, Bruce Catton wisely said:

"I am beginning to believe that this whole mix-up is just one more example of the utter impossibility of solving any part of the Civil War numbers game. It seems to me just about hopeless to be really sure how many soldiers any general really had at any time; all the figures are different, and most of the time the different sets are based on different methods of computation; you have the present-for-duty, the present-for-duty-equipped, the effective-present, and the God knows what else. Maybe the thing to do is to try to strike an average from all the totals available and let it go at that."

Acknowledgments

EVERYTHING that was to be said about the Civil War by those who took part in it has already been said. Now one can only attempt to find out what they really did say. Their written words, which in many cases were carefully put away until all those concerned were dead, are gradually coming to light. These words can be found in our libraries, archives, and private collections, but to locate them often requires a long and difficult paper-chase from one place to another with much retracing of steps and comparison of material which has long been known against that which has only recently been made public.

The people who can best help in such a search are those into whose hands the records, written or printed, have been entrusted. To them every writer who works in the field of history owes a debt of gratitude. The author wishes to thank the institutions, their staffs, and the individuals listed below.

MANUSCRIPT SOURCES

The Manuscripts Division of the Library of Congress is the world's greatest treasure trove for Civil War letters and papers, especially those of the high officials involved. To Dr. David C. Mearns, Chief of the Division, and to Dr. C. Percy Powell the author is indebted for advice on material in the Library's collection and for suggestions about finding needed documents in other collections.

The National Archives, where all Government documents are eventually deposited, is so rich in Civil War military material that much of it has never been explored. But the records are there, and with the patient help of the staff in the sections known as Old Army Records, Old Navy Records, and Treasury Department Records, the author was able to find letters, telegrams, battlefield dispatches, trial testimony, and ledgerbooks which threw new light on many subjects hitherto imperfectly known. He wishes to acknowledge a personal debt to Dr. Richard Wood, to Dr. Wood's successor, Victor Gondos, Jr., and also to Elmer Otis Parker, who went out of their way to be helpful.

He would also like to thank Robert E. Hill, Keeper of the Manuscripts in the New York Public Library, his first assistant Edward B. Morrison, and Miss Jean R. McNiece; Sylvester Vigilante of the New-York Historical Society; William A. Jackson of the Houghton Library at Harvard University; Clyde Walton of the Illinois State Historical Library; Paul M. Angle, Director of the Chicago Historical Society; and Miss Mattie Russell, Curator of Manuscripts of the Duke University Library. And he has cause to be grateful to Dr. Allan Nevins, who made the manuscript and microfilm facilities of the Columbia University Library available.

Specific mention of manuscripts used in the collections listed above appears in the source notes.

PRINTED SOURCES

For guidance and counsel in using the enormous mass of printed material in the Library of Congress the author wants to thank Colonel Willard Webb, Chief of the Reader and Stack Division, whose own military background and special interest in Civil War history made his help particularly valuable.

Many of the books and pamphlets referred to in the source notes were consulted in the very extensive Halliday Collection of Civil War literature of the Brooklyn Public Library. Miss Corinne Sheppard, Miss Louise Turpin, and Marino J. Ruffier made working there a pleasure.

The New York Public Library, the New-York Historical Society, the Harry Elkins Widener Memorial Library of Harvard University, the Boston Athenaeum, and the Washington Public Library supplied most of the other printed sources.

NEWSPAPER SOURCES

The Library of Congress' huge collection of American newspapers had most of the publications needed; others were examined in the New-York Historical Society, and the New York Public Library, the Columbia University Library, and the Illinois State Historical Library made certain much needed newspapers available on microfilm.

MAPS

The National Archives had nearly all the necessary battle maps; others were examined and photostated in the map collections of the Library of Congress and the New York Public Library.

PICTURES

Source credits are printed under each illustration, but the author wishes to thank Miss Alice Lee Parker, Milton Kaplan, and Hirst Milhollen of the Prints and Photographs Division of the Library of Congress and Miss Josephine Cobb of National Archives for their help in finding these pictures.

The author also wants to thank many other people who in one way or another graciously gave of their time and knowledge. They are: Lieutenant Colonel William G. McNamara, U.S.A.R., who has thoroughly explored the Civil War Army records in the National Archives; George Stansfield, Librarian of the National War College; Milton F. Perry, Curator of History at the United States Military Academy, West Point; Rear Admiral John B. Heffernan, U.S.N. (ret.), Director of Naval History; Richard S. West, Jr., of the United States Naval Academy, Annapolis; Philip W. Schulte, Public Information Officer of the United States Civil Service Commission, for information about the old Patent Office building; Stanley W. McClure, Curator of the Lincoln Museum in Washington, for a behind-the-scenes tour of Ford's Theatre; Dr. St. George L. Sioussat, Special Consultant to the Library of Congress, for a long discussion of the career of Andrew Johnson; Lee A. Wallace and Ralph Happel, historians of the National Park Service, for information about the Petersburg, Richmond, and Appomattox battlefields; and Dr. Jay Monaghan for help on some problems concerning Custer; Miss India Thomas, House Regent of the Confederate Museum in Richmond, and the staffs of the Valentine Museum and the Virginia State Library in that city; Clifford Dowdey for long talks about the Confederacy in Richmond; and M. R. Turner of Blackstone, Virginia, who guided the writer (as he once did Douglas Southall Freeman) over Lee's retreat route from Amelia Court House to Appomattox; Bruce Catton for permission to quote from his letters about Civil War battle statistics; Dr. Fletcher M. Green, Chairman of the Department of History of the University of North Carolina, for his efforts to locate certain material about Duff Green; William Townsend, Bennett H. Wall, Maurice G. Baxter, and Charles H. Coleman for assistance in seeking material concerning the elusive "General" Singleton; E. B. Long, Ralph Newman, and Otto Eisenschiml for long discussions about Civil War subjects; Joseph Holt Rose for drawing attention to additional material he had deposited with the Judge Holt Papers in the Manuscripts Division of the Library of Congress; and to Miss Emily B. Warren for information about her father, General Gouverneur Kemble Warren.

None of these people, of course, are in any way responsible for statements or errors made by the author. In Miss Warren's case it is only fair to state that she does not think that her father has been done full justice in the text.

And to those who read and criticized the manuscript, the author is especially grateful. They are, among the forementioned: Colonels McNamara, Webb, and Dr. Powell. Others are: Marcus Goodrich, Carl Haverlin, Maxwell Nurnberg, Mrs. Marie Rodell, Miss Norma Tasman, the author's wife, Lillian, and his daughter, Mrs. Allan Robinson.

Lastly he wants to thank the staff of his publishers, particularly Craig Wylie, Hardwick Moseley, and Miss Helen Phillips.

Source Notes and Bibliography

N O A T T E M P T has been made to list all the material which was consulted for the writing of this book. To do so would require far too many pages and serve no useful purpose. Cited here are the main sources, the exact location of all quoted matter, and the places where hard-to-find anecdotes and odd bits of information may be found. In some cases only one source may be given for an incident which was observed by many people; this does not mean that the other witnesses' accounts were ignored. The author, in so far as he could, has tried to see all the accounts available and has cited the one he thought most nearly complete, truthful, or significant.

He has read with great care such outstanding works on this period as Douglas Southall Freeman's *R. E. Lee* and *Lee's Lieutenants,* Carl Sandburg's *Abraham Lincoln: The War Years,* Bruce Catton's *A Stillness at Appomattox,* and various modern histories and biographies of the men involved, but he has tried to go beyond such books to examine primary source material. This meant spending a great deal of time going over manuscript letters and documents, diaries, battle maps, ships' logs, newspapers, magazines, obscure regimental histories, official records of the War and Navy Departments, and personal narratives. Coming to grips with such material at first hand has enabled him to present much information which should be new even to a well-informed reader of Civil War history. The manuscript has been read in full by authorities whose names are given in the Acknowledgments, while certain parts have been checked by specialists in their own fields.

In order to save space, the appended abbreviations for libraries and often cited works have been used. Since the most important manuscript collections and printed materials are listed, the author feels that a bibliography is not needed. Nor does he think it necessary to list easily available reference works like the *Dictionary of American Biography* or the biographical compilations which give background details about the lives of the men who fought the Civil War.

Location symbols are the standard ones used in library work; when a source is given in the text it is not repeated here; when no year is stated, 1865 is understood. The titles of works only occasionally referred to are given in full in the notes. Page references are not given for pamphlets.

Key to Location Symbols of Manuscripts
and Short Titles of Books, Magazines, and Newspapers
Often Referred to in the Notes

BA: Baltimore *American*
DLC Ms. Div.: Manuscript Division, Library of Congress
DLC Ms. Div., RTL: Robert Todd Lincoln Papers
DNA: National Archives
DNA-OA: Old Army Records
DNA-OA-JAG: Judge Advocate General's Records
DNA-ON: Old Navy Records
DNA-TR: Treasury Department Records

MH: Harvard University Library
MH-H: Houghton Manuscript Collection at Harvard
NN: New York Public Library
NN Ms. Room: Manuscript Division
NYH: New York *Herald*
NYT: New York *Tribune*
NYW: New York *World*
WDC: Washington Daily *Chronicle*
WNI: Washington *National Intelligencer*
WSTR: Washington *Star*

Alexander MMC: E. Porter Alexander, *Military Memoirs of a Confederate* (New York, 1907).
B & L: *Battles and Leaders of the Civil War,* ed. R. V. Johnson and C. C. Buel (New York, 1884, 1888), Vol. IV.
Badeau GP: Adam Badeau, *Grant in Peace* (Hartford, Conn., 1887).
Badeau MHUSG: Adam Badeau, *Military History of Ulysses S. Grant* (New York, 1881), Vol. III.
Bahnson LDW: Henry T. Bahnson, *Last Days of the War,* North Carolina Booklet, Vol. II, No. 12 (Hamlet, N.C., April 1903). Pamphlet.
Bates LTO: David Homer Bates, *Lincoln in the Telegraph Office* (New York, 1907).
Boykin FF: E. M. Boykin, *The Falling Flag* (New York, 1874).
Brooks WLT: Noah Brooks, *Washington in Lincoln's Time* (New York, 1894, 1895).
Browning's Diary: *The Diary of Orville Hickman Browning* (Springfield, Ill., 1925–33). Vol. I, ed. Theodore Calvin Pease and James G. Randall; Vol. II, ed. James G. Randall.
Bruce COR: George A. Bruce, *The Capture and Occupation of Richmond* (n.d., n.p.).
Chamberlain PA: Joshua L. Chamberlain, *The Passing of the Armies* (New York, 1915).

Cooke WG: John Esten Cooke, *The Wearing of the Gray* (New York, 1867).

Crook TFA: William B. Crook, *Through Five Administrations* (New York, 1910).

CWAL: *The Collected Works of Abraham Lincoln* (New Brunswick, N.J., 1953), Vols. I–IX.

De Chambrun PRML: Marquis de Chambrun (Charles Adolphe Pineton), "Personal Recollections of Mr. Lincoln," *Scribner's Magazine*, Jan., Feb. 1893. De Chambrun's *Impressions of Lincoln and the Civil War* (New York, 1952) reprints much of this account.

Eisenschiml WWLM: Otto Eisenschiml, *Why Was Lincoln Murdered?* (Boston, 1937).

Gibbon's Recollections: John Gibbon, *Personal Recollections of the Civil War* (New York, 1928).

Gordon's Reminiscences: John B. Gordon, *Reminiscences of the Civil War* (New York, 1903).

Gorman LLC: J. C. Gorman, *Lee's Last Campaign* (Raleigh, N.C., 1866). Pamphlet.

Grant's Memoirs: *Personal Memoirs of U. S. Grant* (New York, 1894). One-vol. ed.

Humphreys VC: Andrew A. Humphreys, *The Virginia Campaign of '64 and '65* (New York, 1883).

Hyde FGC: Thomas W. Hyde, *Following the Greek Cross* (Boston, 1894).

Keckley BS: Elizabeth Keckley, *Behind the Scenes* (New York, 1868).

Lamon's Recollections: Ward Hill Lamon, *Recollections of Abraham Lincoln, 1847–1865* (Washington, D.C., 1895, 1911).

Longstreet FMA: James Longstreet, *From Manassas to Appomattox* (Philadelphia, 1896).

McCarthy DMSL: Carlton McCarthy, *Detailed Minutiae of Soldier Life* (Richmond, Va., 1882).

MHSM: Military Historical Society of Massachusetts, *The Shenandoah Campaigns of 1862 and 1864 and the Appomattox Campaign of 1865* (Boston, 1907).

Newhall WSLLC: F. C. Newhall, *With General Sheridan in Lee's Last Campaign* (Philadelphia, 1866).

OR: *The War of the Rebellion: A Compilation of Official Records of the Union and Confederate Armies*, 128 vols., plus 3 vols. of folio Atlas (Washington, D.C., 1880–1902).

Owen WA: William Miller Owen, *In Camp and Battle with the Washington Artillery of New Orleans* (Boston, 1885).

Pitman: Benn Pitman, *The Assassination of President Lincoln and the Trial of the Conspirators* (Cincinnati, 1865). Facsimile reprint ed. New York, 1954.

Plum MT: William R. Plum, *The Military Telegraph during the Civil War*, 2 vols. (Chicago, 1882).

Porter CG: Horace Porter, *Campaigning with Grant* (New York, 1897).

Porter IACW: David Dixon Porter, *Incidents and Anecdotes of the Civil War* (New York, 1885).

Ripley CR: Edward H. Ripley, *The Capture and Occupation of Richmond* (New York, 1907).

Schaff SC: Morris Schaff, *The Sunset of the Confederacy* (Boston, 1912).

Sheridan's Argument: *Argument on Behalf of Lieut. Gen. Philip H. Sheridan, U.S.A., Respondent . . . in the case of . . . Gouverneur K. Warren,* by Asa Bird Gardner, Sheridan's counsel (Chicago, 1881).

Sheridan's Memoirs: Philip Henry Sheridan, *Personal Memoirs* (New York, 1888). Enlarged ed. 1902, 2 vols.

Sherman's Memoirs: William T. Sherman, *Memoirs,* 2 vols. (New York, 1875).

SHSP: Southern Historical Society *Papers* (Richmond, Va., 1876 to 1915, issued at irregular intervals after that).

Taylor FYGL: Walter H. Taylor, *Four Years with General Lee* (New York, 1877; Rev. ed., Norfolk, Va., 1906).

Tremain LHSC: Henry Edwin Tremain, *Last Hours of Sheridan's Cavalry* (New York, 1904).

Warren CI: *Proceedings, Findings, and Opinions of the Court of Inquiry . . . in the case of Gouverneur K. Warren,* three parts with maps (Washington, D.C., 1883). Also the Ms. of same in DNA-OA.

Welles's Diary: *Diary of Gideon Welles,* 3 vols. (Boston, 1911).

Whittaker's Custer: Frederick Whittaker, *Gen. George A. Custer* (New York, 1876).

Wise EE: John S. Wise, *The End of an Era* (Boston, 1899).

Chapter 1. Lincoln's Second Inauguration

Page

1. Ice on the Potomac: DLC Ms. Div., Benjamin Brown French Papers. Sherman in Cheraw: Sherman's *Memoirs,* II, 291.

2. NYH account, Mar. 6.
   Mrs. Lincoln drives to Capitol: George C. Ashmun, "Recollections of a Peculiar Service," in *Sketches of War History,* Ohio Commandery of the Loyal Legion (Cincinnati, 1888), Vol. II.

4. Grant's telegram to Lincoln: CWAL, VIII, 330–31; OR, 96:801–2, 824–25.
   Stanton's remark to Lincoln: Lamon's *Recollections,* pp. 249 ff.

8. "It is unsafe for you not to be here on the fourth of March": CWAL VIII, 235.
   Johnson's decision to go to Washington: DLC Ms. Div., Andrew Johnson Papers, letter from R. L. Stanford, Feb. 22.
   "Newspaper clipping from the Boston *Commonwealth*": DLC Ms. Div., Johnson Papers, final unsorted box.

9. NYH account, Mar. 6.

10. Hamlin's unconscious slip: DLC Ms. Div., French Papers, letter to his sister Pamela, Feb. 8.

    Footnote: DLC Ms. Div., Johnson Papers.

    NYW account of Johnson's speech, Mar. 6.

12. Chandler's remark: DLC Ms. Div., Zachariah Chandler Papers.

13. NYH account, Mar. 16.

16. B. B. French identifies John Wilkes Booth: DLC Ms. Div., French Papers.

    "A chance . . . to kill the President": Pitman, p. 45, testimony of Samuel Knapp Chester; Lamon's *Recollections,* pp. 272–73.

17. Whitman quotation: DLC Ms. Div., William E. Barton scrapbook.

18. Execution at Old Capitol: WSTR, Mar. 3.

19. NYW criticism of inaugural address, Mar. 6.

    British reactions: reprinted in BA, Apr. 6.

21. WSTR on East Room reception: Mar. 6.

    Crook on vandalism in the White House: Crook TFA, p. 27.

22. News telegraphed to Pacific Coast: NYH, Mar. 6.

    Senate action on sale of liquor: WDC, Mar. 7.

    Description of Patent Office: DeB. Randolph Keim, *Washington and Its Environs* (Washington, D.C., 1874), pp. 145–51.

23. WDC description of the Patent Office's north hall: Mar. 7.

24. NYW on the Presidential dais: Mar. 7.

Chapter 2. The Singleton-Browning Trading Scheme

Page

29. Tobacco seized in Fredericksburg: OR 96:891, 832.

30. Proclamation blockading Southern ports: CWAL, IV, 338.

    Price of cotton in 1862: Sherman's *Memoirs,* I, 267.

    Price of cotton in Aug. 1864: Boston Board of Trade, *Annual Report,* 1865, p. 67.

31. Cotton consumption in the North: E. J. Donnell, *Chronological and Statistical History of Cotton* (New York, 1872); Appleton's *Annual Cyclopaedia* (New York, 1861–65).

32. Lincoln's letter to Canby: CWAL, VIII, 163–64.

33. The New Almaden case: Milton H. Shutes, *Lincoln and California* (Palo Alto, Calif., 1943), pp. 130 ff.

    Treasury Department records on Robert Lamon and Swett: DNA-TR.

    Singleton "a miracle of meanness": Tyler Dennett, *Lincoln and the Civil War* (New York, 1939), p. 19.

    Singleton's background: *Biographical Encyclopedia of Illinois* (Philadelphia, 1875); P. H. Redmond, *History of Quincy* (Quincy, Ill., 1869); *New York Times,* XX (Feb. 12, 1928), 6.

34. Browning's background: Theodore Calvin Pease, *The Diary of O. H. Browning* (Chicago, 1924). Also the introductions to Browning's *Diary.*

35. Baker's testimony of Feb. 2, 1865: Lafayette C. Baker, *History of the United States Secret Service* (Philadelphia, 1867), pp. 350 ff.
36. Mrs. Helm's attempts to get her cotton out of the Confederacy: Katherine Helm, *Mary, Wife of Lincoln* (New York, 1928), p. 250; R. Gerald McMurtry, *Ben Hardin Helm* (Chicago, 1943), pp. 53, 67.
37. "If you consent": Footnote to text of letter in CWAL, VIII, 267.
   Washburne and Grant: DLC Ms. Div., Elihu B. Washburne Papers for Feb. 1865.
38. Grant's telegram to Stanton: DLC Ms. Div., RTL.
   Lincoln's reply to Grant: CWAL, VIII, 344.
   "Washburne went . . . to present a medal to Grant": Porter CG, p. 393.
39. Lamon's story about Lincoln and Washburne: Lamon's *Recollections,* pp. 187 ff.

Chapter 3. More Plots and Counterplots

Page
40. Crook's description of the Lincoln family's quarters in the White House: Crook TFA, p. 11.
41. The Lincolns attend a performance of *The Magic Flute:* WSTR, Mar. 16.
   Presentation of flag to Gov. Morton: CWAL, VIII, 360–61.
42. Booth at the National Hotel: DNA-OA, Lincoln Assassination Suspects File; Pitman, p. 46.
   Mrs. Surratt's boardinghouse: Pitman, pp. 85–138; also Otto Eisenschiml, *In the Shadow of Lincoln's Death* (New York, 1940), p. 96.
43. The Lincoln conspirators: DNA-OA; Pitman; Eisenschiml WWLM, pp. 250 ff.; George S. Bryan, *The Great American Myth* (New York, 1940), pp. 115 ff.; also various newspaper and magazine clippings and photostats in the author's collection.
44. Statements by Paine and Herold: Ms. affidavits in DNA-OA, Trunk 10; also *Impeachment Investigation,* House of Representatives (Washington, D.C., 1867), Serial No. 1314, p. 674, for Eckert's testimony on what Paine said.
   Lincoln to Grant about Judge Hughes: CWAL, VIII, 353.
46. American consulate's message to Seward: DNA-OA, Lincoln assassination exhibits box; OR, 100:221 (Halleck to Sherman, Apr. 15).

Chapter 4. The Lincolns Go to City Point

Page
49. Vernal equinox: NYT *Almanac* for 1865.
   Washington weather: Accounts of the weather in Washington have

been taken from a day-by-day Ms. record in possession of the author.

Troop movements throughout the book are from OR.

50. Grant's telegraphed invitation to Lincoln: OR, 97:50.

Lincoln's reply: CWAL, VIII, 367.

Mrs. Lincoln's letter to Sumner: MH-H, Charles Sumner Papers.

Ernani at Ford's Theatre: WSTR, Mar. 27.

51. Fox's telegram to Lincoln: DLC Ms. Div., RTL, Mar. 21.

Barnes's account of the voyage to City Point: "With Lincoln from Washington to Richmond in 1865," *Appleton's Magazine,* May 1907.

52. *River Queen* at the Hampton Roads Peace Conference: CWAL, VIII, 286.

Destruction of the *River Queen* in 1911: DNA, Merchant ships' records. There is a description of her in Carl D. Lane, *American Paddle Steamboats* (New York, 1943), p. 128.

57. The Lincolns attend performances of *La Dame Blanche* and *Mireille:* WSTR, Mar. 22, 23; BA, Mar. 23.

River Queen sails from Washington in a storm: WSTR, WDC, WNI, and BA, Mar. 24.

Nautical details, weather, and time schedules of the voyage between Washington and City Point are based on entries in the log of the *Bat:* DNA-ON.

58. Crook is awakened by Mrs. Lincoln: Crook TFA, p. 40.

Lincoln's note to Major James: CWAL, VIII, 373.

59. For the course up the James River: OR *Atlas,* Plates CXXXVII, XCIII.

Jamestown Island and the river mansions: T. J. Trowbridge, *A Picture of the Desolated States* (Hartford, Conn., 1866), p. 216; G. W. Coleman, "Along the Lower James," *Century Magazine,* Jan. 1891.

60. Risley and Mellen go ahead in a revenue cutter: DLC Ms. Div., RTL, Mar. 23.

Singleton and Mrs. Helm at City Point: R. Gerald McMurtry, *Ben Hardin Helm* (Chicago, 1943), p. 67.

Mrs. Helm meets Robert Lincoln: Katherine Helm, *Mary, Wife of Lincoln* (New York, 1928), p. 250.

61. Grant's plans for the spring campaign: Grant's *Memoirs,* p. 598 (end of Chap. XIX).

Chapter 5. The Confederates Try to Break the Union Lines

Page

63. Construction of the earthworks at Petersburg: R. W. Lykes, *Petersburg National Military Park,* Dept. of Interior, Nat'l Park Service (Washington, D.C., 1951; rev. ed., 1956). Pamphlet.

The Union mine: Lykes, *Petersburg;* B & L, IV, 545; W. H. Powell, "The Tragedy of the Crater," *Century Magazine,* Sept. 1887, pp. 760 ff.

64. Description of the earthworks: Badeau MHUSG, III, 3 ff.; Jarratt's Hotel, *Guide to the Fortifications and Battlefields around Petersburg* (Petersburg, Va., 1866). Pamphlet.

67. Gordon's meeting with Lee: Gordon's *Reminiscences,* pp. 385 ff.

71. Walker's statement that purpose of attack was to seize Grant: SHSP, XXXI, John G. Walker, "Gordon's Assault on Ft. Stedman."

Descriptions of Union forts: Lykes, *Petersburg;* OR, **95,** for various commander's reports, especially those of George Ager, John F. Hartranft, John G. Parke, C. Woerner, and Gilbert P. Robinson; OR, **97,** for correspondence; detailed plans of Ft. Stedman and Ft. Haskell in DNA map collection.

74. Major Richardson becomes suspicious: William H. Hodgkins, *The Battle of Fort Stedman* (Boston, 1889). Pamphlet.

The all-night poker game: George L. Kilmer, "Assault and Repulse at Fort Stedman," *Century Magazine,* Sept. 1887, p. 785.

Gordon's account of the attack: Gordon's *Reminiscences,* p. 407.

76. Carson's account: Henry W. Thomas, *History of the Doles-Cooke Brigade* (Atlanta, 1903), p. 37.

78. General McLaughlen's experiences: OR, **95:**331.

79. The heavy firing at Ft. Haskell: B & L, IV, 582.

80. Hartranft's counterattack: B & L, IV, 585.

81. The Union observer who said, "My mind sickens . . . at it": B & L, IV, 583. Written by Kilmer (see above), but text here differs widely.

Chapter 6. Mr. and Mrs. Lincoln Visit the Front

Page

82. Lack of information at Grant's headquarters: Badeau MHUSG, III, 447.

Parke refuses to take command: OR, **95:**318 (Parke's report).

Strange catch of fish: WSTR, Mar. 25.

83. Lincoln's telegram to Stanton: CWAL, VIII, 373.

City Point: detailed map in DNA map collection; also OR *Atlas,* Plate LXXVI.

84. When Grant bought a horse: Grant's *Memoirs,* p. 22.

85. Dana's remark about Grant: Charles A. Dana, *The Life of Ulysses S. Grant* (Springfield, Mass., 1868), p. 403.

Badeau's characterization of Grant: Badeau GP, p. 13.

86. Grant tells Lincoln about attack on Ft. Stedman: John S. Barnes, "With Lincoln from Washington to Richmond in 1865," *Appleton's Magazine,* May 1907.

The Lincolns visit the battlefield: *Loc. cit.*

87. Mrs. Lincoln's jealousy of Mrs. Griffin: Badeau GP, p. 356.
89. The President reviews the troops: OR 97:129; WNI, Mar. 29.
Sheridan greeted by Rawlins: Porter CG, p. 411.
90. Grant's reception of Sheridan: Sheridan's *Memoirs*, II, 126 ff.; Grant's *Memoirs*, pp. 599 ff.
91. The telegraph tent at City Point: Bates LTO, p. 344.
Stanton's telegram to Lincoln: DLC Ms. Div., RTL.
Lincoln's telegrams to Stanton about Ft. Sumter: CWAL, VIII, 375 ff.
Sheridan and Porter note that Lincoln was depressed: Sheridan's *Memoirs*, II, 130; Porter CG, p. 413.
Barnes describes Sheridan's men crossing the river: Barnes, "With Lincoln."
92. Badeau's second ride with Mrs. Lincoln: Badeau GP, pp. 358 ff.
95. Barnes's ordeal: Barnes, "With Lincoln."

Chapter 7. Lincoln Sets the Surrender Terms

Page
99. *Malvern* arrives at City Point: Log of the *Malvern*, DNA-ON.
Grant welcomes Sherman: Porter CG, p. 417.
100. Sherman's account of meeting Lincoln: Letter of Nov. 28, 1872, to I. N. Arnold. Ms. in possession of the Chicago Historical Society.
101. Mrs. Grant scolds the two generals: In the printed version of Sherman's *Memoirs*, II, 325, Mrs. Grant is reported as having said, "Well, you are a pretty pair!" In Sherman's Ms. he wrote that she said, "Well, you are in for it now!" but he changed the original wording. DLC Ms. Div., Sherman Papers.
Sheridan's late arrival at City Point: Sheridan's *Memoirs*, II, 131.
102. Grant's behavior at the conference on the *River Queen*: Badeau MHUSG, III, 436.
103. Porter's version of the conference (written in 1866): Sherman's *Memoirs*, II, 329.
105. A newspaper correspondent describes the men involved: William H. Cunnington, "General Grant's Cabin," *The Blue and the Gray*, May 1893.

Chapter 8. Soldiers in the Rain

Page
107. *Bat* leaves City Point with Sherman: Log of the *Bat*, DNA-ON.
108. Chamberlain's description of the last night before Petersburg: Chamberlain PA, p. 34.
109. The attempt to damage the Southside Railroad in Feb.: OR, 95:365 (Gregg's report).

Lincoln bids farewell to Grant and his staff: Porter CG, p. 424.

110. Description of the country west of Petersburg: OR, 95:797 (Warren's report).

111. Confederate sergeant who defended a fort singlehanded: Theodore Gerrish, *Army Life* (Portland, Me., 1882), p. 231.

112. Joshua L. Chamberlain: No full-length biography of Chamberlain exists. He is dealt with at some length in John J. Pullen's *The Twentieth Maine* (Philadelphia, 1957); the bulk of his papers are in DLC Ms. Div. A few scattered letters are in the Yale University Library. The account of his battle experiences on Mar. 29 is from his own book, Chamberlain PA, Chap. II.

116. Fighting at Ream's Station: Francis A. Walker, *History of the Second Army Corps* (New York, 1886, 1891), Chap. XXII, on Ream's Station (which the author calls "a battle which should never have been fought"), p. 598; also B & L, IV, 571 ff.

117. Sheridan enters Dinwiddie: Tremain LHSC, p. 19; Newhall WSLLC, p. 55; Sheridan's *Memoirs*, II, 140.

118. Grant suggests that some of the horses be sent back: OR, 97:324. Sheridan rides out to see Grant: Sheridan's *Memoirs*, II, 142.

119. "With 'water dripping from every angle' ": Newhall WSLLC, p. 58. "I can drive in the whole cavalry force": Porter CG, p. 428. Sheridan calls on Grant: Grant's *Memoirs*, p. 600.

120. Sheridan visits Warren: Sheridan's *Memoirs*, II, 145. In investigating the complicated details of the ensuing difficulties between Sheridan and Warren, the author has consulted the printed record, Warren CI, and has also studied the manuscript transcriptions of the testimony given in the case, DNA-OA. Even before the Government Printing Office published the Court of Inquiry testimony, Sheridan issued a privately printed reply, cited here as Sheridan's *Argument*.

Warren's career: Emerson Gifford Taylor, *Gouverneur Kemble Warren* (Boston, 1932); Emily Warren Roebling, *The Journal of Rev. Silas Constant* (Philadelphia, 1903), a genealogy which contains much useful material on Warren and his family. His papers are in the Archives of History of the University of the State of New York, Albany, N.Y.

121. "Discouraged teamsters had given up": Newhall WSLLC, p. 68.

122. "One joke became . . . popular": Porter CG, p. 427. Sheridan learns that Confederates were entrenching along the White Oak Road, asks Grant for the Sixth Corps, is offered the Fifth Corps but refuses it: OR, 97:324; Sheridan's *Memoirs*, II, 146 ff.

123. Grant and Meade want to gain White Oak Road: OR, 95:803 ff. (Warren's report). Positions of Pickett's infantry and Fitzhugh Lee's cavalry, etc.: Warren CI, p. 479 (Fitzhugh Lee's testimony).

Chapter 9. Dinwiddie Court House

Page

124. Confederate cavalry appears at 10 A.M.: Newhall WSLLC, p. 63; OR *Atlas,* Plate LXXIV, for the Battle of Dinwiddie Court House; also detailed map in DNA collection.

Footnote on dismounted cavalry—"One of Sheridan's officers": Tremain LHSC, p. 44. Major Tremain was aide-de-camp to General Crook.

125. Weather report: Log of the *Malvern* shows that a strong west wind was blowing at City Point only a few miles away.

Sheridan's military bands: Tremain LHSC, p. 51.

Army of Northern Virginia's "air of abandon": Newhall WSLLC, p. 71.

126. Sheridan mounted on Rienzi: Tremain LHSC, p. 53.

"Sheridan's own account": Sheridan's *Memoirs,* II, 153.

"Commanders were told . . . 'there would be no troop movements' ": Humphreys VC, p. 330; also OR, 97:334 (Grant to Meade), 346 (Ruggles for Meade to corps commanders).

127. Lee's attack on Ayres: Chamberlain PA, pp. 69 ff.

"The Fifth Corps is eternally damned!": Chamberlain PA, p. 72.

Eppa Hunton's praise of the Fifth Corps' countercharge: Warren CI, p. 625.

128. Grant tells Sheridan to expect Warren by midnight: OR, 97:381 (Grant to Sheridan at 10:45 P.M., Mar. 31).

The bridge built across Gravelly Run: OR, 95:820; Chamberlain PA, p. 102.

Chapter 10. The Battle of Five Forks

Page

129. Early encounter with the Confederates in the fog: Newhall WSLLC, pp. 89 ff.

130. "John Brown's Body": DLC Ms. Div., Joshua L. Chamberlain Papers.

Confederate withdrawal before midnight and 2 A.M.: T. T. Munford's Papers in the Duke University Library.

Sheridan's troops meet Ayres's infantrymen: OR, 95:869 (Ayres's report), 1103 (Sheridan's report), 89 (Chronology).

131. The shad-bake incident, although long talked about in the South, was first made public by General T. L. Rosser in the Philadelphia *Weekly Times,* April 5, 1885. There is a copy of a letter which Rosser sent to A. S. Perham, Aug. 29, 1902, in DLC Ms. Div., Chamberlain Papers.

132. Warren's meeting with Sheridan at 11 A.M.: Warren CI, p. 338.

133. Their second meeting at Gravelly Run Church: Warren CI, pp. 396,

391; also, both men's accounts in their reports in OR, **95**, and Sheridan's in Sheridan's *Argument*. The evidence on the Sheridan-Warren affair at Five Forks is so voluminous that only the salient points can be indicated here.

135. Warren's "map based on . . . faulty intelligence": Warren CI, pp. 817, 1168, 1222. Sheridan obviously had only a vague idea of just where the Confederate angle was located. General J. J. Bartlett testified (Warren CI, p. 1168) that Sheridan told Warren it was "somewhere near an old church," but that he did not know whether the church was within the Confederate lines or not. The only church for miles around was the Gravelly Run Church, where this conversation took place, and the angle was three-quarters of a mile west of there. (Gillespie map of Five Forks, DNA map collection.) Warren's original sketch map of the angle is bound into the manuscript transcription of the Court of Inquiry record.

136. "A voice of doom was in the air": Chamberlain PA, p. 116.
The artillery officer sent by Rawlins to find Warren (Captain E. R. Warner): Humphreys VC, p. 356, footnote, important for Humphreys' opinions. He was commander of the Second Corps and knew all the men involved. See also Grant's own testimony in Warren CI, p. 1030.

137. Sheridan on Warren's mental attitude: Warren CI, pp. 114, 1049; Sheridan's *Memoirs*, II, 161.
Griffin tells rumors to Chamberlain: Chamberlain PA, pp. 118–19.
Sun due to set at 6:21: Data on Plate II (Cotton Map No. 2) at end of Sheridan's *Argument*.
Troop movements at opening of attack: OR, **95**, reports by Warren, Crawford, Griffin, and Ayres; Chamberlain PA, pp. 121 ff.; the Duke University Library has a 48-page pamphlet written by Chamberlain on Five Forks (Portland, Me., 1902), which is annotated in the margins by Confederate General T. T. Munford.

138. Rienzi "plunged and curveted": Newhall WSLLC, p. 100.
Mackenzie's troops arrive: Newhall WSLLC, p. 100; OR, **95**:1244 (Mackenzie's report).
Sheridan is angry at Ayres's men: Warren CI, p. 99 (Sheridan's own testimony); Newhall WSLLC, p. 104.

139. Chamberlain's account of taking the guns: Chamberlain PA, p. 146.
The action at the angle: Newhall WSLLC, pp. 105–6; Porter CG, p. 439.

140. W. J. Pegram mortally wounded: A. C. Gordon, *Memories and Memorials of William Gordon McCabe* (Richmond, 1925), I, 164.

141. The shad-bake: Rosser, see above.
Yankee cavalryman on a mule: Newhall WSLLC, p. 119.

142. Warren's attempt to turn Griffin's and Crawford's columns back to

the scene of action: OR, 95:832 ff. (Warren's report) ; Chamberlain PA, pp. 136 ff.; Warren CI, pp. 148, 202, 364, 370, etc.

143. Sheridan's remark to Chamberlain about general officers: Chamberlain PA, p. 130.

"Here Warren took his leave of the corps": Chamberlain PA, pp. 149 ff.

144. Footnote — Grant "spoke very kindly of my services": From a letter from Warren to his wife (Apr. 2) printed in Emerson G. Taylor's *Gouverneur Kemble Warren* (Boston, 1932), p. 228. The remark about Western generals occurs in the same letter. Some light on Warren's falling into disfavor with Grant in May 1864 is given in the footnote in Humphreys VC, p. 356; and in Richard Meade Bache's *Life of General Gordon Meade* (Philadelphia, 1897), p. 529. B & L, IV, 723, prints a summary of the Court of Inquiry's findings; so does Humphreys VC, pp. 358 ff. Sherman's statement that Sheridan "was perfectly justified": Tremain LHSC, p. 79.

145. Townsend's description of Five Forks at night: Written for NYW, Apr. 4; it was reprinted in *Campaigns of a Non-Combatant* (New York, 1866), and in *Rustics in Rebellion* (Chapel Hill, N.C., 1950), a shortened version of the earlier book.

148. Confederate muskets used to corduroy the roads: Tremain LHSC, p. 77.

Horace Porter brings the news of victory to Grant: Porter CG, p. 442.

Admiral Porter takes Lincoln in his barge: Porter IACW, p. 292; also Porter's ms. journal in DLC Ms. Div.

149. The dream Lincoln told to Ward Lamon: Lamon's *Recollections,* p. 116.

Mrs. Lincoln's return to Washington and the fire at Augur's headquarters: OR, 97:446 (Stanton to Lincoln) .

150. Band serenades Admiral and Mrs. Porter: Log of the *Malvern,* DNA-ON.

Porter's story about the President's stay on the *Malvern:* Porter IACW, p. 214.

151. Burning of the transport *General Lyon:* NYH, Apr. 3.

Capture of Ford's Station: Newhall WSLLC, p. 128.

Last train out of Petersburg: Chamberlain PA, p. 192.

152. "Wakeful boys . . . startled the owls": Newhall WSLLC, p. 131.

Other valuable works on the Battle of Five Forks besides those mentioned are: "The Fifth Corps at the Battle of Five Forks" by C. H. Porter and "The Five Forks Campaign" by W. W. Swan, both in MHSM. Also, "Warren at Five Forks" by A. S. Perham, in New York State Historical Association *Quarterly Journal,* July 1923.

Chapter 11. The Attack on Petersburg

Page

153. Troops' reaction to orders for frontal attack: Badeau MHUSG, III, 509.

Effect of the great cannonade on the Confederates: Gorman LLC. ". . . 14,000 infantrymen . . . moved into open ground": Badeau MHUSG, III, 509; Hazard Stevens, "Storming of the Lines of Petersburg," in *Personal Narratives of Events in the War of the Rebellion,* Rhode Island Historical Society (Providence, 1904), Ser. VI, No. 8; OR, **95,** for various commander's reports; OR, **97,** for their correspondence.

155. Lee at the Turnbull house: Longstreet FMA, pp. 604 ff.

156. The shooting of A. P. Hill: SHSP, XII, 185 ff.; also, XI, XIX, XX, and XXVII.

Civil War telegraph: Plum MT, II, 321; George R. Thompson, "Civil War Signals," *Military Affairs,* Winter, 1954.

157. Wright's telegram to Webb of 5:15 A.M.: OR, 97:478.

Grant's telegram to City Point of 6:40 A.M.: OR, **97**:448; of 8:25, *loc. cit.*

Badeau describes Grant under fire: Badeau MHUSG, III, 515 ff.

158. Lee's telegram to Breckinridge of 10:40 A.M.: OR, **97**:1378.

159. Lee under fire at the Turnbull house: Hyde FGC, pp. 258–59; Stevens, "Storming . . . Petersburg"; Confederate eyewitness accounts: Cooke WG, p. 590, and Taylor FYGL, p. 150.

160. Attack on Ft. Gregg: OR, **95,** for reports of the Union commanders involved (Robert S. Foster, John Gibbon, John W. Turner, Thomas M. Harris); also Gibbon's *Recollections,* pp. 300–301. Confederate accounts: Owen WA, pp. 371 ff.; Alexander MMC; Gorman LLC; SHSP. III, VIII, IX, XIX, XXVIII, XXXI.

164. Grant's telegram to City Point at 4:40 P.M.: OR, **97**:449.

Taylor writes out orders for Confederate withdrawal: OR, **97**:1379.

165. Taylor requests leave to get married: Taylor FYGL, p. 276.

166. Blowing up Confederate powder magazines: Gorman LLC.

Lincoln and Porter on deck of the *Malvern:* Porter IACW, p. 292.

167. Grant's telegram to Meade at 7:40 P.M.: OR, **97**:458. Telegram of 9 P.M. instructing Parke to use siege guns on railroad bridge: *Loc. cit.*

Peck enters Petersburg: Lt. George V. Peck, Jr., "A Recruit Before Petersburg," in *Personal Narratives,* Ser. II, No. 8.

168. Surrender of Petersburg: Badeau MHUSG, III, 533.

Grant in Petersburg: Porter CG, pp. 449 ff.

Grant's account of meeting Lincoln: Grant's *Memoirs,* p. 612.

169. Stanton's telegram to Lincoln and Lincoln's reply: CWAL, VIII, 384–85.

Chapter 12. The Fall of Richmond

Page

172. Preparations for the evacuation of Richmond started early: OR, 96:1242 (Breckinridge), 1244 (Lee), 1252, *this especially* (Campbell), 1257 (confidential circular), also Breckinridge, 1265 (Lee), OR, 95:1315, *this especially* (Wright, 2nd report). Also Joseph R. Haw, "The Last of the C. S. Ordnance Department," *Confederate Veteran*, 1926.

"Lee's fatal telegram of 10:40 A.M.": OR, 97:178 (Lee to Breckinridge). Just who handed this message to Davis is an unsolved mystery. Several accounts exist; some say it was a Confederate officer "whose sword clanked as he marched down the aisle"; others say it was the sexton, who in at least one account is described as being a huge Negro elaborately garbed in antique costume.

173. "Every countenance was wild with excitement": *Diary of a Refugee,* by a Lady of Virginia (New York, 1867), p. 343.

Confederate officers at Clover Station get the news by telegraph: Wise EE, p. 413.

174. For the excitement in Richmond that afternoon see J. B. Jones, *A Rebel War Clerk's Diary* (Philadelphia, 1866; reprint, New York, 1935), II, 465 ff.

Midshipmen guard the Confederate Treasury's gold: W. H. Parker, *Recollections of a Naval Officer* (New York, 1883), pp. 350–51; SHSP, IX, M. H. Clark, "Last Days of the Confederate Treasury"; SHSP, XXXII, Dr. John W. Harris, "The Gold of the C. S. Treasury."

Reagan "whittling a stick": S. R. Mallory, "The Last Days of the Confederate Government," *McClure's Magazine,* Dec. 1900, Jan. 1901.

175. Convicts escape from the penitentiary: Mary Tucker Magill, *The Independent,* Jan. 7, 1886.

176. The ambulance bearing the corpse of A. P. Hill: SHSP, XIX, G. Powell Hill, "First Burial of General Hill's Remains."

177. Mayor Mayo: Mallory, "Last Days"; Bruce COR, p. 12; John Cannon, *History of Grant's Campaign for the Capture of Richmond* (London, 1869).

Ewell's account of the burning of Richmond: OR, 95:1293.

178. "I was aroused by what might almost have awakened the dead": "The Fall of Richmond," anon., *Harper's New Monthly Magazine,* June 1866.

"Walter Taylor left his midnight bride": Taylor FYGL, p. 278.

General Alexander's account: Alexander MMC, p. 594.

179. Sulivane's account: B & L, IV, 725.

181. Confederate bands play to cover noise of troop movements: WSTR, Apr. 5.
   Gary's troops: Boykin FF, p. 9.
182. Weitzel, Devens, and Kautz: OR, 95:578–79; Bruce COR, pp. 5–6.
   Two deserters from the 10th Virginia: Bruce COR, p. 7.
   Bruce enters Confederate lines: Bruce COR, pp. 9–10.
183. Wild excitement — men slap gun barrels with glee: Ripley CR.
   The entry into Richmond: Bruce COR, pp. 10 ff.; OR, 95:1212 (Bruce's report).
184. Major Ladd captures the *Patrick Henry*'s flag and is first to enter Richmond: Bruce COR, pp. 15–16.
185. Young artillery officer tries to get ahead of the infantry: Ripley CR.
   First Union flags to fly over Richmond: J. L. De Peyster, *Colors of U.S. First Raised Over Richmond* (Morrisania, N.Y., 1866). Pamphlet.
186. Union bands play Northern airs: Bruce COR, p. 17.
187. The Negroes welcome Union troops: *Harper's*, June 1866, see above; also R. B. Prescott "The Capture of Richmond," in *Civil War Papers*, Commandery of Massachusetts, Loyal Legion (Boston, 1900).
   Troops behave well: *Harper's*, see above.
188. Troops work to put out fire: Ripley CR.
   Union generals establish their headquarters: Bruce COR, pp. 19–21.
   Ord telegraphs Weitzel: OR, 97:535.
   Railroad men find locomotives and cars: OR, 97:534.
189. Telegraph crews string lines: Plum MT, II, 321.
   "Turn down for Richmond": Bates LTO, p. 360; Plum MT, II, 322–23.
   Telegrams of congratulation: OR, 97:592, *passim;* WSTR, Apr. 4.
   Salute of 800 guns: WSTR and other Washington papers for Apr. 3 and 4.
190. Orders sent to all military posts to fire salutes: OR, 97:543.
   Train carrying Davis and his cabinet passes Clover Station: Wise EE, p. 415.
191. Confederate troops at dawn: SHSP, XXXII, M. R. Talcott, "Retreat from Petersburg to Appomattox."

Chapter 13. Lincoln Visits Richmond

Page
193. "Tad was to go along": Of the men who accompanied Lincoln to Richmond, neither Porter nor Barnes mentions Tad; Crook (in Crook TFA, pp. 50–51) definitely says that Tad was with them; so does Beckwith in Bates LTO, p. 354. That day Bruce, who was in Richmond, says he saw Tad (Bruce COR, p. 24, and also

in an earlier letter to John G. Nicolay dated Jan. 1, 1889, DLC Ms. Div., Nicolay Papers). Charles Carleton Coffin, in a dispatch to the Boston *Journal,* dated Richmond, Apr. 4, says Tad was there; he confirmed this to Thomas Nast in a letter dated Boston, July 19, 1866. Yet Captain Charles B. Penrose, who accompanied the party, in a letter printed in *Century Magazine* for June 1890, pp. 306–7, says that Tad was *not* with them and had been taken to Washington with his mother. This latter statement cannot be true; for Lincoln telegraphed (from City Point on Apr. 2) to his wife in Washington that "Tad and I are both well." (OR, 97:447–48; also CWAL, VIII, 384.)

194. Obstructions and mines in the James: Porter IACW, pp. 293–94; R. W. Crowley, "The Confederate Torpedo Service," *Century Magazine,* June 1898; F. T. Miller, *The Photographic History of the Civil War* (New York, 1912), V, 185; Bates LTO, p. 354 n.; SHSP, XXXI, R. L. Maury, "First Marine Torpedoes... in James River."

Cruise up the James: Logs of the *Malvern* and the *Bat,* DNA-ON.

196. *Commodore Perry* aground: William H. Beach, *The New York First (Lincoln) Cavalry* (New York, 1902), p. 492.

Farragut on the *William Allison:* George H. Gordon, *A War Diary of Events in the Great Rebellion, 1863–1865* (Boston, 1882), pp. 396 ff.; Bruce COR, p. 32; Bates LTO, pp. 355–56.

197. Lincoln's story about the old pair of trousers: Porter IACW, p. 29.
198. The landing at Rocketts: Porter IACW, p. 295.
199. "The only sign of welcome I saw": Crook TFA, p. 54.

Porter's story about the girl and her bouquet: Porter IACW, p. 300.

200. "Something that looked like a gun": Crook TFA, p. 54.
201. Bruce sees the Lincoln party pass the Governor's mansion: Letter to Nicolay, see above, MLC Ms. Div., Nicolay Papers; Bruce COR, p. 24.
202. Lincoln asks for a drink of water: John S. Barnes, "With Lincoln from Washington to Richmond in 1865," *Appleton's Magazine,* June 1907.

The little black-and-tan dog: *The Custer Story,* ed. Marguerite Merington (New York, 1950), p. 164.

203. The officers drink Davis' whisky: Crook TFA, p. 55.

Judge Campbell calls on the President: John A. Campbell, *Reminiscences and Documents Relating to the Civil War During... 1865* (Baltimore, 1887); also his *Recollections of the Evacuation of Richmond* (Baltimore, 1880). Both pamphlets.

Lincoln tours Richmond: Crook TFA, p. 55; Bruce COR, pp. 34–35.

204. At the Confederate Capitol: Bruce COR, p. 56; Porter IACW, p. 302.

They pass Libby Prison and Castle Thunder: Bruce's letter to Nicolay, see above, MLC Ms. Div., Nicolay Papers.

Malvern fires a 35-gun salute: Log of the *Malvern*, DNA-ON.
Admiral Porter and Captain Foster: Ripley CR.
205. Porter is now apprehensive about the President's safety: Porter IACW, p. 303.
206. The grand illumination: WSTR, Apr. 5, and other Washington papers of that date.
Johnson's speech: WSTR, Apr. 5, and other Washington papers.
207. Ripley's story about the threat to the President's life: Ripley CR.
208. Judge Campbell and Myers visit Lincoln on the *Malvern:* DLC Ms. Div., Joseph Holt Papers (Myers' "Memorandum" dated Apr. 5, 1865) ; Porter IACW, pp. 304 ff.
Lincoln's account of the conference: CWAL, VIII, 388.
Duff Green: DLC Ms. Div., Duff Green Papers; *Lincoln Lore*, Oct. 1957; Porter IACW, pp. 306 ff.; Crook TFA, pp. 56–57; Fletcher M. Green, "Duff Green, Militant Journalist of the Old School," *American Historical Review*, Jan. 1947.

Chapter 14. The Confederate Retreat Begins

Page
210. The state of affairs at Amelia Court House: OR, 95:1265 (Lee's report) ; Owen WA, pp. 374–75; Boykin FF. See appendix to *R. E. Lee*, by Douglas Southall Freeman (New York, 1935), IV, 509, for a long and careful analysis, entitled "Lee's Failure to Receive Supplies at Amelia Court House."
Description of Amelia: Schaff SC, p. 73.
211. Army trains and troops in the fields nearby: Cooke WG, p. 594.
Lee's scout rides to Jetersville on a mule: Sheridan's *Memoirs*, II, 175.
212. Wise sent north by locomotive: Wise EE, p. 417.
Description of Major Young's scouts: Tremain LHSC, p. 98.
214. Extra caissons burned: Owen WA, p. 375; Bahnson LDW.
"A number . . . did not answer to their names": Schaff SC, p. 76.
Description of Jetersville: Tremain LHSC, p. 111.
"Sheridan felt that Lee had lost his last chance": OR, 95:1107 (Sheridan's report) .
Confederate wagon train attacked near Paineville: OR, 95:1145 (Davies' report) .
215. The stranded girl from Mississippi: Boykin FF, p. 28.
216. Sheridan's message to Grant of Apr. 5: OR, 97:582.
Campbell leads Grant to Sheridan: Porter CG, p. 454.
217. "Sheridan summarized . . . a tense meeting": Sheridan's *Memoirs*, II, 178.
218. Capture of two Union spies: Gordon's *Reminiscences*, p. 426.
The Confederates hear Sheridan's bands: Boykin FF, p. 32.
Panicky Confederates shoot each other: SHSP, XXXI, McHenry Howard, "Closing Scenes of the War About Richmond."

219. Sheridan calls Meade's advance "useless": Sheridan's *Memoirs*, II, 179.
Sheridan arranges to have the Sixth Corps placed near him: Chamberlain PA, p. 207.
Sheridan rides toward Deatonsville: Newhall WSLLC, p. 157.
220. Miller's gunners: Newhall WSLLC, pp. 158 ff.

Chapter 15. From Sayler's Creek to Appomattox Station
Page
222. Young lieutenant in 2nd Rhode Island Infantry: George V. Peck, Jr., "A Recruit Before Petersburg," in *Personal Narratives of Events in the War of the Rebellion*, Rhode Island Historical Society (Providence, 1880), Ser. II, No. 8.
223. "Sis" in the syrup: Theodore Gerrish, *Army Life* (Portland, Me., 1882), p. 252.
224. The fighting along Little Sayler's Creek: OR, 95:1294 (Ewell's report); Robert Stiles, *Four Years Under Marse Robert* (Washington, D.C., 1903), pp. 328 ff.; MHSM, Hazard Stevens, "The Battle of Sayler's Creek"; Schaff SC, pp. 101 ff.; W. R. Turner, "The South's Gethsemane," *The Petersburg Progress Index*, May 1, 1955; *Sayler's Creek Battlefield Park,* a pamphlet published by the Virginia Dep't of Conservation and Development (Richmond, 1955), which describes the Hillsman house; SHSP, XXV, XXXI, XXXII, XLII; J. Warren Kiefer, "Battle of Sailor's Creek," in *Papers Prepared for the Ohio Commandery of the Military Order of the Loyal Legion* (Cincinnati, 1890).
226. Man nearly severed by a Parrott shell: Stiles, *Four Years*, p. 330.
Ewell's remark about tomatoes: SHSP, XXV, R. T. W. Duke, "The Burning of Richmond."
"Has the army been dissolved?": Longstreet FMA, p. 614.
227. Gulch with dead Confederate soldier: Horatio C. King, "Lee's Last Stand," *The Blue and the Gray*, Apr. 1893.
"If the thing is pressed": CWAL, VIII, 389, 392.
228. Confederate generals fraternize with their captors: Newhall WSLLC, p. 187.
229. Custer salutes them: William H. Beach, *First New York (Lincoln) Cavalry* (New York, 1902), p. 504; James H. Stevenson, *Boots and Saddles* (Harrisburg, Pa., 1879), p. 347.
Snow flurries at Burkeville: Eppa Hunton, *Autobiography* (Richmond, Va., 1933), p. 124.
"With that long slinging walk": Newhall WSLLC, p. 191.
Fighting on the High Bridge road: OR, 95:1302; OR, 97:622; OR, 95:682.
230. Man forced off bridge: Bahnson LDW.
Second Corps saves bridge: OR, 95:682.

Boarding-school girls cheer Confederates: Boykin FF, p. 32.

Casks of meat knocked open: Owen WA, p. 377.

Dried French soup in tin foil: Bahnson LDW.

231. Lee loses his temper: Longstreet FMA, p. 413.

Supply wagons burned: OR, 95:683.

Ford at Farmville: Boykin FF, p. 38.

An especially good map of the fighting north of Farmville is in J. W. De Peyster, *La Royale* (New York, 1874), Pt. VII.

Gregg captured: Tremain LHSC, p. 196; OR, 95:1155.

Gordon offers him a horse: Gordon's *Reminiscences*, p. 430.

Grant stops at Farmville hotel: Porter CG, p. 458; Tremain LHSC, p. 198; Newhall WSLLC, p. 194.

232. Three of his commanders call on Grant: Porter CG, p. 458; Gibbon's *Recollections*, pp. 305–6.

Dr. Smith and Grant: Grant's *Memoirs*, p. 662; Schaff SC, pp. 116, 137.

233. Grant's letter to Lee of Apr. 7, 5 P.M.: OR, 97:619.

Longstreet's comment: Longstreet FMA, p. 619.

234. Lee's note to Grant of Apr. 7 ("I have recd your note"): OR, 97:619.

Grant writes, "Peace being my great desire," etc.: OR, 97:641.

A day "of uneventful marching": Badeau MHUSG, III, 592, curiously paralleling Newhall WSLLC, p. 199.

235. Capture of Selma: Schaff SC, p. 143.

Three possibilities reported by Gordon: Gordon's *Reminiscences*, p. 433; see comment in Schaff SC, p. 143.

Pendleton and Lee: Schaff SC, pp. 160–61.

236. Lee consolidates his army into two corps: Schaff SC, p. 153. See comment in Freeman, *R. E. Lee*, IV, 111, 445.

Confederate supply trains captured: Tremain LHSC, pp. 219 ff.

237. Custer saves two girls: Whittaker's *Custer*, pp. 305–6.

The attack of Walker's guns and capture of the Confederate trains at Appomattox Station: Schaff SC, pp. 191 ff.; Newhall WSLLC, p. 200; Tremain LHSC, pp. 213 ff.; OR, 97:654; OR, 95:1282 (Pendleton's report); Sheridan's *Memoirs*, II, 189–90; Boykin FF, p. 118; SHSP, XXXIV, "Diary of Harry Townsend."

238. Confederate food and bad shoes: SHSP XXXI, Frank H. Foote, "Privations and Necessities of the Confederate Soldier."

240. "A sadder looking set . . . I never saw": Comment made by Hicks, a resident of Appomattox Court House in an undated clipping from the New York *Sun, ca.* 16 years later (DLC Ms. Div., Joshua L. Chamberlain Papers, unsorted).

Colonel on white horse shot down: OR, 95:1282; Schaff SC, p. 194.

Wounded sergeant begs to be killed: New York *Sun* clipping, see above.

241. Lee to Grant, Apr. 8: OR, 97:641.
Lee's final council of war: Gordon's *Reminiscences,* p. 435.

Chapter 16. Appomattox Court House

Page
243. Founding of Appomattox: Ralph Happel, *Appomattox Court House National Historical Park,* U.S. Dep't of Interior, Nat'l Park Service (Washington, 1955).
McLean house: *Century Magazine,* May 1900, pp. 156 ff.
244. Union infantrymen belabor the artillery horses: Theodore Gerrish, *Army Life* (Portland, Me., 1882), p. 253.
246. "Gordon's infantry hit the center": Gordon's *Reminiscences,* p. 436.
Two brass Napoleons captured: SHSP, XXXIV, Fletcher T. Massie, "From Petersburg to Appomattox."
Forty rounds of ammunition supplied: McCarthy DMSL, p. 148.
"As if arranged by some skillful stage manager": Badeau MHUSG, III, 597; Gordon's *Reminiscences,* p. 437; Charles F. McKenna, *Under the Maltese Cross* (Pittsburgh, 1910), p. 617.
Negro troops with the Army of the Potomac: Chamberlain PA, p. 232 (Birney's men).
247. The retaking of the two brass Napoleons: Massie, "From Petersburg."
"Fitzhugh Lee had asked Gordon to notify him": OR, 95:1304 (Fitzhugh Lee's report).
Men of the Washington Artillery destroy gun carriages: SHSP, XXXIV, "Diary of H. S. Townsend"; Owen WA, p. 381.
"Everywhere little encounters were taking place": McCarthy DMSL, p. 149.
248. "Three unarmed Confederate surgeons": SHSP, XXVIII, John M. Clayborn, "Personal Recollections of the Last Days of Lee and His Paladins."
249. "One overbold cavalry officer": SHSP, XXXII, T. M. R. Talcott, "Retreat from Petersburg to Appomattox."
"I have fought my corps to a frazzle": Gordon's *Reminiscences,* p. 438.
"Rather die a thousand deaths": Longstreet FMA, p. 421; see comment in Schaff SC, p. 228.
The Confederate emergency conference: Alexander MMC, pp. 603 ff.
250. Sims's flag-of-truce story: *History of the Corn Exchange Regiment* (Philadelphia, 1888), pp. 590–91; SHSP, XXXIII, M. J. Bilmeyer, "The Last Charge at Appomattox"; Schaff SC, p. 239.
Custer's supposed demand for unconditional surrender: Custer, according to several Confederate accounts, was said to have gone to Longstreet and to have behaved so rudely that the old general rebuked him. See Douglas Southall Freeman, *Lee's Lieutenants* (New York, 1944), III, 735, footnote, for a discussion of the

evidence. But note that Michael V. Sheridan, Sheridan's younger brother, who was on the field, wrote to Mrs. Custer that no such thing ever happened (*The Custer Story,* Marguerite Merington, ed., New York, 1950, p. 156).

251. "Sheridan . . . rode . . . toward Appomattox Court House": Sheridan's *Memoirs,* II, 194.
    Gary's men keep fighting: Boykin FF, pp. 57 ff.; Newhall WSLLC, p. 214.
253. The sharpshooter who nearly fired at Sheridan: Gordon's *Reminiscences,* p. 440.
    Grant's sick headache: Grant's *Memoirs,* p. 625.
254. The newspaper correspondent who heard Rawlins read Lee's message: Sylvanus Cadwallader, *Three Years with Grant,* ed. Benjamin P. Thomas (New York, 1955), pp. 318 ff.
255. Grant's message to Lee of Apr. 9 and Lee's reply: OR, 97:664.
    Grant refuses to ride in an ambulance: Porter CG, p. 466.
    "Babcock was sent ahead": Porter CG, p. 467; Taylor, FYGL (rev. ed., 1906), p. 288.
256. "Asking for 'a suspension of hostilities' ": OR, 97:664.
    William Montgomery is mortally wounded: McKenna, *Maltese Cross,* p. 615.
    "Babcock found Lee in an orchard": Porter CG, p. 470.
    Lee and Marshall ride to the McLean house: Papers of *Charles Marshall, an Aide-de-Camp of Lee* (Boston, 1927), p. 268; Schaff SC pp. 235–36.

Chapter 17. History Is Made in a Country Parlor

Page
257. "It was after one o'clock when Grant finally arrived": Chamberlain PA, p. 245; Frederick Driscoll, in his *The Twelve Days Campaign* (Montreal, 1866), says Grant arrived at 2:30.
258. Confederate eyewitness account of the surrender: Charles Marshall, *Appomattox* (Baltimore, 1894); also in *Papers of Charles Marshall, an Aide-de-Camp of Lee* (Boston, 1927), p. 268.
    Union accounts: Porter CG, Chap. XXX; also B & L, IV, 729–46; Horace Porter, "The Surrender at Appomattox Court House"; Badeau MHUSG, III, 601–9; Sheridan's *Memoirs,* II, 200–202; Grant's *Memoirs,* pp. 627–33; Schaff SC, pp. 262–76; Newhall WSLLC, pp. 215–24; Chamberlain PA, p. 246; see comment in Tremain LHSC, Chap. XIII.
    The surrender letter: This with the other pertinent correspondence is in OR, 95:56–58 (Grant's report).
259. Footnote on Mexican surrender at Vera Cruz: *Letters from Lloyd Lewis* (Boston, 1950), p. 42.

Grant's description of the surrender scene: Grant's *Memoirs,* p. 631.

260. Three Union generals (Gibbon, Griffin, Merritt) and three Confederate generals (Longstreet, Gordon, and Pendleton) appointed to arrange details of the surrender; Chamberlain given command of the Union parade at the ceremony: Chamberlain PA, p. 248.

262. Lee's letter to his wife: Robert E. Lee, Jr., *Recollections and Letters of General Robert E. Lee* (New York, 1904), pp. 88–89.

264. The "Redeemers": For a recent study of the part these men played in "redeeming" the former Confederate states in Reconstruction days, see C. Vann Woodward, *Reunion and Reaction, the Compromise of 1877 and the End of Reconstruction* (Boston, 1951; rev. ed., New York, 1956).

The fight for the still unsettled West: For light on the open warfare that went on in the Far West for land and power, see Asa Shinn Mercer, *Banditti of the Plains* (Cheyenne, 1894). An account of the curious publishing history of this much suppressed book can be found in Ramon F. Adams, *Six-Guns and Saddle Leather* (Norman, Okla., 1954).

Military careers of Union officers in the McLean parlor: George W. Cullum, *Biographical Register of the Officers and Graduates of the U. S. Military Academy* (Boston, 1891).

Williams "died of inflammation of the brain": His record in DNA-OA, officers' jacket.

Rawlins and Cuba: Allan Nevins, *Hamilton Fish, the Inner History of the Grant Administration* (New York, 1936), pp. 183 ff.

265. Footnote on Belknap: *Proceedings of the Senate Sitting for the Trial of William W. Belknap . . . on the Articles of Impeachment Exhibited by the House of Representatives* (Washington, D.C., 1876); House *Reports,* 54th Congress, 1st Sess., pp. 186, 345, 791; Nevins, *Hamilton Fish,* Chap. XXXIII; Custer's black mood on the eve of his death: Edgar I. Stewart, *Custer's Luck* (Norman, Okla., 1955), p. 248.

266. Badeau characterizes Grant to Henry Adams: *The Education of Henry Adams* (Boston, 1918), Chap. XVII.

267. Babcock: Matthew Josephson, *The Politicos, 1865–1896* (New York, 1938), p. 120; Nevins, *Hamilton Fish;* E. P. Oberholtzer, *A History of the United States since the Civil War* (New York, 1922), II, 236, *passim;* James Ford Rhodes, *A History of the United States, 1850–1877* (New York, 1906), VI, VII; J. D. Cox, in *The Atlantic Monthly,* Aug. 1895, pp. 164 ff.; also *The Nation* for 1876.

269. The Hayes-Tilden election and its significance: Woodward, *Reunion and Reaction;* Rhodes, *History,* VII; Paul L. Haworth, *The Hayes-Tilden Disputed Presidential Election of 1876* (Cleveland, 1906); Paul H. Buck, *The Road to Reunion, 1865–1900* (Boston, 1937), Chap. IV.

Siegfried Marcus: Ken W. Purdy, *The Kings of the Road* (Boston, 1952) , pp. 210 ff.

Chapter 18. The End of the Army of Northern Virginia

Page

271. Confederates wander across road: *History of the Corn Exchange Regiment* (Philadelphia, 1888) , p. 587.

Gibbon sees General Wilcox wearing a long overcoat: Gibbon's *Recollections,* p. 320.

272. Forsyth's notes of the end of the surrender conference: George A. Forsyth, *Thrilling Days in Army Life* (New York, 1900) , pp. 191 ff.

275. "Relic-hunters charged down": Porter CG, p. 486; Newhall WSLLC, p. 221; Albert D. Richardson, *Personal History of Ulysses S. Grant* (Hartford, Conn., 1868) , p. 488; Sylvanus Cadwallader, *Three Years with Grant,* ed. Benjamin P. Thomas (New York, 1955) , p. 329.

276. The apple tree under which Lee had rested is cut up for souvenirs: undated clipping from New York *Sun* in DLC Ms. Div., Joshua L. Chamberlain Papers.

Confederate officers sell horses and weapons: SHSP, XXXVIII, F. M. Colston, "Recollections of the Last Months of the Army of Northern Virginia."

277. Guns start firing again: Gibbon's *Recollections,* p. 321.

"The indefatigable telegraph corps": Plum MT, II, 326. Plum says that "within two hours after the surrender the line was extended to Grant's [headquarters] at Appomattox Court House."

Grant's telegram to Stanton: OR, 97:663.

278. Grant talks to Ingalls about Mexican mule: Porter CG, p. 488; Grant's *Memoirs,* p. 109.

Behavior of Confederates when Lee returns: McCarthy DMSL, p. 154.

Lee in "a savage mood": Susan L. Blackford, *Memories of Life in and out of the Army of Virginia* (Lynchburg, Va., 1894–96) , II, App.

"A file of men carrying . . . hardtack": McCarthy DMSL, p. 153.

279. Taps at Appomattox: Schaff SC, p. 286.

"Home, Sweet Home": James H. Stevenson, *Boots and Saddles* (Harrisburg, Pa., 1870) , p. 349.

Marshall drafts farewell message for Lee: *Papers of Charles Marshall, an Aide-de-Camp of Lee* (Boston, 1927) , p. 278; B & L, IV, 747. The story of this famous General Orders No. 9, which was issued to Lee's corps commanders and general staff, is told by Dr. Joseph E. Fields in the *Autograph Collectors' Journal* for Jan. and Oct. 1949.

Grant again meets Lee: Grant's *Memoirs,* p. 634.

280. Grant arrives at City Point at 5 A.M., Apr. 12: OR, 97:716 (Dana to Stanton).

Correspondent describes Grant's arrival: William H. Cunnington, "General Grant's Cabin," *The Blue and the Gray,* May 1893.

281. Mrs. Grant and officers' wives prepare supper but fall asleep: Porter CG, p. 493.

Carrying news of Lee's surrender to Sherman's army: Undated, unidentified newspaper clipping in DLC Ms. Div., Chamberlain Papers. This account is reprinted in *Sketches of War History* (Ohio Commandery of the Loyal Legion, Cincinnati, 1888, Vol. II), in which see Augustus J. Ricks, "Carrying the News of Lee's Surrender to the Army of the Ohio."

283. Paroles printed on portable press: Gibbon's *Recollections,* p. 377.

Chamberlain's account of the surrender of the Confederates' arms and battle flags: Chamberlain PA, pp. 258 ff.

287. The field hospital at Burkeville Junction: Wells B. Fox, *What I Remember of the Great Rebellion* (Lansing, Mich., 1892), p. 193; William H. Reed, *Hospital Life in the Army of the Potomac* (Boston, 1866), pp. 167 ff.

Chapter 19. The Lincolns Return to Washington

Page

289. "Their ship left for City Point at 11 A.M.": De Chambrun PRML.

Seward's telegram to Lincoln and Lincoln's reply: CWAL, VIII, 387; also DLC Ms. Div., RTL.

290. Seward injured in carriage accident: WSTR, Apr. 6, and other Washington papers for that day.

291. Mrs. Lincoln's telegram from Ft. Monroe to Stanton: MH-H, Charles Sumner Papers.

"Lincoln received them graciously on the *River Queen*": De Chambrun PRML.

Lincoln returns to the *Malvern:* Log of the *Malvern,* DNA-ON.

Johnson and King at City Point: Porter IACW, p. 287; Crook TFA, p. 44; Ms. diary of General Marsena R. Patrick for Apr. 6, DLC Ms. Div.

294. Mrs. Keckley on Mrs. Lincoln's behavior at dinner: Keckley BS, pp. 166–67.

Porter puts on an extra guard: Porter IACW, p. 318.

William P. Wood and the Secret Service: DNA-OA; James W. Williamson, *Prison Life in the Old Capitol* (West Orange, N. J., 1911); *Impeachment Investigation,* House of Representatives (Washington, D.C., 1867), Serial No. 1314, p. 490.

295. Booth's stay at the National Hotel: Pitman, p. 46.

Description of the *River Queen*'s departure from City Point: De Chambrun PRML.

Time of departure and weather on voyage to Washington: Log of the *Bat*, DNA-ON.

296. Lincoln reads Shakespeare: De Chambrun PRML.

297. Lincoln visits Seward: Frederick W. Seward, *Reminiscences of a War-Time Statesman and Diplomat* (New York, 1916), p. 253.

Chapter 20. Victory Week

Page

298. Brooks's description of Washington on Apr. 10: Brooks WLT, p. 251.

300. Lincoln's activities on Apr. 10: CWAL, VIII, 393–395; Frederick Hill Meserve and Carl Sandburg, *The Photographs of Abraham Lincoln* (New York, 1944), p. 24.

Partial eclipse of the full moon: NYT *Almanac* for 1865.

Weather data: Ms. day-by-day Washington weather report in author's possession.

301. Lamon and the speculators: DLC Ms. Div., RTL (Lamon to Lincoln, Mar. 23).

Lincoln gives Lamon a pass to go to Richmond: CWAL, VIII, 395; Lamon's *Recollections*, p. 280.

302. Lamon and Usher: *Loc. cit.*

Lincoln pardons a half-breed Indian: CWAL, VIII, 398 (Lincoln to James Speed).

Mrs. Lincoln invites De Chambrun to the White House: MH-H, Charles Sumner Papers.

304. Booth in crowd as Lincoln speaks: *Impeachment Investigation,* House of Representatives (Washington, D.C., 1867), Serial No. 1314, p. 674.

Washburne and General Alexander: Alexander MMC, pp. 614–15.

305. "The sooner . . . assassinated the better": New-York Historical Society, Benjamin Brown French ms. letter.

Jefferson Davis arrives in Greensboro, N.C.: A. J. Hanna, *Flight into Oblivion* (Richmond, Va., 1938), pp. 27 ff.

306. Ficklin: Browning's *Diary*, II, 16 ff; DNA-OA-JAG, Lincoln Assassination Suspect File, JAG Letter Book, Apr. to July 1865, Burnett to Augur, May 7. A ms. copy of the O'Beirne report on Ficklin, dated May 25, 1865, is also in the Illinois State Historical Library. Earlier background on Ficklin in J. Wilkinson, *The Narrative of a Blockade Runner* (New York, 1877), p. 84, *passim*.

Bibb: DLC Ms. Div., RTL, Apr. 1, Capt. Worden introduces Bibb to Lincoln; Apr. 12; Bibb introduces R. E. Cox to Lincoln; Bibb introduces Ficklin to Lincoln, DNA-OA-JAG, Lincoln Assassination Suspect File.

307. William P. Kellogg reports Lincoln's remark about finances ruling country for next fifty years: *Abraham Lincoln Quarterly,* Sept. 1945, p. 334.
Lincoln signs a pass for Singleton: CWAL, VIII, 410.
308. Grant arrives in Washington on Apr. 13 and goes to Willard's Hotel: Porter CG, p. 496; Garnett L. Eskew, *Willard's of Washington* (New York, 1954), pp. 45–49.
The draft stopped: OR, 97:744 (Stanton to Dix).
Mrs. Lincoln invites Grant to the White House: Badeau GP, p. 361, has a facsimile of her letter.
310. The last official meeting of the Confederate government: Joseph E. Johnston, *Narrative of Military Operations* (New York, 1874), pp. 396 ff.; Jefferson Davis, *The Rise and Fall of the Confederate Government* (New York, 1881), II, 678–81; J. E. Walmsley, "The Last Meeting of the Confederate Cabinet," *Mississippi Valley Historical Review,* Dec. 1919; Stephen R. Mallory, "Last Days of the Confederate Government," *McClure's Magazine,* Jan. 1901; John H. Reagan, *Memoirs* (New York, 1906), pp. 199 ff.; Jacob D. Cox, *Military Reminiscences of the Civil War* (New York, 1900), II, 489 ff.

Chapter 21. A Darkness over the Land

Page
311. The letter to a soldier dated Apr. 9 predicting the Lincoln assassination was written by Elizabeth A. Blencoe; the document numbers in the Holt Papers are 6223, 6236, 6273, 6276, 6277, 6278.
312. "Mrs. Lincoln was even 'crazier than she used to be' ": DLC Ms. Div., Benjamin Brown French papers.
Oil well struck by lightning: Undated newspaper clipping from the Chicago *Tribune* in NN Theater Collection of Boothiana.
The flag raising at Ft. Sumter: Dr. F. Milton Willis, "Replacing the Flag Upon Sumter," in *Fort Sumter Memorial* (New York, 1915); *The Trip of the Steamer Oceanus to Fort Sumter and Charleston, S.C.* (Brooklyn, N.Y., 1865). The quotations are from the *Oceanus,* pp. 79, 84.
314. Newspaper advertisements announcing theater party at Ford's: WSTR, Apr. 14.
Badeau's account of Mrs. Grant's refusal to attend: Badeau GP, p. 632.
315. Gideon Welles's description of the Cabinet meeting: *Galaxy Magazine,* Apr. 1872, pp. 525 ff.; also Welles's *Diary,* II, 280–83.
316. Grant tells the President that his wife and he will not be able to go to Ford's Theatre: Porter CG, p. 497.
Johnson at the White House: E. D. Neill, "Reminiscences of the Last

Year of President Lincoln's Life," in *Glimpses of the Nation's Struggle* (St. Paul, Minn., 1887).

The Lincolns' last drive: Mrs. Lincoln's letter to Francis B. Carpenter, Nov. 15, 1865, in Carl Sandburg and Paul M. Angle, *Mary Lincoln, Wife and Widow* (New York, 1932), p. 240.

The story about the supposed visit to the Navy Yard and the *Montauk* apparently originated in a letter supposedly written on April 15 (but mailed April 30) by Dr. George B. Todd, who claimed to be present as surgeon of the *Montauk*. The original is in the Wisconsin State Historical Society. NN Ms. Room has a photostat of a typewritten copy of the letter in the George S. Bryan Papers.

317. "I believe there are men who want to take my life": Crook TFA, p. 66.

Booth prepares for the night's work: Pitman, pp. 70–83, *passim;* DNA-OA-JAG, the Lincoln assassination papers, especially those in the exhibits box. See this author's introduction to the facsimile edition of Pitman (New York, 1954), for a discussion of the various printings of the original transcript of the stenographic record of the testimony.

Lincoln asks for Major Eckert as a guard: Bates LTO, p. 367, and Eisenschiml WWLM, Chap. V, for comment.

318. The guard Parker: Eisenschiml WWLM, Chap. III; photostats of Parker's record in the Metropolitan Police, NN Ms. Room, Bryan Papers.

Footnote: NN Ms. Room, Bryan Papers, photostat of a letter from P. E. Jameson dated Sept. 24, 1942, in which Jameson points out that Mrs. Lincoln's mother's name was Eliza Parker. See William H. Townsend, *Lincoln and the Bluegrass Country* (Lexington, Ky., 1955), pp. 29, 47.

319. Card for Ashmun: CWAL, VIII, 413; Ashmun's friend was Judge C. P. Daly of New York (see J. C. Holland, *The Life of Abraham Lincoln,* Springfield, Mass., 1866, p. 518).

Browning at the White House: Browning's *Diary,* II, 18.

Ficklin denounced as a possible conspirator: DNA-OA-JAG, Lincoln Assassination Suspect File. William Leach denounced him to Deputy Provost Marshal Samuel K. Brown on the night of the assassination; on Apr. 15, A. E. Fitzpatrick wrote to Stanton, also denouncing Ficklin and supplying a detailed description.

The Presidential party goes to Ford's Theatre: Pitman, p. 78 (Rathbone's testimony); also ms. affidavits of eyewitnesses in DNA-OA.

320. Location of buildings near Ford's Theatre: Map on front page of NYW for Apr. 18.

Paine had a room at the Herndon House: *Trial of John H. Surratt* (Washington, D.C., 1867), I, 246.

Lloyd Lewis: *Myths After Lincoln* (New York, 1929), p. 405.
For Lincoln's actions on this day see John W. Starr, Jr., *Lincoln's Last Day* (New York, 1922), *New Light on Lincoln's Last Day* (1926), and *Further Light on Lincoln's Last Day* (1930). The last two were privately printed in very small editions.

Chapter 22. Aftermath

Page
322. Footnote: Robert McElroy, *Jefferson Davis* (New York, 1937), II, 488.
324. "Sherman was ready to leave Raleigh": Sherman's *Memoirs*, II, 347. Sherman's description of his meeting with Johnston: Sherman's *Memoirs*, II, 349.
Stanton's telegram to Sherman: OR, 100:221.
326. Johnston tells how Breckinridge and Sherman got along: Wise EE, pp. 450 ff.
328. Sherman sends Hitchcock to Washington: Sherman's *Memoirs*, II, 354, 357.
Grant present at Cabinet meeting: Welles's *Diary*, II, 295.
Grant advises Sherman: Sherman's *Memoirs*, II, 358; Grant's *Memoirs*, p. 645.
329. Sherman feels that Stanton has insulted him: a letter in private hands, which has recently come to light, shows how bitter he was; he wrote it to Rawlins at 3 A.M. on Apr. 29, saying:
> *There has been at no time any trouble about Gen. Johnston's army. It fell and became powerless when Lee was defeated, but its dispersion when the country was already full of Lee's men would have made North Carolina a pandemonium. I desired to avoid that condition of things. The South is broken and ruined and appeals to our pity. To ride the people down with persecutions and military exactions would be like slashing away at the crew of a sinking ship — an outrage — the Secretary has done — he is not the man I supposed him — If he wants to hunt down Jeff. Davis let him use Sheriffs' bailiffs — not hint that I should march hundred's [sic] of miles on a fool's errand — efforts will be made to sow dissension between Grant and myself — that we have political aspirations.*
Sherman refuses to meet Halleck in Richmond: DLC Ms. Div., Benjamin F. Butler Papers, Jan.–Dec. 1865; DLC Ms. Div., Sherman Papers, letter from Halleck to Sherman dated May 8 in which Halleck tries to apologize and says that he was only carrying out "what he knew to be the wishes of the War Department"; Sherman Papers, telegram from Sherman to Grant dated May 10, in which he says he "asked him [Halleck] to keep out of my sight";

Sherman Papers, same date, letter to Halleck in which he says very much the same.

"Washington is corrupt as Hell": *Home Letters of General Sherman,* ed. M. A. DeWolfe Howe (New York, 1909), p. 352.

"Four men . . . dressed in women's clothing": WSTR, Apr. 17.

Riot in Washington: WSTR, Apr. 17.

The false Booths: DNA-OA (Telegrams to Stanton Record Books for Apr.); Washington and New York newspapers.

330. Confederate prisoners at Camp Lookout: WSTR, Apr. 18.

The *Sultana:* Chester D. Berry, *Loss of the* Sultana (Lansing, Mich., 1892); Joseph Taylor, "The *Sultana* Disaster," Indiana Historical Society *Proceedings* (Indianapolis, 1913), V, 161–99; William B. Floyd, "The Burning of the *Sultana,*" *Wisconsin Magazine of History,* XI (1927), 70–76.

331. Johnson charges Confederate complicity in the assassination: WSTR, May 4, and other Washington papers of that date; see David M. De Witt, *The Assassination of Abraham Lincoln* (New York, 1909), Chap. IV for comment.

George N. Sanders accuses Johnson of murdering the President: WSTR, May 6.

Beverly Tucker agrees with him: Montreal *Gazette,* May 4.

Their joint letter offering to be tried at Rouse's Point: DLC Ms. Div., Andrew Johnson Papers, Vol. 62.

332. The arrest of Davis: Jefferson Davis, *The Rise and Fall of the Confederate Government* (New York, 1881), II, 701; Jefferson Davis, *A Memoir by His Wife* (New York, 1890), II, 640; Burton Harrison, "The Capture of Jefferson Davis," *Century Magazine,* Nov. 1883; Halleck's recommendation to Stanton, Robert McElroy, *Jefferson Davis* (New York, 1937), II, 514. McElroy discusses the capture at length; his extensive bibliography describes the anti-Davis cartoons in the Boston Public Library, p. 703; OR 104 for Union reports.

334. Mrs. Surratt kept in irons for the first few days of the trial: De Witt, *Assassination,* p. 280; Benn Pitman statement in NN Ms. Room, Pitman Papers.

Members of the Military Commission inspect Ford's Theatre: WSTR, May 16.

335. Townsend's description of the White House a month after Lincoln's death: NYW, May 20.

336. Mrs. Keckley on Mrs. Lincoln's reactions to her husband's death: Keckley BS, pp. 191–92.

337. Seward sees the Lincoln funeral as in a dream: Frederick W. Seward, *Reminiscences of a War-Time Statesman and Diplomat* (New York, 1916), p. 262.

Mrs. Lincoln leaves the White House on May 22: Dr. W. A. Evans,
   Mrs. Abraham Lincoln (New York, 1932), p. 188 (chronology).

Chapter 23. An End to Valor

Page

338. Sherman's army marched nearly 2000 miles: Sherman's *Memoirs,*
   II, 377.
   Sheridan not at the review: Sheridan's *Memoirs,* II, 208–10; New-
   hall WSLLC, pp. 227 ff.

339. Warren's men cheer him in Petersburg: Chamberlain PA, p. 302.
   Mrs. Custer rides with the regiment: Whittaker's *Custer,* p. 310.

340. Chamberlain's horse uncovers several skeletons: Chamberlain PA,
   pp. 308–9.

341. The thunderstorm: Chamberlain PA, p. 313.

342. The troops enter Washington: WSTR, May 23; WDC, May 24.

343. The reviewing stands at the White House: Brooks WLT, p. 309.
   The troops gather at the Capitol: WSTR, May 24; Tremain LHSC,
   p. 316.
   Decorations on the Capitol: DLC Ms. Div., Benjamin Brown French
   Papers.

344. Custer's balky horse: Whittaker's *Custer,* p. 313.

345. Order of the procession: Tremain LHSC, App. II.

346. The flag of the Treasury Guards: WSTR, May 23; WDC, May 24.
   Trial of the conspirators: WSTR, May 23.

347. Comparison between Eastern and Western troops: Brooks WLT, pp.
   318–19.

348. Sherman cuts Stanton dead: Brooks WLT, p. 316; Ben:Perley Poore,
   Reminiscences of Sixty Years in the National Metropolis (Philadelphia, 1886), II, 191; Sherman's *Memoirs,* II, 377.

349. Brooks describes Sherman: Brooks WLT, p. 318.
   Horace Porter describes the Negroes and the "bummers" in Sherman's
   army: Porter CG, p. 511.

350. "Had the eye of the spirit been opened": Tremain LHSC, p. 549
   (Gen. Francis A. Walker, whose description of the first day's
   review is printed as App. III).

Chapter 24. Beyond the End

Page

352. Whitman quotation: From "Reconciliation" in *Drum-Taps.*
   Shenandoah: Cornelius E. Hunt, *The Shenandoah* (New York, 1866);
   SHSP, XXXII, Captain J. I. Waddell "The *Shenandoah,*" and
   John Grinsball, "The Career of the *Shenandoah.*" The Chicago
   Historical Society has the log of the *Shenandoah.*

353. Three Confederates emerge from the Dismal Swamp fifteen months after Appomattox: Unidentified and undated newspaper clipping in the Civil War Scrapbooks of the Brooklyn Public Library.

Johnson's delayed proclamation of peace for Texas: Nicolay and Hay, "The End of the Rebellion," *Century Magazine,* Feb. 1890, p. 571; Ida M. Tarbell, "Disbanding of the Confederate Army," *McClure's Magazine,* Apr. 1901. Congress established the Texas date as the legal end of the war and it was so considered in cases before the courts.

General Fuller on the bullet in warfare: In his *Grant and Lee* (Bloomington, Ind., 1957), pp. 249–50.

355. Direct cost of the Civil War to the Northern States: Theodore A. Dodge, *A Bird's-Eye View of the Civil War* (Boston, 1883), p. 326.

Civil War pension costs: Letter to the author from the Veterans Administration, Washington, D.C., giving figures to June 30, 1956.

356. "Both parties deprecated war": CWAL, VIII, 332 (Second Inaugural Address).

359. "The last Army mule": *New York Times,* Dec. 15, 1956. The last Army horses are the funeral horses at Fort Myer, Arlington, Va. An effort was made to eliminate them in 1956; because of public pressure, it failed.

The last Union veteran: Albert Woolson of Duluth, Minn., died in 1956 at the age of 109. Two Confederate veterans, both well past 110 years old, survive at the time of this writing (Dec. 15, 1957).

361. Appomattox Court House as it is today: Ralph Happel, *Appomattox National Historical Park,* U. S. Dep't of Interior, Nat'l Park Service (Washington, D.C., 1955). Pamphlet.

362. The restoration of the White House: *Report of the Commission on the Renovation of the Executive Mansion* (Washington, D.C., 1952), pp. 94–96.

Ford's Theatre collapsed in 1893: Stanley W. McClure, "The Lincoln Museum," U.S. Dep't of Interior, Nat'l Park Service (Washington, D.C., 1949), pamphlet. Twenty-two people were killed and 68 injured.

The tomb in the heart of the Capitol: mimeographed information sheet from the office of the Architect of the Capitol.

363. Lincoln quotation: CWAL, IV, 271.

Index

THIS INDEX was prepared by the author, who believes that a simple listing of names and page numbers is practically useless. In order to make room for topical references he has eliminated the names of minor characters and unimportant places.

405

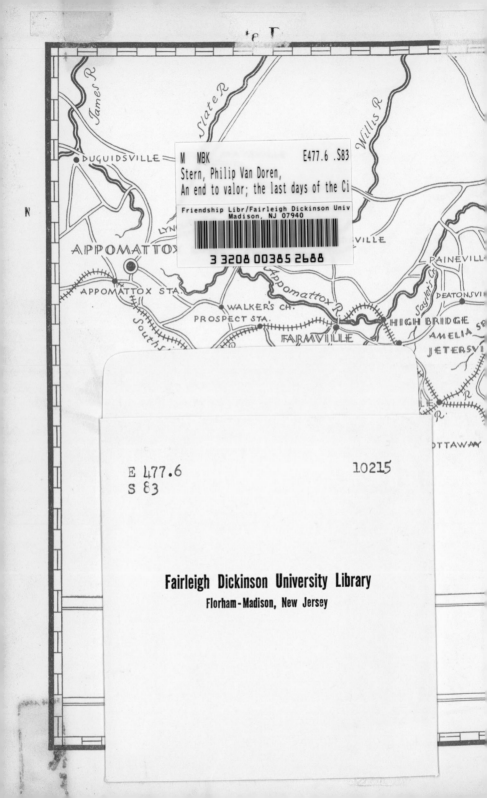